THE END OF STRAIGHT SUPREMACY

Rooted in the politics and theories of early Gay liberation and Radical feminism, Shannon Gilreath's *The End of Straight Supremacy* presents a cohesive theory of Gay life under straight domination. Beginning with a critique of formal equality law centered on the "like-straight" demands of liberal equality theory as highlighted in *Lawrence v. Texas*, Gilreath goes on to criticize the "gay rights" movement itself, challenging the assimilation politics behind the movement's blithe acceptance of discrimination in the guise of free speech and pornography in the name of sexual liberation, as well as same-sex marriage and transsexuality as tools of straight hegemony. Ultimately, Gilreath rejects both the liberal demand for Gay erasure in exchange for meager legal progress and the gay establishment agenda. In so doing, he provides both the vocabulary and analysis necessary to understand and to resist straight supremacy in all its forms. In *The End of Straight Supremacy*, Gilreath calls Gays and their allies to the difficult task of rethinking what liberation and equality really mean.

Shannon Gilreath is the Wake Forest University School of Law Professor for the Interdisciplinary Study of Law and a member of the core faculty of the Women's and Gender Studies Program at Wake Forest University. He is the author of *Sexual Politics: The Gay Person in America Today* and *Sexual Identity Law in Context: Cases and Materials*.

The End of Straight Supremacy

REALIZING GAY LIBERATION

SHANNON GILREATH

Wake Forest University

CAMBRIDGE
UNIVERSITY PRESS

CAMBRIDGE UNIVERSITY PRESS
Cambridge, New York, Melbourne, Madrid, Cape Town,
Singapore, São Paulo, Delhi, Tokyo, Mexico City

Cambridge University Press
32 Avenue of the Americas, New York, NY 10013-2473, USA

www.cambridge.org
Information on this title: www.cambridge.org/9780521181044

First published 2011

Printed in the United States of America

A catalog record for this publication is available from the British Library.

Library of Congress Cataloging in Publication data
Gilreath, Shannon, 1977–
  The end of straight supremacy : realizing gay liberation / Shannon Gilreath.
    p.   cm.
  Includes bibliographical references and index.
  ISBN 978-1-107-00459-7 – ISBN 978-0-521-18104-4 (pbk.)
  1. Gays – United States – Social conditions.   2. Gay rights – United States – History.
  3. Gay liberation movement – United States – History   I. Title.
  HQ76.3.U6G55   2012
  306.76′60973–dc23   2011022029

ISBN 978-1-107-00459-7 Hardback
ISBN 978-0-521-18104-4 Paperback

Women and male homosexuals are united in their queerness.

The Revolution, as we live it and as we imagine it, means destroying the Immovable Structure to create a world in which we can use our holy human energy to sustain our holy human lives … to create a world – a community on this planet – where instead of lying to survive, we can tell the truth and flourish.
Andrea Dworkin, *Woman Hating*

With special thanks to Catharine MacKinnon,
whose kind words,
"Shannon, you honor Andrea with your life and your spirit,"
kept me writing this book – and writing it honestly – when I felt
like giving up.

Contents

Preface

You know, there was a gay community in Germany before the Nazi period which had all the characteristics of the community we have now – including community centers, balls, newspapers, a scientific research institute – everything. I am struck by the ignorance among gay people about the past – no, more even than ignorance: the "will to forget" the German gay holocaust. That we forgot about these hundreds of thousands of people and about the fact that out of one hundred years of gay life, in thirty of them we had a virtual vacuum – that we forgot in such a radical way is, I think, something of a warning.... If there really is a social crisis beginning, gays are in a position similar to that of the Jews in pre-Nazi society.

Guy Hocquenghem (April 1980)

The End of Straight Supremacy appears in the second decade of the twenty-first century – a particularly dangerous time for Gay people. The "will to forget" that Guy Hocquenghem spoke of in an interview in the *Gay Community News* in 1980 is at work today in new and newly frightening ways. Gay people have been particularly good at forgetting what is painful. Given the reality of the pain, it's hard really to resent this coping mechanism. But it has made Gays particularly vulnerable to new forms of oppression. The unique danger of today is that we are continually being erased even as we are told we are being acknowledged. Sometimes this erasure is merely conceptual, a sapping of our community and energy through assimilation. Sometimes it is physical: Sometimes we are killed. Conceptual and physical erasure are forms of violence against us – a violence that is systematic, not random; calculatedly political, not casual; continuous, not episodic. Gay people in recent years have experienced an escalation in this violence. And we are tired. We are tired of being hated. It is easier to close our eyes. To dream. To forget.

The law has done little for us, but much against us. It has propped up a system of straight despotism in which we have been consistently denied meaningful speech as an avenue to power, while those who would destroy us have been given unfettered license to defame us and to mark us for calumny by impressionable people who are made afraid through anti-Gay propaganda, often disseminated as religious doctrine. In virtually every aspect, straight supremacy has been either augmented or directly instantiated through the law. Straight law and the "gay rights" movement – said to oppose straight despotism – have captured Gay Radical energy, in virtually every instance redirecting it away from the possibility of real social change. Caught in this state of straight sado-sublimation,[†] some Gays have put their faith in the Heteroarchy – in straight supremacist institutions, like marriage – striking a bargain that in effect says, "We will change; we will make ourselves palatable to you, if you will stop terrorizing us." Thus, some Gays return to the patriarchal imperatives of the Heteroarchy, often with the idea – which is the central tenet of the modern gay rights movement – that its institutions can be "reformed." Meanwhile, violence against us escalates, and in our state of Gay diaspora we are seldom aware of what is happening to our sisters and brothers for no other reason than on account of their sexuality; and we are oblivious to the increasing likelihood that someday, late or soon, it will be our turn. We would rather forget.

There is another option. We can Remember who we are. We can reclaim our status as Outsiders and with it the moral imperative and authority of our place in a counterculture that flourishes outside patriarchy and resists its demands. To do so we must summon the courage to look honestly at the world around us, at straight supremacy and how it operates, and to name the agents of straight supremacy, even when they are operative in places and through people closest to us. *The End of Straight Supremacy* principally points to such discoveries in the law. Acknowledging this limited scope brings me to the concomitant acknowledgment that I am not here answering every question, or even attempting to raise every question. This is a beginning (for I intend to write again), and it is intended as a springboard for others to make their own discoveries, uncovering the untruths of straight supremacy and reversing the reversals[§] of the Heteroarchy in the law and elsewhere. This is not invention so much as reinvention. Gay people are heirs to a robust Radical heritage

---

[†] By "sado-sublimation" I mean the diversion by the Heteroarchy of Gay creative energy into assimilationist activities of all kinds. The process works with that of sado-sublimination, which Mary Daly and Jane Caputi first defined as "mental manipulation ... involving deliberate perversion of the natural phenomenon of subliminal perception." See Mary Daly & Jane Caputi, Websters' First New Intergalactic Wickedary of the English Language 95 (1987).

[§] I owe this terminology to Mary Daly. See her Pure Lust: Elemental Feminist Philosophy 115 (1984).

of rebellion manifest in the political and legal ethos of Gay liberation, the ground upon which I stand in this book. Gay liberation is in most cases the opposite of the liberal "gay rights" movement. The "gay rights" movement apparently would like to forget (or would like the straight world to forget) that a more Radical Gay Movement/moment existed and still exists. The "gay rights" assimilationist movement has all but blotted out Gay liberation as an important part of our history and our future. Indeed, in the prevailing spirit of our prevailingly "postmodern" age, one might call this new perspective post-Gay; and yet one cannot even say this, for the senescent strategies of an increasingly elitist "gay rights" movement work hard to deny that any *Gay* history exists – which is to say that Gay never really existed. But, today, when threats to our safety are increasing and traps to ensnare us are increasingly beguiling, Gays need to Remember our Radical heritage, thereby Remembering our ability to reconceive, reimagine, and reanimate an insurrection raised before. Challenging and changing the law is one way, perhaps the least bloody, to go about changing our reality.**

** There are, of course, other ways. These are the ways often used against us by the Heteroarchy. They include the tire iron and the crowbar, the knife, and the gun. In generally refusing to respond in kind, Gay people have shown an extraordinary patience.

Acknowledgments

In the course of writing this book I have contracted many debts. Virtually every word of this book was spoken before it was written, during discussions of its ideas before various groups – most memorably at the University of North Carolina, Chapel Hill; the University of Toledo; North Carolina State University, Raleigh; the University of Akron; Pace University; and, of course, Wake Forest University – as well as numerous community and Gay organizations in various parts of the country. In many respects, the opportunity to speak these thoughts in real time contributed to their clarity. Earlier versions of some of the ideas here have also appeared in published form, in the *Journal of Law and Social Change* (Chapter 2); the *Women's Rights Law Reporter* (Chapter 3); the *Wake Forest Law Review* (Chapter 4); the *University of Pennsylvania Law Review, PENNumbra Forum* (Chapter 6); and the *University of Illinois Law Review* (Chapter 7).

Many friends and colleagues read parts of the book in draft form, and conversations with others sparked insights that have greatly enriched the final product. Specifically, I would like to mention Michael Curtis, Ron Wright, Suzanne Reynolds, Art Leonard, Richard Delgado, José Gabilondo, Michael Perry, Ann Scales, Alex Tsesis, Dick Schneider, Chris Coughlin, Ann Rodrigues, Hassan El Menyawi, Mary Deshazer, Luellen Curry, Sid Shapiro, Catharine MacKinnon, Twiss Butler, David Richards, Marc Spindelman, and Chris Kendall. Especially, conversations with my sister-friend Jane Caputi made the book better, and friendly edits – in particular from José Gabilondo and Marc Spindelman – likewise improved it. Of course, I did not always listen to the advice I received – sometimes I vigorously rejected it. Certainly, responsibility for the book is mine.

I am also greatly indebted to the visionaries on whose work I have relied in constructing the arguments in the following pages. The politics and polemics of both Radical feminism and Gay liberation are as indelibly imprinted on this book as they are on my conscience. Many thinkers from these and other perspectives have been extraordinarily helpful. Especially I would like to mention Andrea Dworkin, Catharine MacKinnon, Richard Delgado, Harry Hay, John Stoltenberg, Jane Caputi, Chris Kendall, Marc Spindelman, and Mary Daly. A line in a poem by Maya Angelou reminds us that our "passages have been paid." Truly, here, my ability to say what I am saying has been paid for in part – and at no small price – by these Outsiders and other Outsiders who dared to demand a new way.

Finally, I am grateful for my intellectual base at Wake Forest University and for the support I have received from students, colleagues, and staff members there. I am grateful to Wake Forest's stellar law librarians, especially Jason Sowards, formerly with the Wake Forest law library, to Arlene McClannon and Cynthia Ring, for tech support, and to my research assistants, especially law students Trevor Ostbye and Adam Pastore. I am especially grateful to Wanda Balzano and my colleagues in Women's and Gender Studies at Wake Forest and to Blake Morant, Dean of the Wake Forest University School of Law, who has given me the very critical support of allowing me to go my own way – the way necessary to this and other work.

Shannon Gilreath
February 21, 2011

1

Introduction

The Metaethics of Gay Liberation

The ideas of the ruling class are in every epoch the ruling ideas, i.e. the class which is the ruling material force of society, is at the same time its ruling intellectual force.... The ruling ideas are nothing more than the ideal expression of the dominant material relationships, the dominant material relationships grasped as ideas: hence of the relationships which make the one class the ruling one, therefore, the ideas of its dominance.

Marx and Engels, *The German Ideology*

The important idea for me is that before the conflict (rebellion, struggle) there are no categories of opposition but only of difference. And it is not until the struggle breaks out that the violent reality of the oppositions and the political nature of the differences become manifest. For as long as oppositions (differences) appear as given, already there, before all thought, "natural" – as long as there is no conflict and no struggle – there is no dialectic, there is no change, no movement. The dominant thought refuses to turn inward on itself to apprehend that which questions it.

Monique Wittig, *The Straight Mind and Other Essays*

When you live in a world that's governed by laws you don't understand and can't understand, you can be destroyed mentally by that world.

Andrea Dworkin, *Life and Death*

THE PROJECT OF THIS BOOK

This book takes up the inquiry I began in my first book, *Sexual Politics: The Gay Person in America Today* (2006), and journeys beyond it.[1] It deals with

---

[1] *Sexual Politics* was both angry and hopeful. So, too, is *The End of Straight Supremacy.* The reader of both books will, however, find that the perspective of the latter has been greatly Radicalized. This Radicalism comes with my shift in focus from "gay rights" to Gay liberation.

some big questions, the Big Questions of power, sexuality, and gender, which are themselves the themes around which the following discussion/excavation is organized. Inquiry, with the experience of Gay life as its method, arrives at this quintessential question: Who can one be after a lifetime of being made into no one, no thing – nothing? The discovery this question invites is made all the more difficult because the Heteroarchy[2] has always posed the questions, defined their limits, and usually hidden the answers. The reality of Gay life under heteroarchal law lays bare the relationship between epistemology as a method of knowing and law as a method of power to enforce dominant thought: In the condition that is straight dominance, what is epistemological is taken as ontological.

Any Gay person who manages to stay alive is engaged in a struggle for the freedom of Self. In the process of this struggle, Gays face a beguiling *everyday* – a Scylla and Charybdis that looks like placid water until it is suddenly the swirling vortex consuming you. The "gay rights movement" has plunged into this vortex, rushed headlong into it, seemingly without a thought of the danger. This vortex is the vortex of the Heteroarchy's cleverly constructed everyday, in which they succeed in defining even the Gay struggle for identity on straight terms: the monogamous family ideal, reproduction, marriage, et cetera. Anything not defined by – not moving in and through this context – is made to seem illusory at best, deviant at worst. Sustained attacks on the political system of straight supremacy are thus rendered unlikely, if not unthinkable. After all, if the goal has become assimilating into the straight model, then who would think of destroying this model? Or if revolution is too much to hope for, who would think even of engaging it analytically, when it cannot be seen for the simple reason that it is omnipresent?

Embracing straight values requires Gay people to forget what the Heteroarchy and its everyday has meant for them – their conceptual and, all too often, physical liquidation. *The End of Straight Supremacy* asks that Gays stop Self-censoring and start making the obvious connections between the Heteroarchy's power, the institutions used to perpetuate it, and Gays' own possibilities for freedom. So in addition to Big Questions, this book asks for Big

---

[2] The Heteroarchy is the system of straight over Gay domination. It is an administrative system that exerts control over sex and controls through sex. It is thoroughly sexual. It is based on the religious myth of straight male supremacy; patriarchy is its religion. Its politics is the politics of gender. Its script is the script of male–female relation in the patriarchal model. It creates pseudo-norms of sexuality, which it says are natural, and enacts them into law. Its laws regulate Gay sexuality, identity, creativity, and imagination. Its laws do not regulate the systematic terrorization, capture, and mass murder of Gays. Its aim is the planned, systematic destruction of Gays: *gaynocide.*

Commitments, because making these necessary connections will require that one see not only one's own life, but also its interconnectedness with the lives of Gay people in other places, in other circumstances, existing in other stages and degrees of straight-induced torture. Equality rights, after all, are group-based rights. Making these commitments requires a process of consciousness-raising that takes "Gay" from object to subject. Only when we are able to read the context from this vantage point are we truly able to see the entire pattern of heteroarchal deception for what it is. Only then can we truly be Radical. "Radical" has become a dirty word, but it is derived from the Latin *radix* and means simply "going to the root or source." It is time that Gay people throw off the mind-numbing accoutrements of the Heteroarchy's everyday and get to the root of the heteroarchal domination that is killing us. How many more lives will it take?

Equality, the primary subject of this book, is a Radical idea. Although it is a constant topic in polite liberal discourse, many marginalized people – specifically in the context of this work, Gay people – live whole lives without it. Consequently, I am in pursuit of a legal theory in pursuit of equality, specifically a legal theory that operates in and through the lives of Gay people. In some works, theory has been a clever way of eliding reality. Judicial and academic theorizing about equality has resulted in the perpetuation of the second-class (or even third-class) citizenship of Gay Americans. Theory created in the image of straight dominance, quite frankly, has not fit the reality of Gay lives. Recognition of this and encounters of the past several years with various colleagues, students, and clients persuaded me that a new kind of theory was needed. The resultant work, a theory rooted in Gay lives, is a theory engaged with reality, contending with reality, challenging it, and sometimes calling for its large-scale revision. Its method is not merely the application of the reality of Gay lives to existing legal possibilities. The method of this book is the engagement of law with life, a method often touted, but seldom practiced in typical academic analysis (with some notable feminist exceptions). Its aim is a new order in which homosexuality is something other than the absence of heterosexuality and where Gay people are more than a counterfactual to straight supremacy. Its aim is to envision a world in which Gay people are finally accepted as irreducibly human. In so doing, the book departs significantly from the status quo of asking only for the minima. In sum, the purpose is to root a *meta*ethics of Gay liberation in Gay lives and experiences.

I wanted to subtitle this book "The Metaethics of Gay Liberation," but my editor, for various reasons, persuaded me against it. Nevertheless, I preserved it as the title of this introductory chapter, because it aptly describes the metaethical endeavor of my work here. As commonly understood, "metaethics" is the "study of the meaning and nature of ethical terms, judgments, and arguments."[3] My book is very much that. In the process of making new arguments it analyzes the terms, judgments, and arguments that already exist. But by choosing this subtitle I meant to indicate more than that. There are several definitions of "ethics." One of them, according to *Webster's*, is "a set of principles of right conduct." The prefix "meta" means "higher," "beyond," "more comprehensive"; so I chose it to reflect that some of the arguments I make, about marriage and pornography, for example, aren't strictly legal arguments. With pornography, I don't pose a legal solution to the pornography problem; instead, I argue that the pervasiveness of Gay pornography actually prevents Gays from exercising their First Amendment rights (or any other rights for that matter). So it is more comprehensive than the usual legal/ethical arguments. And, yes, by choosing "meta" I meant to say that an ethics rooted in Gay experiences would be *higher, beyond, superior to* any understanding that heterosexuality has produced, because it would be infused with an understanding and empathy gleaned from being on the receiving end of oppression – from being buried alive in it. "Meta" also indicates change or transformation, and what I hope to accomplish here is a discursive change that is substantive in theory and reality.

In the effort toward this metaethics, I critique the prevailing understandings of equality and free speech, as well as the three sacred cows of the contemporary "gay rights" movement: pornography, (same-sex) marriage, and transsexuality. As to these three, I show that, while they are usually theorized as central to liberation, they are actually engines of oppression, both external and internal. I also show that, while they are usually theorized/engaged separately, they are closely related in theory and practice. Part I of the book, "Equality and Making Meaning," accepts that "gay" is a social construction and an implement of the legal caste system. As such, Gay people have had almost no input or power in shaping the parameters of this legal and political identity, including the conceptualization of equality that has brought us meager gains.[4] I offer a legal analysis for a world in which Gay people would/

---

[3]   The term "metaethics" and my use of it are informed by Mary Daly's book, *Gyn/Ecology: The Metaethics of Radical Feminism* (1978).

[4]   These are limited statements. What I mean here is that Gays live in a legal reality over which we have had little control. I do not mean that there is no Gay Self or no Gay identity to claim – no Gay history. The postmodernist project of claiming negation, of trying zealously to prove that Gays have, in fact, been absent from history and that only our current visibility need be explained (reflected, for example, in the history urged on the Supreme Court in *Lawrence v. Texas*; see Chapter 3, this volume, for expansion) is repugnant to me. As Will Roscoe put it lucidly, "This denial of identity seems to me a uniquely Gay form of self-hatred. I can think of no other contemporary minority whose intellectuals are so deeply invested

could actually matter. Part II, "Equality, Sexuality, and Expression," deals with the collision of two concepts, speech and equality, when sexual minorities are added to the mix. The center of gravity of free speech law has shifted so that the core of speech doctrine is designed to protect anti-identity, anti-equality speech at the expense of the equality rights of Gay and other marginalized people. The chapters in this section examine how the free speech norm is generally manipulated to keep Gay people powerless, as well as posit an alternative approach by which expression *and* equality might receive protection. Part III, "Millennial Equality: A Primer on Gay Liberation in the Twenty-first Century," anticipates the issues looming and applies the theory elaborated in previous chapters to suggest solutions that do not compromise Gay identity for short-term gain.

Some major concepts/themes of the following chapters require prophylactic clarification.

Power/Sexuality/Gender

Sexuality, as it has been defined – indeed, one might say invented – by the heterocrats,[5] is a political system that is all-encompassing. Gender is the regulatory script, if you will, of this system – *Robert's Rules of Order* with a sadistic edge. The politicization of the sex act itself, by straight men, transforming it from an activity into an identity (after Foucault), creates sexuality. Gender, then, was developed as a way to order sexual identity, cutting across categories of sexuality (straight and Gay) to sketch the boundaries of emerging identities in a system the boundaries of which were/are distinctly sexual. In other words, gender determines who does what to whom, sexually speaking. Quite clearly, then, sexuality and gender are not one and the same, but they also cannot be adequately theorized separately. They work *in tandem*.

Sexuality tells us who is fucking: men fucking women or men fucking men or women fucking women. Gender tells us who's fucking *whom*, or to put it a bit more vernacularly, who's on the top and who's on the bottom – again, across categories, for "top" and "bottom" are appellations to which even Gay men remain politically faithful.[6] The importation of straight sexual mores into

---

in erasing their difference." See Will Roscoe, *Afterword: Harry Hay and Gay Politics*, in Radically Gay: Gay Liberation in the Words of Its Founder Harry Hay 347 (Will Roscoe, ed., 1996).

[5]   I use this term for the men and women who make up the Heteroarchy and carry out its edicts.

[6]   As used within the Gay community, a "top" is the insertive partner, while a "bottom" is the receptive partner (fuck-er/fuck-ee). This has nothing at all to do with the actual position of either partner *en flagrante delicto*.

Gay sexuality is testimony to the fact that sexuality, whatever component of it might be biologic, cannot exist unaffected by a system of social inequality. Hierarchy sexualized becomes sexuality. The idea here is that sexuality is social (in the way that feminists have said for some time that gender is social) – in the sense that sexuality – heterosexed – is hierarchical and dominance is sexual. Thus, a proper understanding of sexuality and gender sees sexuality as a product of heterosexual (mostly male) dominance, with the politicization of the sex act creating sexuality as we experience it. The discriminating force that exists within this methodical but deranged system manifests often as gender and discrimination on account of it.

In order to understand how the relationship between sexuality and gender is most commonly undertheorized in gay rights scholarship, consider Janet Halley's analysis of the usual trajectory of Gay antidiscrimination claims. Halley writes:

> [M]ost gay antidiscrimination claims don't involve sodomy at all: the gay plaintiff may never have engaged in anal intercourse, cunnilingus, or fellatio with anyone, much less with another person of his or her own sex; and the feature in the plaintiff that the defendant discriminated against is almost always an act of coming out, or an act of gender nonconformity, not a sex act. Antidiscrimination claims are almost always about public, even civic, relations: what has sodomy got to do with them?[7]

Sodomy (Gay sexuality) has everything to do with them. There really is no separation. "Gay" is both adjective and noun. It is possible (although increasingly unlikely) that there are Self-identifying Gay people who have not had Gay sex, but that is beside the point. The act is inferred from the status as frequently as the status is inferred from the act, if not more so. Claiming that status can theoretically exist without act is akin theoretically to "love the sinner, hate the sin." It is an intellectual limitation that doesn't work well for Gay people as a theology and hasn't worked very well for us as legal theory either.

As some advocates are wont to do, Halley singles out gender as independent of sexuality for a dubious privilege ("an act of gender nonconformity, not a sex act"). But the perceived gender transgression that, concededly, usually triggers heterosexist discrimination against Gays is really a discursive cue about a sex/uality trait that must be punished because the sex/uality involved has been adjudged immoral from the perspective of heterocentric morality. Anti-Gay discrimination might be gendered, but it is also thoroughly sexual.

---

[7] JANET E. HALLEY, DON'T: A READER'S GUIDE TO THE MILITARY'S ANTI-GAY POLICY 13 (1999).

Remembering that it is the politicization of sex itself that created and that maintains sexuality as a system of governance reveals that punishment of gender transgression (which sometimes amounts to little more than fucking someone of the same sex without actually displaying "feminine" attributes [in the case of men]) to ensure that a crisp distinction is maintained between the sexually superior (heterosexual) and sexually inferior (homosexual) castes is sex/uality discrimination. In this analysis we see the place of gender in sexuality and, indeed, the place of sexuality in gender. I do not mean to suggest that gender never operates in other, less obviously sexual capacities – for example, as the script that delineates the perimeters of male over female domination within heterosexuality. But even here gender is operating within a (hetero) sexuality. The root of gender is irreducibly sexual.

In this sex/uality system, the heterosexual defines the homosexual. Homosexuals are defined as rebels because the failure to acquiesce in the sexual politics of gender imperils the system in which men are to be dominant and in which heterosexuality (man over woman) equals dominance. Gays are, therefore, from the straight perspective, outside of – alien to – the gender script, although, as I will show in this book, Gays import some of the most destructive aspects of gender into our own lives in an effort to assimilate. In this system, the discriminatory reaction against gender nonconformity is not a reaction to a different gender script; it is a reaction to a blatant and (from the straight perspective) willful alienation from it.

A useful way to conceptualize this is to consider the discursive content of sexual violence. Women are the object of violence because in a patriarchal culture violence *is* sex, sex *is* violence. As I have posited, the politicization of the sex act, turning it into a weapon for the enforcement of patriarchy, creates gender, which is the social script by and through which society operates. Violence against women is a fulfillment of the social script, from the straight perspective: hence natural, neat, orderly. Thus, what Mary Daly termed *gynocide* is the ever-present reality of life lived by women.

Violence against Gays is different in origination but similar in operation. As objects of systematic violence, Gays are not fulfilling a role – we are outside of the gender script. Instead, Gays stand in direct contravention of the principle that sex must be had between gender unequals and, from the straight perspective, in the case of Gay males at least, for the proposition that men can be sexually violated. In a subject–object social system, in which the subject (the man) becomes the subject by fucking, literally, the object (the woman),[8] the

---

[8] See Catharine A. MacKinnon, Toward a Feminist Theory of the State 124 (1989) ("Man fucks woman; subject verb object").

possibility that men can also be fucked is earthshaking. This is an intolerable risk to the patriarchal/heteroarchal imperative that castes be pure, distinctions crisp, not blurred. In the gender metascript there is no neuter declension; deviations from the caste-based roles must, then, be destroyed.

Violence against Gays was first systematized through prohibitions on sodomy and their attendant death penalties. But as gender-norm violations became more flagrant, obvious outside the realm of sex only, the violence became more widespread and systematic. While gynocide, then, may be seen as a part of gender convention, *gaynocide* is more properly understood as a reaction to that which is totally alien to the gender system – neither subject, nor object, but indescribably *other*.[9] Gaynocide is not a mistake, nor is it random. It is the reality of life lived by Gay people – the systematized domination to the point of death that manifests itself in Gay bashings and murders, but also in less visible ways, namely the epidemic of suicide among Gay youth.[10] It is the product of a socio-legal system that refuses to see the systemic nature of this problem, preferring instead to see individuals harmed by some other individuals, often provoked in particular ways and apologized for, legally, as in the case of the "gay panic" defense.[11] In order to survive this, Gay people must understand what is being done to us. That means that we have to overcome the identity we have been raised to, which has been primarily the masochistic counterpart to heterosexuality's sadism. If gender is their means of getting off, then attacking it is our means of getting over.

Public/Private

This volume necessarily engages and criticizes the prevailing way in which power has been theorized in relation to the law in the form of the public–private distinction. The criticism is necessary given what the public–private

---

9 A theory of the relationship of sexuality to gender (and vice versa), with transsexualism as its locus, is detailed in Chapter 8, this volume.

10 As I wrote this chapter, a spate of Gay youth suicides – dispatches from the holocaust that is Gay life – were reported in the mainstream media. See, e.g., Jesse McKinley, *Several Recent Suicides Put Light on Pressures Facing Gay Teenagers*, N.Y. TIMES, Oct. 4, 2010 (noting the suicide-deaths of thirteen-year-old Seth Walsh, eighteen-year-old Tyler Clementi, fifteen-year-old Billy Lucas, and thirteen-year-old Asher Brown). Most Gay suicides, like most Gay killings, go unnoticed and undocumented. For the staggering statistics on Gay youth suicide, see Chapter 4, this volume. See also SHANNON GILREATH, SEXUAL IDENTITY LAW IN CONTEXT: CASES AND MATERIALS (2007) (collecting data).

11 Zach Christman, *Gay Panic Defense Gets Murder Defendant Off*, NBC Online (2009), http://www.nbcchicago.com/news/local-beat/Gay-Panic-Defense-Gets-Murder-Defendant-Off.html.

distinction has meant for Gays in the wake of *Lawrence v. Texas*, which drew a sharp distinction between the liberty afforded Gays in private, on the one hand, and citizenship more fully understood, on the other.[12] The private, as best understood in the American tradition, has generally been where power is left alone with itself. The Supreme Court's decision protecting a man's possession of obscene (and therefore illegal) material in his home is a prime example.[13] The injuries worked by the public–private distinction are subtle (to those who never experience them) and therefore must be teased out. So let me state *Stanley v. Georgia* again in its own terms: A *man* may not be prosecuted for possession of obscene materials in *his* home.[14] This is the judicial equivalent of "a man's home is his castle." The decision does not inquire into reality to any greater extent than is necessary to accomplish its end, namely to leave power alone with itself. The decision does not consider who else might be in the house. Are there women? Children? Subordinated men? Others on whom the pornography at issue might be used, imposed, forced? What are the consequences for women, children, other men when the pornography user leaves his house? Won't he take what he internalizes from the pornography he uses in private into his public interactions, whether or not they become private? Underlined here is Catharine MacKinnon's observation that "privacy as an ideal has been formulated in liberal terms [and] holds that so long as the public does not interfere, autonomous individuals interact freely and equally."[15]

Women, children, and to this list must be added Gays, also have been relegated to the private, but unlike for straight men, this privatization entails no power. For the women, children, and Gays so relegated, the private most often means invisibility, marginalization, contempt, violence – powerlessness. For example, abortion is relegated to the private (the right to privacy), ensuring that the state need not facilitate access to reproductive control for women – especially not for the women most in need of it (poor and minority women).[16] The right to engage in Gay sex, too, is construed in terms of privacy – either to say that no such privacy exists, so that even Gay people's most intimate

---

[12] See Chapter 3, this volume.
[13] Stanley v. Georgia, 349 U.S. 557 (1969).
[14] Id. at 565. "These are the rights that appellant is asserting in the case before us. He is asserting the right to read or observe what he pleases – the right to satisfy his intellectual and emotional needs in the privacy of his own home. He is asserting the right to be free from state inquiry into the contents of his library."
[15] Catharine A. MacKinnon, Feminism Unmodified: Discourses on Life and Law 99 (1988).
[16] Harris v. McRae, 448 U.S. 297 (1980).

moments may be regulated by the state,[17] or to say that the privacy is nearly absolute, so that those shrouded in it must deal alone with its consequences.[18]

The limits of the private constitute the boundaries of the public, boundaries beyond which Gay people are rarely present. When we are present, we are subordinated. *Lawrence v. Texas* understands the right to have Gay sex as a private right.[19] The Supreme Court is careful to point out that the opinion does not cover "public conduct."[20] Analyzed only in familiar, straight terms, this looks quite reasonable. As Justice Blackmun dissented in *Hardwick*, the issue of what kind of sex a person may have involves the most fundamental of rights – the "right to be let alone."[21] Both Gay and straight are to be let alone after *Lawrence*. But being let alone has an entirely different meaning for Gays than for straights. For Gays it can still mean victimization, this time by the absence of law.[22] And transgressing the boundary into the public has different consequences depending on the group to which one belongs.[23] The status and prerogative of straight people in public still authoritatively constitute the definition of citizenship. For straight people on their own terms, the terms of an individual exercising nearly unfettered liberty (power), the private is a shelter. For Gays, it can be a prison where the deepest deprivations of personhood take place. Privacy rights are prime exemplars of individual rights – the mantra of both conservatism and liberalism converging in a vortex. Privacy rights can be exercised only on an individual basis, even when you are assigned to the private based on your group identity. It is a matter of no small significance, then, that the very conduct by which Gays are defined – homosexual sex – is considered, socially, politically, legally – quintessentially – private.

Equality/Sameness/Difference

Equality rights, by contrast, are group-based rights, public in their very essence. Surely, individuals may suffer discrimination, or may feel its effects,

---

[17] Bowers v. Hardwick, 478 U.S. 186 (1986).

[18] People v. Onofre, 415 N.E.2d 936 (1980); Powell v. Georgia, 510 S.E. 2d 18 (1998).

[19] Lawrence v. Texas, 539 U.S. 558, 578 (2003).

[20] Id.

[21] *Bowers, supra* note 17, at 199 (Blackmun, J., dissenting) (quoting Olmstead v. United States, 277 U.S. 438, 478 [1928]).

[22] Data show that domestic violence in same-sex relationships is at least as great as, if not greater than, that in straight relationships, and underreported to an even greater degree. In many states, access to protective orders in such situations is severely restricted or nonexistent.

[23] Even after *Lawrence*, some states continue to enforce sodomy laws against Gay sex in areas denominated "public," visiting Draconian penalties on Gays when analogous sexual conduct by straights (i.e., vaginal intercourse) in the same setting would warrant considerably less criminal sanction. Often the difference is between felony prosecution and sex-offender

one at a time, but the basis for the discrimination is rooted in group animus – in this context, straight versus Gay – and at stake is the very public definition of citizenship. Access to equal citizenship is controlled by an invention of semantic genius often referred to as the "similarly situated" test – coded in terms of "sameness" (or "likeness") and difference. As applied specifically to the straight–Gay hierarchy, the "similarly situated" formalism means that Gays *may* be deemed sufficiently like straights to warrant some derivative rights status, for example, the abbreviated protection privacy affords, via equal application in the name of equality (as in *Lawrence*). Usually, in such instances, straight people want a right they have not previously enjoyed (or have not enjoyed universally), and they are not overly threatened if Gays are brought along with the tide. At stake is usually a narrow right, for example, the right to engage in consensual sodomy in private, at issue in *Lawrence*. At all times the right is modeled by, after, and for the Heteroarchy, and their needs define its limits.[24] But when access to status in the public space is in contest, whereby public inequalities are challenged on legal grounds (e.g., open access to military service or the civil status of marriage), such deprivations generally are not interpreted as inequalities at all, but rather as reasonable legal distinctions based on legitimate differences warranting different treatment. Put simply, the law recognizes legitimate striving only in terms of what straight people need.

In this book, I posit an alternative approach to equality that would better serve the needs of Gays and other minorities who find their appeals for equal treatment rejected too often because they are not adjudged sufficiently similar to the archetypal class (straights, in the case of Gay equality claims). It is also a conceptualization of equality that explicitly rejects the myopic obsession of the "gay rights movement" to be *like straight* people. I call the alternative approach "substantive equality" in order to differentiate it from the current American approach, which is often called "formal equality." The term "substantive equality" is not new; it is encountered in legal literature as a referent for a variety of methodologies and epistemologies that are neither substantive nor equal. Only rarely has it referred to a methodology that is both substantive and equal, as will become clear.

In my argument for substantive equality, centered on the analysis of *Lawrence v. Texas* in Chapter 3, I am refining and applying a theoretical framework that has some considerable forebears. Specifically, I'd like to mention

registration (for oral/anal sex, that which is paradigmatically Gay, in public) and misdemeanor prosecution and a fine (for vaginal intercourse in public).

[24] See the critique of *Lawrence v. Texas*, Chapter 3, this volume.

Professor Ruth Colker, who has done excellent work on a caste-based analysis of the equality norm.[25] Professor Cass Sunstein, who calls his own work anticaste, must also be mentioned. But Sunstein's work is essentially heteroarchal in that the theory he pursues explicitly rejects Gays and the Gay experience.[26] Professor Kenneth Karst perhaps began the discussion by suggesting the centrality of the Fourteenth Amendment Equal Protection Clause (or what I like to refer to as the "equality norm") to constitutional interpretation, even though in conversations about drafts of chapters for this book he told me he thinks that asking courts to make subordination-grounded inquiries of the kind I advocate is impractical (if not impossible).[27] And to the large extent that my critique centers on power/powerlessness, Andrea Dworkin deserves considerable credit, because it was her writing that first opened my eyes to the idea – the truth – that equality is something other/more than being the close approximation of the oppressor.

But of these notable exceptions to the rule that equality is formalism only, Professor Catharine MacKinnon is the most notable (and noteworthy) of all. Her book, *Sexual Harassment of Working Women*, is an early exposition of a legal analysis that is dominance-centered. It is hard to imagine that any equality scholar writing after her has not been influenced by Professor MacKinnon's work.[28] MacKinnon's subsequent decades of work have been spent developing

---

[25] Ruth Colker, *Anti-Subordination Above All: Sex, Race, and Equal Protection*, 61 N.Y.U. L. Rev. 1003 (1986). Professor Colker does not use the word "caste," but her understanding of equality in terms of freedom from subordination is foundational.

[26] Cass R. Sunstein, *The Anticaste Principle*, 92 Mich. L. Rev. 2410, 2433 n. 74 (1994).

[27] I am grateful to Professor Karst for taking my work seriously and helping me to make it stronger. That graciousness has not always been present in those who share his ultimate assessment that asking courts to treat equality substantively is an impossible endeavor. An almost immediate investment in the system surfaces in recitations of its imperviousness to change. Lawyers, especially liberal lawyers, offer me this defense – this reason – that what I propose won't work, can't work. The law as possibility is coterminous with the law as precedent. Especially do lawyers in academe insist that I accept this. I suppose it is understandable that the abstract level at which most legal academics engage the law with their lives makes the practicality with which I engage it look abstract. It's also understandable, if not admirable, that people whose worth is gleaned from telling other people what the law is in relation to where it has been would be resistant to throwing out what they know – even when what they know doesn't work. The obvious point here is that what I see as not working for those suffering most under our legal system (if not actually to create and impose this same suffering) doesn't register with most academics, because they are not identified with the group(s) doing the suffering. To the density of liberal defeatism currently ruling gay rights, I say simply that sometimes the law changes. Why shouldn't we be the ones who change it?

[28] Although I agree with Professor Ann Scales when she notes that *Sexual Harassment of Working Women* may be the most under-read of Professor MacKinnon's work (see Ann Scales, *Disappearing Medusa: The Fate of Feminist Legal Theory?* 20 Harv. Women's L.J. 34, 39 n. 21 [1997]), I also agree that this is a shame.

and refining her dominance-based theory of inequality. Of those who have written about equality as something substantive, MacKinnon has done the finest job of describing the American theory of equality, which has been in name only, or what she has adroitly named the "stupid theory" of equality, and unmasking it as the tool of domination it has always been.

Citing Professor MacKinnon's work as formative is not, however, without risk (although it is the only fair thing to do). It is risky because conservatives and liberals alike have tried to set up MacKinnon as a straw woman in order to dismiss any substantive interpretive theory that might "mistake" the lives of marginalized people for reality. Conservatives and liberals converge to find reasons not to engage her theorizing, either because they lack the courage to engage it or because they have in fact engaged it in private, at lunches, in the halls of the good old boys' club and found it dangerous to their straight male hegemony. Thus, in their omnipotence, they label it too practical to be intellectual or too intellectual to be practical.

Citing MacKinnon also risks my being dismissed as, in the case of Chris Kendall, "a misguided faggot to do MacKinnon's dirty work."[29] Such attacks are unfair. I believe that the particularized oppression that is straight over Gay goes deeper than the gender paradigm is equipped to uncover or, in the least, that Gay experiences should not be submerged totally in an analytic that was not created to deal with the particularities of our experiences. Consequently, Gay life under straight supremacy needs its own theory of action – one attuned to the specificities of straight-over-Gay domination. That is the purpose of *The End of Straight Supremacy*. Moreover, I do not agree with everything Professor MacKinnon has said, and although she has been a supportive and encouraging friendly acquaintance, I certainly have no reason to believe that she agrees with everything I say.[30] What MacKinnon has given us – those of us who believe that equality can be something substantive and meaningful – is the prerogative to look at inequality under the law as a

---

[29] This is especially true to the extent that MacKinnon's and my views coincide on the issue of pornography. Brenda Cossman, *Return of the Loonies: Feminists Tell Supreme Court That Gay and Lesbian Porn Is Evil*, XTRA! Dec. 30, 1999. This particular "misguided fag" accusation was aimed at Christopher N. Kendall, whose brilliantly argued *Gay Male Pornography: An Issue of Sex Discrimination* (2004) was the first serious sex equality critique of Gay pornography by a Gay male legal scholar. The work of building a sex equality theory specifically applicable to Gay lives has been done most impressively, although not exclusively, by Kendall and by Professor Marc Spindelman.

[30] See Shannon Gilreath, *Some Penetrating Observations on the Fifth Anniversary of Lawrence v. Texas: Privacy, Dominance, and Substantive Equality Theory*, 30 WOMEN'S RIGHTS LAW REPORTER 442, 455, n. 66 (disputing the conclusions MacKinnon draws as to the equality implications of facially "neutral" sodomy laws).

question of power distribution, not simply as one of categorized differences. That point of departure in analyzing any system of inequality makes all of the *difference*. In other words, in order for a theory analyzing the subordination of Gay to straight to be substantive, it must understand the substance of homophobia, not merely the pervasive (but rationalized) manifestations of it. It is a theory that is necessarily as epistemic as it is reactive. I do not think it unduly laudatory to say that by changing the analytic with regard to male over female domination, MacKinnon has made this type of inquiry a serious possibility. The work for an equality practice that takes the lives of marginalized people seriously and finally does something for them deserves to be carried on and made relevant in places it has never been before and, in the process, perhaps amplified or – dare I say – made better. This is the work of *The End of Straight Supremacy*. I say this without hubris, but rather with a sense of purpose. As Andrea Dworkin put it so well, "Women and male homosexuals are united in [our] queerness." Just as Gay liberation historically relied heavily on the theoretical inventions of Radical feminism, the theory of equality presented here does so – proudly.

Free Speech/Expression

A substantial portion of this book engages the standard American conceptualization of freedom of expression, which is free speech absolutism/authoritarianism/fundamentalism[31] – a conceptualization of free speech that is at best disastrously undertheorized, at worst calculatingly homicidal. In her groundbreaking essay, *The Straight Mind*, Monique Wittig spoke of "discourses of heterosexuality" that manage oppression through their totalizing illogic.[32] As Wittig observed, these discourses of heterosexuality "prevent us from speaking unless we speak in their terms."[33] The discourse about discourse in this country, which is to say "free" speech, which is to say "straight talk," is the discourse of heterosexual male hegemony, and the reaction to any suggested alterations in the system have been the most vivid demonstrations of straight male power I have ever witnessed.

The current law of free speech in the United States is, for Gay people, nothing short of a roadmap to death. It has the effect (and convincingly, in multiple aspects, the intent) of robbing Gay people of the ability to speak in

---

[31] I use these terms interchangeably in the primary discussion of this topic in Chapter 4, this volume.

[32] Monique Wittig, The Straight Mind and Other Essays 25 (1992).

[33] Id.

any voice other than that approved for heterosexual discourse (e.g., Don't Ask, Don't Tell), while giving unfettered verbal license to the most resilient murderous impulses of our enemies (e.g., free speech absolutism).[34] Understand this, Gay people will not – cannot – be equal in the United States until the lethal American approach to freedom of expression is rethought and re-acted.

In *The Straight Mind*, Wittig offers pornography as her example of the superordinate discourse of heterosexuality. I certainly agree that pornography constitutes this type of oppressive discourse.[35] But here I would also like to suggest that marriage is another of these discourses that has mostly prevented Gay people from speaking in anything but straight terms. The predominating discourses on pornography and same-sex marriage are composed curiously of the same stuff. Both discourses center, superficially at least, on a morality theme – to a lesser or greater degree depending on who is doing the moralizing, but almost always in decidedly moral terms. Both, however, are really about power – who has it, who wants it, and what those who have it will do to keep it. No amount of moralizing can dissolve what are, at bottom, indissoluble questions of distribution of power. Lest my readers think that an analogy between marriage and pornography/"speech" here is too far-fetched, Professor Douglas Laycock, primary editor and a contributor to the book that was the subject of the book review that became Chapter 7, makes the connection himself, in his simultaneous defense of anti-Gay discrimination and denunciation of hate speech regulation, making essentially my point here in reverse.[36] Professor Laycock apparently believes that enough moralizing about pornography and enough moralizing about same-sex marriage transforms both into moral questions, quite irrespective of, and often in direct opposition to, the real equality concerns that underlie both practices. All of this is accomplished in the guise of what purports to be scholarship supportive of "gay rights."[37] Truly, as Wittig observed, the discourse of heterosexuality is totalizing, and heterosexuality is the totality of the law that emerges out of it. The universalizing nature of the straight mind enacts its ideologies into law, charged with a simultaneous construction and interpretation of reality in straight terms. And as Thelma observed (in the movie *Thelma & Louise*), the law is "some tricky shit."[38]

---

[34] See Chapter 4, this volume.
[35] See Chapter 5, this volume.
[36] Douglas Laycock, Afterword to SAME-SEX MARRIAGE AND RELIGIOUS LIBERTY: EMERGING CONFLICTS 189, 193 (Douglas Laycock et al., eds., 2008).
[37] Id. at 190.
[38] THELMA & LOUISE (Sony Pictures, 1991).

Religion

Although it includes a discussion of religion and religionists, since unfortunately no discussion of Gay liberation can take place without it, this book marks a substantial departure from the theory of *Sexual Politics*, moving beyond the elaborate reformist defense of organized religion in the lives of Gay people found there.[39] Professor Mary Daly rightly recognized that "[p]atriarchy is itself the prevailing religion of the entire planet."[40] Patriarchy is the religion of the men and women who constitute the Heteroarchy.[41] The straight men who are patriarchy and the women who defend them, because they are deluded into believing that they have a real stake in patriarchy, form the Heteroarchy, which has as its sole purpose the containment of the Gay menace – indeed, its ultimate erasure. In light of this realization, the absence of a reformist discussion of religion from this book is not accidental. It is an intentional departure from my earlier work, which sought to defend Gay participation in organized religion. The absence of that defense here is not meant to be a condemnation of those Gays still captured by religious dementia; it is simply movement beyond – from reformism to resistance.

THE METHODOLOGY OF THIS BOOK

The Personality of Pronouns

The first rule of our entire culture is that it is heterosexist. This applies as well to the process by which scholarship is "judged" to be worthwhile and publishable. Hetero-speak is taken to be inherently objective, a voice that is beyond situatedness with no seeming stake or ideological investment that might color its view and, hence, taint its scholarly claims. To say that this objective-hetero is the norm would be the grossest of understatements. In contrast, the Gay writer (at least the Gay writer who does not take pains to sound like a straight writer) is viewed as situated in a position, one that limits his scholarly objectivity and range because it is not heterosexual. Anything said from this subject position will be discounted as biased and untrustworthy. I have encountered

---

[39] See Shannon Gilreath, Sexual Politics: The Gay Person in America Today (2006) (esp. ch. 2).

[40] Mary Daly, Gyn/Ecology: The Metaethics of Radical Feminism 39 (1978). Unfortunately, Daly falls under one of patriarchy's chief deceptions, casting Gay men as the "other" and separating us from our Lesbian (Gay) sisters, in an attempt at some mutilated version of Sisterhood. Despite this failing, Daly's observation regarding religion is generative.

[41] I mean here to include all patriarchal religions: Christianity, Islam, Judaism, Hinduism, and Buddhism.

the stalwartness of this rule in my work before, but never to the extent that I have encountered it while at work on *The End of Straight Supremacy.*

Before publishing a book, academic presses vet manuscripts through a process of multiple reviews by peer scholars or critics; although these readers remain anonymous, the author does have the benefit of reading the reviews themselves. Reading one of the peer reviews of this manuscript, I was reminded of the law of hetero-speak.

This reviewer took explicit issue with my use of the first person, claiming it made the book come off as "precious," an adjective whose gender connotations ought to raise eyebrows. The ambiguity of the third person and its impenetrable pronouns has been favored historically in the academic writing done by powerful people whose identities are so pervasive, so omnipresent that they can afford the game of pretending detachment and throwing their voices through disembodied pronouns, as if the authors were not really of the world about which they write. Most straight-identified academics have the luxury of this kind of standardized/dead writing.

But this is not a luxury available to many Gay people. For a Gay author writing about Gay people to engage in this sort of Self-denial in the guise of academic neutrality would make little sense given the systematic erasure of the Gay Self by the hetero-register of language. Indeed, it might suggest academementia incarnate.[42] The fact is that speaking in the first person is the only honest way for a Gay person to render his or her actual relationship to Heteroarchy – a relationship of alienation, negation, and erasure. It is alien because Gays are ourselves alien from the heteroarchal power structure that not only tells us that we have no Self to express but, through grammar and established style, deprives us of the linguistic register – including pronouns – that would be needed to register an objection, were a Gay one inclined to do so. The ultimate lie, of course, is The Lie that tells us we are simply "disordered" (in the words of the Vatican) straights in need of reordering.[43] No Self

---

[42] Academementia: normal state of persons in academia, marked by varying and progressive degrees; irreversible deterioration of faculties of intellectuals. Mary Daly & Jane Caputi, Websters' First New Intergalactic Wickedary of the English Language 184 (1987).

[43] See Sacred Congregation for the Doctrine of the Faith, Letter on the pastoral care of homosexual persons (Oct. 1, 1986). And see Sacred Congregation for the Doctrine of the Faith, Declaration on Certain Questions Concerning Sexual Ethics § 8 (1975) ("[H]omosexual acts are intrinsically disordered and can in no case be approved of"). This is what José Gabilondo has named the "axiomatic heteronormativity" of Catholic doctrine. See J. Gabilondo, *When God Hates: How Liberal Guilt Lets the New Right Get Away with Murder,* 44 Wake Forest L. Rev. 617, 626 (2009). The Catholic catechism also states that the homosexual "inclination" is "objectively disordered." In this case, as in most, the objective measure of the objective is the straight say-so.

that is authentic, no existentiality, is conceded to us. What is needed, consequently, for and by Gay people, is existential courage and the willingness to break out of the heterosexual register.

The problem is compounded because I am writing about the law, a field that has a very special relationship to notions of authority, power, and personhood. Lawyers usually do what they can to make the law seem inhuman. Most problems are analyzed in terms of decontextualized hypotheticals – assumed people and stylized problems. Lawyers take the stories of people's lives and extract them into something they call "the facts." Many casebooks (the legal texts from which law students are taught) pare down these "facts" to near nothingness. It is the *rule of law*, not human stories, that is important. The impassioned (read: zealous for the law) but dispassionate lawyer is the model. But at some point, especially in the representation of the marginalized, one becomes aware (if one is a good lawyer) that one is dealing with somebody's real life – with somebody's story. After all, the Gay people I know are real people, with all too real injuries, and they need law and a Gay Movement that understands them as they are – not as they might be imagined for the sake of simpler and "straighter" legal doctrine.

The philosophy and narrative ("the facts") of Gay liberation is a story, too. It is a story, often bloody, of the oppression of an entire population of people. Indeed, it constitutes a genus, in the sense of a people identified by an immutable characteristic. Because I am, in addition to a lawyer and an academic, a Gay man, it is a story that is personal, in a first-person kind of way. So in this book you are spared the usual musings of the scientist observing the ant colony. In this book, the ant speaks for himself.[44]

In academentia in the third person, however, knowing less about a subject seems to give you more credibility, and the appearance that you are not present in your own analysis is its cachet. Appellate judges in the United States, for example, even those writing for a solid majority, almost never employ the first person. Indeed, in the law, empathy is suspect. Consider the way that President Obama's suggestion that nominees to the United States Supreme Court should possess empathy ignited a firestorm of criticism.[45] Surely you don't mean that judges should start caring about *actual* people, his critics seemed to be saying. Just the law, please, and its denizens, imagined and

---

[44] The French call this kind of writing from experience *témoignage* and evidently respect it. In the United States it's called "anecdote" and is nearly universally disregarded by the superficially sophisticated, who prefer instead the superficiality of abstraction.

[45] Major Garrett, *Obama Pushes for "Empathic" Supreme Court Justices*, FOXNEWS.COM, May 1, 2009, http://www.foxnews.com/politics/2009/05/01/obama-pushes-empathic-supreme-court-justices/.

disembodied. Maybe this is because legal education seems to pride itself on encouraging dissociation from the empathic impulses most of us have naturally as human beings. But nothing about the law or its supposed majesty demands this. It is enlightening to observe that, in Canada, judges writing in appellate opinions, even for majority opinions, frequently use "I."

The problem is further compounded because I am specifically writing *about* Gay people. As usual, the Gay man is taken to be his most credible when he is invisible or trying valiantly to become so. I was struck by a post last year to the Catholic legal theory blog, *Mirror of Justice*, in which a law professor questioned the objectivity of my work challenging, on equality grounds, so-called religious conscience exemptions to antidiscrimination laws protecting Gays and Lesbians, specifically in this case in the context of marriage equality laws.[46] Essentially, his criticism turned on discounting my work because I have a "horse in the race," as he put it, and, perhaps more disturbingly, because I admit it.[47] This despite the fact that I am constantly saying that I don't think marriage is an appropriate end goal for Gay liberation. It is worth noting here that the professor offering this criticism was also a Jesuit priest. It is enlightening that he would comment on my supposed investment in the debate without realizing his own investment in the system of sexual fascism he theorizes to support.[48] From the perspective of the Heterarchy, my assertion of Self, my first person, my "I," makes me untrustworthy. His "I" is rendered invisible. Why? Because he tries to pass off his "I" – an overt assertion of heteronormative identification that sweeps up not only populations but the institutional machinery of the world's oldest governmental and religious bureaucracy – as so fused with the natural social order as to have nothing to do with him. In contrast, my "I," as a Gay man, makes me immediately suspect, subversive, somehow dishonest. His "I," as a straight man, makes him authoritative – comfortably, academically neutral.[49] It is a double

[46] Robert John Araujo, *Another Interesting Article on Closer Examination*, Mirror of Justice Blog (Dec. 1, 2009, 8:14 P.M.), http://mirrorofjustice.blogs.com/mirrorofjustice/2009/12/another-interesting-article-on-closer-examination.html.

[47] Id.

[48] But this is true of most heterocratic critiques of Gay scholarship, as in, for example, attacks on John Boswell's scholarship in the 1980s and 1990s by professors of Christian-this-and-that (history, ethics, etc.), e.g., the suggestion of Robert Wilkin, professor of the history of Christianity at the University of Virginia, that Boswell's work was merely "advocacy scholarship"; see Larry B. Stammer, *Book's Claims Disturb Church*, Washington Post, June 10, 1994.

[49] Gay writers have this in common with women writers. In analyzing the reception of women writers and women's ideas in the male-dominated space, Andrea Dworkin articulates the male perspective on the legitimacy of women's thought: "Women have stupid ideas that do not deserve to be called ideas. Marabel Morgan writes an awful, silly, terrible book in which

standard that has long been the rule, although its days as a default rule may be numbered.

I don't feign neutrality (nor am I persuaded much by the Jesuit's claim to neutrality), and neither I nor my real peers have the luxury of treating the Heteroarchy and its injuries as some abstract hypothetical used to tease out delicious contradictions and ambiguities in a law classroom. I can't really feign gratitude when the straight hierarchy is simply less cruel than it could be or when, capitulating to social and civil pressure, it is less cruel than it has been and would like to continue to be. Ironically enough, though, quite modestly recognizing my own presence and intellectual agency in a debate about the moral and legal foundations of my existence would seem to mark me for suspicion in the minds of heterocratic thinkers.

Be that as it may, my approach in this regard is an important part of the method of this book. Gay people – the people about whom and for whom I write – are routinely denied the "I am" as an epistemological assertion of Self that is taken for granted by straight society. Law and public institutions are designed to safeguard the straight conception of Self, to enrich it, and to scaffold it. No such institutional framework exists to support Gay Selfhood. Because Gay people have been denied the "I am," they have also been denied the "you," in the *j'accuse* sense. By this I mean that in the absence of an identity of their own making – a position from which to see, speak, name, and accuse – Gays have been denied the ability to advocate effectively against social, political, and economic oppressions. Because of this, what is oppression sometimes feels like freedom, or is claimed as such, to give the victims an identity stake in a power structure in which they are otherwise outsiders.

Consider the phenomenon of "acting straight" as a way out. To be a "masculine" or "straight-acting" Gay man (or feminine Lesbian) is a way of siding with the abusers and claiming straight male dominance (perhaps most obvious in gay pornography). Many times I have heard from Gays a variant of "I'm Gay, but my sexuality doesn't define me." It is a natural reaction born from living in a straight supremacist system that has systematically devalued and scorned Gay sexuality. Hope in this system comes from a cultivated ability

---

she claims that women must exist for their husbands, do sex and be sex for their husbands. D. H. Lawrence writes vile and stupid essays in which he says the same thing basically with many references to the divine phallus; but D. H. Lawrence is smart. Anita Bryant says that cocksucking is a form of human cannibalism; she decries the loss of the child that is the sperm. Norman Mailer believes that lost ejaculations are lost sons and on that basis disparages male homosexuality, masturbation, and contraception. But Anita Bryant is stupid and Norman Mailer is smart." ANDREA DWORKIN, RIGHT WING WOMEN 40–41 (1983) (internal citations omitted).

to blend into the Heteroarchy, diminishing any qualities that might make one stand out, sexually speaking. As I explained in *Sexual Politics*, it is a deadly posture, conditioning the survival of "straight-acting" Gays on the destruction of Gay-identified Gays.[50] The destruction of the moral capacity of Gays as such is a systematized part of straight-over-Gay domination that starts at birth. The result is a straight-conditioned hostility by some Gays toward other Gays, thereby directing the Heteroarchy's deadly attentions onto some other Gay who is less willing to conform (and, thereby, from the perspective of the Gay who has adopted the sadism of the straight perspective, one more deserving of destruction – conceptually and/or physically). Therefore, an important project of Gay liberation, and of this book, is to discern a more authentic "I" – to take back the Self.

How could I be objective about any of this? Indeed, it would be an attempt to sound objective that should produce the kind of suspicion that my peer reviewer intimated. It is this act of Be-speaking that I think is so suspect to the Heteroarchy's academics and reviewers. As Catharine MacKinnon rightly observed in the context of feminism, "[O]bjectivity is the epistemological stance of which objectification is the social process."[51] In a subject–object culture, one must be a subject in order to be objective about much. To be objective about being objectified is to be dead.

Does this make my work "precious"? There are, of course, different dictionary meanings of that adjective.[52] Does my honesty make my work "highly valued" or of "great importance"? I would hope so. This is a welcome interpretation, although it might not be the subjective one intended by the peer reviewer. It certainly makes my work "rare or unique," such that it should "not be wasted." Does it emphatically "express irritation, dislike, contempt … or some other strong emotion"? You bet it does. Is it acknowledging "endearment"? Indeed, it is, for I take my Gay brothers and sisters to be dear ones. I suspect, though, given that this was a criticism, the reviewer more likely meant that my use of the first person makes my work too "fastidious," for

---

[50] Gilreath, Sexual Politics, *supra* note 39, at 33.
[51] MacKinnon, Feminism Unmodified, *supra* note 15 at 50.
[52] The full definition I reference here is from the *Encarta World English Dictionary* (St. Martin's Press, 1999): "pre-cious adj. 1. VALUABLE worth a great deal of money 2. VALUED highly valued, much loved, or considered to be of great importance 3. NOT TO BE WASTED rare or unique and therefore to be used wisely or sparingly or treated with care 4. USED FOR EMPHASIS used for emphasis to express irritation, dislike, contempt, bemusement, or some other strong emotion (informal) 5. FASTIDIOUS OR AFFECTED too carefully refined in language, dress and manners – adv. VERY very, often by way of a complaint – n. TERM OF ENDEARMENT used as a term of affection in talking to somebody."

which dictionary definitions are "demanding" and "scornful." I am proudly these things as well, demanding that the law acknowledge its failure for Gay people and also scorning its intransigence.

On Naming Names: The Straight Problem

Some people will call this book "anti-straight." There is an irony here, because we live in a world that is overwhelmingly, lethally anti-Gay. Traditionally, of course, homosexuality was a punishable crime, protestations about some meaningful distinction between status and conduct notwithstanding.[53] Myriad laws, including constitutional amendments designed to keep heterosupremacist institutions, like marriage, supremacist, continue to exist to remind us of our place. Today, violence against Gays is at epidemic proportions, up many hundredfold in some places. The more we come out, the more visible we become, the more we are brutalized. I hear frequently, through letters, email, the odd phone call, of Gays assaulted, sometimes killed. Few of these crimes make the mainstream media; even fewer are prosecuted. In most states, attacks on Gays aren't even considered "hate crimes," and only after a decade of the most determined activism were we afforded this consideration at the federal level. Group-defamation campaigns are carried out against us on a daily basis, from Fox News to the insertion of insidious propaganda at the grade school level, all defended by liberals as free speech.

The system of straight supremacy is so pervasive that parents turn on their own children, and home life and school life are so hellish that Gay youth take their own lives at a dizzying pace. And the American Heteroarchy exports its buoyant hatred when it gets the chance, with American religious zealots championing the sort of theocratic responses to homosexuality, namely capital punishment, they'd like to see here in places where instability and undereducation ensure it is met with less resistance.[54] Meanwhile, every president, even a liberal one like Obama, attends the National Prayer Breakfast organized by these same murderers. Meanwhile, Gays and supposedly progressive straights have adopted the good-natured delusion, with Anne Frank, that "people are really good at heart,"[55] clinging to the belief that freedom of religion means the freedom to proselytize hatred and then cry foul at any hint of censure.

---

[53] *Bowers, supra* note 17, at 190 (1986).
[54] Consider, for example, recent efforts of some American evangelists to support the death penalty for homosexuality in Uganda.
[55] ANNE FRANK, ANNE FRANK: THE DIARY OF A YOUNG GIRL 237 (1993).

Gays are dying because of this simplemindedness. These are frank observations about power.

When one criticizes the power of people whose power is so pervasive as to be rendered invisible to them, one is accused of attacking one's subject. But, in fact, I am convinced that straight people have the capacity to change their ways. If I did not believe this, this would be a very different book. It would advocate Gay separatism, with land and guns – lots of guns. The reader will see that at various points in the following analysis I feel compelled to make special note that I do not mean to personalize. I'm not suggesting that every straight person is part of what I call in this book the Heteroarchy, the worldview – the practice – of sexuality constructed as a difference and wielded as a weapon. Indeed, some straights have chosen, often at great cost to themselves, to reject the Heteroarchy and the death it manufactures. But I do mean to suggest that, as a class, straight people are powerful vis-à-vis Gay people and that that power is most often exercised in ways that have been massively lethal for Gay people. My job in this book is to point to an emergency, the horrors of which have been not only unanswered but largely unexamined. It has been a bloody affair, and the blood that tracks across these pages belongs to people I know and people I don't know – Gay people – whose blood can only rightfully be laid at the doorstep of the Heteroarchy and its culture of death. Those people bent on destroying Gay lives because their god told them to do it are beyond reach. But there are many more straight people who have remained silent, apathetic in the face of a problem they are often blind to. These straights have both the capacity and the resources to change this. What they need is the will to do it. In order to find this will, they must be made to see the exigency of the circumstances. This they will not do as long as Gay people continue to give them a free pass.

Consequently, part of understanding the particular condition that is straight-over-Gay domination is understanding that real rebellion requires a breaking of illusory loyalties. From Gay people this first act of rebellion requires great existential courage. Gay people exist first in a kind of straight cocoon, internalizing straight values and, inescapably, because they are all we know until we find Gay people, growing to love, admire, and emulate straight people. Some Gay people try hard to fight for Gay rights while at the same time maintaining loyalties to subgroups of straight people. But part of Gay liberation is understanding that some of those loyalties are deadly. One thing is certain: Gays cannot be free of straight domination unless and until we are willing to challenge the dominance of even those subgroups of straight people we like to think of as "our own."

On Naming Names: The Gay "Problem"

Language has its own politics. Anyone writing seriously about Gay issues must confront the initial and important question of what term to use in describing the people for whom and about whom one writes. After writing *Sexual Politics*, I made a choice to use "Gay" (capitalized) inclusively to mean men and women: Gay and Lesbian. This is the convention I have adhered to in *The End of Straight Supremacy*. As a feminist, I am certainly aware of the gendered perceptions of what this choice means. But none of the alternatives seem satisfying to me either. For example, "homosexual" would be the term that most obviously does not denote male exclusively. The use of "homosexual" as inclusive of Gays and Lesbians was vigorously suggested by Twiss Butler in conversation with me. But I decided not to take her advice. Many Gays object to the use of "homosexual" because of its clinical origins. Moreover, despite Ms. Butler's insistence on the inclusiveness of the term, others demur. Mary Daly, for example, in her book *Gyn/Ecology*, recanted the use of "homosexual," calling it a "treacherous term" that "reductionistically 'includes,' that is, excludes, gynocentric be-ing/Lesbianism."[56] I don't really agree with Daly on this, any more than I agree with Ms. Butler that "Gay" is problematic; I reference Daly only to suggest that the inclusive nature of "homosexual" is far from definitively established. Likewise, "queer" has similar problems and is seldom used outside academe. Cumbersome acronyms, like LGBTQ (to mean Lesbian, Gay, bisexual, transgender, and questioning – and there are still longer, more inclusive versions with even more letters), are likewise difficult to use regularly. Moreover, since I do not believe that bisexuality has any real political dimension and is, therefore, outside of my discussion in this book, and since I never claim transsexuality (or the politically correct: transgender identity) as liberation, for reasons dealt with at length in Chapter 8, the use of LGBT in the context of this work would be deceptive.

Also, I think it is inaccurate to say that the use of "Gay" is equivalent to the traditional use of "man" as a bland but unconvincing insistence by men that it includes women. As originally claimed by Gay liberationists, "Gay" was intended to be gender-inclusive. Moreover, I reject the sexism inherent in the archetypal straight logic that demands I see sexism in places where it does not exist. Straights invented sexism and continue to wallow in it. The sexist division of men and women into competing camps that is insisted upon by straight people and by gays (in this case necessarily reflected in the lower-case because they cannot be authentically Gay while merely mimicking the

---

[56] Daly, *supra* note 40, at xi.

Heteroarchy) is as alien to Gay liberation as Gays are alien to the Heteroarchy. As Carl Wittman stated in one of Gay liberation's important formative documents, "A Gay Manifesto":

> Male chauvinism ... is not central to [Gay men]. We can junk it much more easily than straight men can. For we understand oppression. We have largely opted out of a system which oppresses women daily – our egos are not built on putting women down and having them build us up. Also, living in a mostly male world we have become used to playing different roles, doing our own shit-work. And finally, we have a common enemy: the big male chauvinists are also the big anti-gays.... Chick equals nigger equals queer. Think it over.[57]

Professor Daly's analysis of this issue,[58] insisting on Lesbian separatism, insisting that women who identify as "gay" cannot be "Female-identified" and certainly not "Lesbian" (in Daly's sense of the capitalized word), deriding Gay Pride, and seeing the identification of women with "gay rights" as necessarily precluding them from identifying with women's rights, although she never quite explains why, is paradigmatically heterocratic logic, and I reject it.[59] It is intellectually vulnerable because it is rife with the very sexism it purports to reject, failing to comprehend its own investment in a system it vociferously

---

[57] Carl Wittman, *A Gay Manifesto* (1969), reprinted in NEIL MILLER, OUT OF THE PAST: GAY AND LESBIAN HISTORY FROM 1869 TO THE PRESENT 385–387 (1995).

   Nicholas Bamforth provides a lucid introduction to the philosophical differences between "gay rights" and Gay liberation – in the process illuminating the original conceptualization of "gay" as gender-inclusive.

> The word "gay" became popularly associated with non-heterosexual men and women with the rise of the Gay Liberation Front after the 1969 Stonewall Riot in New York, although the word had been widely used as a self-description for some years prior to this. While the liberationists may have popularized the word "gay," however, according to Barry Adam, "[g]ay liberation never thought of itself as a civil rights movement for a particular minority." Instead, the Gay Liberation Front presented itself, on both sides of the Atlantic, as a revolutionary force dedicated to overthrowing, in conjunction with other groups, the existing system of government and society, as well as fixed sexual categories of any sort.

> John D'Emilio has therefore suggested that the idea of "gay rights" – that is, civil rights *under the existing system of government*, a reformist rather than revolutionary demand – came into its own only after the moderate Gay Activists Alliance split away from the New York Gay Liberation Front in November 1969. (Emphasis in original; internal citations omitted)

NICHOLAS BAMFOTH, SEXUALITY, MORALS AND JUSTICE: A THEORY OF LESBIAN AND GAY RIGHTS LAW 64 (1997).

[58] I certainly don't mean to denigrate Professor Daly's work in its totality. Mary Daly's utterly audacious, uncensored writing is a source of inspiration for me, welling up from the oppression that is patriarchy for women (and some men) and answering in poetic authenticity the exigent circumstances that gave (and give) her words their urgency.

[59] See, e.g., DALY, *supra* note 40, at 376. Of such women Daly writes, "She may be 'heterosexual' or 'bisexual' or 'homosexual', but she is not Lesbian" (capitalization in original).

seeks to reverse. A softer version of Daly's logic, one that would allow women to identify with Gay rights as long as the struggle was always and everywhere denominated Gay *and* Lesbian rights, is no less intellectually vulnerable because it is only slightly less heterocratic. Why must Lesbians be necessarily labeled in a way that negatively underscores "otherness" in order to be included in Gay liberation? Are they so negatively "other" by virtue of their being Lesbian (being women?) that they would be invisible if not differently labeled? In fact, a defining feature of the continuing oppression of women through the oppression of Lesbians is the feature of defining Lesbians as different and, therefore, as out of the reach of Gay liberation. QED: women – all women, even Lesbians – belong to all straight men, which is to say to the world of gender polarity, not to themselves (this is the self-imposed "gotcha" that thinkers like Daly miss), and most certainly not to Gay liberation properly. The logic assumes that sexual difference takes priority over personhood.

Thus, the insistence on Lesbian *and* Gay is an insistence on categorizations of difference that, because they constitute difference, cannot be oppositional. As Monique Wittig observed, "[T]hought based on the primacy of difference is the thought of domination."[60] The primacy of difference that pervades heterocratic logic is the ballast of sexism's yoke, and it is just this primacy of difference that the argument developed in this book explicitly rejects. Indulging in the straight fetishism for difference so clouds our thought that it makes critical inquiry, and thus possibilities critical to constituting change, impossible. There can be no hope for an abolition of the current social order in reality if it cannot be accomplished dialectically.[61] By choosing "Gay" I mean to assert as a matter of dialectics the commonality between myself and my Gay brothers and (Lesbian) sisters. I mean to slash the heterocentric dogma that imposes, after Monique Wittig's analysis, the categories "man" and "woman" as natural givens when they are really only political tools.[62] Logic of the "Adam's rib or Adam *is*, Eve is Adam's rib" kind has no place here.[63]

Having said this, I must also acknowledge that this is a book that has grown, at least in part, out of my own experiences as a Gay man. I certainly make no apologies for this. Nor do I owe any, as a Gay liberationist or as a feminist.[64] It

---

[60] WITTIG, *supra* note 32.

[61] I am using "dialectics" here in the manner in which Engels used it, to refer to a process of definitional transitioning that is ongoing.

[62] Wittig, *supra* note 32, at 13–14.

[63] Id. at 5.

[64] Certainly, one can be a feminist and not take an essentialized view, that is, not force women and men into artificially constructed opposing camps. See Andrea Dworkin, *Biological Superiority: The World's Most Dangerous and Deadly Idea* (1977), reprinted in ANDREA DWORKIN, LETTERS FROM A WAR ZONE 110–116 (1993).

is enlightening to note that the sexism critique of "Gay" never seems to turn inward to question itself. No one in such critiques seems to be observing, let alone questioning, the fact that "Lesbian," by definition, cannot include Gay men. It is a term reserved for women exclusively. This is despite the fact that the Gay man who is not also Black or Jewish or a member of some other racial or ethnic minority shares his discrimination with no one if not with Gay women. He cannot share it with straight women, because he is not a woman (although there is common discrimination that is heteroarchal/patriarchal). He cannot share it with straight men, because from the heteroarchal perspective he is a "not-man." It is with his Gay brothers, but also in real Sisterhood with his Lesbian sisters – Gay women – that he finds his strength. The new analysis of the relationships between men and women (at least Gay men and women) born of Gay liberation is dynamic in rejecting heterocentric bias in thought processes and in human relations, and in understanding that the psychic bond between Gay men and women is a change of evolutionary moment. This is Gay Power.

A Note on Capitalization

As is clear to the reader already, in this book I do not always follow conventional rules of capitalization. I capitalize the words "Gay," "Lesbian," and "Black." I do this in recognition of the fact that these categorical labels often describe far more than the mere implication of biological essence. By this I mean that "Gay," "Lesbian," and "Black" often bespeak a cultural, social, and political identity of shared experience that "white" and "straight" do not. The exception is that I don't capitalize "gay" when I am talking about an element that is not really Gay-identified – for example, when I speak of the "gay rights movement," or "gay pornography," or "gay scholarship." This will be clear to the reader in context. I also capitalize "Self" when I am using it to mean "authentic being." I also capitalize the word "Heteroarchy" (a word I made up) in an effort to show the overwhelming infrastructure and enormity of the thing. But I do not capitalize "heterocratic," "heteroarchal," "heterocentric," et cetera. In other places, infrequently, I capitalize words that aren't capitalized in standard usage because it felt right in the moment of writing and in context. Basically, when it comes to the politics of language, I am improvising. This, too, can be liberating.

THE CHALLENGE OF REALIZING GAY LIBERATION

This will be considered an extremist book. I don't here pretend that things are other than they are. My job is not to help straight people feel better about themselves. My job is to point to an emergency. This emergency is the culture of death that is killing Gay people: gaynocide. Until this emergency is made visible, we cannot begin to fight it. Particularly, I am pointing out how the law, both the written law and the norms enforced by a so-called gay rights movement, cossets killers. I want that to stop. Of course, there will be those who say that I have gone too far, as well as those who say that I have committed delegitimizing heresy by placing myself squarely within this debate rather than pretending that I am somewhere outside of it (as if any theorist could be). Nevertheless, since Self-determination by Gay people is found nowhere in straight law, which is all law, surely it deserves a place in a critique of that law, if the critique is to have any authentic Gay integrity. Gay life under straight law ultimately means that Gay people, if we are to survive, must decide, once again, whether an oppressed people can successfully attack their oppressors from a place of powerlessness. Is facing our debasement, honestly, in the ways necessary for success, worth the inevitable pain?

There is less control over us through the law and the church today than at any other time in history. Yes, absolutely, things are better on a good many fronts than they have ever been. We are now in places, visibly, where we had never been before. And why? Not because straight people saw the error of their ways and did the right thing for right's sake. No, because we did it. We changed things – through our sweat and tears and, yes, in too many instances, our blood. So as a matter of history, we are improved. But we also know that beneath the polish of today as it seems, as it is propagandized, runs a river of ahistorical blood. We have to remember that the hierarchy is capable of reorganizing itself; what it cannot successfully rebuff it can absorb, often under the auspices of pseudo-equality for those among the oppressed who can/will assimilate.

It is a shame that "identity politics" has become such a dirty phrase.[65] We need identity politics now more than ever. And when we have the courage to understand that the political is personal, we come to the inescapable revelation that activism is our only chance at survival. In order for that activism to be effective, we must understand the law and politics of the system that oppresses us, even when it purports to be accommodating us. We must also understand the politics of a gay rights movement, purportedly in our interest, that seems to have forgotten most of us. Gay liberation is not about getting more for those Gays who already have the lion's share of security. The issue is not whether,

---

[65] The term "identity politics" was coined by my friend, Black Lesbian feminist Barbara Smith. The term appears in the "Combahee River Collective Statement," a Black feminist manifesto first published in 1978 in Zillah Eisenstein's *Capitalist Patriarchy and the Case for Socialist Feminism*. Barbara Smith co-authored the statement with collective members Demita Frazier and Beverly Smith.

or if, some Gays, those at the top, those few who can be "out" on the job, or at all, without repercussions, those who have the luxury of enough social and financial security to think about things like weddings and children and white picket fences, can have these things in the straight hegemonic image and feel content. People have the right to want what they want, and this point has nothing whatsoever to do with the specificity of any individual situation. The relevant observation is that this is a model of success based on exceptionality. In this model, Gays, and this is to say nothing of the personal cost, whose social résumés most nearly approximate those of their straight counterparts get some security; and the closer the approximation, the more security they get. These tokens are then held up by conservatives and liberals alike as proof positive that change has come. Conservatives say this change is ample proof of the end of a world order and ask what can be done to reverse it. And on the basis of this same tokenism, liberals ask, sardonically, what there is left to accomplish. Somewhere Susie has two mommies ... what more do you people want?

In contrast, Gay liberation asks a question simple in its longing, enormous in its social/political/legal complexity: What might Gay people, as Gay people, contribute? Following on that, what might we say if we were allowed to speak in our own voice? Where might we take the world if we, unmodified, could lead in it? What would power look like by our definition? And how would the law read if it were written by sapient hands and read in empathic voices? I think Gay people, as Gay people, will find the answers to these questions, but only when we understand who our community is and where our loyalties should lie. Gay liberation, thus realized, will sound as a dirge for that "gay rights movement" that has been straight-orchestrated, straight-validated, and straight-assimilated. When straight supremacy is dead and buried, Gay people will know what freedom really is.

PART I

Equality and Making Meaning

2

Law/Morality

Thoughts on Morality, Equality, and Caste

In this chapter, I proceed from the premise that contemporary equality theory does not work for Gay people. I critique equal protection theory, specifically arguing that the current jurisprudence, with its focus on trait immutability, suspect class/classification analysis, and tiered levels of scrutiny, is improperly restrictive of the Constitution's equality norm and generally unproductive for Gay advocacy, and, in any event, is not good, or specifically with regard to immutability analysis, not even settled, law. Consequently, I shift equal protection analysis to focus on state action, omission, and complicity in the perpetration and perpetuation of *caste*-based disadvantage.[1]

This analysis sees trait immutability, a serious stumbling block to many Gay equality claims, as irrelevant to equal protection, which ought properly to prohibit the marginalization of a citizen or group of citizens when that marginalization is based only on the merely descriptive moral disapproval of an identity trait – immutable or otherwise – by majoritarian society, and dispenses with the tiered classification system and its corresponding levels of scrutiny, as well as with the intentionality threshold that marks the entrance to contemporary equal protection. The analysis begun in this chapter is continued in the subsequent chapter's analysis of *Lawrence v. Texas*.[2] The caste understanding of equal protection theorized here becomes the substantive equality alternative to the *Lawrence* Court's privatized-liberty analysis, and it is the basis of my theorizing throughout this book.

---

[1] Caste is "institutionalized inequality." Jo Freeman, *The Legal Basis of the Sexual Caste System*, 5 VALPARAISO L. REV. 203, 230 (1970).

[2] 539 U.S. 558 (2003). *Lawrence*, striking down the states' remaining antisodomy laws, is a victory. However, its evasion of a substantive equality critique cabins its utility for further expansion of Gay citizenship.

In *Sexual Politics,* I said that Gays constitute a subordinated *caste* in the United States.[3] It is this understanding of the reality of Gay life that animates my critique and reformulation of equal protection doctrine.[4] Working within the system gets one only so far. In order to move beyond, we must be aware of the conditions/doctrines of the heteroarchal perspective and of their operation in society and law. *Caste,* then, is a politically intentional invocation/evocation because it is the best descriptor of the actual condition of Gays and Lesbians.[5] The term "caste" is most closely associated with the Brahmanic Indian system of social stratification/hierarchy. Gays are contemporary America's *Untouchables.* The parallels are not subtle. Like Hindu Untouchables, we are said to be dirty, impure, diseased, et cetera, ad nauseum.

[3]   See Shannon Gilreath, Sexual Politics: The Gay Person in America Today 99 (2006) ("In the past century, every state made homosexuality a felony or otherwise criminal offense. The [G]ay person was brutalized, politically marginalized, and shoved into a pariah caste"); see also id. at 90–91 (comparing the treatment of the Indian "Untouchables" under the Nehru administration with the treatment of American Gays).

[4]   For illuminating earlier developments of caste theory, see Freeman, *supra* note 1; Mary Daly, Pure Lust: Elemental Feminist Philosophy (1984); Kenneth Karst, *Why Equality Matters,* 17 Ga. L. Rev. 245 (1983) (although he does not use the term "caste," Professor Karst's early criticism of the "empty tautology that like cases should be treated alike" and that equality has "substantive" content is foundational for this chapter and for my discussion of *Lawrence v. Texas* in the following chapter); Ruth Colker, *Anti-Subordination Above All: Sex, Race, and Equal Protection* 61 N.Y.U. L. Rev. 1003 (1986) (although Professor Colker theorizes in defense of affirmative action programs and does not use the term "caste," her work is foundational to a caste-based understanding of equal protection); Cass Sunstein, *The Anticaste Principle,* 92 Mich. L. Rev. 2410 (1994) (although contaminated by a preoccupation with trait visibility and, therefore, irrelevant for Gays, Professor Sunstein's "anticaste principle" is nevertheless dialectically useful; I should note, however, that Sunstein's focus on visible traits shows a lack of knowledge of the way in which caste actually operated in the Brahmanic tradition from which the term is extracted); Daniel Farber and Suzanna Sherry, *The Pariah Principle,* 13 Const. Comment. 257 (1996). This last theory, certainly more pleasingly alliterative than my caste theory, is, however, faulty because it assumes the immutability of homosexuality (although it does acknowledge that the "pariah principle" would have applicability even where individuals "bear some responsibility for their targeted status" and that "status need not be either immutable or hereditary"). Farber and Sherry write, "[A] group [cannot] be deprived of civil equality based on immutable characteristics such as sexual orientation." I am sympathetic to this view, of course, but such an assumption begs the question and ultimately dooms the principle.

[5]   Caste is the most appropriate descriptor of the condition of Gay people under straight supremacy in multiple ways. "Caste" is derived from the same root as the word "chaste," which is what Gays are told we must be by religionists if we have any hope of escaping their condemnation. This hope is, of course, illusory, a setup for failure, which brings us to the root of "caste"/"chaste," the Sanskrit *śasati,* meaning "he cuts to pieces" (see Mary Daly, Gyn/Ecology: The Metaethics of Radical Feminism 237 (1978)). Gays are cut to pieces by straight supremacy, reduced to our sexuality, with the rest of our humanity hacked away by religious rules and "civil" laws. The result is a Gay life in pieces and the Gay Self in fragments.

Historically, in India, when a member of the Untouchable caste entered the street, he had to shout a warning so that members of higher castes could flee from his contaminating shadow.[6] In America, Gays have been met with the same calculated disgust.[7] In her marvelous little treatise on the politics of disgust as a legal catalyst, philosopher Martha Nussbaum begins with an analysis of the pseudo-/sado-scholarship of anti-Gay muckraker Paul Cameron, whose work, as Nussbaum notes, is published in and disseminated mostly through trumped-up "academic journals" invented by his or other anti-Gay groups. Essentially, Cameron utilizes the politics and language of disgust to urge the caste-based exclusion of Gays from civic life. His "studies" purport to reveal homosexuality as a pathogen and homosexual sex acts as extremely dirty, disease-ridden, public health risks; as he has said: "Screen and quarantine until we come up with a cure.... Homosexuals were hung 300 years ago in our society."[8] Or as his associate Bill Banuchi, executive director of the New York chapter of the Christian Coalition put it, Gays should be required to wear warning labels.[9] Cameron and his allies are a curious subsidiary of a wider, well-organized, extremely well funded movement aimed at perpetuating Gays' status as a pariah caste and reversing hard-won and, generally, meager legal advances. I say that they are a curious subsidiary because they are, in fact, recognized my most liberal academics, like Nussbaum, as the pseudo-/sado-scholars that they are. But it would be a mistake to think of the gaynocidal project as a product of fringe politics. There is in the mainstream academy a virulent gaynocidal politics that passes as acceptable scholarship in ways that similar "scholarship" about Blacks or Jews never would (today). In the same way that good cops never

---

[6] See BARRINGTON MOORE, JR., INJUSTICE: THE SOCIAL BASES OF OBEDIENCE AND REVOLT 59 (1978).

[7] As Barrington Moore, Jr., explains in *Injustice: The Social Bases of Obedience and Revolt*, concepts about pollution and revulsion, or one might say, as Martha Nussbaum does, "disgust" (*infra* note 8), have "political as well as religious" dimensions (id. at 57). "Thus [disgust] serves to conceal unpleasant aspects of the social order from the dominant castes and to enforce these aspects for the latter's benefit" (id.).

[8] MARTHA C. NUSSBAUM, FROM DISGUST TO HUMANITY: SEXUAL ORIENTATION AND CONSTITUTIONAL LAW 7 (2010).

[9] Id. This is a throwback to earlier disgust campaigns against Gays. For example, Anthony Comstock, nineteenth-century founder of New York City's Society for the Suppression of Vice, said:

> These [homosexual] inverts are not fit to live with the rest of mankind. They ought to have branded in their foreheads the word "Unclean," and as the lepers of old, they ought to cry "Unclean! Unclean!" as they go about, and instead of the [sodomy] law making twenty years imprisonment the penalty for their crime, it ought to be imprisonment for life.

See GILREATH, *supra* note 3, at 13.

seem to want to name the crooked cops, most liberal intellectuals refuse to name the purveyors of pseudo-/sado-scholarship.[10] In her discussion of *Romer v. Evans*, for example, Nussbaum names a "few genuinely eminent intellectuals" whose testimony about the depravity of Gays was integral to the state's case.[11] John Finnis at Oxford and Notre Dame, Robert George of Princeton, and Harvey Mansfield of Harvard all testified for the state of Colorado in an effort to justify the most sweeping and baldly anti-Gay legislation since sodomy laws themselves and, it must be said, the most obviously caste-motivated legislation since Jim Crow. Robert George, for example, in his *Romer* testimony, essentially argued for the state-enforced homelessness of Gays as a class. The "new natural law" theory on which George and others rely in order to pathologize Gay identity and to defend Gays' low-caste subordination is little more than reworked Catholic theology presented as legal scholarship, and it arose in direct response to relatively recent advances by women and Gays in the areas of sex, contraception, and sexuality.[12] The emergence of so-called new natural law argument is testament to the enduring need of people to hate, but also of their need for the hate to seem just. Natural law jurisprudence ingeniously moves the hate from the realm of men to the realm of God – of nature – thus ensuring that the stigma is as eternal as it is inescapable. The presence of such a "scholarly" enterprise points to the principal difference in the condition of Gays vis à vis all other subordinated groups today, which is that Gays' low-caste status is actively endorsed and maintained at every level of the social strata, from small-town mayor to U.S. president, from backwoods preacher to prestigious academic.[13] Of all those whom America categorically and institutionally despises, Gays are the most discernibly a caste – the victims of continuous, systematic

---

[10]   There are, mercifully, exceptions to this rule. See, e.g., DAVID A. J. RICHARDS & NICHOLAS BAMFORTH, PATRIARCHAL RELIGION, SEXUALITY, AND GENDER: A CRITIQUE OF NEW NATURAL LAW (2008) (exposing the real motives and motivations of so-called new natural law).

[11]   NUSSBAUM, *supra* note 8, at 109.

[12]   Moreover, the Catholic tradition on which natural law jurisprudence draws has never been very good at getting the nature/natural thing right. After all, the Catholic hierarchy did claim as a central principle of the natural order that the sun revolved around the Earth. What's different now? Well, the implication is that "this time we got it right – trust us." The implacability of power represented by new natural law theory as well as the unmitigated gall its proponents have in claiming a traditional defense of power on other terms, rendering their arguments not merely faintly ridiculous but absurd, makes one encountering new natural law uncertain whether to laugh or cry.

[13]   The fact that purveyors of sado-scholarship have fancy titles after their names or teach at prestigious universities should not confuse us. The word "prestige" is derived from the Latin *praestigiae*, meaning "illusion" or "trick." This should make us suspicious of *prestigious* universities and their products.

violence and institutionalized defamation by attackers held in high esteem as priests, doctors, lawyers, politicians, and teachers.

Omnipresent stigma that is both socially and legally operative is the lot of Untouchables. Indian Untouchables were prevented from entering Hindu temples or other places where the powerful gathered.[14] Likewise, Gays are/were prevented from entering traditional heteroarchal enclaves, like the military,[15] the Boy Scouts,[16] and the institution of marriage. And in many respects/ aspects, Gays, like Hindu Untouchables, have internalized the metaphysics of oppression, believing the system to be somehow rational or preordained or warranted.[17] This internalization, discussed at length throughout this book, fuels "like-straight" argumentation as well as the pornographic conscious- ness of many Gays and, together with deadly sanctions from the Heteroarchy, stymies resistance to heteroarchal oppression. Finally, the Hindu theocracy and the Heteroarchy have encouraged social subdivision among their respec- tive Untouchables in order to ensure disorganization and powerlessness. The peculiar concept, among Hindu Untouchables, of "pure" versus "impure" Untouchables looks a lot like the division of Gays encouraged by heterocrats/ theocrats into nonpracticing homosexuals[18] (the semi-benign status) and those who practice homosexuality (the conduct). It is only the latter category that is said to be targeted by the law (at least in the case of sodomy prohibitions). A division ensues between those Gays who claim the Gay Self, understanding that sexuality is a natural part of that Self, and those who rush into suicidal religious fervor and/or "straight-acting" politics.[19]

These similarities invite us to a deeper understanding of the cur- rent American Heteroarchy/hierarchy through an understanding of caste

---

[14] See MOORE, *supra* note 6, at 59.

[15] I'm thinking, of course, of the recently repealed Don't Ask, Don't Tell, Don't Pursue policy, by which openly Gay and Lesbian people were barred from military service.

[16] Boy Scouts of America v. Dale, 530 U.S. 640 (2000).

[17] See MOORE, *supra* note 6, at 62.

[18] See id. at 58. As I noted, the words "caste" and "chaste" can be traced to the same root. "Caste" is also etymologically akin to the Latin *castus*, meaning "chaste." Chastity under Heteroarchy has always implied Self-negation to various degrees, sometimes to the point of Self-annihilation. The term *sati*, used to name the practice of widow immolation in the Hindu religion and discussed in detail in Chapter 8, this volume, has been translated as "chaste woman." Understood from the heteroarchal perspective, chastity is a sinister pre- scription for Gays. Since Gays are the sex that we do, in Heteroarchy, Gay chastity equates to Gay annihilation.

[19] Among Hindu Untouchables there was conscious mimicry of the customs and taboos of higher castes in an effort to improve status (id.) There was also by Untouchables intracaste enforcement of degrading norms for Untouchables obviously designed and effective in per- petuating higher caste status and power (id. at 60.) The same phenomena exist today among Gays in the United States and elsewhere.

assignment in the Hindu system. In the Hindu system, caste is understood as something extremely rigid but not impossible to change, evocative of the American debate over whether sexual orientation is biological or chosen. In fact, in the Brahmanic tradition, Untouchables are said to *choose* their caste/status by virtue of the doctrine of transmigration of souls, which holds that transgressions ("bad choices") of a prior life dictate present conditions:

> Thus evil and misfortune in this life are due to transgressions, particularly transgressions against the Brahman, in the preceding life. If, on the other hand, according to these beliefs, the individual accepts fate patiently and fulfills the duties of caste, the reward will be to be born into a higher caste in the next reincarnation.[20]

Likewise, a basic tenet of heteroarchal law, theology (the two may be one and the same where Gays are concerned), and, until recently, psychiatry,[21] has been that Gays choose the untouchable condition of homosexuality.[22] The suffering this condition entails is, therefore, self-imposed. Oppression on account of homosexuality is thus just. The treatment of "choice" in this context is a colossal heteroarchal reversal. As Professor Susan Schmeiser observed, "While choice and its conditions of possibility occupy a hallowed place in American culture and politics, its invocation in the context of sexual orientation generally has a more ambivalent, and often sinister, ring."[23] Indeed, choice is usually fetishized by conservatives and liberals in the republican model, who tend to see it (and defend it) even where it does not exist.[24] For heterocrats, the ultimate, constitutionally hallowed choice is that of religion and religious exercise. This choice is interpreted to require accommodation and special rights for religionists.[25] Yet the rhetoric of "choice" for sexual identity has the opposite inference, that of ultimate civic irresponsibility – of *sin*.[26]

---

[20] See id. at 57.

[21] The American Psychiatric Association Board of Trustees dropped homosexuality from its *Diagnostic and Statistical Manual* in 1973.

[22] It has been both untouchable and unspeakable in the law (see Blackstone on homosexuality and Chief Justice Burger's concurrence in *Bowers v. Hardwick*).

[23] Susan R. Schmeiser, *Changing the Immutable*, 41 CONN. L. REV. 1495, 1502 (2009).

[24] I think this is most obvious in argumentation about pornography, with conservatives who claim women choose to be in pornography, and therefore condemn the women's sin, and liberals who claim that payment equals consent, and therefore defend the pornographers' abuses.

[25] See the arguments refuted in Chapter 7, this volume.

[26] The word "sin" is derived from the Indo-European root *es-*, meaning "to be." I'm sure that the patriarchal designation of authentic *being* as theological crime is no accident. Authentic *being*, after all, is the antithesis of the cockamamie rules dreamed up by preachers and prelates.

CURRENT LAW

In contemporary American law, immutability doctrine reinforces this reversal of choice – and a system of injustice as justice – while serving as the linchpin of an (in)equality system that takes caste, in the form of hierarchy based on moral judgment codified in law, as an objective measure of some *difference* that merits legal (normative) disadvantage. The self-reinforcing duplicity of this system, whereby powerful heterocrats (usually judges) mete out *justice* and right *inequality* when they see *similarly situated* persons treated *differently*, is a racket of sheer genius, wherein the already powerful always control the standard by which sameness/difference is measured and, thereby, the mechanism of caste mobility, socially and legally.[27] The truth of my assertion about power insulating itself is revealed in the Court's own insight into its deliberative process in *Washington v. Davis*,[28] requiring proof of intentional differential treatment rather than disparate impact (proof of subordination alone) to establish discrimination in violation of the Fifth and Fourteenth Amendments. Distinguishing Title VII, under which proof of disparate impact is sufficient to establish a prima facie case,[29] the Court opined:

> However this process [the disparate impact (subordination) test] proceeds, it involves a more probing judicial review of, and less deference to, the seemingly reasonable acts of administrators and executives than is appropriate under the Constitution where special racial impact, without discriminatory purpose, is claimed. We are not disposed to adopt this more rigorous standard for the purposes of applying the Fifth and Fourteenth Amendments in cases such as this.

> A rule that a statute designed to serve neutral ends is nevertheless invalid, absent compelling justification, if in practice it benefits or burdens one race more than another would be far-reaching and would raise serious questions about, and perhaps invalidate, a whole range of tax, welfare, public service, regulatory, and licensing statutes that may be more burdensome to the poor and the average black than the more affluent white.

> Given that rule, such consequences would perhaps be likely to follow.[30]

In other words, a genuine subordination-/caste-based inquiry into purportedly neutral and objective laws would expose them as anything but. This frank

---

[27] This is what Catharine MacKinnon was criticizing, in the context of feminism, when she criticized a "differences approach." See CATHARINE MACKINNON, SEXUAL HARASSMENT OF WORKING WOMEN: A CASE OF SEX DISCRIMINATION 4 (1979).

[28] 426 U.S. 229 (1976).

[29] See Griggs v. Duke Power Co., 401 U.S. 424 (1971).

[30] 426 U.S. 229 at 247–248.

admission by the Court also explains why defenders of the sameness/difference approach chiefly have been white (ostensibly straight) men.[31]

In the law, the sameness/difference approach is, like all liberal constructs, focused on individual rights, even when it speaks categorically. First, in its legal manifestation, requiring proof of discriminatory intent in order to establish discrimination, it requires discriminatory motivation by an individual institution or actor. Second, it requires discriminatory impact to be measured in terms of discrete individuals, not groups.[32] Consequently, in critiquing equality arguments based on sameness/difference via trait immutability, my concern is both social and jurisprudential: social because focus on immutability is so important to popular argumentation about the legitimacy of anti-Gay animus generally,[33] and jurisprudential in that immutability has been central in justifying the institutionalization of anti-Gay discrimination in law, as well as central to the increasingly popular (and moderately successful) "like-straight" argument, socially and jurisprudentially, for Gay safety through assimilation.[34]

I think immutability arguments are unsatisfactory socially and legally. No critique of objectification, of dominance as such, can be had when the totality of the formulas available for analysis reduces to the objectivity – the normativity – of the descriptive perceptions of majoritarian morality (your "choices" mark you for maltreatment because we say your "choices" are "bad"). This is the purpose and effect (even when invoked with the best of intentions) of an immutability-based analysis; it keeps purely epistemic notions of right and wrong materially maintained by "science" or other supposedly objective

---

[31] See, e.g., R. BERGER, GOVERNMENT BY JUDICIARY: THE TRANSFORMATION OF THE FOURTEENTH AMENDMENT (1977); A. BICKEL, THE SUPREME COURT AND THE IDEA OF PROGRESS (1970); Peter Westen, *The Empty Idea of Equality*, 95 HARV. L. REV. 537 (1982). It is also why, when on the rare occasion the law does side with the powerless, it is taken to be at its most illegitimate. See Herbert Wechsler, *Toward Neutral Principles of Constitutional Law*, 73 HARV. L. REV. 1 (1959).

[32] See Colker, *supra* note 4, at 1005.

[33] A recent Gallup Poll found that "Americans who believe homosexuals are born with their sexual orientation tend to be much more supportive of gay rights than are those who say homosexuality is due to upbringing and environment (and therefore, perhaps, more of a life-style choice)." http://www.gallup.com/poll/27694/Tolerance-Gay-Rights-Hightwater-Mark.aspx. Many Gay advocates fixate on choice/immutability. Chandler Burr, in theorizing for the Log Cabin Republicans (a Gay Republican group) writes, "At its core, the answer to this question is the only one that matters, the one that determines the most appropriate public policy course, and the one that will win the political struggle over gay rights." *The Only Question That Matters: Do People Choose Their Sexual Orientation?* Log Cabin Republicans White Paper, June 2005, http://www.chandlerburr.com/articles/Burr_White_Paper.html. Although never quite so emphatically, and while still mindbound by the Heteroarchy, I also believed that argumentation from biology was essential and that dissent was irresponsible (see GILREATH, *supra* note 3, at 117–119).

[34] See Chapter 3, this volume.

disciplines, presenting descriptive morality as ontology. In this system, those who are "socially allowed a self are also allowed the luxury of postulating its illusoriness and having that called a philosophical [or religious] position."[35] Immutability allows the powerful to say, simply, "your choice is the prerogative of law, but not your personhood,"[36] while simultaneously regulating both. Or as Thomas Nagel put it, "There is the obvious but important possibility that one can 'hate' an individual's behavior without hating the individual."[37] Since no existentiality is conceded for us, their values look benign, and oppression, if not obfuscated entirely, is presented as collateral. In this system, Gay personality is merely performative and morality is political; politics *are* morals. But the kind of distinction Nagel makes here is intellectually corrupt and belied by reality. Richard Posner tells the truth when he writes: "If you (being male) say that you'd like to have sex with that nice-looking young man but of course will not because you are law-abiding, afraid of AIDS, or whatever, you will stand condemned in the minds of many as a disgusting faggot. Homosexual acts are punished in an effort, however futile, to destroy the inclination."[38] It is the identity that is assumed from the acts; and the acts are subsumed in (and assumed from) the identity. "I am Gay," is a philosophical/ontological statement, not merely a performative one. Despite "love the sinner, hate the sin" blather, it is understood this way by the anti-Gay crowd, too.

The Gay side of the argument from immutability has usually been one of apology: "Don't punish us for something we cannot control." It hasn't worked well, since most religionists think that perfection comes through suffering[39] and that, even if Gays are concededly "born that way," we should not act on it. Straights, of course, are not told that their sexuality is merely performative or that they should refrain from acting on their heterosexuality[40] – thus the hermetic precision of a system that takes its own descriptive value judgments to be definitively objective. Even Gays' supposedly destructive sexual "lifestyles" are not descriptively immoral in the same ways when their ingredients are remixed in the straight recipe. "Unsafe" sex, for example, is roundly condemned as irresponsible and dangerous when it is useful to do so in condemning Gay people

---

[35] CATHARINE A. MACKINNON, TOWARD A FEMINIST THEORY OF THE STATE 210 (1989).

[36] And, concomitantly, "my straight self is not chosen, is natural, and therefore the measure of law."

[37] Thomas Nagel, *Playing Defense in Colorado*, FIRST THINGS, May 1998 at 34, 35.

[38] R. POSNER, SEX AND REASON 232 (1992).

[39] Mother Teresa, with a smile, reported telling a patient suffering terrible agony in the last stages of cancer, "You are suffering like Christ on the cross. So Jesus must be kissing you." The patient replied, "Mother Teresa, please tell Jesus to stop kissing me!"

[40] The exception to this rule occurs when straights' sexual expression looks too much like Gay sex, as in the case of facially "neutral" "sodomy" laws in some states.

(usually Gay men). But that same condom-less sex is a cause célèbre in straight society, where the potential for procreation sanctifies it.[41] When engaged in by straight enthusiasts, "unsafe sex" quickly gives way to pleasanter euphemisms like "in the family way." This "lifestyle choice" even becomes a party theme – we call it the "baby shower." Under the aegis of this kind of epistemologically hermetic doublethink, descriptive morality is presented in society as natural and in the law as neutral.[42] In other words, sexuality is mutable (straights can concede this because they know they have nothing to lose in the concession), and there is justification for punishing some types of sexual expression (those of Gays and Lesbians) because straights, in their majoritarian omnipotence, decree that those sexual expressions are "bad" or "deviant" or "unnatural" or "abnormal" or whatever other referent one might substitute for "not straight." What passes for normal is based entirely on the straight say-so.

British scholar Nicholas Bamforth summarizes immutability's appeal[43]:

> Supporters of immutability claims … maintain that it is … impermissible for the law to penalize a person because of their sexual orientation, and

---

[41] The Roman Catholic Church, the world's largest Christian denomination, actually requires that heterosexual sex be "unsafe" in order for it to be considered holy (procreative).

[42] Adrienne Rich has written that under patriarchy for a woman to be "barren" is the mark of ultimate "human failure." A. RICH, OF WOMAN BORN 249–53 (1976). The unwillingness of many Gays to procreate in the vagina-insert-penis model is a major source of our condemnation by the Heterarchy, where procreation is seen as the ultimate human good – the ultimate fulfillment of nature. Gays are, therefore, "unnatural."

[43] NICHOLAS BAMFORTH, SEXUALITY, MORALS AND JUSTICE: A THEORY OF LESBIAN AND GAY RIGHTS LAW (1997).

On the whole, I think Bamforth provides a brief but lucid account of the problems inherent in the argument from immutability. I do take issue, however, with his view, perhaps inherent in his own preoccupation with the moral model of argumentation, that "even if clear proof [of the biology of sexuality] could be found, theorists would still need to produce a separate moral account of why this particular immutable characteristic was not a valid basis for judging or regulating a person's life" (id. at 204). In the footnote to this assertion, Bamforth goes on to say that any related argument that sexual orientation is irrelevant to an individual's ability to lead a meaningful life is "unsupportable." I don't agree. Equality is not a constitutionally neutral concept, nor is it subsumed in merely moral reasoning. Equality, if it means anything substantive, must mean that personal values, even those based on choices (as most are), cannot be the basis for caste-based disadvantages unless they can be shown to work a normatively demonstrable civic harm (in the "John hit Mary" model), not merely a descriptively moral one (of the "God said so" model). Being equal or unequal in a constitutional system based on equality is first a legal status; only derivatively is it a moral one. Such was the case in *Plessy v. Ferguson*, finding inequality based on descriptive morality legal, and in *Brown v. Board of Education*, finding inequality substantively unequal and therefore illegal. Considerable moral justification preceded and followed *Plessy*, necessarily. Similar moralizing was not necessary after *Brown*; its legality, based upon the central assumption of a legal regime premised on equality – that equality is not neutral about inequality – needed no moralization. In other words, once the objectivity of the "moral" position is exposed as a naked grab for power in a constitutional order supposedly not neutral on abuses through naked power, there is no need for a separate moral inquiry into what ought to be.

arguably to penalize expressions of it in the form of sexual activity. The law does not penalize people due to accidents of birth such as their sex or race, and even seeks to prevent them from being discriminated against on this basis in employment and related contexts – and it would surely be morally arbitrary to treat people unfavorably because of a characteristic which they have acquired via an accident. In consequence, the law cannot consistently – and should not – treat people unfavorably where an analogous accident such as their sexual orientation is in issue.[44]

The last sentence of Professor Bamforth's synopsis reveals immutability's importance to a legal regime intent on seeing only sameness and difference as workable legal categories and, thereby, maintaining its hegemony. It is also a window into why the majority in *Lawrence v. Texas* decided to focus on an abstract notion of "liberty" as opposed to equality. And it reveals why immutability is difficult as a winning strategy – why working within the system has garnered such unsatisfactory results, on the whole, for Gay advocates. How do you prove immutability? More generally, how do you prove causation in a system and to a system that simply changes the definition of causality when it is forced to confront difficult data? Radical feminists in the 1980s presented sociological data establishing the link between pornography and sexual violence against women.[45] The causality was ignored. Other "unbiased" studies appeared to refute it. There is an even greater body of literature, scientific studies and personal accountings, establishing the biologic causality of sexuality.[46] It is ignored.[47]

---

[44] Id. at 203–204.

[45] See Chapter 5, this volume, note 109 and accompanying text.

[46] See SHANNON GILREATH, SEXUAL IDENTITY LAW IN CONTEXT: CASES AND MATERIALS (2006) (ch. 1, collecting studies).

There is also a body of literature arguing the legitimacy of chosen "political lesbianism." See, e.g., SHELIA JEFFREYS, THE LESBIAN HERESY: A FEMINIST PERSPECTIVE ON THE LESBIAN SEXUAL REVOLUTION (1993) ("Many lesbians, after all, have chosen to love women for political reasons, very often after half a lifetime of wifehood and motherhood in which they never thought of being attracted to women"). I don't really buy the idea that sexual orientation is socially constructed, although I think its political meanings certainly are; and thus sexuality reconstituted, as we experience it under Heteroarchy, certainly is. I hope that I am never confronted by someone who asks me to believe that they "love [me] for political reasons." I know too much about how quickly fainthearted political people, even Lesbian feminists, can be to find that kind of love comforting. I also think that the fact that fewer Gay men claim this as their experience of their sexuality speaks to the place of gender in sexuality. And even though there is something appealing in the idea of having men or women embrace homosexuality as a political statement, something about it is unsettling – primarily the idea that anyone could suddenly "choose" to be Gay and then claim to know what that means politically or otherwise. It's an uneasiness akin to the discomfort that some feminists, including myself, feel about male-to-female transsexuals claiming that they suddenly know what being a woman is all about.

[47] It should also be pointed out that the immutability syllogism unwinds if we revisit the question of race as the paradigm immutable trait. If, suddenly, people could choose their race,

Moreover, arguments from immutability are problematic for Gay liberation because they do no more than apologize for the existence of Gay individuals.[48] I don't want to be apologized for, nor do I believe that any Gay person, simply by virtue of being Gay, warrants apology. But from the standpoint of the contemporary immutability perspective, the apology is the totality of the argument. Nothing is said from the immutability perspective about any inherent goodness of being Gay – of Gay claimed as a consciousness, not an imposed, limit on consciousness. The argument overlooks the important difference in identifying as Gay and being identified as gay: Gay is with a purpose toward community; gay is an imposition of inferiority, which, as the Nazis proved, can claim biology as its basis. And since straight sexual morality is not only self-determinatively objective but also homicidal (as Anita Bryant put it, "I'd rather my child be dead than be a homosexual"),[49] there is indeed reason to wonder whether the move to definitize biologic causation won't also make for a eugenics revival.[50] As much as I love Gay people of the present, I care about the well-being of future Gay people too. With Larry Kramer I say, "I love being gay. I love gay people. I think we're better than other people.... I think we're smarter and more talented and more aware ... more tuned in to what's happening, tuned in to the moment, tuned in to our emotions, and other people's emotions, and we're better friends,"[51] and I want us to continue to be around. I say we need a theory of equal protection that doesn't require us to choose temporary safety through assimilation over Self. And I say that the greatest failure of the legal arm of the "gay rights" movement has been its failure to grasp this tension.

and if people chose to be Black instead of white, would being Black become, again, a justifiable basis for imposing legal disadvantages? Or would we accept that in a post–Fourteenth Amendment America hierarchies based on race (or on any characteristic that does not produce demonstrable harm or otherwise limit the ability of a person to contribute meaningfully to the civic endeavor) are patently unconstitutional?

[48] Donna Minkowitz, *Recruit, Recruit, Recruit*, ADVOCATE, Dec. 29, 1992.

[49] Millie Ball, *I'd Rather My Child Be Dead Than Homo*, TIMES-PICAYUNE, June 19, 1977, at 3.

[50] See Janet E. Halley, *Sexual Orientation and the Politics of Biology: A Critique of the Argument from Immutability*, 46 STAN. L. REV. 503, 521–526 (1994). Nicholas Bamforth notes that "[a]bortion was openly suggested in the British tabloid press when the various surveys highlighting the possibility of biological predetermination were first published." BAMFORTH, *supra* note 43, at 232 n. 23. Eugenics, clandestine or otherwise, seems even more likely given the prevailing attitudes exposed by Professor José Gabilondo in *Irrational Exuberance About Babies: The Taste for Heterosexuality and Its Conspicuous Reproduction*, 28 BOSTON COLLEGE THIRD WORLD L. J. 1 (2008), and stated outright in sado-scholarship from the right wing; see e.g., Lynne D. Wardle, *Biological Causes and Consequences of Homosexual Behavior and Their Consequences for Family Law Policies*, 56 DEPAUL L. REV. 997 (2007) (suggesting that homosexuality is a danger to public health).

[51] LARRY KRAMER, THE TRAGEDY OF TODAY'S GAYS 35–36 (2005).

GAYS, EQUAL PROTECTION,
AND THE PROBLEM OF IMMUTABILITY

Gays remain one of the most inequitably treated groups in the twenty-first-century United States. Recently, I discovered a 1973 article, "Is Gay Suspect?", by two nonacademicians, Ellen Chaitin and V. Roy Lefcourt.[52] Reading that article, penned thirteen years before the now-infamous *Bowers v. Hardwick*,[53] thirty years before *Lawrence v. Texas*[54] and *Goodridge v. Dep't of Pub. Health*,[55] and thirty-two years before I started writing this chapter, I was reminded just how little has changed for Gay Americans in terms of legal equality. As a matter of culture, Gays appear on television programs, in the movies, in music videos, and even in cartoon shows,[56] but Gays continue to be subordinated through heteroarchal rules about coupling and marriage, have no federally mandated protection from discrimination in employment or housing,[57] and may lose custody of their children upon divorcing a heterosexual spouse[58] or even upon the dissolution of a same-sex relationship.[59] Gays are blamed for the disintegration of the American family and are the subject of state and federal constitutional amendment efforts to curtail the possibility of same-sex marriage.[60] Many of the same realities were reported by Chaitin and Lefcourt in 1973.[61]

---

[52] 8 LINCOLN LAW REV. 24 (1973).

[53] 478 U.S. 186 (1986).

[54] 539 U.S. 558 (2003).

[55] 798 N.E.2d 941 (Mass. 2003).

[56] See Shannon Gilreath, *Outing Sponge Bob: The Mis-Education of America's Gay Youth*, QUEER DAY (Feb. 21, 2005), http://www.queerday.com/2005/feb/21/outing_spongebob_the_miseducation_of_americas_gay_youth.html.

[57] The U.S. Supreme Court protected Gay and straight against same-sex sexual harassment in *Oncale v. Sundowner Offshore Svcs.*, but the nuanced opinion was careful to construe Title VII as protecting discrimination based on sex – not sexual orientation – which is underscored in Justice Thomas's concurrence. See Oncale v. Sundowner Offshore Svcs., 523 U.S. 75, 82 (1998) (Thomas, J., concurring) ("I concur because the Court stresses that in every sexual harassment case, the plaintiff must plead and ultimately prove Title VII's statutory requirement that there be discrimination 'because of … sex' ").

[58] See, e.g., Pulliam v. Smith, 501 S.E.2d 898 (1998).

[59] In states where second parent adoption is unavailable, the nonbiological/nonadoptive parent often has no legal rights to children of the same-sex relationship once the relationship is terminated. See SEAN CAHILL ET AL., NAT'L GAY AND LESBIAN TASK FORCE, FAMILY POLICY: ISSUES AFFECTING GAY, LESBIAN, BISEXUAL AND TRANSGENDER FAMILIES 77–78 & n. 241 (2003), http://www.thetaskforce.org/downloads/familypolicy/familypolicy-fullversion.pdf.

[60] In addition to the federal Defense of Marriage Act (DOMA) and numerous state DOMAs, thirty-one states have now passed constitutional amendments to prohibit same-sex marriage, and Republicans have raised a proposed federal amendment in successive sessions of Congress.

[61] This is not meant to discount the major progress made, including the repeal of Don't Ask, Don't Tell, the passage of the Shepard–Byrd (Hate Crimes) Act, or the opening of civil

Gays have suffered persecution and discrimination throughout history. In response to the 1986 decision by the U.S. Supreme Court in *Bowers v. Hardwick*, the case that upheld the criminalization of consensual Gay sex acts, Richard Posner made the following observation in his book *Sex and Reason*:

> [S]tatutes which criminalize homosexual behavior express an *irrational fear and loathing* of a group that has been subjected to discrimination, much like that directed against the Jews, with whom indeed homosexuals – who, like Jews, *are despised more for who they are than for what they do* – were frequently bracketed in medieval persecutions. The statutes thus have a quality of invidiousness missing from statutes prohibiting abortion or contraception. The position of the homosexual is difficult at best, even in a tolerant society, which our society is not quite; and it is made worse, though probably not much worse, by statutes that condemn the homosexual's characteristic methods of sexual expression as vile crimes.... There is a gratuitousness, an egregiousness, a cruelty, and a meanness about [such laws].[62]

Judge Posner recognized what Chaitin and Lefcourt recognized before him: "[In] the reality of American society, homosexuals are a minority group with the accompanying characteristics of all harassed and oppressed [minorities], and they are in need of special protection by our legal system to combat these institutionalized injustices."[63]

One logical vehicle for this protection is the Equal Protection Clause of the Fourteenth Amendment.[64] The Equal Protection Clause should be understood "as an attempt to protect disadvantaged groups from discriminatory practices, however deeply engrained and longstanding."[65] The Clause "looks forward, serving to invalidate practices that were widespread at the time of its ratification and that were expected to endure."[66] When attempting to make their cases for equal treatment under the Equal Protection Clause of the Fourteenth Amendment, Gays and their advocates have seized on the most

---

marriage to Gay couples in seven jurisdictions. I acknowledge how far Gays have come in the quest for equal rights and dignity, but I must also, realistically, acknowledge how far we have yet to go.

[62] POSNER, *supra* note 38, at 346 (1992) (emphasis added).

[63] Ellen Chaitin & V. Roy Lefcourt, *Is Gay Suspect?* 8 LINCOLN L. REV. 24, 35 (1973).

[64] "No State shall make or enforce any law which shall abridge the privileges or immunities of citizens of the United States; nor shall any State deprive any person of life, liberty, or property, without due process of law; nor deny to any person within its jurisdiction the equal protection of the laws." The Court has held that Fifth Amendment equal protection is comparable to the Fourteenth Amendment Clause. See, e.g., Bolling v. Sharpe, 347 U.S. 497 (1954).

[65] Cass R. Sunstein, *Sexual Orientation and the Constitution: A Note on the Relationship Between Due Process and Equal Protection*, 55 U. CHI. L. REV. 1161, 1163 (1998).

[66] Id.

obvious biological marker of the Supreme Court's equality paradigm – race. Race, they observe, is immutable, and immutability has, after all, found its way into textbooks and court decisions concerning equal protection analysis. But it is precisely this immutability linchpin, once introduced by Gay advocates and ultimately pulled by the courts, that causes many Gay equal protection claims to come unhinged.[67]

Various legal formulas have evolved in an effort to demystify the U.S. Supreme Court's class-/classification-based approach to equality. Primarily, they take the course of the formula laid out in *High Tech Gays v. Defense Industrial Security Clearance Office*.[68] In *High Tech Gays*, the court held that suspect and quasi-suspect classes for purposes of equal protection analysis are groups that (1) have "suffered a history of discrimination"[69]; (2) "exhibit obvious, immutable, or distinguishing characteristics that define them as a discrete group"; (3) "are a minority or politically powerless."[70]

---

[67] Lower courts have held that Gays and Lesbians meet the criteria of a suspect class for equal protection purposes, yet they have all been reversed on appeal. See, e.g., Equality Foundation of Greater Cincinnati, Inc. v. City of Cincinnati, 860 F. Supp. 417, 436 (S.D. Ohio 1994), *rev'd*, 54 F.3d 261, 267–68 (6th Cir. 1995), *vacated and remanded*, 518 U.S. 1001, 1001 (1996); Able v. United States, 968 F. Supp. 850, 862 (E.D.N.Y. 1997), *rev'd*, 155 F.3d 628, 632 (2d Cir. 1998). In Perry v. Schwarzenegger (704 F. Supp. 2d 921, 1003 (N.D. Cal. 2010), not yet decided on appeal, the trial judge, in dicta, determined that Gays were a suspect class but did so without relying on immutability.

[68] 895 F.2d 563 (9th Cir. 1990).

[69] It is often said that this discrimination must be "invidious," in that it "embodies a gross unfairness that is sufficiently inconsistent with the ideals of equal protection to term it invidious." See Watkins v. United States, 847 F.2d 1329 (9th Cir. 1988) (en banc), *diff. results reached on reh'g*, 875 F.2d 699 (9th Cir. 1989) (en banc), *cert. denied*, 498 U.S. 957 (1990). In *Watkins*, the court associated the immutability query with the invidiousness query. 847 F.2d at 1346.

[70] 895 F.2d at 573.

Modern equal protection analysis was born with *Carolene Products* and its famous Footnote 4. United States v. Carolene Products, 304 U.S. 144, 152 n. 4 (1938). In an opinion in which it basically surrendered in its war on Franklin Roosevelt's New Deal policies, the Court used Footnote 4 to restate its guardianship of individual liberties and to preserve its power of review over such matters in the future. Because the Court specifically marked the rights of "discrete and insular" minorities for an especially searching review, the debate has arisen as to what constitutes "discrete and insular." The "immutability" argument is one attempt at an answer. The full text of Footnote 4 is as follows:

> There may be narrower scope for operation of the presumption of constitutionality when legislation appears on its face to be within a specific prohibition of the Constitution, such as those of the first ten amendments, which are deemed equally specific when held to be embraced within the Fourteenth.

> It is unnecessary to consider now whether legislation which restrict those political processes which can ordinarily be expected to bring about repeal of undesirable legislation, is to be subjected to more exacting judicial scrutiny under the general prohibitions of the Fourteenth Amendment than are most other types of legislation.

No court seems to dispute that Gays have been the subject of historical persecution; indeed, *Bowers* itself – particularly Chief Justice Burger's vitriolic concurrence – settled that point.[71] But many courts have denied Gays suspect class status and strict scrutiny, holding sexual orientation (usually spoken of strictly as homosexuality) to be behavioral and, therefore, not immutable, or holding that Gays do not lack political power in a way that renders them discrete and insular.[72] This was Justice Scalia's argument in his dissent from *Romer v. Evans*.[73] If this argument ever possessed any rationality, it is baseless in today's political climate. Despite massive and often well-funded campaigns to defeat state constitutional amendments aimed at prohibiting Gay marriage, such measures have passed in every jurisdiction in which they have made it onto the ballot – and by wide margins.[74] The simple mathematics involved in voting along group lines demonstrates the political impotence of Gays as a class.

But at the heart of the immutability controversy is the claim that sexual orientation is not a discrete factor by which Gays may be identified as a group. This claim is incorporated by Bruce Ackerman, for example, as follows:

> Nor need we enquire whether similar considerations enter into the review of statutes directed at particular religious, or national, or racial minorities, whether prejudice against discrete and insular minorities may be a special condition, which tends seriously to curtail the operation of those political processes ordinarily to be relied upon to protect minorities, and which may call for a correspondingly more searching judicial inquiry. (Internal citations omitted)

[71] Burger claimed that prohibitions against homosexual conduct had "ancient roots." Bowers v. Hardwick, 478 U.S. 186, 196 (1986) (Burger, C. J., concurring) (quoting majority opinion at 192). That question is certainly debatable, with many historians arguing that widespread repression of Gays is a phenomenon of the past fifty years (see historians' brief in *Lawrence*), but Burger's perception of "ancient" animus says something about the insidiousness of contemporary prejudice against Gays.

[72] 895 F.2d at 573. The whole idea of political powerlessness is more than a little difficult to square with a Supreme Court jurisprudence that allows white male litigants to prevail under a suspect class/ification rationale. See, e.g., Regents of Univ. of California v. Bakke, 438 U.S. 265, 290 (1978) ("[D]iscreteness and insularity [do not] constitute necessary preconditions to a holding that a particular classification is invidious"). But supremacist logic is rarely consistent on anything but the importance of supremacy itself. For an illuminating look at the Court's lexicographic project of shifting subtly from "class" to "classification" in order to entrench power, see EVAN GERSTMANN, THE CONSTITUTIONAL UNDERCLASS: GAYS, LESBIANS, AND THE FAILURE OF CLASS-BASED EQUAL PROTECTION (1999).

[73] 517 U.S. 620, 645–646 (1996) (Scalia, J., dissenting) ("[B]ecause those who engage in homosexual conduct tend to reside in disproportionate numbers in certain communities, have high disposable income, and, of course, care about homosexual-rights issues much more ardently than the public at large, they possess political power much greater than their numbers, both locally and statewide") (internal citations omitted). Justice Scalia curiously argues that we are both concentrated *and* diffuse, numerically nearly nowhere but politically seemingly everywhere.

[74] Arizona was exceptional; passage of a constitutional amendment took two attempts.

As a member of an anonymous group, each homosexual can seek to minimize the personal harm due to prejudice by keeping his or her sexual
preference a tightly held secret. Although this is hardly a fully satisfactory
response, secrecy does enable homosexuals to "exit" from prejudice in a way
that blacks cannot.[75]

Thus, the argument proceeds that Gays are not definable in the way necessary to attain suspect class status. Professor Ackerman concludes that Gays
may be even less politically powerful than more obviously insular and discrete groups, such as African Americans, and that equal protection should
be most concerned with those groups where the members are anonymous
and diffuse and where group detachment is easier. I agree. The detachment
Ackerman notes creates for Gays a problem even worse than "tokenism"[76];
it creates "hiddenism," by which "acting straight" is turned into a sado-
profession and amplified into a sado-professionalism by which closeted Gays
actively work to injure the careers and professional/political/social aspirations
of other Gays. This is what Eve Kosofsky Sedgwick named when she said,
"It is entirely within the experience of gay people to find that a homophobic
figure in power has, if anything, a disproportionate likelihood of being gay
and closeted."[77]

Ackerman's discussion of Gays as an anonymous and diffuse minority conjures a pointed and important equality question. It is not the ability of Gays to
distance ourselves from our "group" that should essentially trouble us; rather
it is the prejudice that drives the desire of some (if not many) Gays to engage
in this group exit that is most troublesome from an equality standpoint. The
ability of Gays to " 'pass' and hide [our] sexual orientation when the going
gets too rough ... while it may have saved a neck from the noose, is in no way
less of a relinquishment of dignity, a loss of freedom, than otherwise inescapable victimization or brutality. Elementally, they are the same."[78] "Escape is
a compromised freedom with a very heavy price."[79]

And, of course, not even all Blacks would fit the conventional definition
of discreteness. African Americans have (particularly historically) engaged in
what is known as "passing," in which an African American with particularly

[75] Bruce Ackerman, *Beyond Carolene Products*, 98 HARV. LAW REV. 713, 730–731 (1985).
[76] By "tokenism" I mean the presence of a few Gays in places we have not been, visibly, before, often for the purpose of signaling (false) progress. These tokens are usually instruments of the Heteroarchy, often working actively to prohibit the advancement of other Gays and being rewarded for such treachery.
[77] EVE KOSOFSKY SEDGWICK, EPISTEMOLOGY OF THE CLOSET 81 (1992).
[78] GILREATH, SEXUAL POLITICS, *supra* note 3, at 129.
[79] ANDREA DWORKIN, SCAPEGOAT: THE JEWS, ISRAEL, AND WOMEN'S LIBERATION 16 (2000).

Caucasian features passes as white to avoid discrimination.[80] But historical analogy notwithstanding, the fact that Gays' caste status is not necessarily marked by spatial segregation can make it harder to see; and yet this same lack of visibility highlights the derivative nature of our status in/to Heteroarchy: the nonbeing of our being, which is the condition of caste under heteroarchal rule. Emphasis on immutability is thus a critical problem for Gays asserting equality claims. It is also largely a problem that arises not from a settled jurisprudence but from a long-standing misconception about equal protection analysis.

HARDWICK'S LONG SHADOW: THE RISE OF IMMUTABILITY

How exactly did the focus on biological immutability of sexual orientation arise in the legal context? It seems to have arisen in a desperate attempt to litigate around the Supreme Court's decision in *Bowers v. Hardwick*.[81] Gay advocates were at a loss as to a conceivable way to protect Gays from various forms of discrimination in employment, housing, and so on, when the nation's highest court had ruled "the conduct that defines the class criminal."[82] *Hardwick*, lower courts reasoned, had foreclosed the possibility of heightened scrutiny for Gay discrimination claims.[83] Hoping to escape the Court's heavy hand, Gay advocates seized on a body of academic literature taking shape in the early 1980s.[84] Most academic treatment centered on the growing belief that sexual orientation was settled by the time of or shortly after birth and was prospectively unchangeable. Attorneys and law professors drew from academic theory and scientific studies on the biologic causation of sexual orientation in the hope of responding to a door opened[85] in the Supreme Court's decision

---

[80]　For a dramatic portrayal of this concept, see generally ALEX HALEY & DAVID STEVENS, QUEEN: THE STORY OF AN AMERICAN FAMILY (1993) (chronicling the life of Haley's grandmother).

[81]　Bowers v. Hardwick, 478 U.S. 186, 191 (1986) (finding no "fundamental right to engage in homosexual sodomy" in refusing to invalidate a state sodomy law).

[82]　Padula v. Webster, 822 F.2d 97, 103 (D.C. Cir. 1987).

[83]　See, e.g., *Padula*, 822 F.2d at 103 ("We therefore think the courts' reasoning in *Hardwick* ... forecloses appellant's efforts to gain suspect class status for practicing homosexuals. It would be quite anomalous, on its face, to declare status defined by conduct that states may constitutionally criminalize as deserving of strict scrutiny under the equal protection clause"); Ben-Shalom v. Marsh, 881 F.2d 454, 464 (7th Cir. 1989) ("If homosexual conduct may constitutionally be criminalized, then homosexuals do not constitute a suspect or quasi-suspect class"); High Tech Gays v. Defense Indus. Sec. Clearance Office, 895 F.2d 563, 571 (9th Cir.) ("[B]ecause homosexual conduct can ... be criminalized, homosexuals cannot constitute a suspect or quasi-suspect class."), *reh'g denied*, 909 F.2d 375 (9th Cir. 1990).

[84]　See, e.g., Richard Delgado, *Fact, Norm, and Standard of Review: The Case for Homosexuality*, 10 U. DAYTON L. REV. 575, 583–585 (1985).

[85]　This is a supposition endorsed by Janet E. Halley and with which I agree. See Halley, *supra* note 50, at 503, 507.

of *Frontiero v. Richardson*.[86] In *Frontiero*, the plurality reasoned that sex discrimination claims deserved heightened constitutional scrutiny because they involve: "a long and unfortunate history of sex discrimination" perpetuated through "stereotyped distinctions between the sexes"; the "high visibility of the sex characteristic: exposing women to 'pervasive … discrimination' "; and the fact that "sex, like race and national origin, is an immutable characteristic determined solely by the accident of birth."[87] The Court's mention of immutability and "accident of birth," together with the tendency of Gay advocates to argue for leniency because "we can't help it" and the tendency of heteroarchal judges to look for reasons to keep Gays powerless, destined immutability to become so central to much of the analysis of Gay equal protection that it has supplanted other factors.

Yet immutability does not figure centrally with any consistency in the Supreme Court's equal protection jurisprudence. In *Lyng v. Castillo*,[88] cited as controlling in *High Tech Gays*, the Supreme Court declined to use strict scrutiny in assessing the constitutionality of provisions of the Federal Food Stamp Act that imposed different requirements on distant relatives or unrelated cohabitants than those for parents and children, holding that close relatives are not a suspect or quasi-suspect class because "as a historical matter, they have not been subjected to discrimination; they do not exhibit obvious, immutable, or distinguishing characteristics that define them as a discrete group; and that they are not a minority or politically powerless."[89] Lawyers know that language matters, but as to equal protection, many seem to forget this important lesson. The conjunction "or," used to link alternatives,[90] gets ignored, and the Court's actual language (obvious, immutable, *or* distinguishing characteristics) gets reduced to immutability only[91] or, at least, to

---

[86] A plurality of the Court concluded that sex-based discrimination warranted strict scrutiny. 411 U.S. 677, 688 (1973). The concurring justices, however, refused to mandate this standard. 411 U.S. at 691–692 (Powell, J., concurring). The Court resolved the scrutiny issue three years later in Craig v. Boren, 429 U.S. 190, 197 (1976), in which a majority of the Court compromised and applied an intermediate level of scrutiny to gender discrimination claims.

[87] *Frontiero*, 411 U.S. at 684–686 (as summarized in Halley, *supra* note 50, at 507). See also Nan D. Hunter, *The Sex Discrimination Argument in Gay Rights Cases*, 9 J. L. & Pol'y 397 (2001) (detailing the work of then–ACLU attorney Ruth Bader Ginsburg in developing the immutability rationale before the courts).

[88] 477 U.S. 635 (1986).

[89] Id. at 638.

[90] See Encarta World English Dictionary (1999 ed.) (Or; CORE MEANING: a conjunction used to link two or more alternatives).

[91] See Anderson v. King County, 138 F.3d 963, 974 (Wash. 2006) (rejecting a challenge to a straight-only marriage law and holding that the challenge failed because "plaintiffs *must make a showing of immutability*, and they have not done so in this case") (emphasis added).

immutability superordinately.[92] This could be due in part to the insistence of Gay advocates and allies on stressing immutability, which continues to be an important part of political and legal strategy.[93]

But the immutability argument, when introduced by Gay advocates, has proved to be friendly fire because of the volatile state of the scientific arguments concerning sexual orientation.[94] Generally, the courts have rejected the immutability claim outright. Even in *Romer v. Evans*, the moment when Gays arguably began to emerge from *Hardwick*'s shadow, the immutability argument fell on deaf judicial ears. The immutability argument presented at trial in *Romer* was a substantially watered down version; the plaintiffs argued that, although sexual orientation is "highly resistant to change," its "etiology" is unknown and "it is not necessary for a trait to be genetically determined for it to be an involuntary trait that is highly resistant to change."[95] But underscoring the danger of muddying the waters with immutability assertions, the court apparently heard, and certainly addressed, a much more stringent argument.[96] The court rejected the immutability claim by a reading of precisely the same science with which the plaintiffs' hoped to buttress it.[97] Be

---

[92] High Tech Gays, 895 F.2d 563 at 573; Woodward v. United States, 871 F.2d 1068, 1076 (Fed. Cir. 1989) ("Members of recognized suspect or quasi-suspect classes … exhibit immutable characteristics, whereas homosexuality is primarily behavioral in nature").

[93] For a lucid discussion of the social and political importance of biologic immutability to the acceptance of Gays (and to Gays' understanding of what Gay is), see Susan R. Schmeiser, *Changing the Immutable*, 41 Conn. L. Rev. 1495 (2009). Schmeiser recounts the reaction to Bill Richardson's statement (during his 2008 Democratic campaign for the presidency), in response to a question posed by Gay singer Melissa Ethridge, that homosexuality is "a choice." The Gay audience booed and hissed (id. at 1500.)

Immutability is the party line of the Human Rights Campaign, the nation's largest LGBT advocacy group. See Human Rights Campaign Foundation, Resource Guide to Coming Out for Gay, Lesbian, Bisexual and Transgender Americans 11 (2004) ("Your Sexuality or Gender Identity Is Not a Choice. It Chooses You"). And it continues, despite its ineffectiveness, to be a part of litigation strategies (see, e.g., Chai Feldblum's admission that, despite misgivings, she continues to make equal protection arguments grounded in immutability).

[94] See, e.g., Baehr v. Lewin, No. 91-1394-05, at 5 (Haw. Cir. Ct. Oct. 1, 1991) (granting defendant's motion for judgment on the pleadings) (holding that homosexuals do not constitute a suspect class, in part because "[t]he issue of whether homosexuality constitutes an immutable trait has generated much dispute in the relevant scientific community"), *rev'd on other grounds*, 852 P.2d 44 (Haw. 1993).

[95] Trial Memorandum on Plaintiffs' Case in Chief at 35 & n. 8, Evans v. Romer, No. 92-CV-7223, 1993 WL 518586 (Colo. Dist. Ct. Dec. 14, 1993).

[96] "Plaintiffs strongly argue that homosexuality is inborn." Evans v. Romer, 1993 WL 518586, at *11.

[97] "The preponderance of credible evidence suggests that there is a biologic or genetic 'component' of sexual orientation, but even Dr. Hamer, the witness who testified that he is 99.5% sure there is *some* genetic influence in forming sexual orientation, admits that sexual orientation is not completely genetic. The ultimate decision on 'nature' vs 'nurture' is a decision for another forum, not this court, and the court makes no determination on this issue." Id.

it true or not, the argument from science has done little to advance the Gay cause in the courts.

In any event, as I have noted, immutability has never been decisively established by the Supreme Court as necessary for a sustainable claim under the Equal Protection Clause. The Court so held in *Bowen v. Gilliard*,[98] when it decided that relatives are not a suspect class. This lack of an immutability requirement could hardly be more evident than in the Supreme Court's decision in *Graham v. Richardson*,[99] holding that aliens constitute a suspect class. Alienage is not immutable[100]; in order to escape the class, one need only become a naturalized citizen.[101] Yet the Court held that "[a]liens as a class are a prime example of a 'discrete and insular minority' ... for whom such heightened judicial solicitude is appropriate."[102] Even if one were to argue that becoming a citizen is not a simple task and that alienage is not transitory, one could hardly argue with seriousness that one can easily change sexual orientations, even if such orientation is, in fact, mutable.[103] As put succinctly in *Watkins v. United States Army*:

> Scientific proof aside, it seems appropriate to ask whether heterosexuals feel capable of changing *their* sexual orientation. Would heterosexuals living in a city that passed an ordinance banning those who engaged in or desired to engage in sex with persons of the *opposite* sex find it easy not only to abstain

---

[98] 483 U.S. 587, 602–603 (1987).

[99] 403 U.S. 365, 376 (1971) (striking an Arizona law that forbade welfare payments to aliens unless they had lived in the country for at least fifteen years).

[100] State courts, as well, have reached suspect class status for Gays without invoking trait immutability. For example, the Oregon Court of Appeals held that "immutability – in the sense of inability to alter or change – is not necessary" because alienage and religious affiliation, which are not immutable, have been held to be suspect classifications. The court held that the definition of a suspect class depends upon whether the characteristic assigned relevance has historically been regarded as defining a distinct and recognizable group and whether that group has been the target of social and political discrimination. Tanner v. Oregon Health Sciences Univ., 971 P.2d 435, 446 (1998).

[101] Some lower courts have, for some time, seen this inconsistency bespeaking a receding importance for immutability; see, e.g., Watkins v. United States Army 875 F.2d 699, 711–728 (9th Cir. 1989)(Norris, J., concurring); Tanner v. Oregon Health Sciences Univ., 971 P.2d 435 (Or. Ct. App. 1998). Scholars, too, have noted immutability's relative unimportance or advocated its outright demise. See J. M. Balkin, *The Constitution of Status*, 106 YALE L. J. 2313, 2323–2324 (1997); Halley, *supra* note 50, at 507.

[102] *Graham*, 403 U.S. at 372.

[103] For an example of the horrors of treatment in the past, see Anonymous, *Electroshock: "The Agony of the Years After,"* in JONATHAN NED KATZ, GAY AMERICAN HISTORY 201 (1992) (1976). The American Psychiatric Association confirms that there is no scientific proof that "reparative therapy" (the so-called "ex-gay" movement) successfully changes sexual orientation and that "[t]he potential risks of 'reparative therapy' are great, including depression, anxiety, and self-destructive behavior."

from heterosexual activity but also to shift the object of their sexual desires to persons of the same sex?[104]

There is additional support for the argument that immutability, by itself, is irrelevant to constitutional inquiry. There are a number of groups with characteristics that are, so far as we can know, immutable, whose claims are not afforded heightened scrutiny for equal protection purposes. For example, neither the traits of intelligence nor physical disability have formed the basis for suspect class status under the Equal Protection Clause.[105] Instead, where immutability is salient, it may be "immutability plus" that is really at work. The *Frontiero* plurality held that strict scrutiny was warranted for gender discrimination claims because gender, in addition to being immutable, "frequently bears no relation to ability to perform or contribute to society."[106] *Frontiero*, then, may stand for the premise that "when a characteristic is both immutable *and* unrelated to the legitimate purposes at hand, discrimination based on it *may* suggest unfairness."[107] One could also plausibly read Justice Brennan's formula in *Frontiero* as having nothing to do with the immutability of any physical trait per se, but rather as focusing on the generally unalterable nature of stereotypes, which frequently bear no relation to the ability of the stereotyped to contribute to society. This kind of caste-based understanding of *Frontiero* is commensurate with Brennan's observation:

> [W]hat differentiates sex from such nonsuspect statuses as intelligence or physical disability, and aligns it with the recognized suspect criteria, is that the sex characteristic frequently bears no relation to ability to perform or contribute to society. As a result, statutory distinctions between the sexes often have the effect of invidiously relegating the entire class of females to inferior legal status without regard to the actual capabilities of its individual members.[108]

---

[104] 875 F.2d at 726 (emphasis in original; citations omitted).

[105] See, e.g., *Frontiero*, 411 U.S. at 686.

[106] Id. at 686 ("[S]ex, like race and national origin, is an immutable characteristic determined solely by the accident of birth.... [W]hat differentiates sex from such nonsuspect statuses as intelligence or physical disability, and aligns it with the recognized suspect criteria, is that the sex characteristic frequently bears no relation to ability to perform or contribute to society"). But see Halley, *supra* note 50, at 508 n. 15 ("There are plenty of careless misreaders of *Frontiero* who construe it to state a freestanding immutability factor uninflected by relatedness. *See, e.g.*, Moss v. Clark, 886 F.2d 686, 690 (4th Cir. 1989) (holding that prisoners do not constitute a suspect classification because the status of incarceration is neither immutable nor an indicator of invidiousness) (citing *Frontiero* on immutability without reference to relatedness)"). For a discussion of how *Frontiero*'s exceptions swallow its theory, see JUDITH A. BAER, EQUALITY UNDER THE CONSTITUTION: RECLAIMING THE FOURTEENTH AMENDMENT 261 (1983).

[107] Halley, *supra* note 50, at 508 (emphasis in original).

[108] 411 U.S. at 686–687.

IF NOT IMMUTABILITY, THEN WHAT?

What, if we eschew immutability as a basis for suspect classification, is the alternative formula for an ethical equal protection analysis? My concern here is not so much with the idea of equal protection as a judicial phenomenon as with getting to the most substantive conception of equal protection possible. Acknowledging the effects of caste and stigma as they operate in reality makes equality substantive.[109] My thesis in this regard is influenced by Michael Perry's 1979 article, "Modern Equal Protection: A Conceptualization and Appraisal,"[110] in which Perry supposed that equal protection is best understood as guarding against the punishment of an individual by the use of certain traits that are irrelevant to an individual's "physical or mental capacity – in the form of native talent, acquired skills, temperament or the like."[111] Race is the paradigm irrelevant trait – what possible effect could the color of one's skin have on one's native abilities? There obviously is no corollary between race and ability. My problem with Perry's analysis is that it failed to include sexual orientation within its wide swath, because Perry believed sexual orientation not to be an immutable characteristic. Perry fell into the same trap of exaggerating the importance of the immutability factor discussed earlier.[112] Nevertheless, Perry's 1979 view of equal protection is foundational. It adequately anticipates the burdens of a caste-based system of inequality in operation, which is to say it recognizes that to be made unequal because of certain disabilities is difficult, but bearable if there is hope of improvement or of accommodation for disability. To be unequal because you are deemed to be ontologically inferior is, on the other hand, to be hopeless. As Perry understood it, government may not give its imprimatur to activity that is aimed at perpetuating the unjust marginalization of a disfavored group by effectively punishing that group's members on the basis of a trait that has no relationship to the group members' physical or mental capacity in the form of native talent, acquired skills, temperament, or the like. Disenfranchisement on the

---

[109] In the next chapter, in order to draw a crisp distinction between liberal formalism and equality that *is* substantive, I call the anticaste theory sketched here "substantive equality."

[110] 79 COLUM. L. REV. 1023 (1979).

[111] Id. at 1066. Perry was prescient in this. In *City of Cleburne v. Cleburne Living Center*, 473 U.S. 432, 444 (1985), the Court held that constitutionally justifiable discrimination required a showing of "real and undeniable differences" between the disadvantaged group and others.

[112] Perry tells me that the "young[er] Michael Perry," who authored the 1979 critique of equal protection at issue here, has "died many times." Email from Michael Perry to Shannon Gilreath (Feb. 28, 2005) (on file with author). I am, as yet, unclear as to Perry's ultimate judgment on the importance of immutability to suspect classification, but I am more certain, as Perry is my former teacher and mentor and friend of many years, that his view about the mutability of the homosexual sexual orientation has changed.

basis of prejudice in the employ of power is the particular evil at which equal protection is aimed.

Perry's explication reveals that equal protection is not simply about a politically identifiable trait; that is to say, we are not merely concerned that circles are drawn around people with an easily discernible trait. The law makes and must be able to make distinctions based on necessary classifications of citizens. For example, the law may allow that those born with immutable handicaps not be hired for jobs when reasonable accommodation cannot bring their functionality in line with the parameters of the job requirements. Or consider that universities are allowed to accept only those who meet stringent academic requirements, while the ability to meet such requirements arguably turns in part on immutable genetic factors over which one has no control. Viewing equal protection as invalidating every conceivable trait-based classification is an unreasonably expansive reading. Conversely, reading equal protection as invalidating state action only in the face of an immutable trait is unreasonably cramped. Rather, equal protection is concerned that members of a group not be punished for a trait that has no relationship to their intrinsic worth to/in society merely because some animosity exists between a dominant group and the group displaying the trait. As Professor Ruth Colker explains:

> We permit distinctions on the basis of intelligence or ability. We only prohibit distinctions that we have good reason to believe are biased or irrational, and it is group-based experiences that primarily inform us as to which kinds of distinctions are biased or irrational. Thus, the anti-subordination principle, by recognizing and drawing on the historical subordination of blacks and women, offers a substantive explanation for why certain distinctions are subjected to closer scrutiny.[113]

The constitutional principle of equal protection, then, recognizes the existence of the political evil of caste-based political subjugation and seeks to eliminate (or, at least, to ameliorate) its degrading effects on the subjected segment of society.[114] This understanding is historically sound. The framers

---

[113] 61 N.Y.U. L. REV. 1003, 1013.

[114] The one thing that is immutable is the effect of the caste oppression once ascribed. In her excellent article, *Changing the Immutable, supra* note 93, Professor Susan Schmeiser draws our attention to the recent decision of the Connecticut Supreme Court in *Kerrigan v. Commissioner of Public Health*, in which the court opened marriage to same-sex Connecticuters. In its brief immutability analysis, the court noted the connection between same-sex attraction and "social and legal ostracism" on account of it (957 A.2d 407, 436 [Conn. 2008]). The Connecticut court's focus on Gays' social definition into a low caste and on legal disadvantage on account of that same caste status may be a first. As Professor Schmeiser notes, "[I]t reminds us that equal protection analysis is centrally concerned with status – not in the sense of one's stable identity, but in the sense of one's access to the rights

of the Fourteenth Amendment realized that the key to transforming the racial prejudices of centuries of physical and moral degradation of Blacks was the use of the government to protect consistently the rights of Blacks.[115] The Reconstruction amendments were aimed at righting the historical ills of racism, but they were also intended to protect members of other unpopular groups – white Republicans in the South, for example.[116] To oversimplify equal protection by transforming it into a concern about "classification" on the basis of "immutability" is therefore contra-contextual.[117] For example, if we were to extend the immutability rationale to its limits, we would have to conclude that the framers of the Fourteenth Amendment would have extended the force of equal protection to those Blacks for whom race was easily identifiable, but not to those who could "pass" as white and, thus, effectively transmute races. Instead, equal protection is ultimately aimed at the type of prejudice and animus that would drive a Black person with a lighter complexion to separate from home and kin when possible. Those who disapprove of applying equal protection analysis to laws that do not explicitly disadvantage Blacks on the basis of race and are not specifically discriminatory ignore the fact that the Fourteenth Amendment is not written with the specificity of the Civil Rights Act of 1866.

The Fourteenth Amendment, approved by Congress in June 1866, spoke in more global terms of unabridged equitable citizenship.[118] It was predicated on an ethical constitutionalism that drew its power from moral dissent and

and protections afforded the majority" (id. 1518.) On this point, Professor Schmeiser cites Professor Richard Ford: "Once status is ascribed, it is 'immutable' in the pragmatic sense that the individual cannot readily alter it. This is the sense in which immutability is relevant to anti-discrimination law" (FORD, RACIAL CULTURE: A CRITIQUE 103 [2005]). Professor Schmeiser argues that immutability may be an appropriate factor for consideration in equal protection analysis when it is understood in this way.

[115] The 1871 enactment of 42 U.S.C. § 1983 is an example. § 1983 is an enforcement provision, supplying a remedy for violations of the trilogy of post–Civil War amendments (Amendments 13, 14, 15), which the Reconstruction Congress knew were likely to happen in the South.

[116] Professor Colker's historical conceptualization of equal protection is technically too narrow. She says, "Historically, the equal protection principle developed to remedy a history of subordination against a particular group in society, blacks. Aspirationally, it reminds us that no group should remain subordinated in our society and that we should therefore take seriously the claims of women and of other discrete minorities that they have been subjected to pervasive discrimination in our society" (Colker, *supra* note 4, 1012.) Obviously, concern about equal protection arose in the context of the slavery question, but it was originally, not merely aspirationally, intended to extend to groups other than Blacks.

[117] Cf. ALEXANDER BICKEL, THE LEAST DANGEROUS BRANCH: THE SUPREME COURT AT THE BAR OF POLITICS (1962).

[118] Even the *Slaughter-House Cases* concede this. 83 U.S. 36, 72 (1872) ("The first section of the fourteenth article, [sic] to which our attention is more specially invited, opens with a definition of citizenship").

genuine concern with "the right to conscience," a central value of American constitutionalism that allowed the framers of the Reconstruction amendments successfully to bring content to the constitutional norm of equality – a content that went appreciably beyond the definition of the equality norm afforded by the courts of the day.[119] The work of the Reconstruction amendments, centering on equality and equal protection, constituted a moral restructuring of the American democratic order based on a respect for universal human rights. When the Court later dropped its famous Footnote 4 in *Carolene Products*,[120] it signaled that, while it was abandoning its New Deal fight about property rights, on this fundamental ideal it could foresee no compromise.

The reader need not rely on my assessment alone, but may instead turn to a hallowed bit of American jurisprudence for which we recently celebrated a fiftieth anniversary: *Brown v. Board of Education*.[121] If race is the paradigm suspect classification and *Brown* is the paradigm race case, then it is only natural to see what *Brown* lends to the discussion.[122] In fact, it is what *Brown* does not say that is instructive. The Court struck down school segregation laws without a single mention of the discrete or insular nature of Blacks as a group; nor did it mention the immutability of race.[123] Rather, the Court acted on the recognition that American racism had for too long enjoyed the life-giving force of constitutional imprimatur. Blacks were degraded and dismissed as unfit even

---

[119] See generally S. Gilreath, *The Technicolor Constitution: Popular Constitutionalism, Ethical Norms, and Legal Pedagogy*, 9 TEXAS J. OF CIVIL LIBERTIES & CIVIL RIGHTS 23–44 (2003).

[120] 303 U.S. 144 (1938).

[121] 347 U.S. 483 (1954).

[122] I should note here that I do not consider *Brown* to be a paradigm *equality* case. *Brown* stressed educational opportunity, albeit in the context of citizenship, but did not stress supremacy or caste in a way that reveals a new, substantive analysis based on caste. (see Chapter 3, this volume, note 76) ("[Education] is an opportunity, where the state has undertaken to provide it, is a right which must be made available to all on equal terms"). Scholars defending *Brown* from attacks that it amounted to *sub rosa* decision making offered the friendly reformism that transmuted *Brown* into a much bolder statement of equality than it actually was. See, e.g., Charles L. Black, *The Lawfulness of the Segregation Decisions*, 69 YALE L. J. 421 (1960); Louis H. Pollack, *Racial Discrimination and Judicial Integrity: A Reply to Professor Wechsler*, 108 PENN. L. REV. 1 (1959). Perhaps it was the realization that a distinctly equality-based decision would require a confrontation with the racial caste system that prompted the Warren Court to take the education route. Or perhaps it was the political reality of the Court's composition of justices. See GERSTMANN, *supra* note 72, at 34–35. Whatever the reason, it was not until *Loving v. Virginia* (1967), striking antimiscegenation laws, that the Court provided a coherent caste-based analysis of racial inequality, naming power distribution through white supremacy as the constitutional evil at issue. Despite these shortcomings, *Brown*, as both an equality icon and a case recognizing, albeit partially, the effects of caste and stigma, is instructive.

[123] As I noted, "immutability" as a judicial term of art did not emerge until *Frontiero*.

to mingle with whites purely on the basis of a trait that bore no relation to the Black person's intrinsic worth or ability.[124]

Thus, as the Court understood it in *Brown*, segregation was not problematic because it was based on some oppressive physiological trait from which targeted group members could not escape. *Brown* made no explanation of race as a genetics issue; instead, it seemed to be focused on something else that, while related, is quite different. *Brown* is cast, although tepidly, in terms of state complicity in the perpetration and perpetuation of social hierarchy.[125] Segregation is constitutionally problematic because it is a mechanism of the socio-legal meaning of race as the basis for distributing power through a system of social and legal discrimination based upon a politicized trait displayed by a group that historically has been the subject of social derision, subjugation, and marginalization. Thirteen years later, in *Loving v. Virginia*, the Court articulated a stronger, caste-based analysis of white supremacy at work through antimiscegenation laws.[126] Importantly, Chief Justice Warren's *Loving* analysis eschewed any immutable trait-based approach and, instead, focused on the Virginia law's illegitimate purpose – the perpetuation of the low-caste status of Blacks under white supremacy.

TRANSLATING EQUAL PROTECTION TO GAYS

Through a caste-based analysis, equal protection analysis for Gays gains plausibility and teeth. One need only read the concurring opinion of Chief

---

[124] In fact, recognition of an intrinsic worth that was being stunted for Blacks by the white practice of educational segregation was an animating premise. See id. at 494 ("To separate them from others of similar age and qualifications solely because of their race generates a feeling of inferiority as to their status in the community that may affect their hearts and minds in a way unlikely ever to be undone.... 'The impact is greater when it has the sanction of the law; for the policy of separating the races is usually interpreted as denoting the inferiority of the negro group' "). Of course, not all critics agree that the Court's guiding principle was quite so clear. See Herbert Wechsler, *Toward Neutral Principles of Constitutional Law*, 73 HARV. L. REV. 1, 31–35 (1959) (decrying the Court's failure to justify its result in *Brown*).

[125] For a similar articulation of the *Brown* analysis, see DAVID A. J. RICHARDS, CONSCIENCE AND THE CONSTITUTION: HISTORY, THEORY, AND LAW OF THE RECONSTRUCTION AMENDMENTS 170–174 (1993). There is good reason to believe that Chief Justice Warren and others wanted to make a stronger caste-based decision in *Brown* but were dissuaded by the politics of the Court and the need for a unanimous opinion. See GERSTMANN, *supra* note 72, at 34–36.

[126] Loving v. Virginia, 388 U.S. 1, 11 (1967) (finding that antimiscegenation laws were unconstitutional because they were "designed to maintain White Supremacy"). For an extended discussion of *Loving* in this context, see Chapter 3, this volume. For a discussion of equal protection after *Loving*, see generally Gerald Gunther, *The Supreme Court, 1971 Term – Foreword: In Search of Evolving Doctrine on a Changing Court: A Model for Newer Equal Protection*, 86 HARV. L. REV. 1 (1972).

Justice Burger in *Bowers v. Hardwick* for evidence of the social ethos that has oppressed Gays as long-suffering victims of a discrimination akin to that perpetrated against Blacks.[127] Burger's opinion resonates with echoes of Gays as *inter christianos non noninandum* – not fit to be named or discussed – invisible *unless* they seek some measure of equality. Then they must be put down. The fear and prejudice against Gays has been scaffolded by government action in the form of laws against sodomy, cross-dressing, same-sex marriage, and Gay adoption. The continuing, corrosive force of prejudice against Gays is sorely evident in the proliferation of state constitutional amendments banning same-sex marriage, which have passed in every state in which they appeared on the ballot, in spite of assimilationist arguments by Gay advocates. The force of homophobia is not found in the suppression of one right, such as sexual privacy or marriage, but rather in the creation and maintenance of a social ethos in which Gay citizens are told that they have nothing to offer their country and that their country has little regard for them. Homophobia has motivated campaigns breathtaking in their discriminatory intent and effect, as in the case of Colorado's Amendment 2, the subject of the Supreme Court's penultimate Gay rights decision in *Romer v. Evans*.

Colorado's Amendment 2 imposed disadvantages on Gays unprecedented in a single piece of legislation. Amendment 2 repealed the antidiscrimination provisions of three Colorado cities, Aspen, Boulder, and Denver, as they applied to Gays and ensured that not even the Colorado legislature could enact antidiscrimination provisions protecting Gay Coloradans.[128] In other words, if Gays wanted to seek protection from anti-Gay discrimination at any level, they would have to amend the Colorado constitution. Amendment 2 is palpable proof of Gays' political impotence. Gays were effectively told in *Bowers* that the courts are not the proper arena in which to fight discrimination; so Gays went to their elected officials. In Colorado, Gays had won a variety of protections at the municipal level and were close to winning statewide Gay rights protections. Since Gays were succeeding on the terms it had set to thwart them, the Heterarchy decided that Gays couldn't use legislative

---

[127] 478 U.S. at 197 (Burger, J., concurring) ("To hold that the act of homosexual sodomy is somehow protected as a fundamental right would be to cast aside millennia of moral teaching").

[128] Amendment 2 read: "No Protected Status Based on Homosexual, Lesbian, or Bisexual Orientation. Neither the State of Colorado, through any of its branches or departments, nor any of its agencies, political subdivisions, municipalities or school districts, shall enact, adopt, or enforce any statute, regulation, ordinance or policy whereby homosexual, lesbian or bisexual orientation, conduct, practices or relationships shall constitute or otherwise be the basis of or entitle any person or class of persons to have or claim any minority status, quota preferences, protected status or claim of discrimination. This Section of the Constitution shall be in all respects self-executing."

means to equality either. Amendment 2 thus enforced an important hetero-cratic maxim: When Gays lose, we lose; when we win, we lose.

It is important to understand exactly what Amendment 2 accomplished. Amendment 2 prohibited pro-Gay legislative action, but not all relief from discrimination based on sexual orientation. Sexual orientation antidiscrimination ordinances/policies were repealed only insofar as they protected Gays and bisexuals. Thus, in a town with such an ordinance after Amendment 2, a straight employer could discriminate against an employee because the employee was Gay; the employee had no legal recourse. But if a Gay employer discriminated against an employee because the employee was straight, the employee had an action. The Supreme Court held that Amendment 2 violated equal protection because it was born of "animosity"[129] causing Gays to be classified and disadvantaged "not to further a proper legislative end but to make them unequal to everyone else."[130]

In reaching its decision, the Court applied "rational basis" review, traditionally the most deferential analysis in the Court's repertoire.[131] Declaring, as the Court did, that merely descriptive moral disapproval of the group designated for legal disadvantage did not satisfy a rational basis inquiry was no small victory. And yet *Romer* cannot be said to be a thoroughly caste-based decision in any substantive sense. The *Romer* Court recognized that Gays are a despised minority, targeted for especial disadvantage and systematically made "unequal to everyone else"; and yet the Court, through its purported application of rational basis, indicated that Gays *were/are* a low caste for legal purposes – a caste whose claims of discrimination are not entitled to the more searching analyses that attend comparable claims predicated on race or gender. In this way, *Romer* highlights the hierarchy-perpetuating force inherent in the three-tiered scrutiny approach. The three-tiered framework is, in the case of Gays, itself antiequalitarian. To be afforded rational basis only, the lowest level of judicial solicitude, when the Court recognizes your

---

[129] Romer v. Evans, 517 U.S. 620, 634 (1996).

[130] Id. at 635.

[131] Surely, the rational basis applied was a heightened rational basis, since traditional rational basis review would accept virtually any imaginable rationale as justificatory. For a discussion of the evolution of heightened rational basis review, see Michael Kent Curtis & Shannon Gilreath, *Transforming Teenagers into Oral Sex Felons: The Persistence of the Crime Against Nature After Lawrence v. Texas*, 43 WAKE FOREST L. REV. 155, 192–197. Yet it could also be said that the Court was signaling that Amendment 2 failed to satisfy even the most minimal rationality, since the Court relied upon much older cases that clearly did utilize low-level rational basis scrutiny. F. S. Royster Guano Co. v. Virginia, 253 U.S. 412 (1920); Railway Express Agency v. New York, 336 U.S. 106 (1949); Williamson v. Lee Optical of Oklahoma, Inc., 348 U.S. 483 [1955]).

group-based disadvantage as an Untouchable, is tantamount to the Court saying you are actually low caste. You may get relief from the most egregious manifestations of caste-based animosity, but not all caste-related disadvantages are problematic. Having a rational basis–type analysis of laws that, say, target left-handers or blue-eyed people, or what have you, might make sense in a reality where such people are not targeted for systemic and systematic caste disadvantage.[132] But when the systemic and systematic disadvantage of a caste is acknowledged and still afforded only minimal scrutiny, a clear message of inferior status is sent. The message is made even more outrageous in a system where straight, white men can claim sex discrimination and have those claims assessed by a heightened scrutiny analysis.[133] After *Romer*, Gays remain at the bottom of the legal equality hierarchy that the three-tiered approach reifies.[134]

Despite Gays' intact low-caste status, the narrow victory of *Romer*, that descriptive morality cannot justify legal disadvantage, was taken as a serious injury to the Heteroarchy. In a rabidly heterocratic dissent, Justice Scalia,

---

[132] In their article, the *Pariah Principle, supra* note 4, Professors Farber and Sherry present an elaborate hypothetical about left-handed people. Their exercise in this regard reveals the principal flaw in most law professor hypotheticals: They cannot operate as a tool to critique the real because they are in no way tethered to reality. First, Farber and Sherry imagine a world where left-handers are "viewed as sinister or at least as gauche" and where the government could "refuse to enact legislation protecting them from private discrimination" without running afoul of their pseudo-caste-based "pariah principle." No theory that is really caste-based could countenance such a result. Farber and Sherry go on to imagine a host of real harms, accidents, etc., caused by left-handers that causes the government to legislate against them. The authors are torn as to whether such action would be legitimate or would produce caste. Certainly, asking left-handers to wear a "scarlet L" would be ridiculous and legally problematic from a caste perspective, as the authors suggest. But their concentration on the actual harms flowing from left-hander inadequacies highlights an important distinction between their understanding of caste and mine: When empirically verifiable harms can be shown to flow from an identifiable trait against which the government wishes to legislate a caste theory of equality is at its weakest state of applicability, for the government is permitted to move against provable harms that speak to an individual's ability for civic contribution. Finally, Farber and Sherry note, "By itself, [the pariah principle] does not necessarily prevent the government from restricting gays and lesbians from some occupations thought to involve peculiar dangers." Like what, exactly? Gays, categorically, make especially bad, uh … airplane pilots, perhaps? Brain surgeons? Law professors? Farber and Sherry give no examples of homosexuality's "peculiar dangers," and I can think of none. When, in *Perry v. Schwarzenegger*, opponents of same-sex marriage were asked to offer evidence of the dangers of homosexuality, they could produce none (2011 U.S. App. LEXIS 74).

   The bottom line is that any caste theory will require judgment calls in close cases. Left-handers might present such a close case in the unreal world Farber and Sherry imagine; Gays, in the real world – in a very real state of subjection – do not.

[133] Adarand Constructors v. Pena, 515 U.S. 200 (1995).

[134] See GERSTMANN, *supra*, note 72.

joined by Chief Justice Rehnquist and Justice Thomas, defended heteroarchal morality as the foundation of law:

> [Amendment 2] is not the manifestation of a " 'bare ... desire to harm' " homosexuals, but is rather a modest attempt by seemingly tolerant Coloradans to preserve traditional sexual mores through use of the laws. That objective, and the means chosen to achieve it, are not only unimpeachable under any constitutional doctrine hitherto pronounced ... ; they have been specifically approved by this Court.[135]

The specific approval was, of course, the Court's decision in *Bowers v. Hardwick*, the invocation of which allowed Scalia to tap into not only stare decisis but the whole of heteroarchal history as understood in *Hardwick*. Heterocrats are especially pleased when they can point to a long history of bigotry to justify continuing heteroarchal/patriarchal oppression. This was evident in the firestorm created when the U.S. Supreme Court forced the gender integration of the Virginia Military Institute (VMI) in *United States v. Virginia*, decided the same year as *Romer*.[136] Traditionally, Virginia had not permitted women to enroll as cadets at VMI. Of course, the usual arguments about the morality of men and women in close quarters, the morale of the cadets, and the need to maintain an ordered and disciplined environment for the all-male population were offered as justifications for retaining the ban on women. The Court, however, decided that the justifications were insufficient to survive constitutional scrutiny and that the VMI policy violated equal protection. A majority of the justices reasoned, quite rightly, that a long-standing tradition of discriminating against women was in no way a justification for compounding historical error by perpetuating it.

In his VMI dissent, Justice Scalia gave us more heterocratic doublethink, declaring that the Court's decisions "ought to be crafted so as to reflect those constant and unbroken national traditions that embody the people's understanding of ambiguous constitutional texts. More specifically, ... 'when a practice not expressly prohibited by the text of the Bill of Rights bears the endorsement of a long tradition of open, widespread, and unchallenged use that dates back to the beginning of the Republic, we have no proper basis for striking it down.' "[137] Extended to its logical limits, Scalia's argument reads that there is no constitutionally mandated reason to end a traditional discrimination unless the Constitution were specifically to say, "Women must

---

[135] Romer at 629.
[136] 518 U.S. 515 (1996).
[137] Id. at 568 (Scalia, J., dissenting) (quoting Rutan v. Republican Party of Ill., 497 U.S. 62, 95 [1990] [Scalia, J., dissenting]).

be allowed entrance to any public educational institution" or "Gays must be allowed to serve in the nation's armed forces." Of course, the Constitution makes no such explicit guarantees, and if such reasoning predominated, not only would Gay equality be impossible, but most of the significant social advances of the preceding century, like the advancement of women's rights or racial desegregation, would never have come to pass. Scalia's argument is a variant of the popular argument that because differences have traditionally been observed – that is, differences in men and women or Gays and straights have traditionally been observed (and manipulated to leave women and Gays powerless) – we should go right on exaggerating those differences, for no better reason than simply because it has always been that way. This is exactly the sort of ingrained caste-based marginalization at which equal protection is rightly aimed. Viewed through the lens of an equal protection analysis that treats equality as substantive, the inclusion of Gays within the equality norm should turn on the existence of a culture of degradation and subjugation of Gays coupled with the political legitimization of that social ethos by state complicity and validation of prejudice. As Professor Ann Scales has written:

> The traditional order cannot be justified by reference to the will of democratic society. Such justifications are part of the positivistic theories of law which neither accurately describe the process of law-making nor account for the historic role of courts in tempering the self-interested mandates of the powerful. The positivist construct of the "sovereign will" factors out all substantive issues of power and value, thus becoming "a trivial generalization" about social conflicts and decisions and a generalization, moreover, which serves as an all-purpose apology for the status quo. The positivist view would have us believe that judicial decisions affecting social norms are usurpations of the majoritarian process, and are, therefore, anomalous episodes in the story of law. To the contrary, the authority of the judiciary to secure the rights of the powerless is of the essence of the Republic, thus imposing upon those ultimate conservators of the Constitution an obligation to intervene when majoritarian arrangements are shown to be oppressive.[138]

Indeed, a system that takes equality seriously would be a system that works to eliminate oppression on all levels. Courts would have to have the latitude to look at laws in context in order to determine which majoritarian arrangements are oppressive. It is upon this observation that Professor Perry, whose earlier work has been foundational for my observations here,

---

[138] 56 Ind. L. J. 375, 342–443 (1980).

and I part company with regard to an appropriate understanding of the equality norm.

It seems to me that Professor Perry's later/contemporary understanding of what the Fourteenth Amendment's equality norm forbids (or allows) is wrong, or at least undertheorized, because his understanding does not incorporate the effects of caste and stigma, thus ignoring the utility of descriptive moral judgments, disguised as normative judgments, as bases for power hierarchy. In discussing *Romer v. Evans*, for example, Perry postulates a law, based in Catholic moral teaching, directed at all sex outside of marriage or all nonprocreative sex, that might have fared differently than Colorado's Amendment 2 for the principal reason that it "might not be grounded even partly in the irrational fear and loathing of homosexuals."[139] Such a law could thus survive equality challenge; indeed, intervention by the courts would be a usurpation of valid majoritarian process.[140] But Perry's formulation of equality here is an empty one from the perspective of Gay liberation. It requires proof of homophobic intent in order to prove inequality and assumes a correlation between intent (or lack thereof) and facial neutrality. This is very much like Justice O'Connor's hypothetically neutral sodomy law, which served as the centerpiece of her concurrence in *Lawrence v. Texas*.[141]

Such an understanding ignores the reality of inequality. A law that burdens *all* nonprocreative or *all* nonmarital sex disproportionately burdens *all* Gays, which is to say *only* Gays *as a group/caste*, and thus becomes a tool for the regulation of Gay identity. Attaching criminal stigma to the sexual practices that define Gays socially, thereby defining them legally, puts Gays in a distinctly lower legal caste – by definition.[142] Straights, on the

[139] Michael J. Perry, We the People: The Fourteenth Amendment and the Supreme Court 140 (1999). This is a sentiment echoed in the work of other philosophers. Professor Robert Audi, for example, with whom I am in general agreement about the role private religious morality should play in public policy making (especially when those views are juxtaposed against those of his sparring partner, Nicholas Wolterstorff), has written, "Controversial issues such as … homosexuality … are easily approached from the points of view of natural law and secular justice." See R. Audi & N. Wolterstorff, Religion in the Public Square: The Place of Religious Convictions in Political Debate 127 (1997). I have yet to see a plausible rationale for regulating homosexuality that does not reduce to religiously motivated animus, although the pseudo-/sado-scholarship of the emergent "new natural law" school has purported to give such reasons. For an illuminating exposé on "new natural law," see David A. J. Richards & Nicholas Bamforth, Patriarchal Religion, Sexuality, and Gender (2008).

[140] Perry elaborates this view in his discussion of *Roe v. Wade*. See Perry, *supra* note 139, ch. 6.

[141] 539 U.S. 558, 579–585 (2003) (O'Connor, J., concurring).

[142] Professor Charles Lawrence has done brilliant work on stigma and its centrality to the formation and perpetuation of caste. See Charles R. Lawrence, *The Id, the Ego, and Equal Protection: Reckoning with Unconscious Racism*, 39 Stan. L. Rev. 317 (1987). Lawrence, too, would not require proof of discriminatory intent to make equal protection operative.

other hand, can escape this caste, or rather are never technically assigned to it, since sex that is paradigmatically straight (from the heteroarchal perspective) is paradigmatically procreative. Group-based distinctions, legally and socially, are thus drawn only as to one group – Gays – while straights are not defined by and thus not stigmatized or caste-typed by the law's target. Perry goes on to reason that a law that accomplishes this same end but that actually facially discriminates on the basis of sexual orientation ("a law directed at nonmarital sex between two persons of the same sex") could not survive equal protection challenge.[143] Perry's theory of equality thus reduces legal equality to a purely lexical exercise, making equality something even less than liberal formalism; it makes of equality a mere tautology.

Perry understands that the equality norm means that the law cannot "discriminate against any group on the *basis* of a view to the effect that members of the disfavored group are not truly or fully human – that they are, at best, defective, even debased or degraded, human beings."[144] It is his focus on intentionality that dooms Perry's theory to the same unworkability that has plagued the Supreme Court's equal protection jurisprudence since *Washington v. Davis*. Rather, equality jurisprudence ought to be concerned not only with prohibiting intentionally discriminatory laws, but also with liberating human beings from inequality that already exists. Neither the Court's prevailing understanding of equal protection nor Perry's understanding gets us to any resolution of the problems of conditions of inequality already existing in a system supposedly not neutral on the equality question. In other words, neither theory understands that the law can be a source of prejudice even in instances when it isn't directly reflective of prejudice. Conversely, an understanding of equality that takes Gay experience seriously, and that would thus *work* for Gay people, would focus on a law's effect – that is: Does a law based only on descriptive majoritarian morality, as a law against all nonprocreative sex is, produce or perpetuate lower-caste status for one group in a way that it does not for others? If the answer to the query is yes, then the law works an impermissible inequality. In this formulation, equality is substantive. Restated in substantive terms, the equality question becomes: Is there a right to be free from caste-based stigma imputed on bases that do not correspond to demonstrably provable harms to society? If equality means anything, it must surely produce an affirmative answer to this query.

[143] Perry, *supra* note 139, at 141.
[144] Id. at 145.

EQUALITY AND MORALITY

There is much discussion today about the proper place of religion and religious morality in American politics and law.[145] Yet the Constitution provides for Americans an independent morality of reason, republican government, and democratic justice. The Equal Protection Clause was aimed primarily at righting centuries of racial degradation and subjugation of American Blacks. Blacks were held captive by a morality that made no place for them and that not only defined them by a trait that was part of their physiological definition but also *redefined* – constructed – that trait into something wholly separate from its essential biology in order to use it as a tool for subjection. *Brown* was thus a step toward righting the immorality of *Plessy v. Ferguson*,[146] in which the Court drew circles around American Blacks on the basis of a trait that bore no relationship to their personhood. Equal protection forbids the forced isolation of groups of people into untouchable categories, exempt from basic freedoms of self-determination and liberty of conscience, that subject caste members to numerous legal burdens not borne by citizens outside the caste.[147]

In his oft-invoked *Plessy* dissent, Justice Harlan intoned that "[t]here is no caste here.... We boast of the freedom enjoyed by our people above all other peoples. But it is difficult to reconcile that boast with a state of the law which,

---

[145] See, e.g., ROBERT F. DRINAN, S.J., CAN GOD AND CAESAR CO-EXIST? BALANCING RELIGIOUS FREEDOM & INTERNATIONAL LAW (2004) (particularly ch. 4, "Religious Freedom in the United States") (discussing the interrelationship of government and religion in the promotion of morality and stability); MICHAEL J. PERRY, LOVE AND POWER: THE ROLE OF RELIGION AND MORALITY IN AMERICAN POLITICS (1991) (addressing the role of religious morality in the politics of a morally pluralistic society); ROBERT AUDI & NICHOLAS WOLTERSTORFF, RELIGION IN THE PUBLIC SQUARE (1997) (presenting differing viewpoints on the appropriateness of religious morality in politics).

[146] Compare Brown v. Board of Educ., 347 U.S. 483 (1954) with Plessy v. Ferguson, 163 U.S. 537 (1896).

[147] For a decidedly narrower "caste-based" equal protection articulation, *see* Cass Sunstein, *The Anticaste Principle*, 92 MICH. L. REV. 2410 (1994). Sunstein articulates his anticaste principle as follows:

> [T]he anticaste principle forbids social and legal practices from translating highly visible and morally irrelevant differences into systemic social disadvantage, unless there is a very good reason for society to do so. On this view, a special problem of inequality arises when members of a group suffer from a range of disadvantages because of a group-based characteristic that is both visible for all to see and irrelevant from a moral point of view. This form of inequality is likely to be unusually persistent and to extend into multiple social spheres, indeed into the interstices of everyday life.

Id. at 2411–2412. Sunstein's focus on trait visibility, however, would bring discrimination against women and Blacks into the anticaste purview but would leave Jews and Gays outside of the principle. See id. at 2438, 2444.

practically, puts the brand of servitude and degradation upon a large class of our fellow-citizens, our equals before the law."[148] In *Plyler v. Doe*, the Court, in striking a law depriving illegal alien children of a public education, noted that "[t]he Equal Protection Clause was intended to work nothing less than the abolition of all caste-based ... legislation."[149] Likewise, the Court has noted that the Constitution does not permit states to "divide citizens into ... permanent classes."[150] This interpretation of the Fourteenth Amendment seems consistent with the defense of the Amendment proffered during the Reconstruction debates by Senator Howard, who declared the Amendment's major purpose to "abolish all class legislation ... and ... the injustice of subjecting one caste of persons to a code not applicable to another."[151]

Equal protection is rightly invoked to right historical wrongs in which a group is held in bondage by a prevailing cultural morality, imprisoning them in a lesser caste in contravention of equality. Constitutional equal protection doctrine, if interpreted and applied substantively, may be the only *real* morality involved in these repressive equations. The morality, be it religious or otherwise, that has historically belittled Gays has been *descriptive*, offering only a restatement of societal prejudices: Discrimination against Gays is justified because Gays are *immoral*. If the implied morality here is merely a restatement of social mores of fear and hatred of Gays, then the issue is indeed one of moral import. The problem inheres in the extension of this logic. By this definition of morality, even the Nazis were moral when they began a systematic campaign to murder Europe's Jews.[152] Surely, Americans should reject the mere regurgitation of phobias and neuroses as moral authority. In order to draw legal and political boundaries around groups of citizens, we need a normative morality – one that is prescriptive and based on reason. Normative morality is based on fairness and an essential consistency in the way we apply our moral prescriptions to members of society. Such is the central thrust of the Equal Protection Clause: All citizens must be treated equally under the law – unless there is a justifiable reason, beyond mere collective prejudice, for imposing legal burdens. Such reason arises only when the trait that is the subject of the moral judgment is directly related to the person's physical or mental capacity in the form of native talent, acquired skills, temperament, or

[148] Plessy v. Ferguson, 163 U.S. 537, 559; 562 (1896) (Harlan, J., dissenting).

[149] 457 U.S. 202, 213 (1982).

[150] Zobel v. Williams, 457 U.S. 55, 64 (1982) ("It would permit the states to divide citizens into expanding numbers of permanent classes. Such a result would be clearly impermissible").

[151] Cong. Globe, 39th Cong. 1st Sess. 2766 (1866).

[152] For an elaboration of this point, see Richard Mohr, Gays/Justice: A Study of Ethics, Society, and Law 31 (1998).

the like. By this definition, the fact that many – or even most – people dislike Gays is not reason enough to sanction discrimination against us.

Here, we might tweak (or perhaps more fully develop) Professor Perry's original definition of equal protection. We might say that equal protection is meant to prohibit the marginalization of a citizen or group of citizens on the basis of a merely descriptive moral disapproval of a trait, or the display of a trait, immutable or otherwise. This is the answer to the inevitable but ultimately false moral conundrums asserting that favorable legal treatment for Gays will lead to leniency regarding rape, incest, bestiality, murder, and a host of other horribles. Viewed in light of a moral imperative, the answer is quite simple – there is an independent, normative basis, beyond the merely descriptive, for condemning these "choices." These activities are inherently injurious to their victims, and society's just condemnation goes well beyond any merely descriptive dislike or discomfort.[153]

From this perspective, use of the political process to coerce disfavored individuals into different ways of being – or at least of seeming – would be forbidden by the Equal Protection Clause. Thus, Gay rights advocates would do well to shift the debate to this sort of question: Is a person displaying a particular trait (homosexuality) being coerced into altering the display of that trait to fit conventional norms or otherwise be punished? This query echoes Judge Rheinhart's dissenting view in *Watkins v. U.S. Army*: Sodomy may be an issue of privacy, but homosexuality is an issue of identity.[154] Under the substantive definition of equality derived from a caste perspective, discriminatory laws are unconstitutional, in violation of equal protection, if they create or perpetuate the powerlessness and low-caste status of a definable caste through imposition of disadvantage on account of merely descriptive moral

---

[153] Some critics might regard my normative reasoning here as ultimately merely descriptive and, thus, self-defeating. They might say that my rationale, exemplified by the differences I perceive between partners in a same-sex relationship and murderers or rapists, is little more than my preference for a society in which we do not kill or sexually violate our fellow citizens (in much the same way that religious fundamentalists prefer only heterosexual families or missionary sex). But I submit that there is a reasonable, rational difference. The reasoning of my critics is the same kind of thinking that led Arthur Leff to conclude that "normative [legal] thought crawled out of the swamp and died in the desert." Arthur Allen Leff, Commentary, *Economic Analysis of Law: Some Realism About Nominalism*, 60 VA. L. REV. 451, 454 (1974). Normative thought is more than just nose counting and loud voices. Like Professor Leff, I am not prepared to give up on normative thought. I may not be able to articulate it beyond its irritating simplicity, but, damn it, "napalming babies *is* bad.... *And the 'law' has always known it; that is the source of its tension and complexity.*" Id. at 481 (emphasis in original).

[154] Watkins v. U.S. Army, 847 F.2d 1329, 1353 (9th Cir. 1988) (en banc) (Reinhardt, J., dissenting), *diff. results reached on reh'g*, 875 F.2d 699, 724–28 (9th Cir. 1989) (en banc), *cert. denied*, 498 U.S. 957 (1990).

judgments about caste-associated traits that do not translate to limited ability or capacity for meaningful citizenship. Equal protection, then, guards against a type of moral slavery that would cause one to alter one's identity to avoid peril at the whim of the dominant society.[155] By contrast, the sameness/difference approach requires targeted minorities to become "like" the majority in order to be seen as worthy of equal treatment, often to such an extreme that the identity of the minority is completely blotted out by the analysis. Enter *Lawrence v. Texas*.

In 2003, in *Lawrence*, the U.S. Supreme Court had the opportunity to engage the caste oppression of Gays and Lesbians and refused to do so. *Lawrence*, the subject of the next chapter, proves that liberal morality, even when it captures five votes on a conservative Court and even when the resulting opinion reads like a Maya Angelou poem, cannot operate as an effective critique of the real, which is to say an effective engagement of the reality of the distribution of social power, because it refuses to recognize the effects of power as empirically verifiable. However sympathetic the Court's prose, the question of Gay equality is reduced to some other question (one of privacy or "liberty") rather than seen as *the question* calling for analysis and action. Rather than citing the evidence of Gays' subordination as proof of Gays' difference, as the *Bowers* Court did, the *Lawrence* Court used the evidence of that same oppression to elevate Gays to the level of the heterosexual universal, completely disappearing us in the process. The result for Gays after *Lawrence* is that that we are only sometimes categorically beyond the law's stigma, but we are always, to borrow a phrase from Catharine MacKinnon, "a category beyond history."[156]

---

[155] David A. J. Richards coined the term "moral slavery" in IDENTITY AND THE CASE FOR GAY RIGHTS: RACE, GENDER, RELIGION AS ANALOGIES 56 (1999).

I originally sketched these thoughts on immutability in 2005, and they were published in 2006; see *Of Fruit Flies and Men: Rethinking Immutability in Equal Protection Analysis – with a View toward a Constitutional Moral Imperative*, 9 JOURNAL OF LAW AND SOCIAL CHANGE 1 (2006). The approach was echoed in the California Supreme Court's decision in *In re Marriage Cases*, 183 P.3d 384, 442–443 (Cal. 2008), in which the court held that "[b]ecause a person's sexual orientation is so integral an aspect of one's identity, it is not appropriate to require a person to repudiate or change his or her sexual orientation in order to avoid discriminatory treatment."

[156] MACKINNON, *supra* note 35, at 59.

3

Law/Power

The Appropriation of Gay Identity in
Lawrence v. Texas – *and the Substantive Alternative*

I think [judges] have failed adequately to recognize their duty of weighing considerations of social advantage. The duty is inevitable, and the result of the often proclaimed judicial aversion to deal with such considerations is simply to leave the very
ground and foundation of judgments inarticulate, and often unconscious.

Oliver Wendell Holmes, "The Path of the Law"[1]

In the summer of 2003, the U.S. Supreme Court decided *Lawrence v. Texas*,
invalidating the states' remaining sodomy laws.[2] Justice Kennedy's majority
opinion proceeded through a due process analysis to invalidate a Texas law,
unequal on its face, that criminalized same-sex sex. Many Gay rights advocates greeted the decision with enthusiastic abandon.[3] But exactly what was
decided in *Lawrence*? Exactly what did we get? As I see it, the Court made
a glancing pass at equality jurisprudence,[4] but its mere passing reference is
highlighted by the fact that certiorari was granted on the question of whether

---

[1]   Oliver Wendell Holmes, *The Path of the Law*, 10 HARV. L. REV. 457, 467 (1897).

[2]   539 U.S. 558 (2003).

[3]   See, e.g., John Rechy, *Finally, Dignity and Respect – But at Such a Cost*, L.A. TIMES, June 29,
2003 (describing Lawrence as an "unqualified victory"); E. J. Graff, *The High Court Finally
Gets It Right*, BOSTON GLOBE, June 29, 2003 (referring to *Lawrence* as "our *Brown v. Board
of Education*, declaring us full citizens, entitled to all the rights and freedoms held by our
siblings, colleagues, and friends"). Legal academics, too, including William Eskridge, Tobias
Wolff, and Richard Lazarus, praised the *Lawrence* decision unreservedly. See Katherine M.
Franke, *The Domesticated Liberty of* Lawrence v. Texas, 104 COLUM. L. REV. 1399 (2004)
(collecting citations to such commentary at 1399–1400, n. 2). In the interest of full disclosure,
I should say that even I got in on the act. In the not so distant past, my commentary on the
Lawrence decision was decidedly rosier. See, e.g., Shannon Gilreath, *Of Fruit Flies and Men:
Rethinking Immutability in Equal Protection Analysis – With a View Toward a Constitutional
Moral Imperative*, 9 J. L. & SOC. CHANGE 1 (2006) (esp. Section III et. seq.).

[4]   "Equality of treatment and the due process right to demand respect for conduct protected by
the substantive guarantee of liberty are linked in important respects, and a decision on the
latter point advances both interests." *Lawrence*, 539 U.S. at 575.

the Texas law violated equal protection[5]; and equality arguments were made by lawyers for Lawrence and Garner and by advocates for the amici curiae.[6] As has been typical in equality adjudication, the questions most in need of answers were the very questions avoided by the Court. This chapter asks those questions and posits answers – specifically, a rethinking of the equality norm with the reality of the Gay experience as its method. Importantly, it exposes that *Lawrence's* equivalence is not the same as equality. Equivalence is about approximation – assimilation on the oppressor's terms. Equality is about free-dom – about who gets to make the rules.

I explain how the privacy rationale employed in *Lawrence*, its equality pro-motion notwithstanding, actually delivered equivalence under the law – not real (substantive) equality – thus serving to further entrench heterodomi-nance.[7] An applied equality rationale of the kind I advocate here would have avoided this result and would have created access to foreclosed public spaces that currently operate as institutionalized, heterodominated hierarchy in con-travention of equality. Curiously, a substantive equality analysis also would have avoided Justice Scalia's feared disruption of other forms of traditional morals legislation (e.g., bigamy, prostitution), which Scalia believes are left vulnerable by the *Lawrence* majority's substantive liberty approach.[8]

Proceeding through several observations about privacy theory's failings to an ultimate criticism of the equality analysis (or lack thereof) of the *Lawrence* opinion itself, I am ultimately critical of the long-standing notion that "equal protection of the laws" must be taken to mean that persons "similarly situ-ated" are to be treated the same under the law.[9] I argue that the "similarly

[5] "Whether petitioners' criminal convictions under the Texas 'Homosexual Conduct' law – which criminalizes sexual intimacy by same-sex couples, but not identical behavior by differ-ent-sex couples – violate the Fourteenth Amendment guarantee of equal protection of laws." *Lawrence*, 539 U.S. at 564.

[6] See Brief of Petitioner at 32, Lawrence v. Texas, 539 U.S. 558 (No. 02-102); Brief for Mary Robinson et al. as Amici Curiae Supporting Petitioners, at 22–23, Lawrence v. Texas, 539 U.S. 558 (No. 02-102); Brief for Human Rights Campaign et al. as Amici Curiae Supporting Petitioners, at 14, Lawrence v. Texas, 539 U.S. 558 (No. 02-102).

[7] I should note at the outset that *Lawrence* is not strictly speaking a "privacy" decision. Rather, the Court recognized the right at issue as a "liberty" and employs this language throughout its decision. Nevertheless, the Court's close association of the right at issue in *Lawrence* with the contraception and abortion decisions, in my opinion, inextricably links it to the Court's privacy jurisprudence. Katherine Franke has described the right recognized in *Lawrence* as a "privatized liberty," and that is good enough for me. See Franke, *supra* note 3, at 1404.

[8] *Lawrence*, 539 U.S. at 590 (Scalia, J., dissenting).

[9] In *Barbier v. Connolly*, the Court held that "[c]lass legislation, discriminating against some and favoring others, is prohibited; but legislation which, in carrying out a public purpose, is limited in its application, if within the sphere of its operation it affects alike all persons simi-larly situated, is not within the [fourteenth] amendment." Barbier v. Connolly, 113.U.S. 27, 32

situated" test is especially dangerous for Gay equality interests. Specifically, I examine some of the jurisprudential trade-offs implicit in privacy doctrine rather than equal protection ideas to ground the type of liberty the Court considered in *Lawrence*. I consider the specific risk that privacy doctrine poses for Gays – mainly that our identity rests on being "assimilated" into a heterosexual model from which we are always already excluded. I propose an alternative grounding for the legal rights of Gays sought in *Lawrence*, which I call substantive equality, looking through mere legal forms to recognize the undeniable context of social dominance in which sexual minorities seek limited recognition.[10] This approach has two special virtues: It can override arguments for discrimination based on religion, and it is strong medicine against the stigma imposed on identity groups that are otherwise subordinated, both in law and in fact. Finally, I conclude with a consideration of the role of prudence in constitutional decision making and with a warning that prudence should not be used as an excuse to shirk remedying denials of equality, like those the Gay litigants charged in *Lawrence*.

LAWRENCE, ROE, AND PRIVACY

Commentary on constitutional law has historically operated as debate about the meaning of seminal cases. My commentary here is no exception. It considers in its analysis the meaning of several other so-called seminal cases. In an area like constitutional law with very little settled law but a great deal of theory, commentary can hope to do little more than to figure out how a new case fits into the web of precedent. With this principle in mind, it may be useful to begin any constitutional analysis with *Roe v. Wade*,[11] unquestionably the most controversial, emotionally contentious, and feared decision in modern constitutional law.[12] Certainly, any meaningful discussion of *Lawrence* must

(1884). As this chapter will show, this concept has been the core of the Court's often stunted equality decisions ever since.

[10] As I explained in Chapter 1, this volume, "substantive equality" is a phrase encountered in legal literature as a referent, with notable exceptions, for a variety of methodologies and epistemologies that are neither substantive nor equal. In this chapter, I use the phrase to refer to a methodology that is both substantive and equal, as will become clear. In my substantive equality analysis of *Lawrence* (as opposed to what we got from the Court), I am refining and applying a theoretical framework that has some considerable forebears. See Chapter 1, this volume, note 28 and accompanying text.

[11] 410 U.S. 113 (1973).

[12] For a discussion of *Roe*'s centrality to constitutional analysis see generally H. N. HIRSCH, A THEORY OF LIBERTY: THE CONSTITUTION AND MINORITIES (1992). I say *Roe* is the most feared of contemporary constitutional cases because even "liberal" jurisprudes seem to feel the need to expend a great deal of effort apologizing for it. See, e.g., MICHAEL J. PERRY,

begin with *Roe*. *Lawrence* is the culmination of a series of departures from essentialist equality analysis that have led to disastrous results, the archetype of which is *Roe v. Wade*.[13] To understand where Gay people may be going post-*Lawrence*, we must understand the jurisprudential framework into which the *Lawrence* decision fits. Justice Kennedy places it squarely in the line of privacy cases that originated with *Griswold v. Connecticut*,[14] by stating that the liberty compromised by the Texas law was akin to "personal decisions relating to marriage, procreation, contraception, [and] family relationships."[15] This effectively took Lawrence and Garner's essential equality claim, lying at the heart of the Fourteenth Amendment, and moved it to the vulnerable and unstable constitutional periphery where privacy dwells. The location of the constitutional claim here makes sense, if one looks at the evolution of the Court's sex equality jurisprudence that cabined the abortion right almost as soon as it recognized it. *Roe* connected a woman's right to choose an abortion with its contraception jurisprudence, holding that the privacy right recognized in *Griswold* was "broad enough to encompass a woman's decision whether or not to terminate her pregnancy."[16]

But the Court could just as easily have applied an equality analysis in *Roe*.[17] In that case, a pregnant woman, "Jane Roe," and others, challenged the constitutionality of the Texas criminal ban on abortions, which provided no exception for saving the mother's life. The law made it a crime to procure or to attempt an abortion. Jane Roe was actually a carnival worker named Norma McCorvey. McCorvey, twenty-one years old at the time, claimed to have been gang-raped on her way back to her motel in a small Georgia town.[18]

MORALITY, POLITICS, AND THE LAW, 161–179 (1988); John Hart Ely, *The Wages of Crying Wolf: A Comment on* Roe v. Wade, 82 YALE L. J. 920 (1973).

13   410 U.S. 113, 162–163 (1973). *Roe* guaranteed the right to abortion, counterbalanced against other considerations, by denominating it a private choice.

14   381 U.S. 479, 485 (1965) (holding that a right to privacy exists in the Constitution that prevents the states from prohibiting the sale of contraceptives).

15   *Lawrence*, 539 U.S. at 574 (citing Planned Parenthood v. Casey, 505 U.S. 833, 851 [1992]).

16   *Roe*, 410 U.S. at 153.

17   Professor Kenneth Karst pursued an equality rationale for *Roe* in *Foreword: Equal Citizenship Under the Fourteenth Amendment*, 91 HARV. L. REV. 1 (1977). After I finished drafting this chapter, a colleague introduced me to Jack Balkin's article, *Abortion and Original Meaning*, 24 CONST. COMMENT. (2007) (Yale Law School, Public Law Working Paper No. 128), in which Professor Balkin makes some very similar (and, therefore, in my mind, eminently insightful) equality-based observations about the abortion right. I did not have the benefit of Balkin's article in sketching my own critique, but I recommend it to all interested in an equality defense of the right of women to seek an abortion.

18   McCorvey would later recant much of this story when she became a "born-again" spokesperson for the anti-choice movement. See Douglas S. Wood, *Who Is 'Jane Roe'?* CNN, June 18, 2003, http://www.cnn.com/2003/LAW/01/21/mccorvey.interview/.

McCorvey was a high school dropout; she was divorced and had a five-year-old daughter; she earned very little money. Pregnancy meant that she could not continue her work. McCorvey believed that abortion was her only option. Virtually no American, I dare say, is unaware of the outcome of her case: The Supreme Court found that the Texas abortion ban violated McCorvey's right to "privacy."[19]

An intellectually honest Court should surely have recognized that abortion is the ultimate sex equality question. Only women are existentially affected by the choice of whether to carry a fetus to term.[20] Certainly, that was true for McCorvey. In the case of antiabortion restrictions, laws made primarily by men serve to force a woman to endure the burden of pregnancy – a burden *only* she can endure. What could more obviously implicate equal protection of the laws than that quandary?[21]

But the Court placed the right to choose an abortion on the outer fringes of constitutional thought. The idea of privacy inhabits and delineates this fringe. "Like a Greek chorus, or a bad dream,"[22] the privacy debate haunts modern constitutional commentary. By locating abortion rights on this fringe, the Court ensured that women's equality quickly became subsumed by the needs of male-dominated, heterocentric society. Women's equality was translated through the rhetoric of individual rights into the realm of descriptive moral counterbalancing – which means that the needs of the heterosexual male most always win. By couching the *Roe* holding in privacy, the Court made possible the future subordination of women's collective equality needs to the desires of male supremacy.

Privacy's inadequacy is made plain in the Court's 1981 decision in *Harris v. McRae*, in which the Court held that the right to privacy did not require that federal Medicaid funds be available to finance abortion needs arising from medical necessity.[23] Privacy, the Court held, guaranteed only a woman's

---

[19] Roe, 410 U.S. at 162–165.

[20] It is too obvious to be said that only women can give birth. But it is also predominantly women who provide the majority of childcare after the birth. Women's careers are compromised. And the majority of single-parent homes are headed by women. See Karst, *supra* note 17, at 53–59.

[21] Madam Justice Bertha Wilson of the Canadian Supreme Court recognized this with great eloquence, writing, "It is probably impossible for a man to respond, even imaginatively, to [the abortion] dilemma not just because it is outside the realm of his personal experience … but because he can relate to it only by objectifying it." R. v. Morgentaler, [1988] 1 S.C.R. 30, 172 (Wilson, J., concurring), http://csc.lexum.umontreal.ca/en/1988/1988rcs1–30/1988rcs1–30.html.

[22] Hirsch, *supra* note 12, at 30. See also Karst, *supra* note 17.

[23] 448 U.S. 297, 311 (1980).

"decision" whether to terminate her pregnancy.[24] Privacy imposed no duty on government to see that women's abortion choice was in any way meaningful.[25] In less than a decade, *Roe's* privacy jurisprudence devolved to this. The interests of (heterosexual) men – manifest primarily in the sectarian perspectives of religion designed by men for men – outweighed the highly circumscribed privacy interest of women.[26]

Privacy is, of course, the perfect vehicle for dominance. Privacy provides no space or place for a myriad of rights, not the least of which is equality, that are otherwise guaranteed to heterosociety (read: men) for the very reason that such rights are not the prerogative of the private realm when the access point is heterosexual maleness. Nowhere is this more visible than in the abortion cases. Women enjoy a private right, which essentially means that the right's only guaranteed public dimension is what men are willing to facilitate for women. If the male power structure does not see fit to make even medically necessary abortions affordable, then that is that. The private–public denomination ensures that government need not be the catalyst for any change in the status quo. Woman's "decision" is inviolable; the operation of that decision is left to what she can work out with men on their terms. The very fact that abortion is privacy ensures that government will not intervene in the realm of autonomous, individualistic decision making. The women in *Harris* needed something more than mere choice to make their privacy meaningful, or as Catharine MacKinnon put it, they "needed something positive, not abdication [by the state] to make their privacy

[24] Id. at 316.

[25] Id. at 318.

[26] My analysis of the abortion right might lead one to ask why, if these suppositions about privacy and male supremacy are accurate, abortion was ever constitutionally legalized at all. One potential answer to this query is found in Catharine A. MacKinnon's sex equality critique of the abortion question, namely:

> In the context of a sexual critique of gender inequality, abortion promises to women sex with men on the same reproductive terms as men have sex with women.... [A]bortion facilitates women's heterosexual availability.... The availability of abortion removes the one remaining legitimized reason [the potential of unwanted pregnancy] that women have had for refusing sex besides the headache.

CATHERINE A. MACKINNON, FEMINISM UNMODIFIED 99 (1987). MacKinnon's concentration on the "heterosexual availability" of women dovetails with my argument that couching Gay rights equality claims in terms of privacy serves to further insulate the interests of male-dominated heterosociety. One could easily make the same observation about *Griswold* itself. By making contraceptives readily available, the Court removed another barrier to the pursuit of heterosexual male sexual aggressiveness. Or as Andrea Dworkin, in her inimitable cut-to-the-chase style, once said, "Getting laid was at stake." ANDREA DWORKIN, RIGHT-WING WOMEN 95 (1983).

effective."[27] They needed equality – substantive equality – but the Court studiously avoided it.[28]

Exactly how this analytic retrospective of the abortion cases applies to Gay rights becomes clear in the great jurisprudential joke of the *Lawrence* decision – the Court's implication that Gay people actually have any privacy to be safeguarded. The Court's precedents make clear that no such privacy exists for Gay people *qua* Gay people. The sudden equation of homosexual sex with heterosexual sex that *Lawrence* accomplishes creates a privacy dimension for sure, but despite Kennedy's assurances, it is not a privacy right that necessarily advances Gay equality interests.[29]

PRIVACY AND ASSIMILATION

Lawrence is largely a decision about the protection of sex generally – specifically of "sexual intimacy," which the Court equates primarily to all sex, presumptively consensual,[30] in the heterosexual image. In this way, the Court avoids the equality concerns at stake in *Hardwick*,[31] namely that only homosexual sex is neither presumptively free nor constitutionally protected. The Court's concern with liberty's substance meant that the Court extended heterosociety's presumptive right to sexual privacy to homosexuals, so long as the Gay sex being had sufficiently resembles heterosexual sex. This assimilation principle, reduced to equivalence, undergirds the *Lawrence* decision and permeates it.[32]

There are, generally speaking, two primary and alternative paths to equality for Gay people. These are what I have elsewhere termed the "assimilationist"

[27] C. A. MacKinnon, Toward a Feminist Theory of the State 192–193 (1989). Many points in this chapter's retrospective on *Roe*, privacy, and abortion jurisprudence are indebted to Catharine MacKinnon. See especially, C. A. MacKinnon, Toward a Feminist Theory of the State (ch. 10: "Abortion: On Public and Private") as foundational.

[28] It should come as no great surprise, then, that the Court believed that the federal government had no power to intervene in that most private realm where sex abuse takes place. See U.S. v. Morrison, 529 U.S. 598 (2000) (striking down the Violence Against Women Act).

[29] See *Lawrence*, 539 U.S. 588 (2003).

[30] See *Lawrence*, 539 U.S. at 567 (discussing rights of adults to enter into relationships within the confines of their homes). The presumption of consent bothers sex equality theorists like Professor Marc Spindelman (see Spindelman, *Surviving Lawrence v. Texas, infra* note 35). It bothers me, too.

[31] Bowers v. Hardwick, 478 U.S. 186, 190 (1986).

[32] "Persons in a homosexual relationship may seek autonomy for these purposes, just as heterosexual persons do." *Lawrence*, 539 U.S. at 574. As Angela Harris notes, "*Lawrence* looks like an attempt to rebrand patriarchy by making it gay-friendly." Angela P. Harris, *From Stonewall to the Suburbs? Toward a Political Economy of Sexuality*, 14 Wm. & Mary Bill Rts. J. 1539, 1577 (2006) (emphasis added).

and "integrationist" approaches.[33] A substantial politics surrounds this discussion in the Gay community itself. One need not, however, know much about the movement politics to see, quite clearly, that the *Lawrence* Court chose the assimilationist path. The assimilationist approach says to Gay people that equality is defined in terms of equivalence to the preexisting heteronormative standard.[34] "Gay person," says the assimilationist, "if you want equality with straight people, the approach is simple: Be the same as straight people." This is exactly what most Gay rights advocates, and ultimately the Court, said in *Lawrence*. Gay people deserve equality because they are constitutionally (morally, socially, jurisprudentially) equivalent to straight people. Much of the Court's logic, indeed most of the pro–Gay rights briefs submitted on appeal,[35] argues that Gay people are deserving of equal protection in their sexual activity precisely because that activity sufficiently mirrors heterosexual sexual activity, which is (of course) the presumptive good.[36] The Court's very

---

[33] SHANNON GILREATH, SEXUAL POLITICS: THE GAY PERSON IN AMERICA TODAY, 37–38 (2006).

[34] Id.

[35] See, e.g., Brief for Constitutional Law Professors, et al. as Amici Curiae Supporting Petitioners, Lawrence v. Texas, 539 U.S. 558 (2003) (No. 02-102) [hereinafter Law Professors]. In an effort to demonstrate to the Court just how much Gay people are like straight people, the brief highlights "facts" that are so obvious that they sound totally absurd when read aloud: "[Gay people] shop, cook, and eat together, celebrate the holidays together, and share one another's families.... They rely on each other for companionship and support." Id. at 13.

The amicus brief filed by the ACLU likewise focuses on the domestic normalcy of Gay people. "As adults, [Gay people] form intimate relationships with one another, often have or adopt children, and interact with groups of relatives that make up their extended families." Brief for the American Civil Liberties Union and the ACLU of Texas as Amici Curiae Supporting Petitioner at 8, Lawrence v. Texas, 539 U.S. 558 (No. 02-102).

Similar "like-straight" characterizations of Gay life are to be found in the amici briefs of the Human Rights Campaign and the National Lesbian and Gay Law Association. For an excellent summary of the briefs and discussion, see Marc Spindelman, *Surviving* Lawrence v. Texas, 102 MICH. L. REV. 1615, 1619–1621 (2004). Spindelman's work critiquing like-straight politics is excellent and foundational. In addition to the article note, see M. Spindelman, *Homosexuality's Horizon*, 54 EMORY L. J. 1362 (2005).

The urgency of the pro-Gay groups to connect Gays with the acceptable straight paradigm is overwhelming in these briefs. Their arguments reduce to an essence: Gays are sufficiently like straights to merit constitutional protection for their sexual behavior, because that sexual behavior is sufficiently domesticated to straight acceptability. One notable exception is the brief for the Cato Institute by Professor William Eskridge. Eskridge specifically argues that "[t]he Texas Homosexual Conduct Law violates the Equal Protection Clause ... for it targets gay people as an outlaw class because of antigay animus." Brief for CATO Institute, et al. as Amici Curiae Supporting Petitioners, at 18, Lawrence v. Texas, 539 U.S. 558 (No. 02-102).

[36] As the Law Professors' brief put it, since the Court had recognized the undeniable importance of heterosexual intimacy, this recognition should be "for gay people no less than for heterosexuals." Law Professors, *supra* note 35, at 13.

discussion of the history of sodomy prohibitions connects these demeaning laws by the ways in which they influenced the *heterosexual* sexual experience (remember, the presumptive good) to show their constitutional deficiencies.[37] The Court's treatment of sodomy prohibitions in this way has equal protection ramifications to be sure. Unfortunately, the question of whether the Court's analysis will morph into a later argument that will claim that antisodomy laws (associated as they now are primarily with the heterosexual experience) do not provide evidence of a history of "invidious" discrimination against Gays as is required by generally accepted equal protection analysis cannot yet be answered. I hope not.

Situating *Lawrence* as the natural outgrowth of the reproductive privacy cases, the Court is able to declare that "[p]ersons in a homosexual relationship may seek autonomy for these purposes [defining one's own concept of existence, of meaning, of the universe, and the mystery of human life], just as heterosexual persons do."[38] The Court's assimilation of homosexual sex into the heterosexual norm is thereby complete. Gay people do not deserve protections as Gay people, but rather as the legal equivalent of the heterosexual "Mini-me." We receive protection because we are sufficiently like straight people to merit protection. Viewing the Court's decision in this way brings new meaning to the Court's assertion that a decision grounded in "liberty," in fact, advances equality. Indeed, the *Lawrence* majority assures, concerned as they were with Justice O'Connor's envisioned ban on heterosexual sodomy,[39] that heterosexual men can now get their dicks sucked without fear of prosecution. The Equal Protection Clause means that Gay men receive the protection by default.

The Court's assimilation strategy becomes clear in its nearly wholesale adoption of Justice Stevens's *Hardwick* dissent as the controlling analysis in *Lawrence*.[40] Perhaps Justice Stevens was troubled by something more, but his dissent proceeds on the logic that Georgia's law at issue in

---

[37] Students sometimes ask me, Does homosexuality have a history? After *Lawrence*, the answer to that question, at least legally, appears to be yes, if history means what historians make of an actual experience. See Brief for Professors of History George Chauncey, et al. as Amici Curiae Supporting Petitioners, Lawrence v. Texas, 539 U.S. 558 (No. 02-102).

[38] *Lawrence*, 539 U.S. at 574.

[39] "Were we to hold the statute invalid under the Equal Protection Clause some might question whether a prohibition would be valid if drawn differently, say, to prohibit the conduct both between same-sex and different-sex participants." *Lawrence*, 539 U.S. at 575. Indeed, Justice O'Connor raised precisely this question. Id. at 584–585 (O'Connor, J., concurring).

[40] "Justice Stevens' analysis, in our view, should have been controlling in *Bowers* and should control here." Id. at 578.

Hardwick was constitutionally faulty because it treaded on *heterosexual* autonomy:

> [I]ndividual decisions by married persons, concerning the intimacies of their physical relationship, even when not intended to produce offspring, are a form of "liberty" protected by the Due Process Clause of the Fourteenth Amendment. Moreover, this protection extends to intimate choices by unmarried as well as married persons.[41]

> Paradoxical as it may seem, our prior cases thus establish that a State may not prohibit sodomy within "the sacred precincts of marital bedrooms," or, indeed, between unmarried heterosexual adults. In all events, it is perfectly clear that the State of Georgia may not totally prohibit the conduct proscribed.[42]

Justice Stevens is preoccupied with the notion that to "totally prohibit" sodomy would collide with the privacy rights of heterosexuals – as established, both married and single, by the very line of privacy cases the Court relies upon in its articulation of the liberty of sexual intimacy.[43] Stevens believed that such a prohibition clearly violated these heterosexual rights.[44] This starting move by Stevens reflects his inability to abstract himself from the dictates of his own identity position, from which he can only analogize or generalize. He then, by an equal application theory, extended heterosexual privilege to the homosexual, made as he is in the heterosexual's image:

> Although the meaning of the principle that "all men are created equal" is not always clear, it surely must mean that every free citizen has the same interest in "liberty" that the members of the [heterosexual] majority share. From the standpoint of the individual, the homosexual and the heterosexual have the same interest in deciding how he will live his own life, and, more narrowly, how he will conduct himself in his personal and voluntary associations with his companions. State intrusion into the private conduct of either is equally burdensome.[45]

The Court's transmutation of Stevens's *Hardwick* dissent into Kennedy's *Lawrence* majority opinion gives life to its dubious prophecy:

> Equality of treatment and the due process right to demand respect for conduct protected by the substantive guarantee of liberty are linked in important

---

[41]   *Lawrence*, 539 U.S. at 578 (quoting Bowers v. Hardwick, 478 U.S. 186, 216 [1986]).
[42]   *Hardwick*, 478 U.S. at 218 (Stevens, J., dissenting) (internal citations omitted).
[43]   Id. (Stevens, J., dissenting).
[44]   Id. at 219.
[45]   Id. at 218–219 (Stevens, J., dissenting).

respects, and a decision on the latter point advances both interests. If protected conduct is made criminal and the law which does so remains unexamined for its substantive validity, its stigma might remain even if it were not enforceable as drawn for equal protection reasons.[46]

This is a curious formula. As Marc Spindelman observed, "[T]he Court vindicates sexual liberty by recognizing heterosexuals' sexual rights and advances 'equality of treatment' by extending liberty to [Gays]. Rights that are made to the king's measure are fit for a queen."[47] This is distributive justice at its acme. The more the Court critically evaluates the rights of Gays, the more it concentrates on the presumptive rights of heterosexuals.

Would not the Court have taken a more honest jurisprudential look at the plight of Gay Americans had it engaged in a substantive equality analysis? That is to say, had it seen the hierarchical and, therefore, anti-equality dimensions of a law that criminalizes homosexual expressions of intimacy (or even nonintimate sex) – the very conduct by which Gays as totally sexualized beings are defined – even if such laws facially applied to heterosexuals, too.[48] One needs no analogies to marriage or romanticized heterosexual intimacy to see this. Justice O'Connor's nominally equal protection-based concurrence hints at this problem,[49] but her analysis of the issues stops far short of substantive equality (although it may constitute a classic formal equality analysis).[50] By refusing to acknowledge hierarchy in this way, the Court scaffolds it. The

---

[46] *Lawrence*, 539 U.S. at 575.

[47] Spindelman, *supra* note 35, at 1630.

[48] "Sodomy ... is such an intrinsic characteristic of homosexuals, and so exclusive to us, that it constitutes a rhetorical proxy for us. It is our metonym." Janet E. Halley, *Reasoning About Sodomy: Act and Identity in and after* Bowers v. Hardwick, 79 VA. L. REV. 1721, 1737 (1993).

[49] "Rather than relying on the substantive component of the Fourteenth Amendment's Due Process Clause, as the Court does, I base my conclusion on the Fourteenth Amendment's Equal Protection Clause." *Lawrence*, 539 U.S. at 579 (O'Connor, J., concurring).

[50] Justice O'Connor, of course, begins with the faulty premise that equal protection "'is essentially a direction that all persons similarly situated should be treated alike'." Id. (quoting Cleburne v. Cleburne Living Center, Inc., 473 U.S. 432, 439 [1985]). She goes on to recognize that the effects of the existence of the Texas statute go far beyond the potential for criminal prosecution. Id. at 581–582. But the "similarly situated" principle blinds Justice O'Connor to the caste-creating effects of the statute, were its facial discrimination removed. "The Equal Protection Clause 'neither knows nor tolerates classes among citizens'." Id. at 584 (citing Romer v. Evans, 517 U.S. 620, 623 (1996) (quoting Plessy v. Ferguson, 163 U.S. 537, 559 (1896) (Harlan, J., dissenting)). "Whether a sodomy law ... is neutral both in effect and application ... is an issue that need not be decided today." Id. What Justice O'Connor fails to realize is that a sodomy law can never be neutral in "effect," even if it were to be neutral in application. Even in such an imaginary regime, heterosexuals would always be punished for engaging in acts common to homosexuals, not for any quality of their superior heterosexual orientation.

superior constitutional status of heterosexuals is both the doorway and the ceiling of homosexual rights.

And what's wrong with that? *Lawrence*'s celebrants will ask. Well, nothing if you believe, as the Court apparently did, that equality is a numbers game, counting rights, quantities, and uniformities: likes alike and unalikes unalike.[51] But if you believe that true equality cannot be found in acquiescence in a system where the oppressed must assume the appearance of the oppressor in order to enjoy freedom, then the Court's analysis presents serious moral and philosophical dilemmas. If freedom for Gays is to be had only in the legal institutionalization of compulsory heterosexuality, in the mere mimicry of the privileged, is it really freedom at all? Does real equality lie in the exchange of Gay identity for the implicit safety of heteronormative assimilation?

My point of departure with Justice Kennedy is not on the question of whether same-sex sex ought to be the object of special and especially oppressive regulatory intrusion. Certainly, I believe that it should not be. On this, the ultimate outcome, the *Lawrence* majority and I are in total agreement. No, the point of departure is whether in reaching this conclusion the Court should have examined the substantively unequal trappings of the heterosexual hierarchy – the Heteroarchy itself. By ignoring its existence, the Court legitimates it. In operation, it does this by taking the due process privacy route instead of the substantive equality route. Perhaps, the majority truly believed (or at least it did not consider the alternative) that its privacy-based decision was the best possible outcome for Gay people. Whatever the reality, surely the Court believed – it must have understood – that a privacy analysis was the least bumpy route to the desired outcome. Rights are delivered, no doubt, but it should be clear that equality is not part of the delivery.

Lawrence, its equality outcome notwithstanding, further isolates Gays rather than providing them equal citizenship. From the very outset of its opinion, the *Lawrence* majority, in the parlance of privacy, makes clear that what they are articulating is an individuated and individuating right. "Liberty," Kennedy posits, "protects *the person* [read: individual] from unwarranted government intrusions into … private places."[52] This pronouncement, coupled with the historiography the Court embraces – a history that disconnects antisodomy

---

[51] "Likes alike, unalikes unalike" is a useful coinage I have heard Catharine MacKinnon employ in public lectures – for example, at the University of North Carolina, Chapel Hill (Feb. 18, 2009).

[52] *Lawrence*, 539 U.S. at 562 (emphasis added).

persecutions from the Gay experience – avoids the class-based an
a substantive equality approach would have required and, thereby,
(or at least looks through) the Gay *community*.[53] As the *Lawrence* deciso....
Gay people, we have no identity or worth of our own, nothing that is separate
from the heteronormative definition. So long as that definition is intact, Gay
people can continue with the "lifestyle" choices that Justice Kennedy concedes by analogy from straight identity. In the Court's analysis, heterosexuals are again the heroes of the constitutional drama, and Gay people are the
mendicants. The use of privacy, not equality, reifies the bitter heteronormative
prerequisite Gay people face daily: To be free we must be *like*, we must be
palatable to the Heterarchy.

Justice Kennedy's explication of liberty seems to presuppose that Gay
people have the same inner self recognized for straight people and denied
to Gay people in *Hardwick*. What Kennedy drastically misapprehends, however, is whether this inner self can be free in the isolation to which Kennedy's
majority opinion assigns it. *Lawrence* announced a curious rule: Gay people
have a right to define their own destinies, which includes, the Court says,
their intimacies. But that destiny seems to extend only as far as the door
of the new Closet the Court creates. Gay people will not be sent to jail for
consensual sex in private, but any illumination of these "bond[s] that [may
be] more enduring"[54] to an unwilling heterosexual establishment is subject
to the hammer of heteronormative conformity. Aside from marriage, which
Kennedy so obviously elides,[55] lower courts have held *Lawrence* to cover only
the most closeted of sex – the most private – so that oral sex, for example,
can still be punished more harshly than paradigmatic heterosexual sex (vaginal) if it occurs in public,[56] or for hire,[57] or even when state legislatures have
gone to great pains to decriminalize the conduct, as have many states with
oral sex between minors close in age.[58] Even rapists may have their sentences

---

[53] The imperative of an equality norm that recognizes group realities has been understood
from perspectives other than Gay liberation as well. "With the inability to assert a group reality – an ability that only the subordinated need – comes the shift away from realities of power
in the world and toward the search for 'identity'.... It changes the subject, as it were, or tries
to." CROSSROADS, DIRECTIONS, AND A NEW CRITICAL RACE THEORY 75 (Francisco Valdes
et al., eds., 2002).

[54] *Lawrence*, 539 U.S. at 567.

[55] Id. at 578 ("[This case] does not involve whether the government must give formal recognition to any relationship that homosexual persons seek to enter").

[56] See, e.g., *In re* R.L.C., 635 S.E.2d 1, 5 (N.C. Ct. App. 2006) ("It was undisputed that the
conduct occurred in a car parked in a bowling alley parking lot. The crimes against nature
statute remains applicable where public conduct is involved").

[57] See, e.g., State v. Thomas, 891 So.2d 1233 (La. 2005).

[58] See *In re* R.L.C., 635 S.E.2d at 5–8 (Elmore, J., dissenting).

enhanced if they violate their victims orally or anally.[59] This is not to suggest – in any way – that the rapist is sympathetic; rather I am suggesting that rape is made no worse simply because the form it takes is a violent mirror of traditionally homosexual sex acts.[60] All of these painful associations make it difficult for Gays to have the free inner self Kennedy's opinion imagines for us. *Lawrence* allows bigoted judges, reminiscent of Chief Justice Burger in *Hardwick*, to continue to enact homophobia into law.

Of course, a necessary precursor to the Court's approach is the a priori assertion, taken as gospel, that heterosexuality is the measure of the good.[61] Heterosexuality is citizenship, presumptively and really. The assimilationist standard says Gays are to be judged equivalent to the "good" when we are sufficiently proximate to the heterosexual paradigm. In the case of Lawrence and Garner, a Gay couple happened to be engaging in a sex act that a substantial number of straight couples engage in; therefore, those acts and the participants deserve protection based upon the heterosexual paradigm.[62] As I will

---

[59] See, e.g., Wilson v. State, 631 S.E.2d 391, 392 (Ga. Ct. App. 2006).

> [I]f a seventeen-year-old male who engages in an act of sodomy with a female under the age of sixteen years is convicted of aggravated child molestation, he is subject to a mandatory sentence of ten years imprisonment without possibility of parole. If, however, that same teenage male engages in an act of sexual intercourse with the same female child and is convicted of statutory rape, he is guilty of only a misdemeanor.

> Id.

[60] As to Catharine MacKinnon's assertion that "[a] forced sodomy statute enforced equally without regard to sex or sexual orientation would [survive substantive sex equality scrutiny]," I vigorously disagree. See Catharine A. MacKinnon, *The Road Not Taken: Sex Equality in Lawrence v. Texas*, 65 Ohio St. L. J. 1081, 1093 (2004). Taken at face value, this statement means that forcible oral sex might still be the object of more onerous criminal punishment than, say, forced vaginal intercourse. My conceptualization of substantive equality would find this statute to be a violation *simpliciter*. To punish forced oral or anal sex more harshly than forced vaginal sex, respecting the reality that the acts of oral and anal sex are so central to the iconography of Gay identity, perpetuates the existence of the very kind of caste – in this case a highly sexualized version – which is inimical to substantive equality. Rather, a permissible law aimed at the evil of forced sex would be a law against rape – unwanted sex of any kind. But a criminal system that allows an escalation of punishment for rape because the act of rape itself was the violent mirror of the acts by which Gay people interact sexually is, in a phrase, substantively unequal.

[61] See, e.g., José Gabilondo, *Irrational Exuberance About Babies: The Taste for Heterosexuality and Its Conspicuous Reproduction*, 28 B.C. Third World L. J. 1 (2008).

[62] See William D. Mosher et al., U.S. Dep't of Health & Human Services, Sexual Behavior and Selected Health Measures: Men and Women 15–44 Years of Age, United States, 2002, at 3 (2005), www.cdc.gov/nchs/data/ad/ad362.pdf (reporting that 90% of males and 88% of females between twenty-five and forty-four years of age had engaged in oral sex with a member of the opposite sex. The figures for anal sex were 40% for males and 35% for females. Among males twenty-two to twenty-four years of age, 7.4% reported

explain, a substantive equality analysis of the situation in *Lawrence* would not have required assimilation, but a privacy analysis is perfectly comfortable with that outcome. Privacy protects Gay sexual conduct because it (as suggested by current data) is substantially equivalent to heterosexual sexual conduct. The conduct at issue (oral and anal sex) must be, and presumptively should be, protected for heterosexuals. Gay people get the benefit of this protection, too. But make no mistake – heterosexuality is the referent for the decision. The individuated right of sexual autonomy elucidated in *Lawrence* has no room for the group realities that define the place of the Gay individual in American society, law, and politics. These defining issues of dominance and hierarchy are both the symptom and the root cause of sodomy prohibitions aimed at same-sex sexual expression, but they are not discussed. Why?

Here is why. The canonical development of the "right to privacy" has never really been about what is "private" in the most common sense of the word. It has not been about what should be secreted by necessity, locked away because it is shameful or perverse (although the privacy cases could understandably be interpreted in this way as well: sex practices, condom use, unwanted pregnancy, abortion as the destruction of "life," the possession of obscene materials, oral sex, etc.)[63]; rather "privacy" as it has emerged jurisprudentially is much more about the power (and that word "power" is important) to define one's own sense of self, one's own personhood, and one's own moral register. At issue in the privacy cases has been the right and ability to define the "good" life for one's own self. Viewed in this light, the essential equality problem in *Lawrence* becomes clearer.

The problem, obviously, is not *Lawrence*'s outcome – the decriminalization of oral and anal sex. There is an equality there. The Court's privacy perspective, however, is fraught with equality challenges. Who is the definitional measure in *Lawrence*? Is it Lawrence and Garner? Or is it the Heterarchy's evolved definition of what is morally problematic (or no longer morally problematic)? Heterosociety's definition of what is properly protected sexual conduct is at issue; its history defines sodomy prohibitions for the Court; and ultimately its acquiescence in the practices (equivalency) drives *Lawrence*'s

---

engaging in sex with another male; 12.4% of females between fifteen and twenty-four years of age reported engaging in sex with another female).

[63] Even in its secular manifestations, sodomy is deemed abominable and detestable, as in an 1837 North Carolina statute that read "the abominable and detestable crime against nature, not [to] be named among Christians." N.C. Gen. Stat. § 34–6 (1837). Sodomy, this thing that Gay people do, treads in privacy so deep that the acts dare not even be said aloud. It is private because it is "abominable," "detestable," "horrible," "against nature." It is all these things exponentially because it is private – because it cannot be examined or questioned in the light of day.

decriminalization of sodomy, just as its obsessions with Gay sex previously animated sodomy's criminalization. Equality as equivalency (sexual being to sexual being, couple to couple) emerges from the *Lawrence* decision's privacy guarantee. Substantive equality – that which considers questions of hierarchy and dominance – does not.[64] The only real importance of constitutionally protected privacy – the ability to define one's own destiny – collapses under the crushing weight of heterosexual domination. Even on this question of sexual privacy, heterosexuals are the measure of worth. Gays are delivered from non-person status because of their equivalency with straights, not because of any inherent equal worth. The destined good has been defined for Gay people, but not by Gay people.[65]

---

[64] This has been an inherent flaw in the metaphysics of equality from its early American development. Consider this revelation from the congressional debates on the Fourteenth Amendment. "When a distinction is made between two married people or two *femmes sole*, then it is unequal legislation; but where all of the same class are dealt with in the same way then there is no pretense of inequality." CONG. GLOBE, 39th Cong., 1st Sess. 1064 (1865) (quoting Congressman Thaddeus Stevens). Michael Kent Curtis has observed:

> The principle against class or caste legislation was accepted by people like … Representative Stevens. But [he] thought it did not apply [to women generally] because of then-widely held assumptions about the nature of gender differences. In another context (that of suffrage and Section 2 of the Fourteenth Amendment), Senator Howard explained that by "the law of nature … women and children were not regarded as the equals of men." The congressional debates and social practices of 1866–68 suggest that, for most, the class or caste principle was not expected to change the inferior role the law typically assigned to married women.

Michael Kent Curtis, *The Fourteenth Amendment: Recalling What the Court Forgot*, 56 DRAKE L. REV. 911, 994 (2008) (internal citations omitted).
  Despite this obvious shortcoming, Professor Curtis believes strongly in the redemptive power of the "similarly situated" conception of equality when in the hands of courts willing to apply the premise to evolved social facts. My problem is that this conception is, itself, a caste. Substantive equality theory of the type I propose in this paper would not depend needlessly on rationality inquiries – that is, whether the government can rationalize a reason for the discrimination (e.g., "nature," "morality"). Instead, the courts would ask whether the law in operation (as distinct from motivation) has the effect of instituting or perpetuating a caste. By this definition, women deserved equality as much in 1866 as they do in 2009. And this entitlement does not depend on the willingness of male-dominated society to determine that women are really not much different from men. But because courts operated – and continue to operate – under the flawed "similarly situated" standard, women still do not have equality.

[65] Another meritorious criticism of the *Lawrence* majority opinion, although one tangential to this discussion, is the criticism that *Lawrence* is a substantial departure from the privacy canon altogether. This is so because the majority requires privacy in the traditional sense (read: secrecy [to a degree]) in order for the liberty it announces to be exercised in any meaningful way. The *Lawrence* majority speaks in the sweeping language of destiny but then requires that those engaging in "sodomy" do so closed off, behind closed doors. Justice Kennedy underscores this when he says, "Liberty protects the person from unwarranted government intrusion into a dwelling or other *private* places." Lawrence v. Texas, 539

The *Lawrence* majority essentially says: Look at what antisodomy laws prohibit (oral and anal sex).[66] These are expressions of sexual intimacy common to straight and Gay alike (just as the expression of sexual intimacy at all is common to Gay and straight alike). If it must be protected for straight people, as Justice Stevens proclaims in *Hardwick*, then Gay people should get the benefit of that protection too.[67] Any difference between Gay sexual intimacy and straight sexual intimacy – at least any difference to the point of constitutional significance – is in the Court's view a fantasy of the Texas legislature.[68] In this very basic observation, surely the Court is right. But what the Court's approach misses and thereby validates is the fact that the heterosexual hierarchy of power at work when the Texas legislature imagined a legally significant difference in Gay and straight intimacy produces real as well as imaginary differences – differences that become inequalities. Real difference emerges, often in the form of psychic or cognitive differences. The eight-hundred-pound gorilla in the *Lawrence* opinion is this question: Why should Gay people have to be perceived as *like* straight people (indeed, with such myopic obsession that even gay rights groups believe heterosexuality to be the presumptive measure of goodness) in order to receive protection as equal citizens? Why is heterosexuality the access point to citizenship, so that Gay people – Gay people who want to make a claim for equal citizenship in a legal order (a world order) made by straight people – have to show that they are the same as heterosexuals in all the ways that really matter and that they are only accidentally homosexual as a consequence of birth.

This is the ultimate failing of the Court's decision to go the privacy route. Whatever lurks beneath the rock of formal equality (likes alike, unalikes unalike) – whatever must be squashed so that substantive equality can thrive – goes undiscovered. Of course, any time one criticizes the establishment with the ground of Gay liberation as one's base, one must immediately answer calls that

---

U.S. 558, 562 (2003). Or "[A]dults may choose to enter upon this relationship in the confines of their homes and their own private lives and still retain their dignity as free persons." Id. at 567. Kennedy's analogy between the activity at issue in *Lawrence* and the obscenity cases, like *Stanley v. Georgia*, 394 U.S. 557, 568 (1969) (privacy protects the right to possess obscene (otherwise illegal) material in the home) helps make it plain. *Lawrence*, 539 U.S. at 567. This type of privacy is as much cage as sanctuary. It is exactly the same conception of privacy manifest in the military's "Don't Ask, Don't Tell" policy allowing Gay servicemembers to serve so long as they keep their sexual proclivities entirely secret. See generally Shannon Gilreath, *Sexually Speaking: "Don't Ask, Don't Tell" and the First Amendment after* Lawrence v. Texas, 14 Duke J. Gender L. & Pol'y 953 (2007).

[66] *Lawrence*, 539 U.S. at 563.
[67] Bowers v. Hardwick, 478 U.S. 186, 218–219 (1986) (Stevens, J., dissenting).
[68] *Lawrence*, 539 U.S. at 564.

one is advocating for special rights. In relation to my criticism of the *Lawrence* decision in this chapter, I should answer this anticipated criticism now. I can understand intellectually this criticism: "Isn't Gilreath asking to be regarded as both the same and different? Isn't he asking to have it both ways?" My answer is: "So what?" This is exactly what straight people have: equality under the law and preservation of their identities as straight people. *Lawrence* illustrates this perfectly. Straight people are like Gay people when they want to be (when they want to engage in sodomy) and they are different from Gay people when they want to be, too (when they want to get married, for example). So for Gay people to be equal and different at the same time is, in a word, fair.

SUBSTANTIVE EQUALITY AND *LOVING V. VIRGINIA*

Substantive Equality

A different approach was open to the Court, however, one, though never fully realized, that threads its way through our constitutionalism from its earliest theoretical formulation – from Jefferson's *Declaration* to the Fourteenth Amendment. Equality was the approach not taken, the question not answered (not even seriously asked), in *Lawrence v. Texas*. This approach is one concerned not with similarities and differences, but with the distribution of power.[69] Sexual orientation is a question of power, of heterodomination and of Gay subordination. Substantive equality recognizes that inequality is not inherent, but constructed. From this perspective, sexual orientation may not qualify as a difference at all, except that it has been constructed into one by

---

[69] Feminist advocates have understood the necessity of eschewing a similarities test in favor of a power differential approach for some time. For an excellent exposition for the woman-centric argument that "sameness" and "difference" in equality theory should be replaced by "a deeper understanding of gender as a system of power relations," see Joan C. Williams, *Deconstructing Gender*, 87 MICH. L. REV. 797, 836 (1989). Catharine MacKinnon elucidates a version of this dominance-over-difference approach to equality analysis as far back as 1979. See generally CATHARINE A. MACKINNON, SEXUAL HARASSMENT OF WORKING WOMEN (1979). She continues to refine the theory in subsequent work; see, e.g., CATHARINE A. MACKINNON, FEMINISM UNMODIFIED: DISCOURSES ON LIFE AND LAW 37 (1987) (examining the sameness/difference approach as derivative of Aristotelian theory).

I remain convinced that the inequality of Gays to straights, with its particularized prejudices, now almost uniquely rationalized as acceptable religious expression, normatively moral when actually only descriptively so, deserves a theory of its own. Nevertheless, earlier feminist theorizing on the failings of "similarly situated" analysis and the possibilities of a realistic judicial look at majoritarian dominance is of much merit to Gay liberation. The link between women and Gays and their social, religious, and legal inequality is impossible to deny. For an excellent exposition of the connection, see generally DAVID A. J. RICHARDS, WOMEN, GAYS, AND THE CONSTITUTION (1998).

the Heteroarchy, who have used it as a tool for dominance. From the assumptions of heterosexual male supremacy come categorical distinctions that matter, which have been gender and sexual orientation. In this invented reality, difference is consequential only as a tool for social power. Justice Kennedy's privacy rationale recognized that a constructed difference existed and should be unconstitutional because, as the majority understood it, the difference (the sex of sexual partners) was an artificial one.[70] The individuated nature of the privacy right, however, ensured that the Court stopped there, without exposing and considering the root cause of the epistemological distinctions drawn by the Texas law. The kind of substantive equality approach I envision would have gone further. It would have given Gays access to the standard by which differences are measured and power meted out, rather than, as the *Lawrence* Court did, rest on the determination (albeit right) that resulted when it measured one group's (Gays) differences against the standard set by the group (straights) that constructed the differences.[71]

Now, if the Court is to cease asking questions of categorized difference, what questions should the Court ask? In the sort of substantive equality approach I suggest, the Court, instead of asking whether Gays and straights were sufficiently alike or sufficiently different or were in the appropriate box for purposes of criminalization, would have asked whether the law promoted the dominance of one group with the consequence of the subordination of the target group, in a socio-political reality in which the groups are, in fact, unequal in power, and where the socio-political (and legal) hierarchy excludes the target group from power. In short, this approach is the revivification of Justice Harlan's much-lauded *Plessy* dissent: "There is no caste here."[72] This approach, of course, requires the Court to realize things it may not wish to realize. It requires the Court to depart from a historical jurisprudence of formal equality only, and to begin to ask questions that are so hard because they are so simple. It requires the Court to distinguish the oppressed from the oppressor, victim from victimizer, powerless from powerful. It requires that the Court examine equality (or more often inequality) as it *really* exists – in reality – not merely in the abstract world of judges and law professors.

---

[70] *Lawrence*, 539 U.S. at 575, 578–579.

[71] I continue to believe that

> [e]quality ... is the combination of personal and civic freedom; it is a combination of the private and the public. While it is fair to say that one cannot enjoy civic freedom without first possessing personal liberty, one is not free until one has a role in shaping the public mechanisms that govern one's destiny.

> GILREATH, SEXUAL POLITICS, *supra* note 33, at 129–130.

[72] Plessy v. Ferguson, 163 U.S. 537, 559 (1896) (Harlan, J., dissenting).

Some constitutional scholars are disquieted by my shift from a "difference" to a "dominance" theory of equal protection. For example, in conversations about this essay, Professor Michael Kent Curtis raised the following
hypothetical:

> Suppose a young man in a small Southern town wants to enter nursing
> school. The nursing program in closest proximity to the young man is part of
> a woman-only college. He is denied admission based on his sex. The young
> man brings an equal protection challenge seeking access to the woman-
> only program. Shouldn't the young man receive equal opportunity?

The young man is a sympathetic plaintiff. He is not wealthy; he is caring for
a sick mother; and he wants to enter a noble profession. He cannot do so in
the manner most convenient for him solely because of an accident of birth –
his sex. In *Mississippi University for Women v. Hogan*, the case from which
Professor Curtis's hypothetical is drawn, the Supreme Court ruled – applying
the formal "likes alike; unalikes, unalike" equality theory – that refusal to
admit the young man solely on the basis of his sex was a violation of equal
protection.[73]

Professor Curtis believes that *Hogan* was rightly decided and that my shift to
a dominance-over-difference equality analysis like the one I posit for *Lawrence*
would require contrary results. The sex-based classification in question doesn't,
at first blush, appear to be constructed to promote the dominance of women
over men, and men as a target group likely are not subordinated by it (given
what we know about the employment realities of men and women); the hierarchy is not constructed to subordinate men – on the contrary, the hierarchy cuts
the other way; and the power differential is, in reality (if reality is composed
of something more than isolated counterfactuals), weighted heavily in favor of
men. Therefore, wouldn't substantive equality theory mean that the sympathetic male plaintiff loses?

Maybe. But this result does not *necessarily* follow from the theory.
Substantive equality looks at inequality as it really exists, which requires that
the court examine the power structure at play and the attendant moral register
in its entirety as a complement to individuated decision making. In this type
of analysis, the male plaintiff may still win if he can show that the segregation
of the nursing profession has the net effect of relegating women to a subordinate status. An economy that attempts to define certain professions as "for
women only" may indeed have such an effect. Again, maybe. Reasoning like

---

73 See Miss. Univ. for Women v. Hogan, 458 U.S. 718, 733 (1982).

this, albeit a bit more patronizing, seems to be the basis for Justice O'Connor's majority opinion in *Hogan*.[74]

Sex stereotyping notwithstanding, in other circumstances in which a male plaintiff seeks access into the relatively few enclaves enjoyed and controlled by women, substantive equality may well order his loss in the courts. Equality should not be used as a battering ram by which a member of the majority can shatter the few enclaves carved out by the minority for themselves. This would defy the substantive imperative and return us to mere formal equality. Such a result ignores the reality by which majority and minority – in the hypothetical example: men (heterosexual men, at least) and women – live their lives. In that reality, "differences" constructed by the majority into legal significances have already given the heterosexual male myriad advantages, which may explain why certain woman-only enclaves may be a necessary evolution in the first place. In these instances, the use of sameness/difference theory to open new inroads for the majority simply serves to magnify the advantages they already enjoy. Such an approach turns equality theory into an affirmative action program for the already powerful.

Exceptional cases and counterfactuals, like *Hogan*, become convenient weapons for attacks on substantive equality theory. Unfortunately, they usually ignore the group realities that define minority existences. Only in a legal order grounded in heterosexual male supremacy would "driving further," as the plaintiff in *Hogan* would have had to do in order to enter a coed school, be judged an imposition equal to the destruction of a learning model formulated specifically to address the needs of a less powerful minority. Haven't the women of Mississippi University for Women lost exponentially more than the individual male plaintiff has gained? Shouldn't this, at least in an equality analysis – perhaps especially in an equality analysis – matter?

The focus on the needs of the *individual* plaintiff, divorced from group realities, is natural in a legal order that systematically, pathologically advantages the already advantaged. In reality, however, while heterosexual men may be able to live their lives primarily as individuals, many minorities, especially women and Gays, live realities defined almost entirely by their group status. In such a world order, no caste is created by single-sex or single-sexuality learning environments, like the Harvey Milk School for Gay students in New York City.[75] Such educational environments merely take into account group realities that define existence.

---

[74] 458 U.S. at 729–731.
[75] Hetrick Martin Institute: Home of the Harvey Milk School, http://www.hmi.org (last visited May 9, 2009).

I would defend educational experiments, like the Harvey Milk School, by suggesting that such environments may be necessary to account for – in a more than merely ameliorative way – the realities faced by Gay youth. I could defend all-women or "historically Black" institutions on similar bases. Such environments created by the powerless as a power base illumine the sharp distinction between *separation* and *segregation*. The former is an instrument of survival; the latter is an implementation of caste. Viewed in this way, it makes no sense to destroy these ecologies of survival because one member of the majority must suffer the burden of "driving further." Indeed, such a result is the opposite of equality – it is a net loss for equality.

Loving v. Virginia

The paradigm for a substantive equality analysis of the questions presented by *Lawrence* is not found in the contraception cases and their endangered privacy. The paradigm case is *Loving v. Virginia*,[76] in which the Court struck down antimiscegenation laws as discriminatory tools to maintain white supremacy.[77]

---

[76]   Loving v. Virginia, 388 U.S. 1 (1967). I have not chosen *Brown v. Board*, 347 U.S. 483 (1954) as my paradigm (though it is the most commonly touted equality case), because I do not believe *Brown*, in fact, to be a substantive equality case. By my reading of it, *Brown*, unlike *Loving*, announces no new equality theory. The *Brown* Court simply applied the *Plessy* Court's formal equality analysis (the likeness/difference approach) to evolved social facts. Id. at 492–493. In other words, the Court decided that Black people were sufficiently like white people to merit integration. Viewed in this way, *Brown* is the mirror of *Lawrence*: The minority "wins" because it has sufficiently – in the eyes of a court constituted by the majority – come to resemble the majority (or has the potential to). There is an equality there, for sure, but one without substance.

[77]   *Loving*, 388 U.S. 1, 11 (1967). It is interesting that the justices dissenting in *Hardwick* apparently thought *Loving* to be the most analogous precedent, too. Justices Stevens and Blackmun, both joined by Justices Brennan and Marshall, wrote dissents that relied on *Loving*. Justice Blackmun noted that "[t]he parallel between *Loving* and this case is almost uncanny." Bowers v. Hardwick, 478 U.S. 186, 210 n.5 (1986) (Blackmun, J., dissenting). Likewise, in a footnote, Justice Stevens notes the parallels between the crimes of miscegenation and sodomy. Id. at 216 n. 9 (Stevens, J., dissenting).

The *Loving* analogy has also been made by academics. For a brilliant analysis, see Andrew Koppelman, *The Miscegenation Analogy: Sodomy Law as Sex Discrimination*, 98 YALE L. J. 145 (1988). Professor Koppelman and I cover some of the same ground, albeit from distinctly different starting points – he from the already well framed law of sex discrimination and I from the far less well framed law and theory of Gay liberation.

It is no surprise that *Loving* should figure so prominently in the thinking and rethinking of Gay equality claims. The relationship between *Loving* and *Lawrence* provides a historical analogy, but it, in multiple ways, provides a converged reality as well. Gay people have never been owned as chattel property (at least not *as* Gay people – surely there were slaves who happened to be both Black and Gay); otherwise, their treatment has been similarly tragic. Like Blacks, Gay people have been subject to systemic abuses, sexual and other physical violence,

In the following discussion, I do not mean to suggest that *Loving* is unproblematic for Gay liberation. It very obviously is not a Gay liberation decision; we are still waiting on that decision. From a Gay liberationist perspective, it cannot escape notice that *Loving* valorizes a certain type of relationship and, indeed, a certain type of sexuality. These important points for exploration are neglected here. The important aspect of *Loving* for a discussion of substantive, caste-based equal protection is the refusal of the *Loving* Court to be constrained in its equality analysis because the Virginia law prohibited Black people from marrying white people as well as white people from marrying Black people (mirroring the sort of equal application sodomy law the Court envisioned would be problematic for equality analysis in *Lawrence*). Instead, the Court looked at the overarching problems of power and hierarchy. The Court invalidated the Virginia law at issue in *Loving* because it was "designed to maintain White Supremacy."[78] This focus is also a departure from the "trait-based" jurisprudence that has come to define equality doctrine. The Court spent no time expostulating on the evils of classifications drawn on the paradigmatic trait – race. Rather the Court focused on the power relationships at play in a system of supremacy – power hierarchy, which "violates the central meaning of the Equal Protection Clause."[79] The one exception was Justice Stewart, who argued that "it is simply not possible for a state law to be valid under our Constitution which makes the criminality of an act depend upon the race of the actor."[80] Race was determinative for him. No other justice joined his opinion, and Chief Justice Warren's majority opinion is indubitably concerned with the consequences of power and caste.

Sodomy laws, no less than antimiscegenation laws, are designed to maintain supremacy – this time, Heterosexual Supremacy – what Adrienne Rich coined "compulsory heterosexuality."[81] Moreover, the *Loving* Court was not deterred by the possibility of a racially neutral restriction on marriage. Instead, the Court recognized and focused on the substantive inequalities of power that motivated the law in the first place, writing, "[W]e find the racial classifications in these statutes repugnant to the Fourteenth Amendment, even

---

condoned and, indeed, often encouraged by the American legal order from the top down. Blacks, Gays, and women have all been systematically sexualized by their governments. But these realities of the lives lived by the powerless or less powerful are seldom the stuff of which decisions are made in formal equality adjudication.

[78] Id.

[79] Id. at 12. See also Chapter 2, this volume, for a discussion of the failure of the Court's trait-based jurisprudence.

[80] Id. at 13 (Stewart, J., concurring) (internal citations omitted).

[81] This concept appears in Rich's classic essay, *Compulsory Heterosexuality and Lesbian Existence*, 5 SIGNS: JOURNAL OF WOMEN IN CULTURE AND SOCIETY 4 (1980).

assuming an even-handed state purpose to protect the 'integrity' of all races."[82] The law operated to institutionalize a caste, and that was enough to constitutionally condemn it.

A similar observation by an intellectually honest Court regarding Justice O'Connor's hypothetical facially neutral sodomy law in *Lawrence* would be this: The mere existence of sodomy laws, whether they target only Gays or all people equally, given the real inequalities between Gay and straight, discriminates on the basis of sexual orientation in a way that entrenches heterosexual dominance in violation of the Equal Protection Clause of the Fourteenth Amendment.[83] This is so because, while straight people apparently engage in acts of oral and anal sex with great frequency, the conduct is inextricably associated with Gay people. The unavoidable association of Gay people with sodomy has been the means by which the Heteroarchy fictionalized the caste. An honest recognition of this reality would have accomplished the result the majority wanted without resort to the spuriousness of privacy.[84]

---

[82] Loving v. Virginia at 12 n. 11.

[83] For example, in striking an anti-Gay Act in South Africa, Justice Ackermann of the South African Constitutional Court focused on the ways in which the mere *"existence* of a law which punishes a form of sexual expression for gay men degrades and devalues gay men in our broader society." *Nat'l Coal. for Gay & Lesbian Equal. v Minister of Justice & Others* 1999 (1) SA 6 (CC) at 30 (S. Afr.) (emphasis added). See also id. at 14–26, 27–39. This is different from Justice Kennedy's focus on the stigma attached to *convictions* under such laws.

[84] Moreover, even in the current equal protection framework, a facially neutral sodomy statute need not be a major hurdle for a Gay plaintiff bringing a discrimination action. Facial neutrality is not proof that the law does not target Gays. A plaintiff need not "prove that the challenged action rested solely on racially discriminatory purposes.... When there is a proof that a discriminatory purpose has been a motivating factor in the decision, this judicial deference is no longer justified." Vill. of Arlington Heights v. Metro. Hous. Dev. Corp., 429 U.S. 252, 265–266 (1977). Homophobia may or may not have been the original motivator of antisodomy legislation, but it certainly has been a prime motivator in the statutes' retention. This is rarely disputed. Consider the 1981 decision of the House of Representatives to overrule a decision of the District of Columbia City Council to repeal the District's sodomy law. The House debate focused on homosexual sodomy, not heterosexual activity. "A vote to table or postpone a vote to legalize sodomous [sic] homosexual liaisons," declared Rep. Philip Crane, resolution sponsor. 127 Cong. Rec. 27, 749 (1981). See also remarks of Rep. Parren Mitchell noting and criticizing the debates' nearly exclusive focus on homosexual sex. Id. For a discussion, see Koppelman, *supra* note 77.

Of course, *Hardwick* itself ought to close the debate on the meaning of facially neutral sodomy laws. The Georgia law at issue applied equally to Gays and straights, but Georgia defended it almost exclusively in light of the evils of homosexuality; and Justice White, writing for the Court, followed the House of Representatives in his opinion's exclusive focus on homosexuality. The result of these observations, even if we accept the work of historians who want to delink Gays and sodomy prohibitions (see Brief for Professors of History George Chauncey, et al. as Amici Curiae Supporting Petitioners, Lawrence v. Texas, 539 U.S. 558 [2003] [No. 02–102]), ought to be this: The antisodomy law is facially neutral. So

By failing to follow the substantive equality approach, *Lawrence*'s victory became a limitation almost the moment it arrived. Perhaps this was intended. After all, if marriage laws based on racial classifications are unconstitutional because of their caste-maintaining consequences – if hierarchies of suprem-acy and dominance are bad in this realm – why are marriage statutes based on sexual orientation not so? Perhaps this was the unarticulated worry that motivated the Court's choice of approaches.[85] The privacy approach, by con-trast, allows the Court to stop short of this outcome. Marriage involves more than the nonintervention privacy requires. Marriage requires legal recogni-tion by the state.[86] So marriage – the current holy grail of the gay rights move-ment – is beyond *Lawrence*'s scope.[87] Essentially, *Lawrence* holds that Gay "dignity" is inviolable only when the law recognizes it as unregulable.[88] When it is not so recognized, it is neither inviolable nor free. It is in private, where the Court locates it, that equality is most vulnerable. The *Lawrence* decision reinforced the private–public demarcation that has been the inevitable result of the Court's privacy jurisprudence.[89]

---

what? Homophobia need not be the sole reason for the statute; it need only be a "motivating factor." See Vill. of Arlington Heights, 429 U.S. at 265–266; *accord* Pers. Adm'r of Mass. v. Feeney, 442 U.S. 265, 276–277 (1979).

 Moreover, the substantive equality theory elaborated here, one that sees dominance before difference, would scrap this requirement altogether. Substantive equality theory would require no proof of a legislative *mens rea* of "reckless" or "knowing" disadvantage to the target group before a law should fall as an unconstitutional breach of equality. Instead the Court would inquire as to whether the law at issue has the *effect* of instituting or perpetuating a caste. If it does, then the government would have the duty of proving that the classification did not legalize identity prejudice.

[85] *Loving*, after all, came thirteen years after *Brown*. The Court denied certiorari in miscege-nation cases twice before the *Loving* decision, once in 1954, just months after *Brown* was handed down in Jackson v. Alabama, 348 U.S. 888 (1954), and again in 1956 in Naim v. Naim, 350 U.S. 985 (1956). After the 1967 *Loving* decision, the Court declared – seventeen years later – that the interracial nature of a parent's subsequent relationship could not be a basis for a custody decision regarding children of a prior relationship. Palmore v. Sidoti, 466 U.S. 429 (1984). This slow progress might be seen as a shirking of constitutional duty by the Court, or it might be seen as "prudence." See Koppelman, *supra* note 77, at 162 ("The prospect of the Court attempting to impose such results on a resistant society is, and should be, a daunting one"). Whatever the proper description, the Court's "one bombshell at a time" approach to earlier social issues may portend a long road to a gay rights vindication of marriage equality. Gay marriage is certainly no less explosive than was interracial marriage.

[86] For an argument, see Carlos A. Ball, *The Positive in the Fundamental Right to Marry: Same-Sex Marriage in the Aftermath of* Lawrence v. Texas, 88 MINN. L. REV. 1184 (2004).

[87] *Lawrence*, 539 U.S. at 578.

[88] See generally *Lawrence*, 539 U.S. 558.

[89] See Harris, *supra* note 32, at 1544 ("Embracing *Lawrence*, even with the hope of somehow turning it against itself, is a strategy that risks us getting lost, once again, in the mazes of the public/private distinction").

A substantive equality analysis would have avoided these problems. It also would have avoided the "problems" that give Justice Scalia most pause about the *Lawrence* decision (at least, that is, if you take Scalia's dissent at face value rather than viewing it simply as rationalized bigotry). Scalia believed that the majority's privacy rationale and its resulting decriminalization of sodomy necessarily meant the decriminalization of bigamous marriage, same-sex marriage, incest, prostitution, adultery, fornication, bestiality, and obscenity.[90] Scalia interestingly concedes that since majoritarian morality cannot trump individual privacy, laws criminally prohibiting these practices must fall. Substantive equality analysis would find Scalia only partially right. As I explained, substantive equality would result in the fulfillment of Scalia's prophecy about same-sex marriage. But substantive equality's insistence that the Court make realistic distinctions between the powerful and powerless would ensure that the others in Scalia's parade of horribles would find no refuge in equality because they entail real power inequities and real harms.

Polygamous marriage could continue to be criminalized on the basis of gender inequities usually entailed in the reality of these relationships. Thus, the laws would stand as shields against an institution (the polygamous marriage) that usually compounds existing sex inequalities between men and women, thereby serving to entrench male supremacy. Laws prohibiting bestiality would stand, if for no other reason than the obvious power inequality between animals and humans. Prostitution and pornography entail obvious harms to women – obvious to all but those who do not want to see them. Their prohibitions would likely remain undisturbed. Laws prohibiting rape and incest and other laws prohibiting coerced sex would remain intact because of the obvious harms and power inequities of forced sex crimes.

SUBSTANTIVE EQUALITY AND MORALITY: A NOTE

An analogy between *Loving* and *Lawrence* is also important because it illumines the faultiness, constitutionally speaking at least, of transmuting the old talisman "love the sinner, hate the sin," into jurisprudential theory. The "possibility that one can 'hate' an individual's behavior without hating the individual"[91] has been a stumbling block even to those who are largely sensitive to claims for equal citizenship made by Gay people. Professor Michael Perry,

---

[90]　Id.
[91]　See Robert F. Nagel, *Playing Defense in Colorado*, FIRST THINGS, May 1998, at 34, 35. For my original critique of Nagel's position, see GILREATH, SEXUAL POLITICS, *supra* note 33, at 49.

for instance, wonders whether an "irrational fear and loathing"[92] of homosexuals really motivates many of the laws that deny Gays equal citizenship – for example, the opposition to extend civil marriage to Gay couples. Perry wonders whether such resistance is rather a genuine expression of religiously based moral disapproval (presumptively more benign?) for homosexual activity, and thus a reluctance to "incentivize" it. Andrew Koppelman, a consistent proponent of marriage equality, also argues, "Not all antigay views ... deny the personhood and equal citizenship of gay people.... There is a serious discussion to be had here about sexuality and morality."[93] Now, opposition to Gay "conduct" (or conduct most commonly presumed "Gay") may be, as Perry and Koppelman see it, a genuine expression of religious morality. Or it may be, as I see it, a convenient rationalization for bigotry. Or it may be both. What *Loving's* equality analysis makes quite plain, however, is that the answer to this conundrum makes absolutely no difference in the way the Court should adjudicate an equality-based claim under the Fourteenth Amendment. Religious justifications supporting anti-equality legal regimes have not served as a shield from constitutional scrutiny.[94] Indeed, the Virginia trial judge who sentenced Richard and Mildred Loving to banishment for the *conduct* of engaging in interracial marriage buttressed his decision by concluding that interracial marriage violated the laws of "the Creator."[95]

> Almighty God created the races white, black, yellow, malay [*sic*] and red, and he placed them on separate continents. And but for the interference with his arrangement there would be no cause for such marriages. The fact that he separated the races shows that he did not intend for the races to mix.[96]

Was this religious pronouncement a reflection of the deeply held moral conviction of the Virginia electorate, or was it a rationalization and mechanism (a very effective one) for the maintenance of White Supremacy? The Court made no effort to solve the dilemma, because it was constitutionally irrelevant. Regardless of whether the impetus for the miscegenation statute was one of moral force, the sentiments in legal operation denied equality to Blacks.

Indisputably, the religious teaching of the natural separation of the races was part and parcel of the southern establishment that kept Blacks powerless.

---

[92] MICHAEL J. PERRY, THE CONSTITUTION, THE SUPREME COURT, AND HUMAN RIGHTS (forthcoming) (quoting RICHARD POSNER, SEX AND REASON [1992]). I read Professor Perry's book in manuscript form.

[93] Andrew Koppelman, *You Can't Hurry Love: Why Antidiscrimination Protections for Gay People Should Have Religious Exemptions*, 72 BROOK. L. REV. 125, 145 (2006).

[94] See Chapter 7, this volume.

[95] Loving v. Virginia, 388 U.S. 1, 3 (1967).

[96] Id.

Pro-segregation southern ministers frequently argued that Blacks were God's creation too and should be treated compassionately, but that

> the destiny to which the Almighty has assigned [the races] on this continent … require[s] that they should be kept distinct and separate, and that connections and alliances so unnatural that God and nature seem to forbid them, should be prohibited by positive law, and be subject to no evasion.[97]

It's really for their own good, see?

Anti-Gay laws also rest on powerful religious convictions. Some such expressions mirror those of pro-segregation preachers in that they affirm that Gays should be treated with "respect, compassion and sensitivity."[98] Only their "conduct" (having sex with same-sex partners or marrying someone of the same sex) is morally dubious and objectionable.[99] No such posturing mattered

---

[97] Kinney v. Commonwealth, 71 Va. 858, 869 (1878). Arguably, this kind of legal imposition of sectarian definitions of "destiny" would even violate the right to privacy, insofar as that right has been construed to protect an individual's ability to control his or her own destiny and to define his or her own relationship with the universe.

[98] UNITED STATES CONFERENCE OF CATHOLIC BISHOPS ADMINISTRATIVE COMMITTEE, PROMOTE, PROTECT, PRESERVE MARRIAGE: STATEMENT ON MARRIAGE AND HOMOSEXUAL UNIONS (2003), http://www.usccb.org/comm/archives/2003/03-179.shtml. This concededly pretty language rings rather hollow to many Gay people, considering that the Vatican has also labeled Gays "inherently disordered" and equates our mere contact with children with child abuse. See CONGREGATION FOR THE DOCTRINE OF THE FAITH, CONSIDERATIONS REGARDING PROPOSALS TO GIVE LEGAL RECOGNITION TO UNIONS BETWEEN HOMOSEXUAL PERSONS, June 3, 2003, http://www.vatican.va/roman_curia/congregations/cfaith/documents/rc_con_cfaith_doc_20030731_homosexual-unions_en.html; Neela Banerjee, *Bishops Back Guidelines Urging Gay Celibacy*, N.Y. TIMES, Nov. 14, 2006, http://www.nytimes.com/2006/11/14/us/14cnd-bishops.html?ex=1321160400&en=280c5b982a28458f&ei=5088&partner=rssnyt&emc=rss.

[99] See UNITED STATES CONFERENCE OF CATHOLIC BISHOPS ADMINISTRATIVE COMMITTEE, *supra* note 98. Similar morality arguments were used to deny women equal citizenship. Consider Justice Bradley's explanation of his decision in *Bradwell v. Illinois* in which the Court upheld laws prohibiting the "conduct" of a woman practicing law: "The paramount destiny and mission of woman are to fulfill the noble and benign offices of wife and mother. This is the law of the Creator." 83 U.S. 130, 141 (1873).
Or this attack on women abolitionists:

> We invite your attention to the dangers which at present seem to threaten the female character with widespread and permanent injury. The appropriate duties and influence of women are clearly stated in the New Testament. Those duties, and that influence are unobtrusive and private, but the sources of mighty power. When the mild, dependent, softening influence upon the sternness of man's opinions is fully exercised, society feels the effect of it in a thousand forms. The power of woman is her dependence, flowing from the consciousness of that weakness which God has given her for her protection.

ELEANOR FLEXNER, CENTURY OF STRUGGLE: THE WOMAN'S RIGHTS MOVEMENT IN THE UNITED STATES 42 (1975) (1959) (quoting a pastoral letter).

to the *Loving* Court. All that mattered was that Virginia's antimiscegenation law, whatever its religious justification, served to entrench the power of the white hierarchy – a consequence that struck at "the central meaning of the Equal Protection Clause."[100]

PRIVACY, EQUALITY, STIGMA, AND POWER: SOME FINAL THOUGHTS ON *LOVING'S* LESSON

I find it curious that the Court would find the answers to its concerns over "stigma" in due process as opposed to the substantive dimensions of equality.[101] Sartre once observed that anti-Semites define "the Jew."[102] How heteronormativity and homophobia define the "Gay" person was the proper departure point for the *Lawrence* decision, yet it is given only passing reference. Kenneth Plummer has observed[103]:

> The single most important factor about homosexuality as it exists in this culture is the perceived hostility of the societal reactions that surround it.... [This hostility] renders the business of becoming a homosexual a process that is characterized by problems of access, problems of guilt and problems of identity. It leads to the emergence of a subculture of homosexuality. It leads to a series of interaction problems involved with concealing the discreditable stigma. And it inhibits the development of stable relationships

---

Or "The Creator has endowed the bodies of women with the noble mission of motherhood.... Any woman who violates this great trust by *participating* in homosexuality not only degrades herself socially but also destroys the purpose for which God created her." Allan Bérubé & John D'Emilio, *The Military and Lesbians During the McCarthy Years*, 9 SIGNS 759, 769 (1984) (emphasis added).

Condemnation of the *conduct* at issue in these statements was done to protect and further "respect, compassion and sensitivity" toward women, not to deny a woman's personhood (allegedly). Indeed, the "hate the sin, love the sinner" camp would argue that the condemnation is there solely so that personhood may be fully recognized. This is the argument with regard to homosexuals. The abiding insult of such pronouncements is that the pontificators purport to know what is good for Gays better than Gays know it for ourselves. Enforcing this descriptive "good" by the power of the state is exactly what makes such laws violate the substantive equality guaranteed by the Fourteenth Amendment. For further discussion see Shannon Gilreath, *The Technicolor Constitution: Popular Constitutionalism, Ethical Norms, and Legal Pedagogy*, 9 TEX. J. C.l. & C.R. 23, 33–36 (2003). For further discussion of this existentialist flimflam in the marriage context, see Chapter 6, this volume.

[100] *Loving*, 388 U.S. at 12.

[101] See generally Lawrence v. Texas, 539 U.S. 558, 575 (2003).

[102] JEAN-PAUL SARTRE, ANTI-SEMITE AND JEW 143 (George J. Becker, trans., 1948). Sartre's observation was certainly true in Nazi era Germany. See Chapter 4, this volume.

[103] The source materials by Kenneth Plummer and Kenneth Karst cited here are also cited in *Sex Equality*, by Catharine MacKinnon, to whom I am indebted for pointing them out.

among homosexuals to a considerable degree. Homosexuality as a social experience simply cannot be understood without an analysis of the societal reactions towards it.[104]

The analysis Plummer suggests is exactly the analysis the Court's privacy decision avoids. Privacy analysis asks, "Where may power be exercised? What are its spatial limits?" Substantive equality analysis, by contrast, asks "What is power? What does a group deprived of power look like? And what would redistribution of power take?"

Professor Kenneth Karst has offered the following analysis of power as it relates to stigmatization and inequality:

> The principle of equal citizenship presumptively insists that the organized society treat each individual as a person, one who is worthy of respect, one who "belongs." Stated negatively, the principle presumptively forbids the organized society to treat an individual either as a member of an inferior or dependent caste or as a nonparticipant. Accordingly, the principle guards against degradation or the imposition of stigma. The inverse relationship between stigma and recognition as a person is evident. "By definition, … we believe that the person with a stigma is not quite human." The relationship between stigma and inequality is also clear: while not all inequalities stigmatize, the essence of any stigma lies in the fact that the affected individual is regarded as an unequal in some respect. A society devoted to the idea of equal citizenship, then, will repudiate those inequalities that impose the stigma of caste and thus "belie the principle that people are of equal ultimate worth."[105]

The privacy-based decision in *Lawrence* merely removed one possible place in which the stigma that is "homosexuality" may legally operate. It does little, if anything, to investigate the "how" and "why" of the stigma the majority presumes; indeed, it purposefully stops short of such an analysis. If, as Professor Karst has suggested, equality is ultimately reducible "to a claim to be free from stigma,"[106] has the *Lawrence* Court really done anything at all to address substantively the equality question before it? *Lawrence* tells us that

---

[104] Kenneth Plummer, Sexual Stigma: An Interactionist Account 102 (1975) (citation omitted).

[105] Kenneth L. Karst, *The Supreme Court, 1976 Term – Forward: Equal Citizenship Under the Fourteenth Amendment*, 91 Harv. L. Rev. 1, 6 (1977) (internal citations omitted). I use Professor Kart's characteristically forceful and elegant language here for my own ends. I should mention that in his recent article, *The Liberties of Equal Citizens: Groups and the Due Process Clause*, Professor Karst adopts a view contrary to mine and embraces the Court's liberty-through-due-process disposition of the *Lawrence* claims. 55 UCLA L. Rev. 99 (2007).

[106] Kenneth L. Karst, *Why Equality Matters*, 17 Ga. L. Rev. 245, 249 (1983).

the government may not force its institutionalized stigma in the form of the criminal law into the private confines of the bedroom. Despite the poetry of language Justice Kennedy employs, the *Lawrence* decision practicably goes no further – nor could it. Essentially, the decision reinforces the need for "the Closet." The most wounding aspect of *Lawrence* is perhaps the fact that its gesture toward "equality of treatment" operates as the latch dropped on the Closet door.

By limiting recognition of Gay rights to the decriminalization of consensual sex in private, *Lawrence* thus draws a line across which the liberty it supposes does not operate, or at least across which liberty's operability remains questionable. The majority then undertheorizes to the point of nonexistence the way the line demarcating the private from the public is constantly susceptible to repressive heterocentric definition.[107] The stark contrast between private and public assumes for Gays a dual reality with which no other category of citizen is asked to contend. The liberty presupposed by the *Lawrence* majority ought to mean more than the availability of a defined space in which one may live freely so long as one lives detached from the rest of society.

The Fourteenth Amendment forbids the arbitrary isolation of groups of people into untouchable categories exempt from basic moral freedoms of self-determination and liberty of conscience that subject caste members to burdens not borne by citizens outside of the caste.[108] One lesson we should

[107] Indeed, Professor Angela Harris points out that with the ascendancy of "neoliberal" politics, especially consolidated under the Reagan presidency, the public sphere is shrinking (as are the legal remedies that usually operate in it) as rights and citizenship are increasingly defined into the private realm. She quotes Lauren Berlant for the proposition that "since '68, the sphere of discipline and definition for proper citizenship in the United States has become progressively more private, more sexual and familial, and more concerned with personal morality." Harris, *supra* note 32, at 1560 (quoting LAUREN BERLANT, THE QUEEN OF AMERICA GOES TO WASHINGTON CITY: ESSAYS ON SEX AND CITIZENSHIP 177 [1997]). As Harris notes, this family-centered view of citizenship is trended heteronormative and, as politicized, generally involves the drama of the straight family norm in constant conflict with "evil queers and selfish feminists bent on destroying the 'family'. " Id. at 1560–1561.

[108] I explore this dimension of equal protection fully in Chapter 2, this volume. For a similar but narrower caste-based theory, see Cass R. Sunstein, *The Anticaste Principle*, 92 MICH. L. REV. 2410 (1994).

Critics have observed that my conceptualization of the equality norm leaves the question of the poor unanswered. Surely poverty is a caste that ought to be incorporated into any meaningful antisubordination theory of the kind that my "dominance-over-difference" theory purports to be. I share Professor Mari Matsuda's belief that, in any jurisprudential theory that matters, theorists must maintain a "multiple consciousness" that allows them to "operate both within the abstractions of standard jurisprudential discourse, *and* within the details of [their] own special knowledge." Mari J. Matsuda, *When the First Quail Calls: Multiple Consciousness as Jurisprudential Method*, 11 WOMEN'S RTS. L. REP. 7, 9 (1989); see also Darren Lenard Hutchinson, *"Gay Rights" for "Gay Whites"? Race, Sexual Identity, and Equal Protection*

take from *Lawrence* is that equality should not depend upon uniformity. As Justice Albie Sachs of the South African Constitutional Court so elegantly stated, "Equality means equal concern and respect across difference."[109] The

Discourse, 85 CORNELL L. REV. 1358 (2000) (arguing that failure to analyze Gay rights claims in terms of race and class results in the faulty essentialism of using white, economically privileged Gays as a proxy for all Gays). Nevertheless, even a theory attuned to multiple consciousnesses must categorize to avoid the inevitably unworkable nature of a theory that is too narrow because it is too individuated or too broad because it approaches sweeping metatheory.

The Gay struggle is a particularized struggle. The power differential that results from the heterosexual hierarchy against Gay people's interests is often unique. For Gay liberation theory to matter, and for any conceptualization of an equality norm that is informed by it to matter, some identifiable expression of the "Gay experience" must be distilled, not to the isolationist extreme of essentialism, but in order to define a theme, which for Gay liberation is necessarily the theme of straight against Gay. The search for this kind of definition may mean that in certain situations the experiences of those in parallel castes are suppressed to a degree. This may be a necessary (but concededly disappointing) side effect of constructing a theory with coherence that will possess any authority.

Fully understanding, as Barbara Smith observed, that the effect of multiple oppression is "not merely arithmetic" (see Barbara Smith, *Notes for Yet Another Paper on Black Feminism, or Will the Real Enemy Please Stand Up?* 5 CONDITIONS 123 [1979]), my solution is to treat poverty as an intensifier of the underlying prejudice discussed by the theory (be that, for example, anti-Gay, anti-Black, or anti-woman prejudice). In this way, my theory operates on the assumption that there are particularized inequities of the experience that is straight against Gay, or white against Black, or men against women, which are the primary inequities that I envisioned when pursuing the dominance-over-difference approach. Certainly, these inequities may be intensified when their victims also have the misfortune of being poor, so that a poor Gay person will feel more acutely the weight of straight oppression (usually) than will a Gay person who is better off financially. Economic privilege is often ameliorative of identity prejudice.

It is, however, important to note (and I make no representations to the contrary) that my dominance theory is aimed at a particular kind of subordination – that which may be denominated "identity subordination." This type of subordination often (usually) transcends social class to be operative at any and every level of economic strata. For example, less well off straights may coalesce politically to visit anti-Gay prejudice on Gays in a higher economic stratum. Or take, for example, James Baldwin's observation that neither the wealth nor fame he had achieved as a Black man entitled him to the use of a whites-only phone booth in Jim Crow Alabama – a privilege even the poorest white was accorded. Baldwin's success may have been ameliorative of anti-Black prejudice because he could board a train and leave Alabama, but it did not destroy the subordination.

Or take as an example the observation of critical race theory that a poor white man, when asked whether he would trade places with a more affluent Black man – if he could – would refuse to do so. It is with this type of identity subordination, which generally transcends economic class, that my theory is most concerned. I remain convinced that a poor straight man is inherently better off than is a poor Gay man. Despite what is lost for want of it, the theory I articulate here does not purport to be a general theory addressing all social inequality. I hereby invite the critique and subversion of my own theory for the good of the creation of one that does.

[109] *Nat'l Coal. for Gay & Lesbian Equal. v Minister of Justice & Others* 1999 (1) SA 6 (CC) at 128, ¶¶ 110–135 (S. Afr.) (Sachs, J., concurring).

assimilation demand inherent in Justice Kennedy's reasoning does not even imagine that any constitutionally significant difference exists between Gay and straight – or that such difference could exist in other situations. The decriminalization of sodomy accomplished little more than the signal of an emerging tolerance of, or perhaps acquiescence in, behavior, once descriptively deviant, by dominant straight society. The behavior is, nevertheless, still deviant enough to warrant its relegation to the privacy of the Closet. This stigma is even preserved for straight "sodomites."[110]

The Court's hypothetical facially neutral sodomy law (most fully explored in O'Connor's concurrence) begs the question of why such a facially neutral statute was enacted in the first place. Does the law's theoretical applicability to straights make it any less stigmatic? Consider, again, the Court's treatment of the interracial marriage ban at issue in *Loving*. Virginia argued that the ban treated Blacks and whites equally. The only discrimination, argued Virginia, was against people who sought to participate in interracial marriages, and that categorization crossed racial lines.[111] Black people could not marry white people and white people could not marry Black people. In this way, Blacks and whites were truly equal and no "racial" discrimination existed at all. This factual scenario led to the Court's emphasis on "White Supremacy."[112] Virginia's appeal to formalism in equality was rejected by the Court, which understood that Virginia's aim with its antimiscegenation law was to preserve the race hierarchy. The significant source of power in any caste system is the ability to determine the "inferior" from the "superior," and a significant source of power in Virginia's racial caste system was the ability to tell Black from white. In a Virginia with legalized racial mixing, the ability to tell the "superior" from the "inferior" would erode. Understood in this way, as the Court understood it, Virginia's miscegenation ban violated the very core of equal protection.

Consider now the analogous argument for purposes of sexual orientation. A substantive equality analysis, like that at work in *Loving*, would ask more than simply whether a sodomy ban applies to straight and Gay alike (where O'Connor's analysis stops). If such a facially neutral statute existed, a substantive equality analysis would ask why the prohibition was likewise applied to straights and what are the effects of its operation. The answer, of course, is the same answer as that buttressing the miscegenation ban at issue in *Loving*:

---

[110] This was the case in North Carolina in 2003, and in other states as well. For a thorough discussion, see generally Michael Kent Curtis & Shannon Gilreath, *Transforming Teenagers into Oral Sex Felons: The Persistence of the Crime Against Nature after* Lawrence v. Texas, 43 WAKE FOREST L. REV. 155 (2008).

[111] Loving v. Virginia, 388 U.S. 1, 8 (1967).

[112] Id. at 11.

Prohibiting straight actors from engaging in sexual activity usually associated with homosexuals (oral and anal sex) keeps the sexual caste distinction pure – it makes it easier to define the sexually "superior" from those stigmatized as sexually "inferior." Under a conceptualization of equal protection that prohibits the marginalization of a citizen or group of citizens merely on the basis of a descriptive moral disapproval of a trait, or display of a trait, immutable or otherwise,[113] the antisodomy law at issue in *Lawrence* is as constitutionally infirm as the antimiscegenation law in *Loving*.

PRUDENCE AND JURISPRUDENCE: A NOTE

As mentioned, constitutional commentary is largely a theoretical exercise, although one that can have compelling applications and effects. At any given moment, the Court faces practical limitations that the law professor does not. In fact, any agent of change that is judicial, legislative, or executive faces the very real and profound problem of the popular will. Abraham Lincoln, for example, consistently maintained that slavery was wrong. But as to the best means of eradicating slavery, Lincoln was open to equivocation, even doubt.[114] Lincoln believed that as a practical matter "the great mass of white people" would not permit immediate unqualified change in the status of Blacks.[115] "A universal feeling, whether well or ill-founded, can not be safely disregarded."[116]

Justice Ruth Bader Ginsburg has expressed similar feeling in relation to *Roe v. Wade*.[117] *Roe*, doubtlessly, had some extraordinarily disastrous results from the perspective of liberal politics. *Roe* galvanized the evangelical electorate and has been a consistently reliable clarion call to get these myopic, single-issue voters to the polls. The polarization *Roe* caused was central to the ascendancy of Ronald Reagan. And the tendency to see the women's movement as coterminous with the pro-choice movement has been, over all, detrimental to women's equality interests.

My disagreement with *Roe* has been jurisprudential: It has been a disagreement with the Court's philosophy and judicial methodology. I have

---

[113] This is explored fully in Chapter 2, this volume.

[114] For a fascinating discussion of Lincoln and the slavery question, see PAUL ESCOTT, "WHAT SHALL WE DO WITH THE NEGRO?" WHITE RACISM, ABRAHAM LINCOLN, AND CIVIL WAR AMERICANS (2009).

[115] Cass R. Sunstein, *Homosexuality and the Constitution*, 70 IND. L. J. 1, 23 (1994) (quoting an Abraham Lincoln speech at Peoria, Illinois [Oct. 16, 1854]).

[116] Id.

[117] See Ruth Bader Ginsburg, *Some Thoughts on Autonomy and Equality in Relation to* Roe v. Wade, 63 N.C. L. REV. 375 (1985).

not disagreed with *Roe's* outcome: that McCorvey could procure an abortion. But the aforementioned societal backlash is serious reason to be skeptical of *Roe's* wisdom. I think Gay rights advocates – even those of us who would consider ourselves more radical, as Gay liberationists – should resist allowing our needs and the adjudication of our rights to become the next *Roe v. Wade.*

When one has nothing, and consequently has everything to gain, a little pragmatism goes a long way. Of course, the "gay rights" movement, hijacked as it now is by "liberals" who are disconnected from the way most Gay people live their lives, has not been long on pragmatism. One need look no further than the disastrous way much of the Gay establishment handled a chance at federal employment antidiscrimination laws to see this. Hundreds of Gay organizations (one must read their dedication loosely) actively opposed the Employment Non-Discrimination Act in 2007, which would have secured much-needed protection for millions of Gay people, because the legislation, as revised in Congress, did not reach the aspiration of protecting transsexuals too.[118] The approach of these antiemployment rights groups within the movement is emblematic of a movement intuition that mistakes pragmatism for lack of principle.[119]

I have some sympathy with the unpragmatic. As Professor Marc Spindelman has observed, "Pragmatic or prudential considerations always potentially modulate a principle's sweep."[120] But I would tweak this explanation a bit to say that prudential considerations modulate a principle's *application*, not "sweep," as Professor Spindelman suggests. Principles are sweeping precisely because they are principles. It is the application of the principle that, sometimes for prudential reasons (and sometimes sadly because of cowardice or careerism), does not always live up to its sweep.

In my courses dealing with law and sexuality, I want students to think about not only what the law is, but what it should be as well. As I cover the marriage materials, I invariably ask students which court, the Vermont Supreme Court in *Baker v. State*[121] or the Massachusetts Supreme Judicial Court in *Goodridge v. Department of Public Health,*[122] had the better approach to

---

[118] See Carolyn Lochhead, *Gay Rights Bill Snags on Blurred Perceptions of Identity, Orientation,* S.F. Chron., Oct. 3, 2007, http://www.sfgate.com/cgi-bin/article.cgi?file=/c/a/2007/10/03/MN6RSIH93.DTL.

[119] For a discussion, see Shannon Gilreath, *In Defense of the Employment Non-Discrimination Act,* Gay City News, Oct. 25, 2007.

[120] Marc S. Spindelman, *Reorienting* Bowers v. Hardwick, 79 N.C. L. Rev. 359, 431 (2001).

[121] 744 A.2d 864 (Vt. 1999).

[122] 798 N.E.2d 941 (Mass. 2003).

bringing marriage equality to Gay people.[123] Many students believe that the *Goodridge* court got it right in ordering that only "marriage," and no analogous construct of the legislature, like the civil union scheme that emerged from *Baker*, would do.[124] These same students often overlook the important concerns the *Baker* majority had in mind when it left it to the Vermont legislature to craft the legal vehicle by which the equality the court mandated would be delivered.[125]

In dissent, Justice Denise Johnson argued that the court should have issued civil marriage licenses immediately.[126] In a display of bare political calculation, majority and dissent traded accusations – Justice Johnson holding that the majority had "abdicate[d] [its] constitutional duty"[127] and the majority charging that Johnson's claims were "insulated from reality."[128]

This rather acid disagreement between Chief Justice Amestoy for the majority and Justice Johnson exposes the argument over pragmatism that I have been talking about. Amestoy is unwilling to order the remedy of marriage, the only remedy Johnson believes plausible, because of the "disruptive and unforeseen consequences" such action may introduce.[129] Clearly, he fears the possibility of a constitutional amendment overturning such a wide-sweeping remedy as Justice Johnson posits. In fact, Amestoy makes note of just those sorts of amendments reversing prior marriage equality rulings in Hawaii and Alaska.[130] Amestoy is prescient here, for in the wake of *Goodridge* the ensuing popular backlash spawned many state constitutional amendments precluding Gay couples from marriage and a similar, failed attempt at the federal level.[131]

Justice Johnson's reply to these concerns is ambivalence: "If the people of Vermont wish to overturn a constitutionally based decision, as happened in

---

[123] For an excellent discussion of the judicial politics at work in these marriage decisions, see ANDREW KOPPELMAN, THE GAY RIGHTS QUESTION IN CONTEMPORARY AMERICAN LAW 141–154 (2002).

[124] See *Goodridge*, 798 N.E.2d at 969 (holding that barring an individual from the protections, benefits, and obligations of civil marriage solely because that person would marry a person of the same sex violates the Massachusetts Constitution); *Baker*, 744 A.2d at 886 (holding that plaintiffs were entitled to obtain the same benefits and protections afforded by Vermont law to married opposite-sex couples, but leaving it to the legislature to establish same-sex marriage or an alternative statutory scheme like "domestic partnerships" or "registered partnerships").

[125] *Baker*, 744 A.2d at 887.

[126] Id. at 898 (Johnson, J., concurring in part and dissenting in part).

[127] Id.

[128] Id. at 888.

[129] Id. at 887.

[130] *Baker*, 744 A.2d at 888.

[131] See SHANNON GILREATH, SEXUAL IDENTITY LAW IN CONTEXT: CASES AND MATERIALS 726–728 (2007) (collecting citations).

Alaska and Hawaii, they may do so."[132] Justice Johnson is concerned with what the law *is* and with the most "straightforward and effective" way of effectuating it.[133] Chief Justice Amestoy is concerned with what the law *should be*. He knows that marriage equality for Gays will not have a long shelf life if it is achieved through a decision that makes sweeping alterations to the marriage norm. Chief Justice Amestoy hopes to ensure equality by making his decision as politically palatable as possible. He understands that sometimes, as Andrew Koppelman put it, "[j]udges must be politicians for the sake of the things that should be beyond politics."[134]

All of this is not to suggest that prudence dictates that the Court could not have applied a substantive equality analysis of the sort I envision in *Lawrence*. On the contrary, prudence requires only that the Court modulate the immediate reach of the theory's application. Again, *Loving* is instructive. We see this sort of modulated approach at work in the progression from *Brown* to *Loving*. The Court, of course, has nearly unfettered discretion in deciding which cases it will consider on certiorari. The Court used that discretion prudentially in refusing to hear two equality challenges to antimiscegenation legislation prior to the *Loving* decision. Apparently, the Court believed that the risk of deciding the interracial marriage question so soon after *Brown* was too great.

The Court could have reacted similarly with a substantive equality analysis in *Lawrence*. It could have analyzed the *Lawrence* claim as one of substantive equality dimension, thereby addressing the damaging role of hierarchy and anti-equality effects of institutionalized caste. The Court could then have modulated the holding's reach by using its discretion to avoid addressing the marriage question until such time as it becomes politically feasible.

CONCLUSION

Lawrence v. Texas is an important decision. Gay people as human beings are present in the Supreme Court's jurisprudence for the first time. If the decision had accomplished nothing else, this sharp contrast to *Bowers v. Hardwick*, in which Michael Hardwick, the plaintiff, was totally invisible, entirely disappeared by the sexual act that became his proxy, is a momentous thing. Of course, the decision brought other important achievements. The sex acts of consenting Gay adults in private can no longer be criminal, and criminal Gay sex regulations can no longer be the basis for invidious civic burdens.

[132] *Baker*, 744 A.2d at 904 n.7 (Johnson, J., concurring in part and dissenting in part).
[133] Id. at 901 (Johnson, J., concurring in part and dissenting in part).
[134] KOPPELMAN, THE GAY RIGHTS QUESTION, *supra* note 123, at 143.

But in celebrating *Lawrence* as an accomplishment, we should not be blind to the underlying heterosexist dogma that motivated its structure as much as its outcome. In constitutional law, structure is important. My major gripe with *Lawrence* is that it was a missed (or perhaps avoided) opportunity for a real structural analysis of the heterosexual hierarchy at work in the creation of anti-Gay laws and the anti-Gay caste in general. The Court avoids the deeper issues, leaving largely intact the system of heterodominance under which Gay Americans labor daily and for which the state is either an accomplice or a direct sponsor.

Equality and the due process framework of the *Lawrence* decision are in tension. Substantive equality cannot exist – will not exist – until equality is examined substantively. What I have dubbed the "substantive equality" approach is a departure from the "similarly situated" brand of formal equality that has been, with rare exception, the ceiling of the Court's equality jurisprudence for nearly one hundred and fifty years. It is both a marked departure from this formalism and an invitation to begin thinking about equality as the highest constitutional good. Equality thus conceptualized is substantive in and of itself. To borrow from Thoreau,[135] castles built in the air are not necessarily futile labors; after all, that is where castles belong. But these castles need firm foundations if they are to last. The liberty and freedom of conscience presupposed by the *Lawrence* majority are beautiful things; they deserve a place in gossamer realms. Now, I say, put the foundations under them. Equality is the foundation. Equality will make us free.

---

[135] HENRY DAVID THOREAU, WALDEN 362 (1902) (1854) ("If you have built castles in the air, your work need not be lost; that is where they should be. Now put the foundations under them").

PART II

Equality, Sexuality, and Expression

4

Speech/Hate Propaganda

A *Comment on* Harper v. Poway Unified School District

The struggle to break the form is paramount. Because we are otherwise contained in forms that deny us the possibility of realizing a form (a technique) to escape the fire in which we are being consumed.

> Julian Beck, *The Life of the Theatre*

Cruelty is an idea in practice.

> Antonin Artaud, *Collected Works*

The attempt to split bias from violence has been this society's most enduring and fatal rationalization.

> Patricia Williams, *Spirit-Murdering the Messenger*

Without words ... not one Jew would have been gassed.

> Andrea Dworkin, *Scapegoat*

> It's a simple message really,
> these two words
> fired bent
> as a head hits cement,
> followed by the slow awareness
> of spreading pain.
> They are mouthed so calmly
> from a gun
> loaded with only two words:
> "die faggot."

> Joseph Ross, *Imagine the Shock (Poetic Voices Without Borders*, vol. 2)

Discussion of campaigns to silence Gay voices and Gay identity, through, for example, Don't Ask, Don't Tell or through policies attempting to prevent Gay youth from organizing in schools, is fairly commonplace in the literature on

Gays' legal status. It is not difficult to see that Gays have been systematically prevented from speaking. In this chapter, I explore the underexplored and inverse problem of *too much* speech – specifically in the form of the cacophonous propaganda campaign to dehumanize Gays and dispirit our allies.

As with the Nazi propaganda campaign to dehumanize Jews by normalizing anti-Semitism, thus making violence against Jews easy (to which I analogize later), when Gay hating becomes the norm – is normalized through state-sponsored propaganda (called "free speech" or "free expression") – then killing and other forms of abuse of Gays become easy. In response to the emergency of which such a system is an essential part, this chapter offers a substantive equality theory of freedom of speech. In doing so, it examines what I term "anti-identity" speech and its effects on its targets. Anti-identity speech, as a method of categorization, is broader and more appropriate than "hate speech." Anti-identity speech does not require the use of individualized insults or epithets and can be delivered quite effectively and aggressively with a smile and a soft voice. To understand the nuance, one must think of James Dobson, not David Duke. Its targets are almost always minorities who are unpopular because of certain inescapable identifying traits. They are always traditionally marginalized and systematically disadvantaged peoples.

Reforming a system of speech that is built upon power prerogatives, as ours is, is no easy task. The old canard that restricting the speech of Nazis and Klansmen and inciters of murder would eventually lead to censorship of Gay and other minority voices en masse has been extremely effective and convincing, even to many Gay people. So has been the canard that words do not harm. The effectiveness of this stems from the ease with which civil libertarians of the ACLU variety, whom I dub speech authoritarians, and other liberals, who do not understand much about real life as it exists for subordinated peoples, dismiss as anecdotal actual testimony of people harmed by propaganda campaigns of subordination and the attackers they cosset. So some Gay people listen to the Heteroarchy's lawyers and politicians and believe them when they say that anti-identity speech and its consequences must be tolerated for some abstract "good."

Unfortunately for the duped among us, time is not on their side. The massively escalating tide of violence against Gays and Lesbians in this country, fueled by the anti-identity speech campaigns this chapter details, means somebody else's experience of violence, easily dismissed as anecdotal, will with increasing certainty be visited as undeniable personal trauma. At that point what has been *said* about you is no longer so easily separated from what has been *done* to you on that account. And at that point the real questions crystallize: Are you worth more than the oppression you are buried in? And can anything be done to stop it? A substantive equality theory of free speech says we can use the possibility of the law to stop it and that we really have no other choice but to try. For even when confronting something as "settled" as First Amendment law, Gay liberation cannot afford to be programmatic; it has to be elementally entrepreneurial.

Thus, because this chapter focuses on the rights of victims and not obsessively on the rights of their oppressors, as most free speech scholarship does, it is not a discussion of free speech as it relates to "justice." Any conversation about justice in an American legal system that is, in effect, broken for identity minorities reduces to a conversation about the administration of injustice. In fact, in this climate, the very action of applying a Gay-centric analytic to *free speech* would be the perpetuation of a misnomer. For Gay people, speech has not been equal or just, and it certainly has not been *free*.[1] Examining the topic through the lens of the Gay experience is a considerable shift away from discussions of "justice" and "fairness," usually the watchwords of powerful people employed to preserve their power, to a genuine look at free speech as it relates to *freedom*.

Any such examination of anti-identity speech through the lens of Gay experience must necessarily come to terms with the fact that our attackers usually deny us the existential status they concede to their other victims. They do not even imagine that our situation could be existentialist.[2] And, of course, this assertion is part of their anti-identity speech campaign against us.[3] The anti-identity attacks against us are all the more insidious because the speech intersects with assertions of religious belief. These interests converge to render the speech off-limits, regardless of its effects on its targets. This view has been so insidious that it has also infected the "liberal" academy.[4] Apparently,

---

[1] Conservative values and liberal politics converge to offer us tolerance at best. Neither side seems to want change very much, preferring instead to talk in sound bites about "meeting in the middle of the road." Anybody who has lived a Gay person's life knows that standing in the middle of the road will get you run over with impunity. So equality hangs in the air, in the insistence of liberals that Gays are getting it, or of conservatives that Gays already have special rights instead of it, or as a rallying cry for Gays who are in a constant struggle for it. In whatever form, it is rhetorically ever-present; in reality, never-present.

[2] For a general discussion, see Shannon Gilreath, Sexual Politics: The Gay Person in America Today (2006), at 49–50. For an example of such denial, see Michael W. McConnell, *What Would It Mean to Have a "First Amendment" for Sexual Orientation?* in Sexual Orientation and Human Rights in American Religious Discourse 252 (Saul M. Olyan & Martha C. Nussbaum, eds., 1998).

[3] The exception may be the Catholic Church. The Church's categorization of Gays as "inherently disordered" does concede an element of existentiality. The Church's treatment of Gays, however, does not indicate that this conceded existentiality matters.

[4] Andrew Koppelman, *You Can't Hurry Love: Why Antidiscrimination Protections for Gay People Should Have Religious Exemptions*, 72 Brook. L. Rev. 125 (2006).

only the powerful, through the religions they have created for themselves, have the uniquely "American" capacity to determine their own destinies. Thus, the speech of homophobes becomes like the lives of their victims: bitter and unanswerable.

Two recent circuit court decisions bring these issues into sharp focus and serve as the vehicles for my discussion here, beginning with the Ninth Circuit's decision in *Harper v. Poway Unified School District*,[5] upholding a high school's ban of a student's T-shirt with a degrading message about homosexuality. Judge Reinhardt, writing for the panel majority, held that degrading messages about the identity of certain minority groups could be constitutionally proscribed in the public grade school setting by applying the first prong of the analysis set forth in *Tinker v. Des Moines Independent Community School District*,[6] which held that speech that "impinges on the rights of other students" may be constitutionally proscribed.[7] To my knowledge, this is the first time any court has actually applied this particular prong of the *Tinker* analysis, as opposed to the more familiar "substantial disruption" prong.[8]

Judge Reinhardt's opinion is, of course, not without controversy. It was met by a withering dissent from Judge Kozinski and by criticism from the academy.[9] In this chapter, I explain why, considering the First Amendment and the free speech norm, along with the Fourteenth Amendment and the equality norm, Judge Reinhardt's decision is correct.

Harper raises the usual questions about the limits of free speech for public school students, but it also raises taboo questions about the parameters of the free speech norm itself. Moreover, it marks a rare case in which judges are willing to talk about speech in a social context and to consider the *real* harm to the targets of anti-identity speech. *Harper* is a judicial look at such speech through the lens of "minority experience" – in this case, the Gay experience. In that respect, the decision is remarkable for the broader questions it raises. Indeed, the compassionate among us, conscious of human experience, find

---

[5] 445 F.3d 1166 (2006).

[6] Tinker v. Des Moines Indep. Cmty. Sch. Dist., 393 U.S. 503, 509 (1969).

[7] *Harper*, 445 F.3d at 1177–1178 (quoting *Tinker*, 393 U.S. at 509).

[8] *Harper* quotes the Tenth Circuit's ruling in *West v. Derby Unified School District*, 206 F.3d 1358 (10th Cir. 2000), that the display of the Confederate flag might "interfere with the rights of other students to be secure and let alone." Id. at 1178 (quoting *West*, 206 F.3d at 1366). But the *West* court actually interpreted the "rights of other students" as coextensive with "material and substantial disruption of school discipline." *West*, 206 F.3d at 1366.

[9] See, e.g., Posting of Eugene Volokh to the Volokh Conspiracy, http://volokh.com/archives/archive_2006_04_16–2006_04_22.shtml#1145577196 (Apr. 20, 2006, 19:53 EDT) (being entitled *Sorry Your Viewpoint Is Excluded from First Amendment Protection*).

ourselves asking these questions over and over, as derivatives of the darkest aspects of human history:

How could Americans who espouse the view that "all men are created equal" subjugate a race into slavery, transforming people into chattel to be beaten and prodded and worked for profit without so much as a nod to their dignity?

How could Christians of the Dark Ages be convinced that women were witches, resulting in the burning (and other horrendous) deaths of more than 9 million women?[10]

How could the German populace – with less or more knowledge depending on one's historical perspective – watch as their government ghettoized Jews and pulled down synagogues, melting stars of David into golden lamps eventually to be shaded by the human skin of some of the 6 million Jews murdered by the Nazis?[11]

How could some human beings be convinced of the rectitude of slamming passenger jets into office buildings heavily populated with civilians?[12]

Some readers will say that these atrocities could not be committed by Americans today. Perhaps not. But contemporary America has its targets and its victims. What we cannot match in historical magnitude we make up for in tenacity. It is the *how* and *why* of it that puzzles us.

Harper provides for us the beginning of a partial answer, which is to say simply this: *Words matter.* Language matters. These scenarios have in common a systematic dehumanization of the target effectuated by language. Of course, this did not happen in a blinding flash, but more as creeping twilight. First, there was innuendo set buzzing by the powerful. Then, there was targeted propaganda. Mere *words* devolved into physical violence. First, the victims were robbed of their humanity – that is essential – and, finally, they were robbed of their lives.

Harper did not involve the second step of the process; it did not involve the actual destruction of the Gay victim by physical violence, only his or her conceptual destruction. But *Harper* is a discrete look at the wider *how* and *why* of the second step. *Harper* also raises the question of what we may do, consistent with our free speech norm, when the victim's well-being is threatened by words unaccompanied by immediate physical violence.

The other illustrative and closely related case, *Nuxoll* ex rel. *Nuxoll v. Indian Prairie School District No. 204*,[13] involved similar facts and a similar

---

[10] Andrea Dworkin, Woman Hating 129–130 (1974).

[11] Max I. Dimont, Jews, God, and History 373 (2004).

[12] The reference here is, of course, to the 9/11 disaster.

[13] 523 F.3d 668 (7th Cir. 2008). The lower court decision, as *Zamecnik v. Indian Prairie School District*, cited *Harper* approvingly. Zamecnik v. Indian Prairie Sch. Dist. No. 204, No. 07-C-1586,

concession as to the operation of the *Tinker* test on student anti-Gay speech, but with a very different analysis and outcome. Both cases involve the problem of anti-identity speech as it is manifested in schools, where its targets are at their most vulnerable and in the greatest need of protection; but my concerns about anti-identity, anti-equality speech certainly are not confined to the school setting.[14] In that regard, cases like *Harper* and *Nuxoll* are doubly important because, while at first blush they appear to be discrete situations with discrete solutions, they inevitably raise discomforting questions about speech – particularly so-called hate speech – in general. Thus, the arguments presented in this chapter, grounded in substantive equality, are relevant to numerous situations in which the conceptual liquidation of the person is effectuated by speech or expression that then finds refuge in the free speech clause of the First Amendment. As such, they are relevant to anti-harassment, anti-bullying, and anti–hate speech laws. Harassing, bullying, and hate-filled speech are problematic on whatever plane and, indeed, may be constitutionally regulable on any plane.

THE CASES AND THEIR THEORIES

Harper v. Poway Unified School District *(9th Cir. 2006)*

In 2004 Tyler Chase Harper, a sophomore at Poway High School, in Poway, California, wore a T-shirt to school that read, "I Will Not Accept What God Has Condemned" on the front and "Homosexuality Is Shameful 'Romans 1:27'" on the back. The next day, presumably to avoid the fashion faux pas of being seen in the same outfit twice, Mr. Harper wore a shirt that read, "Be Ashamed, Our School Embraced What God Has Condemned." Apparently, Harper wore the shirts in protest of the recently observed "Day of Silence," by which Gay students and their allies drew attention to the inequality faced by Gays and Lesbians in society.[15]

2007 WL 4569720, at *4 (N.D. Ill. Dec. 21, 2007), *rev'd subnom.* Nuxoll *ex rel* Nuxoll v. Indian Prairie Sch. Dist. No. 204, 523 F.3d 668 (7th Cir. 2008). In *Nuxoll*, Judge Posner drops any reference to *Harper*.

[14] As a matter of practicality, grappling with anti-identity speech in schools is an efficient starting point. It is in school that this speech and its purveyors are at their most pernicious and harmful. Students, who are still constructing their views of self and of the world and who, at least in the grade school (K–12) setting, are unable to escape from damaging speech targeting their personhood, are particularly vulnerable. The setting also presents, because of the Supreme Court's decision in *Tinker* (and related cases), the best opportunity for the regulation of anti-identity speech. Consequently, it may present the best instructional model for developing arguments against anti-identity speech on other planes.

[15] *Harper* at 1171.

On the second day, a teacher asked Harper to remove the shirt, and he refused. He was then sent to the principal's office.[16] He again refused to remove the shirt and indicated that he wanted to be suspended.[17] He was required to stay in the principal's office for the remainder of the day but was not suspended or disciplined in any other way.[18] Harper and the Alliance Defense Fund filed suit in the U.S. District Court for the Southern District of California.[19] The district judge sided with the school, and appeal was taken to the Ninth Circuit.

Judge Reinhardt's majority opinion in *Harper* begins with the question to be decided: May a public high school prohibit students from wearing T-shirts with messages that *condemn* and *denigrate* other students on the basis of their sexual orientation?[20] A series of altercations had already occurred at the Poway High School, so that the substantial disruption necessary to regulate speech consistent with *Tinker* was, arguably, established.[21] But the court did not pursue this usual method of student-speech analysis. Instead, the court relied on the first of the two *Tinker* prongs, permitting schools to prohibit speech that "'intrudes upon … the rights of other students'" or "'colli[des] with the rights of other students to be secure and to be let alone'."[22] Because students in K–12 schools are "discovering who and what they are," they are often insecure. "Generally, they are vulnerable to cruel, inhuman, and prejudiced treatment by others."[23] On that basis, Judge Reinhardt concluded, "[W]hile Harper's shirt embodies the very sort of political speech that would be afforded First Amendment protection outside of the public school setting,[24] his rights in the case before us must be determined 'in light of [those] special characteristics'."[25] Thus:

> Public school students who may be injured by verbal assaults on the basis of
> a core identifying characteristic such as race, religion, or sexual orientation,

---

[16] Id. at 1172.

[17] Id.

[18] Id. at 1173.

[19] Harper v. Poway Unified Sch. Dist., 345 F. Supp. 2d 1096 (S.D. Cal. 2004).

[20] *Harper*, 445 F. 3d at 1170 (emphasis added).

[21] Id. at 1171. This was the course the district court took in dismissing Harper's suit. Id. at 1175. School officials recalled that these physical altercations were, specifically, the results of "anti-homosexual" speech. Id. at 1171. Some members of the community, presumably parents, had called the school threatening to do "something about" the school's "condoning" of the "Day of Silence" organized by the Gay-Straight Student Alliance. Id. at 1172–1173 n. 7.

[22] Id. at 1175 (quoting Tinker v. Des Moines Indep. Cmty. Sch. Dist., 393 U.S. 503, 508 (1969) (alteration in original).

[23] Id. at 1176.

[24] Id. This is a point that I in no way concede.

[25] Id. (quoting *Tinker*, 393 U.S. at 506) (alteration in original).

have a right to be free from such attacks while on school campuses.... Being secure involves not only freedom from physical assaults but from psychological attacks that cause young people to question their self-worth and their rightful place in society ... [an interest] perhaps most important "when persons are 'powerless to avoid' it."[26]

The majority further held:

> Speech that attacks high school students who are members of minority groups that have historically been oppressed, subjected to verbal and physical abuse, and made to feel inferior, serves to injure and intimidate them, as well as to damage their sense of security and interfere with their opportunity to learn. The demeaning of young gay and lesbian students in a school environment is detrimental not only to their psychological health and well-being, but also to their educational development.[27]

The majority went on to cite studies and statistical data that supported the court's finding that Gay youth subjected to anti-identity speech suffer actual harm as a result of assaultive speech.[28] Directly engaging Judge Kozinski's dissent, the majority shows an intellectual courage often missing from judicial opinions regarding Gay rights: "Perhaps our dissenting colleague believes that one can condemn homosexuality without condemning homosexuals. If so, he is wrong. To say that homosexuality is shameful is to say, necessarily, that gays and lesbians are shameful."[29]

Troubling for the dissent and other objectors is the distinction that the majority draws between anti-identity assaults and other expressions of political viewpoint. The court notes the stark difference between speech campaigns that strike at the core, existential characteristic by which a person is defined into a lesser caste and speech that may, for example, insult a person's political affiliation.[30]

Perhaps more troubling for the defenders of a "free" speech system built on the premise of securing speech rights for powerful people who already

---

[26] Id. at 1178 (quoting Hill v. Colorado, 530 U.S. 730, 716 (2000)).
[27] Id. at 1178–1179 (footnote omitted).
[28] Id. at 1179.
[29] Id. at 1181.
[30] The court gave the example of "T-shirts proclaiming, 'Young Republicans Suck' or 'Young Democrats Suck.' ... 'Similarly, T-shirts that denigrate the President, his administration, or his policies, or otherwise invite political disagreement or debate, including debates over the war in Iraq,' would not fall within the 'rights of others' *Tinker* prong." Id. at 1182. As the majority observed in a footnote, "[A]nti-war T-shirts ... constitute neither an attack on the basis of a student's core identifying characteristic nor on the basis of his minority status." *Harper*, 445 F.3d at 1182 n. 27.

have them, as our system is, is the majority's pointed distinction between "a historically oppressed minority group that has been the victim of serious prejudice and discrimination and a group that has always enjoyed a preferred social, economic and political status."[31] Thus, as the dissent notes, the majority's theory of restriction does not encompass speech aimed at discrediting the preferred status of Christians or whites.[32] The pointed judicial recognition of a theory that distinguishes between the powerful and the powerless must sound like a dirge to the believers in a system that allows for anti-identity saturation propaganda aimed at marginalized people but provides no basis for those marginalized to gain an equal voice.

In dissent, Judge Kozinski disagreed with the majority's holding that Tyler Chase Harper's T-shirt intruded on the rights of Gay students in any substantial way, characterizing the message as a normal part of "ordinary . . . discourse in high school corridors and lunch rooms."[33] But, primarily, Judge Kozinski took issue with the majority's formula because, he said, it amounted to viewpoint discrimination:

> Given the history of violent confrontation between those who support the Day of Silence and those who oppose it, the school authorities may have been justified in banning the subject altogether by denying both sides permission to express their views during the school day. . . . I find it far more problematic – and more than a little ironic – to try to solve the problem of violent confrontations by gagging only those who oppose the Day of Silence and the point of view it represents.[34]

---

[31] Id. at 1183 n. 28.

[32] Id. Although, as the majority noted, the second prong of *Tinker*, the "substantial disruption" prong, is still operable and may supply some relief in those circumstances. Id.

[33] *Harper*, 445 F.3d at 1194 (Kozinski, J., dissenting).

[34] Id. at 1197 (Kozinski, J., dissenting). This studied judicial inability to distinguish between the powerful and the powerless reminds me of James Baldwin's observation:

> The powerless, by definition, can never . . . make the world pay for what they feel or fear except by the suicidal endeavor which makes them fanatics or revolutionaries, or both; whereas, those in power can be urbane and charming and invite you to those which they know you will never own. The powerless must do their own dirty work. The powerful have it done for them.

JAMES BALDWIN, NO NAME IN THE STREET 93–94 (1972).

In a legal world where we pretend that there is no distinction between the powerful and powerless, the powerful have their dirty work done by laws and judges. Moreover, the pious handwringing by the dissent and some scholars (see, e.g., Michael Kent Curtis, *Be Careful What You Wish For: Gays, Dueling High School T-Shirts, and the Perils of Suppression*, 44 WAKE FOREST L. REV. 431 (2009)) over what it might mean to regulate anti-Gay "political" expression (i.e., "Homosexuality Is Shameful" or even "Be Happy, Not Gay (as in *Nuxoll*)") but not restrain pro-equality speech, such as "Gay Is Good" or "Gay, Fine by Me," is to misunderstand entirely the qualitative difference inherent in the expression. Indeed, to see "Gay Is Good" as merely a political statement

Judge Kozinski also insisted that Harper's "Homosexuality Is Shameful" message amounted only to casual offense and that "'[t]he mere fact that expressive activity causes hurt feelings, offense, or resentment does not render the expression unprotected'."[35] Kozinski goes on to refute the majority's characterization of "anti-identity" speech as that speech that targets a person on the basis of a core identifying characteristic related to the person's minority status. "What makes a minority?" Kozinski effectively asked.

> [D]o we look to the national community, the state, the locality or the school? In a school that has 60 percent black students and 40 percent white students, will the school be able to ban T-shirts with anti-black racist messages but not those with anti-white racist messages, or vice versa?
>
> … If the Pope speaks out against gay marriage, can gay students wear to school T-shirts saying "Catholics Are Bigots," or will they be demeaning the core characteristic of a religious minority?[36]

"The fundamental problem with the majority's approach," he concluded, "is that it has no anchor anywhere in the record or in the law."[37]

Nuxoll v. Indian Prairie School District *(7th Cir. 2008)*

The *Nuxoll* case also involves the limits of anti-Gay speech in public schools. Also in response to the Day of Silence, Alexander Nuxoll, a high

---

about the acceptability of homosexuality generally is to see it as only an outsider to the Movement would. It is not merely a statement of attitude; it is an assertion of identity. Most Gay youth have grown up feeling – indeed, being made to feel – that they are somehow bad, monstrous, undesirable. And Gays, especially Gay youth and Gays from poor or small-town backgrounds, have been denied forums to discuss any issues remotely relevant to their lives. So the slogan "Gay Is Good" and its derivatives are a coming to speech for Gays in a world that has otherwise conceptually (and often physically) liquidated them. Moreover, "Gay Is Good" is a conscious dismantling of caste hierarchies within the Gay community itself. For most of our lives, Gay people are under intense pressure to pass, to seem straight. The passing norm, through the institutionalization of the Closet, is enforced from earliest memory and in every conceivable venue, including the churches. In the Baptist churches of my youth, "effeminate" male church members were tolerated, if snickered at behind their backs, so long as they participated in the charade that they were straight. In the Catholic Church, at least until the Church needed a scapegoat for the pedophilia problem, priests were allowed to be Gay so long as their superiors did not have to confront the reality of it. And the ultimate passing norm, Don't Ask, Don't Tell, has become as much a part of the legal fabric and imagination of our country as the Miranda warnings. "Gay Is Good" challenges this social hierarchy, works to alter it. It says to closeted Gays that self-fragmentation is not the only way to survive the world. It also undercuts the notion that the liberal individualism that sanctions the opportunism inherent in passing is acceptable in the Movement.

[35] *Harper*, 445 F.3d at 1200 n. 10 (Kozinski, J., dissenting) (quoting Sypniewski v. Warren Hills Reg'l Bd. of Educ., 307 F.3d 243, 264–65 (3d Cir. 2002)).

[36] Id.

[37] Id.

school student, wanted to wear a T-shirt bearing the words "Be Happy, Not Gay" but was prohibited from doing so by a school policy forbidding the making of derogatory comments referring to the race, ethnicity, religion, gender, sexual orientation, or disability of another student.[38] Writing for the panel, Judge Richard Posner granted Nuxoll's request for a preliminary injunction against the policy as applied to his T-shirt. Posner, however, asserted that such a policy is sound if the restricted comments are sufficiently derogatory to interfere with the educational purpose of the school. Posner's theory is distinguishable from that of the Ninth Circuit in *Harper*, which was a theory specifically grounded in the rights of students to be free from assaultive speech in school. Judge Posner is not terribly interested in anyone's identity or subordination; he believes the constitutional focus more properly rests on the rights of the school itself to maintain an orderly learning environment:

> [W]e cannot accept the defendants' argument that the rule is valid because all it does is protect the "rights" of the students against whom derogatory comments are directed. Of course a school can – often it must – protect students from the invasion of their legal rights by other students. But people do not have a legal right to prevent criticism of their beliefs or for that matter their way of life....
>
> The school is on stronger ground in arguing that the rule strikes a reasonable balance between the competing interests – free speech and ordered learning – at stake in the case.[39]

Posner's shift here is important, because it is a shift in focus away from equality rights to institutional rights. Nevertheless, the realities of the lives of Gay youth are important to vindicate this institutional interest. In *Nuxoll*, Judge Posner cited a number of studies demonstrating that Gay youth subjected to anti-identity speech face real psychological harm that may affect their performance in school. He took this information and transmuted it from the universe of power and caste (the focus of the *Harper* court) back to the universe of substantial disruption – the watchwords of institutional stability: "[I]f there is reason to think that a particular type of student speech will lead to a decline in students' test scores, an upsurge in truancy, or other symptoms of a sick school – symptoms therefore of substantial disruption – the school can forbid the speech."[40]

---

[38] Nuxoll *ex rel.* Nuxoll v. Indian Prairie Sch. Dist., 523 F.3d 668, 670 (7th Cir. 2008).
[39] Id. at 672.
[40] Id. at 674.

"So," Posner continued, "[Nuxoll] is not entitled to a preliminary injunction against the rule."[41] That is, Nuxoll is not entitled to a preliminary injunction that would allow him to make *any* negative comments about homosexuals that stop short of fighting words. But with respect to his "Be Happy, Not Gay" message, Posner granted him his injunction.[42] Why? The "why" for Posner is that forbidding the message "Don't be gay" stretches the school's policy "too far."[43] By Posner's thinking, "Don't be gay" is not derogatory enough[44]; it is only "tepidly negative."[45] "Be Happy, Not Gay," even in a context of hostility to Gays that Posner explicitly recognizes, cannot be expected to have the sort of negative effect on Gay students necessary to create the requisite substantial disruption to the institutional interest he believes the school's policy justifiably safeguards. Any evidence that the message "Don't be gay" may have this negative psychological effect is, for Posner, "highly speculative."[46]

Protection of anti-Gay speech is often accomplished through the clever lie, judicial and otherwise, that the speech is not targeting Gay people, only homosexual *acts*. Plaintiff Nuxoll and the powerful anti-Gay interests litigating for him were careful to acknowledge that a school could regulate the use of individuated attacks crossing the threshold of "fighting words," and they purported to comment only that "homosexual *behavior* is contrary to the teachings of the bible, damaging to the participants and society at large, and does not lead to happiness."[47] This is a clever characterization of the attack at issue, but it is not reality. Judge Rovner, although ultimately she does not care, is quite clear on this fallacy, writing in her concurrence:

> My brothers also wonder whether this slogan is actually derogatory, noting that it is a play on the words "happy" and "gay." That it is a play on words does not change its ultimate meaning, however. Nuxoll tells us that he intends the slogan to convey the message that "homosexual behavior is contrary to the teachings of the bible, damaging to the participants and society at large, and does not lead to happiness." Throughout his brief, he claims to be criticizing homosexual "conduct" and "behavior" although his four-word polemic "Be Happy, Not Gay" does little to convey this message and instead seems to attack homosexual identity. Nonetheless, the statement is clearly intended to derogate homosexuals.[48]

[41] Id. at 675.
[42] Id. at 676.
[43] Id. at 675.
[44] Id. at 676.
[45] Id. at 676.
[46] Id.
[47] Id. at 678–679 (Rovner, J., concurring) (emphasis added).
[48] Id. at (Rovner, J., concurring) (citation omitted).

Of course, it is. As the concurrence also points out, Nuxoll's T-shirt slogan is a double play on words, because the word "gay," formerly "happy," now "homosexual," has been transformed into a general insult. Nevertheless, the concurrence continues, "I suspect that similar uses of the word 'gay' abound in the halls of Neuqua Valley High School and virtually every other high school in the United States without causing any substantial interruption to the educational process."[49]

I wonder how many Gay students' testimonies informed that conclusion.

SUBSTANTIVE EQUALITY THEORY AND SPEECH

While I am in principal agreement with the *Harper* majority, I have some disagreement with the majority's theory. For the rest of this chapter to be coherent, it is necessary at this point to leap ahead a bit intellectually and articulate exactly what restrictions on speech I see as permissible – even necessary. The rest of the chapter is my effort to explain the "why" and "how" of the theory I now articulate. My theory of speech is one grounded in the idea of substantive equality, explained in Chapters 2 and 3 – a grounding that raises prickly questions about hierarchy and power. Equality in this country cannot be understood, in any substantive way, apart from an understanding of power and how power operates to create and then to maintain a caste system where there are identifiable oppressor and oppressed classes.[50] Thus, an understanding of free speech that is informed by a commitment to substantive equality necessarily also must confront power hierarchy.

In a system of government committed to equality, it is entirely consistent with a commitment to free speech to draw a distinction between speech that has as its aim genuine political debate and discussion and speech that has as its aim the silence and demoralization of others. In this, the Ninth Circuit and I are in agreement. I think it is important, however, to set out the exact basis for this distinction. The Ninth Circuit understandably grounded its opinion on *Tinker*.[51] But I believe there are more substantial constitutional reasons to draw

---

[49] Id. at 679.

[50] This theory, most fully expounded in Chapters 2 and 3, this volume, has been central to my work from the start, from Shannon Gilreath, *Cruel and Unusual Punishment and the Eighth Amendment as a Mandate for Human Dignity: Another Look at Original Intent*, 25 T. Jefferson L. Rev. 559 (2003), through Gilreath, Sexual Politics, *supra* note 2, and through this chapter.

[51] I do not explore in detail the cases, beginning with *Tinker*, in which the Supreme Court has formulated special tests by which to adjudicate free speech claims involving public school youth. For purposes of my discussion, I assume that the reader has a basic familiarity with the Court's school-speech theory.

a distinction between speech that encourages political debate and speech that demoralizes and silences. Indeed, there is a powerful argument that the government has a constitutional obligation to ensure the equal dignity and equal participation of historically disenfranchised people and to protect them from speech that effectuates subordination.

Everyone knows that the First Amendment protects – along with other things – freedom of speech. What is not as clear is exactly what the framers of that provision were protecting. The Constitution, from the point of view of its powerful framers, was a means to the end of securing the power they already had. The "have-nots" were left in the same position they were in before the Constitution. In myriad ways, the speech of the Founders depended upon the silence they imposed on the people they conspired to render legally invisible. There is no denying that the Constitution originally valued Black people as three-fifths of a person and that many of the Founders considered Blacks part of the "property" that they pointedly sought to secure by the Constitution's very letter. Beyond this, when many of us consider the constitutive mind that gave us the Constitution, we see only our stark absence (or the absence of those like us). There certainly were no women among the Framers, although there were men who owned women, effectively, as chattel property. There probably were some Gay men among the Framers, but certainly none who could admit they were so. Whatever else they were, we can say that our founding fathers were presumptively straight, a standard for citizenship that hasn't changed much down to this minute.

Despite evidence of the Founders' failings, there is some evidence that even they did not intend an inviolate right of speech that would shield egregious personal attacks. Benjamin Franklin remarked of the free speech clause of the Pennsylvania Constitution: "[I]f it means liberty to calumniate another, there ought to be some limit."[52] And there is other evidence that the Founders viewed free speech as operating appropriately on an understanding of power and oppression. In correspondence with the inhabitants of Quebec, in 1774, the Continental Congress explained:

> The last right we shall mention regards the freedom of the press. The importance of this consists, besides advancement of truth, science, morality and arts in general, in its diffusion of liberal sentiment on the administration of government, its ready communication of thoughts between subjects, and its consequential promotion of union among them, whereby oppressive officials are shamed or intimidated into more honorable and just modes of conducting affairs.[53]

[52] Zechariah Chafee, Jr., Free Speech in the United States 17 (1941).
[53] Id.

But the system evolved into something quite different, with the powerful hatching a clever analogy to describe a system of free speech that focuses on the right of powerful people to remain powerful, at the expense of the victims of that power, in terms only the powerful understand. The "marketplace of ideas"[54] recalls power, property, and money. It says nothing of whole segments of the population it excludes – women: men's property then, undervalued and underpaid now; African Americans: slaves then, disproportionately poor and disenfranchised now; Gay people: totally invisible then, only marginally more visible now. In many cases, these people cannot afford the marketplace of the powerful. The price is simply too high. And the powerful make certain, by laws they make and judges they appoint, that the price point rarely moves.

The marketplace of ideas analogy assumes, either implicitly or explicitly, that there are no false ideas, only ideas to be picked or chosen, much in the same way that one would select apples at a market. There may be good or bad apples, better or worse apples, but no "false" apples. In the marketplace of ideas, there are good apples (fairness and civility, civic respect, and political correctness) and there are bad apples (bigotry, hate, and malevolence). Presumably, consumers may choose freely and, presumably, they will, more often than not, choose the good apples, eventually marginalizing the purveyors of bad apples or driving them from the market altogether. The analogy is flawed in several important respects. First, the analogy does not account for monopolists as they appear in the marketplace of ideas – and they do, indeed, exist in this metaphorical marketplace, too. The very purpose of anti-identity speech is to monopolize the debate to the exclusion of the targeted group. So a better analogy would be a market where no Blacks or Gays or women were allowed to shop; when they try to enter, they are driven away by vicious, dehumanizing verbal attacks. When the attackers see that the law offers no response, their next attack is more vicious and likely physical.

Also, it is obvious, perhaps too obvious to be said, that ideas are not apples. There *are* false ideas.[55] In the American democratic order, we have determined

---

54 For a discussion of the "marketplace of ideas" theory, see *Abrams v. United States*, 250 U.S. 616, 630 (1919) (Holmes, J., dissenting) ("[T]he ultimate good desired is better reached by free trade in ideas – that the best test of truth is the power of the thought to get itself accepted in the competition of the market, and that truth is the only ground upon which their wishes safely can be carried out").

55 Of course, in the speech context, although not explicitly in an anti-equality speech context, the Supreme Court has held: "Under the First Amendment there is no such thing as a false idea. However pernicious an opinion may seem, we depend for its correction not on the conscience of judges and juries but on the competition of other ideas." Gertz v. Robert Welch, Inc., 418 U.S. 323, 339–340 (1974). The Court's cavalier overlay of bourgeois capitalism on free speech continues to undermine equality when it contends with speech.

that the equality of every person is a paramount principle[56] – perhaps the ultimate principle of ordered liberty. Equality is a fundamental right of every citizen. Thus, expression that is targeted to undermine equality, to subjugate an individual or group purely because of group identity, and to exclude the victim from meaningful, equal citizenship is – constitutionally speaking – false.

The Fourteenth Amendment marked a seismic shift in the ground on which First Amendment tradition rests. With the addition of the Fourteenth Amendment, the Constitution, for the first time, guaranteed equality – facially, at least. A constitutional commitment to equality, if it means anything at all, must at least mean that certain people cannot be forced into a caste system, into an existence as second-class citizens, because powerful people regard them as somehow less valuable.

The exercise of equality, its meaningful exercise, at least, depends on speech, both the right to speak – a positive right to your own voice[57] – and the negative right to be free from speech that dehumanizes you. Congruent with this negative right, U.S. law has evolved to see some types of speech, once permitted, subsequently prohibited, such as a sign reading, "No Blacks Served Here,"[58] or the words of a boss, "Fuck me or you're fired."[59] Indeed, the law no longer categorizes such speech in terms of "speech" at all, although it certainly does constitute speech. Instead, we now label these words by reference to what they *do*: discriminate. There is a paradigm shift in these situations from the realm of *words only* to the realm of *action* – speech as action. In these cases, the courts have weighed the competing rights of the speaker with those of the people affected by such speech and have held that the equality rights involved were more important than the right to unfettered speech. The development of laws prohibiting sexual harassment in the workplace (in order to effectuate some equality between the sexes) is an example of considering speech for what action it constitutes.[60]

In these situations, we are not concerned with viewpoint or the attendant ramifications of viewpoint discrimination. Really, what more forceful

---

[56] U.S. Const. amend. XIV, § 1.
[57] This is most obvious in the context of Don't Ask, Don't Tell and in the struggle for its repeal.
[58] For example, Blow v. North Carolina, 379 U.S. 684, 684–685 (1965) (finding that a restaurant serving "whites only" violated the Civil Rights Act of 1964).
[59] Stockett v. Tolin, 791 F. Supp. 1536, 1543 (S.D. Fla. 1992).
[60] Despite the widespread acceptance of these legal improvements, some scholars continue to insist that even these concessions to equality are unconstitutional. See, e.g., Eugene Volokh, Comment, *Freedom of Speech and Workplace Harassment*, 39 UCLA L. Rev. 1791, 1797 (1992). Such protestations, however, proceed from a theory that privileges the right to speak over the right to equality – a posture I, obviously, do not adopt.

articulation of a point of view is there than "No Blacks Served Here" or "Fuck me or you're fired"? One sends the unmistakable message that Blacks are inferior, while the other sends the same message about women: Blacks are unfit for service with whites, and women are fit only to serve as fuck dolls. We do not inquire whether a policy that prohibits "Fuck me or you're fired" but permits women to petition for equal pay for equal work is "viewpoint-neutral," precisely because the viewpoint expressed by "Fuck me or you're fired" is restricted only incidentally to the regulation of discriminatory conduct. Put another way, we do not restrict such speech in the workplace for what it says – at least not only for what it says – but rather for what it does (which is to harass women out of the workplace or, at least, to condition their participation on their sexual submission to male bosses). The law of speech, informed by the law of equality, has evolved to deal with these harmful actions in reasonable ways. Nevertheless, similar speech, which we might colloquially define as "hate speech" but which I prefer to define as "anti-identity" speech, in the parlance of the *Harper* court, or perhaps as "anti-equality speech," targeting traditionally marginalized groups, still abounds.

In such cases, the courts have held that the right of the Nazi,[61] the Klansman,[62] the pornographer,[63] or the homophobe[64] to "speak" outweighs the equality interests of the targets of such speech – that is, *if* the equality interest has been seriously considered at all. In these cases, equality and speech are treated as trains departing from separate stations and on separate tracks. In reality, however, the two are on a collision course. The great interpretive challenge is to reconcile the two commitments, recognizing that they represent competing interests in some instances and complementary interests in others. When the two commitments do collide, equality should prevail as the subsequent and preeminent principle of liberty.

Consequently, a theory of free speech consistent with equality begins here: Speech that has as its aim or effect the subordination and second-class status of historically disenfranchised minorities offends equality and can be restricted

---

[61] Collin v. Smith, 578 F.2d 1197 (7th Cir. 1978) (striking down a Village of Skokie, Illinois, ordinance making it a misdemeanor to disseminate any material – including "public display of markings and clothing of symbolic significance" – promoting and inciting racial or religious hatred). In *Collin*, Skokie leaders wanted to use this ordinance to prohibit Nazis from demonstrating in Skokie, a town with a large population of Jewish Holocaust survivors. Id.

[62] Brandenburg v. Ohio, 395 U.S. 444 (1969).

[63] Am. Booksellers Ass'n v. Hudnut, 771 F.2d 323 (7th Cir. 1985), *aff'd without opinion*, 475 U.S. 1001 (1986) (invalidating a law that would have given women a sex-discrimination remedy against pornography).

[64] See, e.g., Chambers v. Babbitt, 145 F. Supp. 2d 1068 (D. Minn. 2001).

in reasonable ways. In such discrete instances, the speech is analyzed and regulated on the basis of harm, not viewpoint. The speech is restricted for what it does – erode equality – not for what it says. To put it another way, equality provides the compelling state interest for restrictions of anti-identity, or anti-equality, speech.

A theory thus articulated requires a conceptualization of the end product of anti-identity speech as actual harm – something more than "hurt feelings, offense, or resentment." It also requires a showing that restrictions are related in constitutionally significant ways to the defense of equality. This calls into question a number of popular myths anchoring the absolutist view of free speech, as well as demands their answer through a realistic look at the inter-relation of language, history, and context.

SPEECH AND HARM

When historians write our history books, when they write down the lives of those great people who have created our past and shaped our destinies, when they write of their lives and loves and deaths, they have the enviable advantage, in most instances, of having never known their subjects. They have not seen the twinkle of life and promise in their eyes; they have not heard their voices, known their habits, watched the corners of their mouths crinkle into a smile, or held their hands in moments despairing of hope. In short, they have not known what makes their subjects so inexorably, ineluctably human. Their stories can be written methodically, incrementally – scientifically.

It is an entirely different and terrifying matter to know the people about whom and for whom one writes.[65] It is an entirely different and entirely ter-rifying matter to confront the death, not of some specter in the dusty annals of history, but of a young man gone too soon, often under abhorrent circum-stances and, worst of all, for no good reason. It makes history, of which these dead people are now also a part, all the more personal and the more urgent. The history of free speech in this country is not one that has included the people about whom I write. And the present, etiolated by its place in his-tory's shadow, has no room for them either. Free speech, as it is determined by those powerful people who decide what the First Amendment means for the rest of us, is about protecting the "rights" of the Nazis, the Klansman, the misogynists, and the Gay bashers. It has nothing – nothing at all – to do with

---

[65] Gay people have been totally sexualized by our oppressors, and we have sexualized politics by bucking traditional heterosupremacist norms. Consequently, for Gays, the personal is political. This author's experience has been no exception.

the victim. Comfort and security are the prerogative of the powerful; harm is somebody else's reality.

For a discussion of anti-identity speech to be meaningful, there must be a realization that speech, in certain discrete circumstances, equates to actual harm. This realization made the *Harper* majority's theory possible; the failure to realize this same concept of speech as harm on Judge Kozinski's part animated his dissent. Judge Posner, by contrast, in *Nuxoll*, recognized that speech can be harm, but then obfuscated that harm by transferring it to the institution of the school, ignoring entirely the real-life aspects of the situation before him.

Conceptualizing speech as harm – understanding that words do not operate in a vacuum – is of paramount importance to any equalitarian theory of speech that matters. Words do not operate in a vacuum but rather are inevitably plugged into a social context. That context is often determinative of when words are words *only* and when they move beyond *mere words* to constitute actions – dehumanization, degradation, and subjugation. Social context is inseparable from power hierarchy that everywhere operates in and through that same context.

SUBORDINATION THROUGH LANGUAGE: THE PARABLE OF "COLERIDGE JACKSON"

Coleridge Jackson had nothing to fear. He weighed sixty pounds more than his sons and one hundred pounds more than his wife. His neighbors knew he wouldn't take tea for the fever; and the gents at the pool hall walked gently in his presence. So everybody used to wonder why Coleridge would come home, take off his shoes, hang up his coat, and beat the water and the will out of his puny little family. Everybody wondered, even Coleridge wondered, the next day or even later that same night. Everybody wondered except Coleridge's weaselly little sack of bones white boss, with his envious eyes. He knew; he always knew. And when people told him about Coleridge's family – about the black eyes, the bruised faces, the broken bones – how that scrawny man laughed. And the next day he treated Coleridge nicely – like Coleridge had just done him the biggest favor. But then, right after lunch, he'd start in on Coleridge again: "Hey, come here, Sambo. Can't you work any faster? Who on earth needs a lazy nigger?" But Coleridge would just stand there, not saying a word, his eyes sliding away, lurking at something somewhere else.[66]

---

[66] This parable of Coleridge Jackson is adapted by the author from the poem "Coleridge Jackson," by Maya Angelou. For a script of the original, see Maya Angelou, *Coleridge Jackson*, in THE COMPLETE COLLECTED POEMS OF MAYA ANGELOU 234, 234–236 (1994).

"Coleridge Jackson" is a story about the power of language to effect what it describes. What it describes, in the case of Coleridge Jackson and countless other marginalized and stigmatized people, is the process of dehumanization. Dehumanization is the transformation of someone first into some*thing* and finally into no*thing*.

The question "Who on earth needs a lazy nigger?" spoken by a white bigot and given a certain veracity by institutional scaffolding, becomes internalized, becomes internecine. The oppressed person begins to wonder if he, indeed, may be that thing that his oppressors say he is. Dehumanization is a very effective means of changing someone into nothing because it ensures that the messages one hears from *others* about oneself eventually become the messages one hears from oneself about oneself, and that is all the more damaging. It has happened this way to the Black man – the finely sinuous proliferation of the myth that he is desperate and dangerous – until, finally, even the Reverend Jesse Jackson proclaims his relief at discovering the footsteps heard in a darkened alley belonged to a white man.[67]

Dehumanization is real, and it happens most often to stigmatized people. It is real life for them. It is a life by which they are transformed into a target. The language of dehumanization does not necessarily betray physical violence, yet it inhabits it. This language – what I call anti-identity speech – while paradigmatically cruel, is not always overtly violent. But there is real cruelty that does not have in it overt violence.[68]

Cruelty happens to the marginalized in our society on a daily basis. Perhaps no group in this country experiences this as "ordinary" more than Gays and Lesbians. When one thinks about the everyday lives of Gay people, particularly Gay youth, it is hard not to think of those lives as an exercise in cruelty – at least, that is, if one is taking an honest look. Professor Mari Matsuda notes that "[t]he places where the law does not go to redress harm have tended to be the places where women, children, people of color, and poor people live."[69] For me, as a Gay writer, the glaring omission from her list is my own people – Gay people. But it is not unthinkable that Gay people would be omitted from such a list; we are almost always omitted from protection, almost offhandedly, even by

---

[67] In a November 29, 1993, article in the *Chicago Sun-Times*, Jackson is quoted as saying, "There is nothing more painful to me at this stage in my life than to walk down the street and hear footsteps and start thinking about robbery, … [t]hen look around and see somebody white and feel relieved." Mary A. Johnson, *Crime: New Frontier: Jesse Jackson Calls It Top Civil-Rights Issue*, CHI. SUN-TIMES, Nov. 29, 1993.

[68] See Andrea Dworkin, *Pornography Happens*, in LIFE AND DEATH: UNAPOLOGETIC WRITINGS ON THE CONTINUING WAR AGAINST WOMEN 129 (1997).

[69] Mari J. Matsuda, *Public Response to Racist Speech: Considering the Victim's Story*, 87 MICH. L. REV. 2320, 2322 (1989).

those people who, if they thought about it, would likely include us. This sort of omission is exactly the reason that Gay people present the archetypal class for explaining the need for reasonable regulation of anti-identity speech.

Evidence

A response to anti-identity speech must assume, of course, that the targets of the speech matter. And, for a great many people, Gays and the other minorities usually targeted for their identities simply do not matter. Consider the following:

- 97 percent of students in public high schools report regularly hearing homophobic remarks by their peers.[70]
- The typical high school student hears anti-Gay slurs more than twenty-five times a day.
- 53 percent of students report hearing homophobic comments made by school staff.
- 80 percent of Gay and Lesbian youth report severe social isolation.
- 78 percent of school administrators say they know of no Lesbian or Gay students in their schools; yet, astoundingly, 94 percent of them claim they feel their schools are safe places for these young people.
- 26 percent of adolescent Gay men report having to leave home as a result of conflicts with their families over their sexual orientation.
- 19 percent of Gay men and 25 percent of Lesbians report suffering physical violence at the hands of family members as a result of their sexual orientation.
- 42 percent of homeless youth self-identify as Gay or Lesbian.
- 15 percent of Lesbian, Gay, and bisexual youth have been injured so badly in a physical attack at school that they have had to seek the services of a doctor or nurse.
- 30 percent of Gay and bisexual adolescent males attempt suicide at least once.
- Gay and Lesbian youth represent 30 percent of all teen suicides. Extrapolation shows that this means a successful suicide attempt by a Gay teen in this country every five hours and forty-eight minutes.

We have to push beyond the shock of these facts and accept that we are confronting ordinary life for real people. For them, the hurt is more than

---

[70] This and the following statistics on Gay youth are taken from SHANNON GILREATH, SEXUAL IDENTITY LAW IN CONTEXT: CASES AND MATERIALS 125 (2007).

something astonishing on the page of a book. For them, the hurt and the harm are ordinary. This harm is what Judge Reinhart recognized in *Harper*.

The harm of anti-identity messages is obviously not unique to Gay people, nor is it even at its most well documented when targeted at Gay people. Since race and race theory are the preferred, more comfortable paradigms of the academy, scholars who study these things have focused on the harms of racist speech. Their findings are telling. Children as young as three are conscious of race and racism, and they make value judgments about race and their own racial identities based on the speech they hear.[71] Psychologist Kenneth Clark noted that "'[h]uman beings ... whose daily experience tells them that almost nowhere in society are they respected and granted the ordinary dignity and courtesy accorded to others will, as a matter of course, begin to doubt their own worth'."[72] The paternalistic arguments that speech authoritarians most often employ – let the insult roll off or talk back – are hardly options for most minority youth. "A child who finds himself rejected and attacked ... is not likely to develop dignity and poise.... On the contrary he develops defenses. Like a dwarf in a world of menacing giants, he cannot fight on equal terms."[73]

A report commissioned by the American Association of University Women Educational Foundation shows that the most damaging, shameful epithet, from the perspective of damaged, stigmatized school youth themselves, is that

---

[71] As to the effects of racial labeling, Professors Delgado and Stefancic record:

> [A]t a young age, minority children exhibit self-hatred because of their color, and major- ity children learn to associate dark skin with undesirability and ugliness. When pre- sented with otherwise identical dolls, a black child preferred the light-skinned one as a friend; she said that the dark-skinned one looked dirty or "not nice." Another child hated her skin color so intensely that she "vigorously lathered her arms and face with soap in an effort to wash away the dirt." She told the experimenter, "This morning I scrubbed and scrubbed and it came almost white." When asked about making a little girl out of clay, a black child said that her group should use the white clay rather than the brown "because it will make a better girl." When asked to describe dolls which had the physical characteristics of black people, young children chose adjectives such as "rough, funny, stupid, silly, smelly, stinky, dirty." Three-fourths of a group of four-year-old black chil- dren favored white play companions; over half felt themselves inferior to whites. Some engaged in denial or falsification.

> RICHARD DELGADO & JEAN STEFANCIC, UNDERSTANDING WORDS THAT WOUND 94–95 (2004) (citing MARY ELLEN GOODMAN, RACE AWARENESS IN YOUNG CHILDREN 36–60 (1964)).

[72] RICHARD DELGADO & JEAN STEFANCIC, MUST WE DEFEND NAZIS? HATE SPEECH, PORNOGRAPHY, AND THE NEW FIRST AMENDMENT 5 (1997) (quoting KENNETH B. CLARK, DARK GHETTO: DILEMMAS OF SOCIAL POWER 63–64 (1965)).

[73] DELGADO & STEFANCIC, WORDS THAT WOUND, *supra* note 71, at 10 (quoting GORDON W. ALLPORT, THE NATURE OF PREJUDICE 139 (1954)).

of Gay or Lesbian.[74] The homophobic slur has driven avowed heterosexual youth to suicide.[75]

The experience of Gay youth targeted by anti-identity speech is lucidly articulated by Michelangelo Signorile, who has written of his personal experiences growing up in New York.[76] Signorile's experience presents a classic case of name-calling escalating to violence. He explains how verbal harassment changed him from a happy, extroverted boy into, first, a subdued, quiet youth, then into a belligerent bully. He writes:

> [B]y the third or fourth grade things began to change: Suddenly, the boys were calling me a faggot. My happy nature grew more subdued....
>
> My personality development was stunted and deformed. I had been a bubbly, smart kid when I entered school, but now I was defensive and belligerent. Whereas I might have developed into one of those kids who was funny, irrepressible and well liked, instead I was a "faggot," laughed at and ostracized.

---

74 Am. Ass'n of Univ. Women Educ. Found., Hostile Hallways: The AAUW Survey on Sexual Harassment in America's Schools 20 (June 1993).

75 Deborah Locke, *Youth's Intolerance of 'Different' Can Destroy Lives*, St. Paul Pioneer Press, Jan. 2, 1997.

   The word "Gay" does not have this power over youth alone. In 2000 Danny Overstreet, a Gay man, was murdered in Roanoke, Virginia, by an assailant who was "allegedly driven to murder by the trauma he suffered by simply having the last name 'Gay.'" Shannon Gilreath, *A Climate of Violence Against Gay People*, Raleigh News & Observer, May 28, 2008. Six others were seriously injured in Ronald Gay's shooting spree outside a Gay bar. Id.

   A sort of *Twilight Zone* converse of people who do not believe that the word "Gay" can be stigmatizing are those people, either obtuse or incredibly stupid, who fail to see how "faggot" can be offensive (to say the least) to Gays. For example, Pittsburgh Steelers linebacker Joey Porter called opponent Kellen Winslow, Jr., a "fag" after a contentious game in 2006. Ed Bouchette, *Steelers Notebook: Porter Apologizes but Not to Winslow*, Pittsburgh Post-Gazette, Dec. 13, 2006, http://www.post-gazette.com/pg/06347/745642–66.stm. After his homophobic remarks drew fire, Porter "apologized" by calling his use of the epithet a "poor choice of words" and rationalizing that "how we used that word freely, me growing up using it, I didn't think nothing [sic] of it like that.... I apologize to anyone I offended on it [sic]." Despite being inarticulate, Porter wasn't completely oblivious: He did realize that "fag" was offensive, and he intended it to be – at least to Kellen Winslow. He summed up: "I didn't mean to offend nobody [sic] but Kellen Winslow. Pretty much, that's it about that." Id.

   I found the most interesting report on the incident to come from journalist Keith Boykin, who wrote on his website that Porter had "*accused*" opponent Kellen Winslow, Jr. of being a 'fag'" (emphasis added). Given that Boykin is an out Gay man himself, his description of Porter's homophobic slur as an accusation, as though actually being a "fag" connotes something normatively immoral as opposed to a homophobe's verbal practice of homophobia, is particularly telling. See Keith Boykin, *Steelers Player Calls Opponent a Fag*, Dec. 9, 2006, http://www.keithboykin.com/arch/2006/12/09/steelers_player (last visited Apr. 21, 2009).

76 Michelangelo Signorile, Queer in America: Sex, the Media, and the Closets of Power (2003).

> All my time and energy were consumed with trying to prove I wasn't this horrible thing, this sissy-faggot-queer....
>
> ... Every day was hell, and I began to dread going to school. I did everything I could to avoid being noticed. I stayed quiet and tried not to answer questions. I didn't even laugh at jokes....
>
> ... I was literally afraid for my safety, so I lived with the shame.[77]

In another passage, Signorile explains how the verbal assaults escalated into violence: "Sometimes they would gang up on me and beat me up."[78] As is often the result of a persistent campaign of dehumanization, Signorile eventually internalized the abuse he suffered at the hands of his peers:

> All the years of name-calling had taken their toll: I hated myself. Why, I began to ask myself over and over, do I want to live any longer? Why do I want to go through any more of this? I contemplated suicide. Over and over I'd go through the scenarios: Take all the pills in the medicine cabinet. Jump off the Staten Island Ferry into the harbor. Run into oncoming traffic. Slit my wrists.[79]

Signorile's self-hating also led him to other dangerous behavior patterns. He experimented with drugs and, while still a young teen, had sex with adults as old as three times his age. Eventually, he, too, began to harass others and resorted to "bashing queers" in an effort to destroy the part of himself he most hated (or to prove, to himself and others, that he was not this hated thing). Testament to the sheer effectiveness of anti-identity messages is the fact that Signorile was so horrified and "ashamed" (exactly what Tyler Harper suggested Gays should be) that he did not reveal his anguish to anyone who did not already know – not even his parents.

Signorile survived his ordeal. Sadly, many Gay youth do not. If you think that Signorile's account is merely anecdotal or too individualized, ample research backs up his account as far from unique or counterfactual.[80]

Numerous studies have shown a direct correlation between perceived homosexuality in youth and suicidality, with bullying, shaming, and peer ostracism mediating this relationship. A 2005 study by the University of Pittsburgh School of Social Work revealed that, in addition to being more likely than heterosexual youth to be bullied, Gay adolescents are more likely to be threatened or

---

[77] Id. at 23–25.

[78] Id. at 25.

[79] Id. at 31 (emphasis omitted).

[80] Cases also reflect this. See, e.g., Nabozny v. Podlesny, 92 F.3d 446 (7th Cir. 1996); Montgomery v. Indep. Sch. Dist. No. 709, 109 F. Supp. 2d 1081 (D. Minn. 2000).

injured with a weapon at school and to miss school because they feel unsafe.[81] The same study found a direct relationship to suicide among Gay youth.

Another study shows that Gay youth who are subject to verbal harassment and isolation from peers and family members are "two to three times more likely to attempt suicide than their heterosexual peers and may account for 30% of suicides among youth annually."[82] The same study recounts that

> 45% of the gay men and 20% of the lesbians surveyed were victims of verbal and physical assaults in secondary schools[, that 54% of school counselors] agreed that students often degrade fellow students whom they discover are homosexual, and that 67% strongly agreed that homosexual students are more likely than others to feel isolated and rejected.... 28% of homosexual youth were dropping out of secondary school because of discomfort and fear.[83]

Additionally, Gay youth experiencing isolation and degradation persisted in other patterns of high-risk behavior, including risky sex, increasing their probability of HIV infection.[84] According to this study, "speech" did not usually stop there: 32.7 percent of Gay youth were threatened with a weapon at school, compared with just 7.1 percent of straight youth; 68.1 percent of Gay youth were involved in physical altercations, compared with 37.6 percent of straight youth; 25.1 percent missed school out of fear, compared with 5.1 percent of straight youth; and 35.3 percent had attempted suicide, compared with 9.9 percent of straight youth.[85]

In addition to the greater likelihood that they will be victimized, the psychological consequences of victimization may be more severe for Gay youth than

---

[81] Mark S. Friedman et al., *The Impact of Gender-Role Nonconforming Behavior, Bullying, and Social Support on Suicidality Among Gay Male Youth*, 38 J. ADOLESCENT HEALTH 621, 621 (2006).

[82] Robert Garofalo et al., *The Association Between Health Risk Behaviors and Sexual Orientation Among a School-Based Sample of Adolescents*, 101 PEDIATRICS 895, 895 (1998).

[83] Id. at 895–896.

[84] Id.

[85] Id. at 898. Figures vary for the percentage of Lesbian and Gay youths who have attempted suicide, but all published reports have suggested disproportionately high rates among Gay youth. See PAUL GIBSON, U.S. DEP'T OF HEALTH & HUMAN SERVS., GAY MALE AND LESBIAN YOUTH SUICIDE 110–142 (1989) (reporting a 35% suicide rate); Scott L. Hershberger & Anthony R. D'Augelli, *The Impact of Victimization on the Mental Health and Suicidality of Lesbian, Gay, and Bisexual Youths*, DEVELOPMENTAL PSYCHOL., Jan. 1995, at 64–74 (reporting 42%); A. D. Martin & E. S. Hetrick, *The Stigmatization of the Gay and Lesbian Adolescent*, J. HOMOSEXUALITY (1988), at 163, 172 (reporting 21%). The statistics should be compared with corresponding rates among straight youth, which range from 8% to 13%. See Hershberger & D'Augelli, *supra*, at 66.

for heterosexual youth. In addition to suicidality, Gay youth evidence "substantially more health risk behavior" than their straight counterparts and are more likely to smoke and use alcohol and drugs.[86] Another study directly links the "debilitating effects of growing up in a homophobic society" to increased suicide attempts, running away from home, and school truancy.[87] One study reported the average GPA of harassed Gay youth at "half a grade lower than students experiencing less harassment (2.6 versus 3.1)."[88] The same students studied were more likely to report that they did not plan to go to college.[89]

As to Judge Posner's contention that the slogan "Be Happy, Not Gay" could not be adequately established as anti-Gay, Posner needed only to ask school students themselves. While 75.4 percent of students report hearing easily identifiable derogatory remarks, such as "faggot" or "dyke," in schools, nearly nine out of ten (89.2 percent) report "frequently or often" hearing "that's so gay" and its equivalents; and perhaps more importantly, *contra* Posner, they report understanding it to mean "stupid or worthless."[90]

There are also physical consequences for the victims of anti-identity speech that do not result from the battery that often eventuates from the speech. For example, I recently attended a large fund-raising affair for a national Gay organization. As I walked from my hotel to the meeting, a group of Christian psychotics were on the street corners with microphones and nauseating signs prescribing the death penalty for homosexuals. Now, I am used to saying unpopular things, and I am used to serious academic disagreements, but I have never felt more invaded or violated than I did as I walked by this tiny cadre spewing its venom. My muscles tightened, heart raced, fists clinched, lips pressed tight. I felt humiliation and impotent fury all at once. It was real stress. Later I thought about what it must be like for the millions of Gays and Lesbians, people of color, and women for whom this sort of dehumanization is a daily affair. It is no wonder that the number-one killer of women,

---

[86] Daniel E. Bontempo & Anthony R. D'Augelli, *Effects of at-School Victimization and Sexual Orientation on Lesbian, Gay, or Bisexual Youths' Health Risk Behavior*, 30 J. ADOLESCENT HEALTH 364, 371 (2002).

[87] Rich C. Savin-Williams, *Verbal and Physical Abuse as Stressors in the Lives of Lesbian, Gay Male, and Bisexual Youths: Associations with School Problems, Running Away, Substance Abuse, Prostitution, and Suicide*, 62 J. CONSULTING & CLINICAL PSYCHOL. 261, 262, 266 (1994).

[88] GLSEN, *GLSEN's 2005 National School Climate Survey Sheds New Light on Experiences of Lesbian, Gay, Bisexual and Transgender (LGBT) Students*, Apr. 26, 2006, http://www.glsen. org/cgi-bin/iowa/all/library/record /1927.html?state=research (last visited Apr. 21, 2009).

[89] Id. ("Overall, [Gay] students were twice as likely as the general population of students to report they were not planning to pursue any post secondary education").

[90] Id.

particularly African American women, is heart disease, no doubt occasioned by high stress levels.[91] It is no wonder that Gays commit suicide at disproportionately alarming rates. Stress kills. The anti-identity climate that academics call "the marketplace of ideas" kills.

In addition, Professors Richard Delgado and Jean Stefancic point out that the damages of hate speech go beyond psychic and physical injury alone. Delgado and Stefancic posit that hate speech produces tangible economic harms as well.[92] Surely, what they say is true. Imagine having to focus on your professional and economic development in an environment that constantly enforces your nothingness, where the speech of the bigot is unfettered and where, essentially, no legal recourse shields you from the bigot's most resilient impulses to degrade and dehumanize you. Gays and Lesbians in this country do not have to imagine that state of being – they have lived it and continue to live it.[93]

And, of course, physical violence is often overt. The well-publicized case of Matthew Shepard is notorious.[94] Matthew Shepard was somebody's son, somebody's family, somebody's friend. On the night of October 6, 1998, he was lashed to a crude fence in rural Wyoming, beaten into a coma with the handle of a pistol, and left there to die. He finally did – five days later. The passerby who found him said that his body was so crumpled and small against the vast Wyoming landscape that he was mistaken for a scarecrow that had slipped loose from its pole. His face had been beaten beyond recognition. In fact, his face was so crusted with blood that the only skin visible was in two vertical lines down his face – where his tears had washed away the blood.

The only thing unique about what happened to Matt Shepard is that the media seemed to care.[95] Mostly, violence against and killing of Gays and

[91] AM. HEART ASS'N, FACTS ABOUT WOMEN AND CARDIOVASCULAR DISEASES (2007), http://www.americanheart.org/presenter.jhtml?identifier=2876; AM. HEART ASS'N, EDUCATION ABOUT HEART DISEASE IS CRUCIAL FOR AFRICAN AMERICAN WOMEN (2007), http://www.americanheart.org/presenter.jhtml?identifier=2222.

[92] DELGADO & STEFANCIC, WORDS THAT WOUND, *supra* note 71, at 15.

[93] Title VII and Title IX do not offer specific protection to Gays and Lesbians as Gays and Lesbians. Even the meager victories, like *Oncale*, offer little hope. See Oncale v. Sundowner Offshore Servs., Inc., 523 U.S. 75 (1998) (holding that same-sex sexual harassment is actionable under Title VII so long as that harassment is motivated by genuine sexual desire or by an antipathy toward the presence of the targeted sex in the workplace by a member of the same sex).

[94] Howard Chua-Eoan, *That's Not a Scarecrow*, TIME, Oct. 19, 1998.

[95] Matt Shepard's death is particularly poignant for me because Shepard (had he lived) and I both turned thirty-one during the year in which I began writing this book. The year 2008 also happens to mark the tenth anniversary of Matt's death. In the ten years since his death, violence against Gays and Lesbians remains rampant and has actually risen. It remains to be

Lesbians go unreported (at least, not reported on), and the killing and the victims remain invisible. In Texas, between 1993 and 1995, eight Gay men were systematically stalked, terrorized, and murdered by teenage boys.[96] The real-world effects of anti-identity speech are evident in these killings. For example, an Oregon man who murdered two Lesbians execution style said, "I have no compassion for lesbians, or bisexual or ... gay men. I can't deal with it."[97] In another incident, a reporter challenged a group of teen boys who confessed they were looking to beat up "faggots."[98] One boy replied that faggots were not really human and that it was like "smashing pumpkins on Halloween."[99]

In May 2007, twenty-year-old Sean Kennedy was murdered in Greenville, South Carolina, by a young man who called him "faggot" while punching him so hard that he broke every bone in Sean's face.[100] Sean fell to the pavement; the impact caused his brain to separate from his brain stem, killing him. Shortly after driving away, Sean's killer left a message on the cell phone of one of Sean's friends: "Tell your faggot friend that when he wakes up he owes me $500 for my broken hand."[101]

In February 2008, eighth-grader Lawrence "Larry" King was murdered by a fellow student, Brandon McInerney, in a California middle school.[102] Larry was labeled "Gay" by fellow students and subjected to a pattern of verbal abuse and taunts. Larry took a page from the civil libertarians' manual and talked back to his attackers. When they taunted him, he taunted them right back, openly flirting with them.[103] Fourteen-year-old McInerney ended things when he shot Larry in the back of the head during a class.[104] In both the Kennedy and King cases, a pattern of assaultive speech preceded the killings.[105]

Rape, the weapon just short of murder, is also employed. In one case, a twelve-year-old boy was attacked and raped three nights in a row by four other sixth-graders and two older boys at a school-sponsored camp.[106] Teachers ignored much of the anti-Gay speech and Gay-baiting that preceded the

seen what impact recently enacted federal legislation aimed at anti-Gay crimes will have on the climate of pervasive anti-Gay violence.

[96] H. G. Bissinger, *The Killing Trail*, VANITY FAIR, Feb. 1995, at 80–89, 142–145.

[97] Charles Burress, *Confessed Stockton Slayer Tells Motive*, S.F. CHRON., Aug. 22, 1996.

[98] *Eight Teenagers Arrested in Weekend Assault on Gay Men*, L.A. TIMES, Apr. 16, 1996.

[99] Id.

[100] See Gilreath, *A Climate of Violence*, *supra* note 75; Steven Petrow, *They Shoot Gays, Don't They?* INDEP. WKLY., June 25, 2008.

[101] Id.; *see also* Petrow, *supra* note 100.

[102] Rebecca Cathcart, *Boy's Killing, Labeled a Hate Crime, Stuns a Town*, N.Y. TIMES, Feb. 23, 2008.

[103] Greg Risling, *Shooting of Gay Student Sparks Outcry*, USA TODAY, Mar. 28, 2008.

[104] See Petrow, *supra* note 100.

[105] Id.

[106] Erin Van Bronkhorst, *Study: Gay Kids Being Raped in Schools*, BAY WINDOWS, Sept. 7, 1995.

attack.[107] Social workers noted that anti-Gay rhetoric often devolves into physical violence when it goes unchecked.[108] Recently, a Lesbian reported that she was brutally raped at her home in Charlotte, North Carolina. The woman, who chose not to disclose her identity to the one local TV station that covered the crime, said that while brutalizing her, her attacker made it clear that he was raping her *because* she was a Lesbian. These are but a few examples of the inseparability of words and violence.

At this point, it is necessary for me to anticipate criticism. Critics will say that neither Harper's speech nor that of Nuxoll represents anti-identity speech, with a requisite connection to harm, as I have defined it. Neither Harper nor Nuxoll resorted to the usual epithets: faggot, dyke, and the like. So do the messages at issue, "Homosexuality Is Shameful" and "Be Happy, Not Gay," constitute anti-identity speech that is harm, or are they words only, without harm? Judge Posner believed Nuxoll's message was only the latter – at least, he held that Nuxoll's message did not meet the threshold for regulation. He reached this conclusion despite plaintiff Nuxoll's testimony that he *intended* the slogan as a derogatory commentary.[109] Posner held that "Not Gay" is only "tepidly negative," not "demeaning."[110]

> [I]t is highly speculative that allowing the plaintiff to wear a T-shirt that says "Be Happy, Not Gay" would have even a slight tendency to provoke [harassment of gay students, which was already documented at the school], or for that matter to poison the educational atmosphere. Speculation that it might is, under the ruling precedents, and on the scanty record compiled thus far in the litigation, too thin a reed on which to hang a prohibition of the exercise of a student's free speech.[111]

I believe both messages constitute anti-identity speech as harm in the ways that I have articulated. Both messages could be aggrandized into political speech, but they are not. Neither message is deliberative debate on the good or ill of a political choice; rather, the messages are targeted anti-identity speech constituting a coercive proclamation of the inequality of an identifiable minority group. Mari Matsuda rightly identifies this type of speech as "cold" hate speech.[112] It is not the evident name-calling, epithet-filled hate speech we

---

[107] Id.

[108] Joyce Hunter & Robert Schaecher, *Gay and Lesbian Adolescents*, in Encyclopedia of Social Work 1055, 1058 (Richard L. Edwards et al., eds., 19th ed., 1995).

[109] Nuxoll *ex rel.* Nuxoll v. Indian Prairie Sch. Dist. No. 204, 523 F.3d 668, 676 (7th Cir. 2008).

[110] Id.

[111] Id.

[112] Matsuda, *supra* note 69, at 2320, 2366. Patricia Williams calls it "spirit murder." See Patricia Williams, *Spirit-Murdering the Messenger: The Discourse of Fingerpointing and the Law's Response to Racism*, 42 U. Miami L. Rev. 127, 129 (1987).

often think of. But it is just as damaging. In fact, I believe it is, in many cases, more damaging. Its dressed-down, almost civil tone makes it less recognizable, less shocking, and thereby more insidious. In this way, it is reminiscent of "cold" forms of anti-Semitic speech: the Holocaust lie literature[113] or the various conspiracy theories about Jews surreptitiously buying control of the government,[114] for example. Insofar as the targeted groups are concerned, of course, there is little difference in effect; but insofar as the majority of listeners is concerned, the "cold" hate speech is more effective. Anti-identity speech that appears to be a civic warning or political observation is less alarming to people than explicit attack and serves to desensitize audiences to more obvious attacks that inevitably come later.[115] These are the messages that must take root before there can be swastikas or burning crosses – or blatant incitements to murder. They create the foundation.

This was a method used extremely effectively by the Nazis during their rise to and consolidation of power. The Nazi experience demonstrates that effective anti-identity propaganda can take many forms. In fact, Judge Posner's disposition of the phrase "Not Gay" reminded me of a much earlier decision by another court that could not quite bring itself to recognize the power of language in light of the social context in which the language operated or to interpret the law in light of facts as they really existed.

In the 1920s, Joseph Goebbels, later Hitler's official propaganda minister, organized an anti-Jew campaign in the very effective form of cartoons.[116] The cartoons focused on one character, a Jewish police officer. The man derisively nicknamed "Isidor" was caricatured, in among other atrocious ways, with his neck in a crude noose. The caption read, "For him too, Ash Wednesday will come."[117] The cartoons became the vehicle by which the Nazis imparted all manner of nefarious characteristics to Germany's Jewish citizens. The police official on whom "Isidor" was based sued Goebbels to stop the publication of the libelous cartoons. Goebbels, his lawyers making full use of all the available "democratic" protections of free speech – after all, such "democratic" protections are always available to the powerful – got Goebbels acquitted. The court upheld the acquittal reasoning that the word Jew was equivalent to the word Protestant or Catholic. Surely one could not be sued for libeling another

---

[113] Matsuda, *supra* note 69, at 2366–2367.

[114] Id.

[115] Posner implicitly recognizes this in *Nuxoll*. See *Nuxoll*, 523 F.3d at 672.

[116] SAUL FRIEDLANDER, NAZI GERMANY AND THE JEWS 104 (1997).

[117] The police official on whom *Isidor* was based was actually Dr. Bernard Weiss. See generally id. for more on this story and similar episodes. See also Andrea Dworkin, *The Power of Words*, in LETTERS FROM A WAR ZONE: WRITINGS, 1976–1989, at 27, 27–28 (1993).

by calling him a Protestant or a Catholic. "How could there be injury from calling a Jew a Jew?"

This pre-Nazi court was guilty of the same error that many U.S. courts commit today – the error Judge Posner commits in *Nuxoll*: the error of theorizing speech in a way that completely divorces it from social reality. Had there been no history of rampant prejudice and discrimination against Jews, the pronouncement by the German court would have made sense. But in the world of 1920s Germany, and in the twenty-first-century world we live in now, theorizing free speech in this way – divorced from context – puts it on a completely different plane – an inhuman plane – like a tornado that never touches the ground. Goebbels understood that language was not divorced from its social context, but the court did not. Goebbels used anti-identity language to construct genocide, and he used democratic notions of free speech to shield genocide. The courts did nothing to stop him.

Speech authoritarians have convinced the courts that the same studiously blinkered approach is necessary for a robust free speech system in the United States. The problem with this idea is that it does not work. It does not result in free or even free-*er* speech. Language can be used to illuminate and to educate – to promote understanding. But language can also be used to perpetuate ignorance and inequality and to coerce others not to rebel. That is how language is predominantly used against Gays and Lesbians today. Language is used against the target group as a weapon to provoke fear and hatred. We are told that this speech is nevertheless worthy of protection because it is about ideas, part of the great "marketplace of ideas." But this speech from the bargain basement of the marketplace of ideas[118] is not about the discussion of an idea. Its very objective is to monopolize the discussion and to close the debate. Judge Posner's *Nuxoll* decision is made all the more deplorable because he *does* recognize the cause behind the litigation. Presumably, he does not believe – or cannot understand – the cause to conceptually liquidate Gays to be as dangerous as it really is. The desensitization that anti-identity speech accomplishes works to protect it even with the likes of federal appellate judges, who, one may assume, are as far removed from the reality of public school hallways as is possible. Distance, in this case, is not critical distance. My chief

---

[118] The "bargain basement of the marketplace of ideas" is the useful coinage of Evelina Giobbe. Evelina Giobbe, *The Bargain Basement in the Marketplace of Ideas*, in THE PRICE WE PAY: THE CASE AGAINST RACIST SPEECH, HATE PROPAGANDA, AND PORNOGRAPHY 58, 58–60 (Laura Lederer & Richard Delgado eds., 1995).

disagreement with Judge Posner stems from my belief that legal principles ought to have some grounding in reality. Posner apparently believes that reality should be theorized to fit principles.

Analogy: Der Stürmer *Politics and Anti-Identity Speech* *(Speech as Action)*

A chief medium for the Nazi's anti-Jew campaign was *Der Stürmer,* a cheap newspaper published by Julius Streicher, a Nazi Party member from Nuremburg, Franconia. Streicher was merciless and relentless and quite productive in his campaign against Germany's Jews. *Der Stürmer,* especially immediately prior to Nazi control, was the most widely read and circulated paper in Germany.[119] *Der Stürmer,* while it certainly had its disgusting and utterly pornographic side, also contained what might be called – in the parlance of contemporary free speech discourse – political viewpoint. This is undeniably true, insofar as every utterance expresses a viewpoint. But what is most salient for purposes of my discussion here is that *Der Stürmer* and its copycat rags were important propaganda machines in the dissemination by saturation of the particular anti-Jew *viewpoint* that defined Nazi fascism. *Der Stürmer* is the acme of viewpoint as saturation propaganda, and of propaganda as action. Streicher was a confidant of Adolf Hitler and reportedly had an enormous influence on Hitler's thinking. "*Der Führer* [was] always greatly quickened in his anti-Jewish feeling by contact with the notorious Julius Streicher."[120]

Surely, the comparisons I make at this point will be criticized. There is always shock when one takes the horror of something that happened and is well documented historically and then analogizes to what is happening now in striking parallels but is perhaps less obvious because there is no historical spotlight. After the Holocaust, women writers like Sylvia Plath, Muriel Rukeyser, and Andrea Dworkin made connections in their work between what Nazi society had done to the Jews and what they felt their own society was doing to women. Their work was repeatedly denounced as disrespectful, in the least. My analogy here of what anti-Gay religionists are doing to Gays in this country with what anti-Semites did to Jews in Nazi Germany will surely receive the same reaction, perhaps because people who are not experiencing it cannot see it at work. What was claimed to be hyperbole has

[119] LOUIS W. BONDY, RACKETEERS OF HATRED: JULIUS STREICHER AND THE JEW-BAITERS' INTERNATIONAL 45 (1946).
[120] Id. at 31.

more than once become history with the passage of time. Those of us whose observations are based in reality see things quite differently, and the cross-over from Jews to Gays is easy enough. The analogy is important because it deflates the erroneous classification of coercion and incitement to hatred as permissible "viewpoint" under the First Amendment. Supposed viewpoint neutrality is a constant refrain of free speech absolutism. Writing in response to the *Harper* decision, Professor Eugene Volokh articulates the absolutist case perfectly, writing in *Harper's* wake that a sacrosanct "viewpoint" had been "excluded" from the equally sacrosanct First Amendment.[121] Volokh, like Judge Posner in *Nuxoll*, confuses what he sees as the casual insult of Harper's message, something he calls "viewpoint," with what is, in reality, saturation propaganda. But as Louis Bondy noted in his study of Nazi Jew-baiting, concluded just after World War II and while Julius Streicher awaited his trial for war crimes:

> It seems ... necessary to be well acquainted with the methods by which the Nazis tried to spread their doctrines.... "It cannot happen here" is too easy an attitude to take up.... [A]ll those who wish to see human liberties preserved will have to be on their guard against any recurrence of the events of the last decade.[122]

Gays know that Bondy was prescient in this, for we have seen the shape of the wrath Bondy chronicles and bear witness in intimate, personal ways to its devastating consequences.

The Nazi regime depended on saturation propaganda to motivate, coerce, terrorize, and proselytize. Many people who experienced the worst of both physical and verbal violence at the hands of the Nazis specifically prayed for an end to the latter. David Rubinowicz, twelve years old, wrote this in his diary: "When the village constable had put [an advertisement accusing Jews of deceit in business dealings] up, some people came along, and their laughter gave me a headache from the shame that the Jews suffer nowadays. God give that this shame may soon cease."[123] The anti-Gay campaign in this country, currently still slightly more constrained by law than was Nazi fascism, operates in parallel ways. Messages like those at issue in *Harper*, therefore, must be understood in context.

By focusing on Harper's "shameful" message I do not mean to suggest that this is the worst kind of message that Gay people encounter. Far from it. But by concentrating on Harper's message in this way I do mean to suggest that

---

[121] Volokh, *supra* note 9.
[122] BONDY, *supra* note 119, at 253.
[123] DAVID RUBINOWICZ, THE DIARY OF DAVID RUBINOWICZ 43 (Derek Bowman, trans., 1982).

this message and its abundant variants *are* harmful. In fact, they may be more insidious in nature and degree than more emotionally shocking variants, like "faggot." The point of the message, of course, is to shame the Gay person who encounters it, to degrade and to demoralize. The purveyors of hate messages are usually upfront about this particular goal.[124] But a corresponding and equally effective purpose is to shame those who might associate with the Gay person. This is a page right out of the *Stürmer* playbook.

The readers of *Der Stürmer* were not, of course, principally Jewish, although some Jews read it in an attempt to stay informed of the anti-Semitic tidal wave it portended. Mostly, *Der Stürmer*'s readers were the suggestible masses, perhaps already disposed to anti-Semitic thought to one degree or another, for whom there was, aside from Jew-inspired counter demonstration tainted by its very association with Jews to start with, little counterweight. Streicher published messages not only demonizing the Jews, but also demonizing those who might give the Jews some sympathy. "We know that there are still people who pity the Jew. They are not worthy of living in [Nuremburg] nor are they worthy of belonging to this city nor are they worthy of belonging to this nation of which you are a proud part."[125]

Harper's message that homosexuality is "shameful" and that those who are sympathetic are "condemned" is evocative of exactly the same sort of feeling. *Der Stürmer* also printed letters shaming community members who were known to do business or otherwise associate with Jews. One representative letter chastised a certain Johann Jacob, a member of the Nazi Party, because he had, in a public place, called Jews "friends."[126] In addition to Jacob's name, even the date of his "offense" was printed.[127] Another chapter attacked a priest for refusing to accommodate the Nazi gospel of hate and, instead, defending Jews.[128]

Der Stürmer advocated direct social boycott of Jews and their supporters. It was a particularly effective campaign. There is a clever revisionist myth of history that ordinary Germans would not have supported the Holocaust had they known what was actually happening.[129] But history unrevised suggests that the same ordinary people, had Germany come out on the winning side of the war, would have done nothing about the Holocaust, if not

---

[124] See Nuxoll *ex rel.* Nuxoll v. Indian Prairie Sch. Dist. No. 204, 523 F.3d 668, 670 (7th Cir. 2008).

[125] BONDY, *supra* note 119, at 37.

[126] Id. at 51.

[127] Id.

[128] Id. at 52.

[129] ALEXANDER TSESIS, DESTRUCTIVE MESSAGES: HOW HATE SPEECH PAVES THE WAY FOR HARMFUL SOCIAL MOVEMENTS 11–27 (2002).

support it.[130] The campaign against Gays under the guise of political debate about social policy accomplishes the same end.

Despite Judge Posner's protest in *Nuxoll* that children cannot possibly affect society in such a way as to render their speech important,[131] the methodology of *Der Stürmer* shows otherwise. It shows exactly how messages carried by young people are effective – and essential – in any propaganda campaign. As early as July 1924, *Der Stürmer* advocated for the expulsion of Jewish children from schools because "grown-up Germans could not be expected to perceive in the Jew a person of alien race if they had been forced in their childhood to accept the Jew as their playmate."[132]

Streicher understood as well as modern Christian fundamentalist pundit James Dobson does that "[t]hose who control what young people are taught, and what they experience, what they see, hear, think, and believe will determine the future course of the nation."[133] This is precisely the concern that animates messages like that at issue in *Harper*, the religious zealots who prod them along, and the powerful organized interests, like the Alliance Defense Fund, that defend anti-equality speech each time it is challenged. If young people are deprived of messages like Harper's in schools where a substantial part of their mental and emotional personalities are formed, they may stop believing that Gays are aliens whose "father was the devil."[134]

As even Judge Posner recognized, the real goal of the anti-Gay initiative is not only the elimination of pro-Gay speech in schools, but the unfettered insinuation of anti-Gay messages at all levels.[135] Such was the case with *Der*

---

[130] Klaus Saur, the son of Nazi leader Karl Saur, had an argument with his mother after World War II, described in detail by his younger brother:

> It was between Klaus and my mother. They had seen a discussion on television about the war and a Jewish person had been interviewed. My mother had said a typical German expression, "That is one that should have gone to the gas chambers." And my brother was furious and told her it was stupid to say such things. And she was really shocked that he was so angry. "It's just an expression, it doesn't mean anything," she told him.... Klaus was firm with her. "Those stupid sentences are what eventually led to the types of things that happened in the war, he told her."

Quoted in ANDREA DWORKIN, SCAPEGOAT: THE JEWS, ISRAEL, AND WOMEN'S LIBERATION 149 (2000), at 143.

[131] Nuxoll *ex rel.* Nuxoll v. Indian Prairie Sch. Dist. No. 204, 523 F.3d 668, 671 (7th Cir. 2008) ("The contribution that kids can make to the marketplace of ideas and opinions is modest").

[132] BONDY, *supra* note 119, at 52.

[133] Shannon Gilreath, *First Amendments*, NEW HUMANIST, May/June 2005, at 10–11 (quoting James Dobson).

[134] BONDY, *supra* note 119, at 52.

[135] *Nuxoll*, 523 F.3d at 672.

Stürmer. Streicher's ambition was not simply that pro-Jew sentiment be banished from schools, but also that anti-Jew messages pervade the schools. As *Der Stürmer* testifies, "[O]ften we wish we could have with us in the class room the people who still fail to understand the mean and shameful deeds of the Jew."[136] Underneath this letter was the printed motto, "[T]he Jew is wagging his venomous tongue, that's why he would be sent to Dachau concentration camp."[137] Young people, who are extraordinarily impressionable, were receptive. Students in Pomerania sent a letter to *Der Stürmer* extolling the anti-Jew plays they performed each Saturday. "We can hardly wait until it is Saturday again," they chirped.[138] Streicher's publishing company also produced schoolbooks for young people to reinforce Nazi ideology in the classroom, containing graphs and explanations of "racial types" and "racial pollution," an eerie parallel to similar efforts by anti-Gay fundamentalist forces in the United States.[139] The Nazis understood then what radical Islamists know now but Posner apparently does not: Children used as suicide bombers are every bit as effective as adult suicide bombers – perhaps more so.

I admit that it is difficult for us to imagine how all of this could happen on such a raw and obvious level. It took, of course, the complicity of the people, but it is also a testament to what people can be conditioned to accept given enough time and effort, especially when that effort is itself dressed up by its perpetrators as the endangered, embattled ideology – another tactic employed by anti-Gay propagandists.[140] Would we be shocked to read this poem for children? "A devil walks through our lands, / he is Gay, well known to us, / a murderer, polluter, and terrorist. / Corrupt he must even the young, / he wants all people to die, / don't ever have anything to do with Gays, / then you will be glad and happy." Replace "Gay" with "Jew" and you have exactly the kind of poem that was officially approved for use by children in the Nazi era.[141] One wonders if the children, or certainly the parents, did not register shock at such words. It seems not. The systematic corruption of their minds against the Jew desensitized them even to such blatant attacks. One wonders if it began with

---

[136] BONDY, *supra* note 119, at 53.

[137] Id.

[138] Id.

[139] Id. at 54.

[140] The idea that "moral values" or "conservative values," or whatever referent one wants to use for a fundamentalist Christian worldview, are somehow under siege by a menacing Gay agenda is so prevalent that it needs no citation. On the liberal affection for giving subordinating ideologies equal time in the name of "balance," see José Gabilondo, *When God Hates: How Liberal Guilt Lets the New Right Get Away with Murder*, 44 WAKE FOREST L. REV. 617 (2009).

[141] BONDY, *supra* note 119, at 54–55.

something as simple as "Be Aryan, Not Jewish." Judge Posner seemed to realize a similarly sinister mission on the part of the Alliance Defense Fund and
its allies, but he, like the Weimar court, did nothing to stop it.[142]

Another explicit parallel exists between *Der Stürmer* and anti-identity
T-shirts. Streicher was not content to let anti-Jew sentiments be uttered and
dissipate (if such a thing is possible); he wanted them to be ever-present for a
compelled audience. To that end, Streicher and Nazi officials orchestrated
showcases (*Stürmerkasten*) to carry *Der Stürmer's* message beyond those who
would willingly subscribe. Whole issues of *Der Stürmer* were displayed behind
glass for all to see, usually constructed along important thoroughfares, where
few could avoid them.[143] Anti-identity T-shirts serve the same purpose. An
anti-identity utterance is sent out and may be confined by time or place. The
T-shirt, by contrast, is ever-present, with its damaging message ever-ready.
No one who sits in the classroom or walks down the hall can escape it. The
Jews of Nazi Germany were powerless to offer any but the same advice Judge
Kozinski now glibly offers Gay youth: Avoid it; try not to look. As in the anti-
Gay campaign, in the Nazi regime, language was a primary weapon:

> The quantity and intensity of verbal violence, which included the widespread
> posting of signs (which Germans and Jews saw daily) that forbade Jews' phys-
> ical and social existence among Germans ... should be seen as an assault
> in its own right, having been intended to produce profound damage – emo-
> tional, psychological, and social. ... The wounds that people suffer by having
> to listen [to] [or view] publicly ... such vituperation and by not being able to
> respond – can be as bad as the humiliation of a public beating.[144]

An important point to keep in mind in the analogy between *Der Stürmer*
and "Homosexuality Is Shameful" is that these messages do not operate in
isolation. They are immediately part of the social context in which they exist.
Everything in life is part of it; we cannot compartmentalize away the stuff
we do not like. This was my chief criticism of the Weimar court's handling
of Dr. Weiss's libel suit (the "Isidor" case). There, indeed, may be no harm in
calling a Jew a Jew in certain social contexts; Weimar Germany was not such
a context.

Anti-identity messages aimed at Gays necessarily operate in social context
too. In that sense, Harper's message of shame and reproach does not operate
in the abstract, as speech trapped in some space-time continuum. Instead, it is

---

[142] Nuxoll *ex rel.* Nuxoll v. Indian Prairie Sch. Dist. No. 204, 523 F.3d 668, 671 (7th Cir. 2008).
[143] See, e.g., BONDY, *supra* note 119.
[144] DANIEL JONAH GOLDHAGEN, HITLER'S WILLING EXECUTIONERS: ORDINARY GERMANS AND
THE HOLOCAUST 126 (1996).

immediately plugged into a social and political context charged with hate for homosexuality and homosexuals. The pervasive anti-equality climate faced by Gays in this country makes the institutionalization of a message like Harper's in an environment in which exposure to the message is compelled even more insidious. This knowledge is exactly why Julius Streicher wanted *Der Stürmer* in public schools, and it is exactly why the Alliance Defense Fund wants "Homosexuality Is Shameful" in public schools. As both Streicher, speaking for a group-hating right then, and James Dobson, speaking for a group-hating right now, noted, appropriately indoctrinated youth make good adult warriors.

Adult messages are compelling evidence of the verity of the theory. Indeed, the parallels between anti-Semitic speech of the *Der Stürmer* variety and anti-Gay speech now are overwhelming – not obvious only to those who do not wish to see. The idea that anti-identity prejudice facing Gays and Lesbians is so outside the mainstream that it can be ignored is balderdash. Anti-identity speech labeling Gays as the maniacal "other" abounds and finds the receptive ear of many policy makers. Julius Streicher wrote, "[T]he wire-pullers behind every disaster that has overtaken the people is the eternal Jew."[145] In the wildly popular Nazi propaganda film, *The Eternal Jew*, it is asserted: "At the beginning of the twentieth century, the Jews sit at the junction of the world financial markets. They are an international power. Although only one percent of the world's population, with the help of their capital, they terrorize the world stock exchanges, world opinion, and world politics."[146] Compare that with the testimony before Congress of Robert Knight, leader of the right-wing Family Research Council, an unabashedly bigoted group given prime time by Congress. Knight asserts: "Homosexuals display political control far beyond their numbers. A tiny fraction of the population (about one percent), homosexuals have one of the largest and fastest growing Political Action Committees in the country (the Human Rights Campaign) and give millions of dollars to candidates."[147] Like Jews, Gays are a threat because we are supposedly better educated, have better jobs, and make more money than other people.[148]

[145] BONDY, *supra* note 119, at 39.

[146] THE HOLOCAUST HISTORY PROJECT, STILL IMAGES FROM DER EWIGE JEW (1998), http://www. holocaust-history.org/der-ewige-jude/stills.shtml (last visited Apr. 21, 2009) (quoting from the film THE ETERNAL JEW (Deutsche Film Gesellschaft 1940)).

[147] *Employment Non-Discrimination Act of 1994: Hearing on S. 2238 Before the S. Comm. on Labor and Human Resources*, 103d Cong. 93 (1994) [hereinafter *Hearing*] (statement of Robert Knight, Family Research Council).

[148] Compare THE HOLOCAUST HISTORY PROJECT, *supra* note 146 ("Fifty-two out of every 100 doctors were Jews. Of every 100 merchants, 60 were Jews. The average wealth of Germans was 810 marks; the average wealth of Jews 10,000 marks"), *with Hearing, supra* note 147, at 93

And these are not merely the rants of wackos on the periphery of political power. They are the official speech of political leaders (perhaps no less wacko). For example, recently addressing a Republican group, Oklahoma representative Sally Kern asserted that "[homosexuality is] the biggest threat our nation has, even more than terrorism or Islam."[149] Moreover, she claimed that "the homosexual agenda is destroying the nation"; "no society that has totally embraced homosexuality has lasted for more than, you know, a few decades"; and "what's happening now is they're going after, in schools, two-year-olds."[150] The parallel between these assertions and those of Streicher toward Jews is chilling. Like Kern, Streicher was insistent that "the Jew was the root of all political, social, and economic evil in Germany and in the whole world. Parallel to this theme was the patent insistence that this evil must be feared, hated and eventually destroyed."[151] Similar heterosexist hallucinations permeate U.S. courts, right up to the level of the nation's highest court. Justice Scalia's anti-Gay dissent in *Romer v. Evans* echoes anti-Jew propaganda when he describes efforts to strip Gays of antidiscrimination protections as "a modest attempt by seemingly tolerant Coloradans to preserve traditional sexual mores against the efforts of a politically powerful minority."[152]

Another common *Der Stürmer* tactic is to libel Gays by repeating what Gays themselves have allegedly said, even when the perpetrators of the anti-equality speech know that the imputed remarks are neither accurate nor accurately attributed. It is like one supremely deceptive election-year ad that never stops circulating. Streicher was a master at this, reprinting and distributing *The Protocols of the Learned Elders of Zion* as if it were true.[153] This "secret plan of a cabal of Jews to control the world" was actually the creation of the secret police of the czar to whip up a pogrom against Russian Jews.[154] Streicher used it to whip up the ultimate pogrom: the Holocaust.

(statement of Robert Knight, Family Research Council) ("[H]omosexuals have higher than average per-capita annual incomes ... are more likely to hold college degrees ... [and are more likely to] have professional or managerial positions").

[149] *Kern: Gays Biggest Threat to Nation, Killed 100,000*, ON TOP, Oct. 10, 2008, http://www.ontopmag.com/Chapter.aspx?id=2522&MediaType=1&Category=26 (last visited Apr. 21, 2009).

[150] *Homophobic Official May Have Gay Son*, DALLAS VOICE, Mar. 13, 2008, http://www.dallasvoice.com/artman/publish/printer_8341.php (last visited Apr. 21, 2009). Kern's remarks were secretly recorded by the Gay and Lesbian Victory Fund and leaked to various media.

[151] WILLIAM P. VARGA, THE NUMBER ONE NAZI JEW-BAITER: A POLITICAL BIOGRAPHY OF JULIUS STREICHER, HITLER'S CHIEF ANTI-SEMITIC PROPAGANDIST 94 (1981).

[152] Romer v. Evans, 517 U.S. 620, 636 (1996) (Scalia, J., dissenting).

[153] DWORKIN, SCAPEGOAT, *supra* note 130, at 149.

[154] Id.

The anti-Gay camp are also masters at such deception. In my home state of North Carolina, Mary Francis Forrester,[155] the wife of James Forrester, a state senator,[156] recently wrote an opinion piece for the right-wing Christian Action League website, in which she opened with a quotation from the February 15, 1987, issue of the now-defunct *Gay Community News*[157]:

> We shall sodomize your sons.... We shall seduce them in your schools, in your dormitories, in your gymnasiums, in your locker rooms ... in your youth groups.... Your sons shall become our minions and do our bidding.... They will come to crave and adore us. All laws banning homosexual activity will be revoked. Instead legislation shall be passed which engenders love between men. Our writers and artists will make love between men fashionable.... We shall raise private armies ... to defeat you. The family unit will be abolished. Perfect boys will be conceived and grown in the genetic laboratory.... All churches who condemn us will be closed. Our only gods are handsome young men. All males who insist on remaining stupidly heterosexual will be tried in homosexual courts of justice and will become invisible men. Tremble, hetero swine, when we appear before you without our masks.[158]

Forrester's selective excerpt conveniently leaves out the beginning (remember: context is everything) of the essay she quotes. Michael Swift, the essay's author, begins: "This essay is an outré, madness, a tragic, cruel fantasy, an eruption of inner rage, on how the oppressed desperately dream of being the oppressor."[159]

The fact that what she cites as proof of a "revolutionary" homosexual agenda is actually a literary exercise – high satire – is nowhere mentioned. Forrester's editorial is filled will other calculated inaccuracies. For instance, she writes: "Did you know that the average life span of a homosexual is 39 years as opposed to 78 for heterosexual women and 76 for heterosexual men?"[160] But as

---

[155] Forrester is also the former director of Concerned Women for America of North Carolina and currently serves as its legislative liaison and media coordinator. See CONCERNED WOMEN FOR AMERICA OF NORTH CAROLINA (Spring 2008), at 5, http://states.cwfa.org/images/content / spring08ncnews.pdf.

[156] Senator Forrester is the sponsor of a state constitutional amendment, which he reintroduces each legislative session, to ban Gay marriage and to bar legal recognition of contractual relationships between Gays that might approximate marriage. See S. 13, 2007 Gen. Assem., Reg. Sess. (N.C. 2007), http://ncleg.net/sessions/2007/bills/senate/pdf/s13v1.pdf.

[157] Forrester inaccurately dates the piece to 1986. *See* Matt Comer, *Wife of N.C. State Senator Pens Hate-Filled Op-Ed*, Mar. 13, 2008, http://www.interstateq.com/archives/2621.

[158] Id. (quoting Michael Swift, GAY COMMUNITY NEWS, Feb. 15, 1987).

[159] Id. Again, Forrester misattributes the piece to "Mark" Swift. But as journalist Matt Comer points out, even this may have been a pen name. Id.

[160] Jim Burroway, *Certified Cameronite: Mary Frances Forrester*, BOX TURTLE BULL., Mar. 17, 2008, http://www.boxturtlebulletin.com/2008 /03/17/1647. This same misinformation,

journalist Matt Comer explains, Forrester draws these numbers from discredited studies, methodologically flawed, looking at the life spans of men with AIDS.[161] While these studies have been discredited even as to their relation to the effects of AIDS, Forrester, in typical right-wing fashion, conflates all Gay men with men living with AIDS. Also echoing *Der Stürmer,* Forrester notes that "societies that condoned homosexual behavior did not survive past one generation."[162] This statement is easily exposed as factually inaccurate in antiquity and modernity.

Religion as Culture War

It cannot escape observation[163] that Forrester's and Kern's assertions and Harper's and Nuxoll's[164] messages are linked directly to a pervasive religious paranoia that fuels anti-identity rhetoric and worse.[165] Religion was also a

---

echoing Nazi propaganda that Jews were physically inferior to Aryans, was also part of Sally Kern's speech. Id.

[161] The studies in question are by Paul Cameron, whose so-called scientific studies were reported by the Southern Poverty Law Center in 2005 to be "echoes [of] Nazi Germany." See *Report: Anti-Gay Movement Gains Momentum,* SPLC REPORT, June, 2005, http://www.splcenter. org/center/splcreprt/artocle.jsp?aid=152. The SPLC was too generous. Cameron's accounts are not merely "echoes"; he is, in fact, one of Nazi Germany's greatest revisionists.

[162] See Comer, *supra* note 157.

[163] The term "Culture War" here is an allusion to Justice Scalia's dissent from *Romer v. Evans* (in which the Court struck down as a violation of equal protection a Colorado constitutional amendment that repealed all state and municipal antidiscrimination protections for LGBT people [and for LGBT people *only*]), in which he begins with his famous *Kulturkampf* reference. Romer v. Evans, 517 U.S. 620, 636 (1996) (Scalia, J., dissenting). I've always found this reference by a famously Catholic judge to be exceedingly odd. The word means literally "culture struggle" or "culture war." But it refers to a particular episode in German history: the German government's suppression of the Roman Catholic Church (for refusal to go along with Bismarck's nationalistic policies). Church suppression of this kind would violate the religion clauses of the First Amendment, and presumably Scalia, as a Catholic, would want the federal government to step in if such suppression took place at the state level.

[164] Harper's message was explicitly religious, and at least the *Nuxoll* concurrence believed Nuxoll's message to be religious, defending it by finding that "[t]here is a significant difference between expressing one's religiously-based disapproval of homosexuality and targeting LGBT students for harassment. Though probably offensive to most LGBT students, the former is not likely by itself to create a hostile environment." See Nuxoll *ex rel.* Nuxoll v. Indian Prairie Sch. Dist. No. 204, 523 F.3d 668, 679 (7th Cir. 2008) (Rovner, J. concurring). The fact that both teens were represented by the Alliance Defense Fund is solid evidence that their messages were part of a larger religious initiative.

[165] The examples I cite at this point in the discussion are just that, merely examples, and the actual recitation of such libelous claims could go on ad infinitem. My stellar research assistants filled three large three-ring binders with claims about Gays ranging from inflated incomes to the routine consumption of blood. As in Nazi anti-Semitism, a predominant theme in right-wing Christian anti-Gay rhetoric is that Gays are degenerate and depraved;

weapon in Julius Streicher's arsenal. Streicher argued: "To my mind, a good German is a good Christian. Instead of continuing a system which divides Christian children and teaches them different religious beliefs, we should unite our teaching and our educational goals. Let them all learn together that our worst enemy is the Jew."[166]

Echoing (in fact, predating) Harper and Kern, televangelist Pat Robertson exhorts: "Homosexuality is an abomination. The practices of those people is [*sic*] appalling. It is a pathology."[167] And Robertson all but coined the sentiment that Judge Posner could not bring himself to label anti-Gay when Robertson decreed that "[t]he term gay is the most serious misuse of the English language. They're not gay, they're very, very depressed and miserable."[168] Warning that hurricanes could hit Orlando, Florida, because of Gay events held there, Robertson laid bare the eerie *Der Stürmer* link between anti-Gay and anti-Semitic hate: "[T]he acceptance of homosexuality is the last step in the decline of *Gentile* civilization."[169] The religious warfare is not merely implicit. Robertson has warned, "[Gays seek] to destroy all Christians."[170] Likewise, Jerry Falwell warned that "the homosexual steamroller will literally crush all decent men, women, and children who get in its way … and our nation will pay a terrible price!"[171] Streicher blamed the Jews for the world wars and for calamities of his day.[172] Both Robertson and Falwell blamed Gays for the terrorist attacks on the World Trade Center, and Robertson blamed Gays for the fact that Hurricane Katrina destroyed much of New Orleans.[173] Powerful religious leaders use their

> that they are child molesters (committing 80% of all child molestations by one libelous report); are sexually depraved; and want to undermine home and family. Such assertions chillingly recall the blood libel used for centuries to instigate pogroms against Europe's Jews and, eventually, the Holocaust itself. The essence of the blood libel, a myth with obscure origins in the Dark Ages, is that Jews must be feared and ultimately destroyed because they lure children to their destruction. So, too, for Gays.

[166] VARGA, *supra* note 151, at 109.

[167] *700 Club* (Christian Broadcasting Network television broadcast June 6, 1988) (quote available at http://gainesvillehumanists.org/patr.htm).

[168] *The Religious Right and Anti-Gay Speech: Messengers of Love or Purveyors of Hate?*, http://www.wiredstrategies.com/robertson.html [hereinafter *Religious Right*].

[169] Id. (quoting Pat Robertson from TIME magazine, Oct. 26, 1998) (emphasis added).

[170] PEOPLE FOR THE AM. WAY, HOSTILE CLIMATE 9 (1997).

[171] Id. at 15.

[172] The Holocaust History Project, *Short Essay: Who Was Julius Streicher?* http://www.holocaust-history.org/short-essays/julius-streicher.shtml (last visited Apr. 21, 2009) (indicating that Streicher reported that the Jews had murdered the king of Yugoslavia [whose murderer was not Jewish]).

[173] *Rev. Falwell Blamed for Terrorist Attacks: Partial Transcript of Comments from the September 13, 2001 Telecast of 700 Club*, http://www.actupny.org/YELL/falwell.html (last visited Apr. 21, 2009); Posting of Dan Savage to Slog News and Arts Blog of the Stranger, http://slog.thestranger.com (Sept. 13, 2005, 10:51 PDT).

clout to sway elections, too. Jerry Falwell publicly denounced former vice president Al Gore for "endors[ing] deviant homosexual behavior … attempting to glorify and legitimize perversion."[174] Senator John McCain, having publicly denounced Jerry Falwell, who declared that "God Hates Homosexuality" in the 2004 election, made highly publicized amends with the televangelist in the run-up to the 2008 election.[175] McCain received the endorsement of another anti-Gay mastermind, televangelist John Hagee, in the 2008 race.[176]

Gary Bauer, who heads the right-wing Family Research Council, has warned that "involvement in homosexuality can kill you."[177] The anti-Gay speech that everyone from the ACLU to the Alliance Defense Fund is defending certainly can. Benjamin Matthew Williams, the thirty-one-year-old white supremacist who entered the home of a Gay couple in northern California and shot them to death in their bed, defended his actions by asserting, "I'm not guilty of murder. I'm guilty of obeying the laws of the creator."[178] Like young Tyler Harper, Williams believes that God has condemned homosexuals. Williams also believes that the biblically endorsed punishment for the "sin" of homosexuality is death. It is more than merely trivial that the staunchest opposition to laws curbing anti-Gay rhetoric in other democracies comes from religious groups.[179] In the United States, also, powerful religious interest groups, like the Alliance Defense Fund, are the staunchest defenders of anti-equality speech, especially speech attacking Gays, in schools and elsewhere.[180] Whatever else may remain of the "Wall of Separation," there is no separation in this.[181]

---

[174] *Religious Right, supra* note 168.

[175] Libby Quaid, *McCain's Sharp Tongue: An Achilles Heel?* HUFFINGTON POST, Feb. 16, 2008, http://www.huffingtonpost.com/2008/02/16/mccains-sharp-tongue-an_n_87012.html.

[176] Posting of Max Blumenthal to The Nation: State of Change Blog, http://www.thenation.com/blogs/campaignmatters (June 2, 2008, 6:50 EST). Among other things, Hagee has said that the Anti-Christ "will be a homosexual Jew." Id.

[177] Candace Chellew, *Esqueertology: Gay Christians' Right to Hope*, http://www.whosoever.org/v3i4/hope.html (last visited Apr. 21, 2009) (quoting Gary Bauer).

[178] Mike Hudson, *Anti-gay Violence Frequent Across the Nation, Activists Say*, ROANOKE TIMES, Sept. 30, 2000, http://rtonline1.roanoke.com/rt_specials/shooting/story19.html.

[179] Richard Roth & Ruth Gledhill, *Inciting Hatred Against Gays Could Lead to 7 Years in Prison*, TIMES (London), Oct. 9, 2007.

[180] Alliance Defense Fund News Center, *ADF Attorneys Appeal Poway "T-Shirt" Case to U.S. Supreme Court*, Oct. 27, 2006, http://www.alliancedefensefund.org/news/story.aspx?cid=3902 (noting that ADF attorneys represented Chase Harper); Alliance Defense Fund News Center, *ADF Attorney Available to Media After Hearing in "Be Happy, Not Gay" Case*, Apr. 3, 2008, http://www.alliancedefensefund.org/news/story.aspx?cid=4459 (noting that ADF attorneys represented Alex Nuxoll).

[181] The extent to which the religious origins of anti-Gay initiatives and speech should further insulate those initiatives and speech is debated. See, e.g., Kristi L. Bowman, *Public School Students' Religious Speech and Viewpoint Discrimination*, 110 W. VA. L. REV. 187 (2007); George W. Dent,

The Nazis proved over and over again that words were necessary to debase prey and legitimize lies and to encourage complicity in crimes. Their slogans were incitement, a saturation propaganda that normalized the subhuman status of the "other" (in the case of the Nazis, Jews, *and* homosexuals).[182] The Religious Right campaign against Gays understands propaganda as well as the Nazis did. Once their slogans are part of everyday reality, "the deviant (in sociological terms) ... [will] stand out in bold relief."[183] Is it any wonder that Larry King is dead, that Sean Kennedy is dead, that countless, nameless others are dead? Of course, words alone did not kill them. That is a simplistic defense that does not deserve credibility. Words alone did not kill them, but a social environment of hate, of which words are a part, cosseted their killers in contextual support. As Andrea Dworkin observed of German police who murdered Jews, "[T]he social environment ... made them heroes or good soldiers or good Germans or just one of the ... boys."[184] "Jew" (then and now), like "Gay" (then and now), was a word that stigmatized and killed. Isaiah Berlin made the connection: "The Nazis were led to believe by those who preached to them by word of mouth or printed words that there existed people, correctly described as subhuman.... [I]f you believe it, because someone has told you so, and you trust this persuader, then you arrive at a state of mind where, in a sense quite rationally, you believe it necessary to exterminate Jews."[185] Religious or otherwise, anti-identity speech is more than viewpoint or abstraction; it is dangerous. Coercion is not a viewpoint. Incitement is not a viewpoint. Neither is murder.

SPEECH AND EQUALITY

Once anti-identity speech is regarded as action inducing harm, a speech theory that has its foundation in equality can emerge. No group systematically shamed, degraded, and dehumanized can possess equality. German courts manipulated free speech doctrine in many of the same ways it is currently manipulated in the United States. The German courts held that only

---

Jr., *Civil Rights for Whom? Gay Rights Versus Religious Freedom*, 95 Ky. L. J. 553 (2007); John E. Taylor, *Why Student Religious Speech Is Speech*, 110 W. Va. L. Rev. 223 (2007).

[182] Because the general orientation of history is heterosexual, the Nazis' Gay victims often are historically invisible, but important scholarship chronicling the mass murder of Gays in the Holocaust does exist. See, e.g., Richard Plant, The Pink Triangle: The Nazi War Against Homosexuals (1986).

[183] Dworkin, Scapegoat, *supra* note 130, at 149 (2000).

[184] Id. at 151.

[185] Id. at 141.

individuals could be libeled, thereby protecting favored groups but allowing powerful, socially dominant groups to systematically degrade others. This particular speech doctrine contributed directly to the rise of the Nazis.[186]

Certainly, the doctrine espoused by the German courts made possible the systematic defamation of Jews in ways that cast them in ill-repute and made them easy scapegoats. When the Allies occupied Germany, they had to confront this problem head-on. They did so quite reasonably, by licensing German presses.[187] This was particularly the case in the American zone. When these presses published material inconsistent with the Allied agenda, the licenses were revoked. There was also school curriculum reform to combat the Nazi ideology among German youth.

In the United States, viewpoint theory says nothing whatever of equality. It does not take equality into account. What makes a viewpoint is a matter of power. Power hierarchy, subordination and domination, is the stuff U.S. law is made of. Gay people are subjugated in this country, relegated to a lesser caste, precisely because it is the viewpoint, so expressed, of powerful people. The reason proposing regulation of coercion and incitement is cast as viewpoint discrimination is precisely that powerful people disagree with it.[188] There is certainly genuine social disagreement about whether Gay people should be able to exist as Gay people.[189] Neither ten years of *Will & Grace* nor four seasons of *Queer Eye for the Straight Guy* has changed that. But the content/viewpoint approach obfuscates the fact that the focus on anti-identity speech as a discrete category of harmful speech is not content-based. It is harm-based – focused entirely on the harm in action that the speech produces.[190]

In *Nuxoll*, Judge Posner's principal departure from the approach taken by the *Harper* majority is summed up in his belief that

> people do not have a legal right to prevent criticism of their beliefs or for that matter their way of life. There is no indication that the negative comments that the plaintiff wants to make about homosexuals or homosexuality names or otherwise targets an individual or is defamatory. Anyway, though

---

[186] See David Riseman, *Democracy and Defamation: Control of Group Libel*, 42 COLUM. L. REV. 727, 728–730 (1942).

[187] See JOHN GIMBEL, THE AMERICAN OCCUPATION OF GERMANY: POLITICS AND THE MILITARY, 1945–1949, at 246–247 (1968).

[188] I don't mean to make this personal. I'm not suggesting that every individual bigot is powerful. But I am suggesting that, as a matter of social hierarchy, white, heterosexual, male bigots are powerful as a class and that the law scaffolds that power. Academic apologists for the state of the law are there to buoy up the status quo when it begins to lag. Especially when they suggest that bigots are not powerful, they betray the magnitude of that power.

[189] Robert F. Nagel, *Playing Defense in Colorado*, FIRST THINGS, May 1998, at 34, 34–35.

[190] The most common forms of harm are coercion and incitement, as I have explained.

Beauharnais v. Illinois has never been overruled, no one thinks the First Amendment would today be interpreted to allow group defamation to be prohibited.[191]

Judge Posner is quite wrong in his assessment that statements denigrating Gays are not defamatory. But he is also wrong, as a matter of theory, in his point of departure. Posner's concentration on defamation and its theory is only half the story. The theory of group defamation does not adequately reflect what is accomplished through anti-identity speech. Defamation law survives, of course, as it is applied to individuals, its derivative applications to groups in *Beauharnais v. Illinois* perhaps having been discredited, especially insofar as group libel claims are concerned. Since *New York Times Co. v. Sullivan*,[192] safeguards against group-based defamation have been severely circumscribed out of fear that laws against group defamation may compromise legitimate expressions of political viewpoint.[193] In this sense, group defamation is approached as a theory about the expression of ideas, which it inevitably is. It is not – overtly, anyway – a theory about discrimination, which is at the heart of the controversy over anti-identity messages. Discrimination accomplished through words, even insomuch as it expresses a viewpoint, has never been shielded from legal regulation by the First Amendment.

Discrimination and inequality have always, in a very real sense, been the product of something somebody said. "We don't serve blacks here,"[194] "No Jews,"[195] "Walk more femininely, talk more femininely, dress more femininely, wear makeup, have your hair styled, and wear jewelry,"[196] and "Fuck me or you're fired"[197] are all verbal expressions of certain viewpoints. All have been held regulable. All speech expresses some idea[198]; as Justice Holmes observed,

---

[191] Nuxoll *ex rel.* Nuxoll v. Indian Prairie Sch. Dist. No. 204, 523 F.3d 668, 672 (7th Cir. 2008) (citations omitted).

[192] 376 U.S. 254 (1964).

[193] It should not be overlooked that the evolution of defamation law in the United States tracks its treatment by German courts as the Nazis rose to power. German courts generally held that only individuals could be defamed, not groups. David Riseman explains how this approach to the law of defamation was instrumental in the Nazi campaign to subordinate Jews and to impose inferiority systematically through mass propaganda campaigns. See Riseman, *supra* note 186, at 728–29, 1282.

[194] See, e.g., Blow v. North Carolina, 379 U.S. 684 (1965) (finding that a restaurant serving "whites only" violated the Civil Rights Act of 1964).

[195] This sort of segregation was common, of course, to Germany in the Nazi era.

[196] Price Waterhouse v. Hopkins, 490 U.S. 228, 235 (1989) (Brennan, J., concurring) (Justice Brennan believed such statements constituted sex stereotyping in violation of Title VII).

[197] Stockett v. Tolen, 791 F. Supp. 1536, 1543 (S.D. Fla. 1992).

[198] This seemed to be a bedrock First Amendment principle until the dissenters in *Morse v. Frederick* (the famous "Bong Hits 4 Jesus" case) questioned whether Frederick's speech was

"A word is not a crystal, transparent and unchanged, it is the skin of a living thought and may vary greatly in color and content according to the circumstances and the time in which it is used."[199] But we, today, recognize certain expressions and the acts they constitute – acts of discrimination – as affronts to the equality norm embodied in the Fourteenth Amendment. They are more than the expression of an idea; they are discriminatory acts that violate the Constitution. Words that are more than mere words – words whose expressions of contempt and discriminatory animus are then acted out in *real* manifestations – are constitutionally suspect and regulable. The law's concern is not with what the speech says (at least not only that) but with what it *does*.

Because anti-identity speech is at once both defamation and discrimination,[200] a substantive equality theory of group defamation would necessarily center on the subordination (the harm) accomplished through the dissemination of the anti-identity message – inequality in verbal form. The dissemination of anti-identity messages about historically marginalized groups facing systemic and systematic disadvantage creates social inequality, which becomes political and legal inequality. Without the prejudice perpetuated by anti-identity expression, power hierarchies could not exist, and systems of social subordination that scaffold power through the promotion of inequality would not exist. Inequality of opportunity is controlled through the coercive imposition of a lower caste status. The impossibility of equality of opportunity in an atmosphere of derision and contempt is exactly what the *Harper* majority recognized[201] – as did Judge Posner,[202] although he missed entirely the connection between the atmosphere of contempt and the speech that creates the atmosphere.

Speech that says, quite authoritatively because it encounters no official resistance, that a group is second-class or no-class is precisely how caste systems are built and maintained. Words create the hierarchies and people fill them. If we are ever to reach the heart of darkness where the Heteroarchy is made to seem

---

not simply "nonsense," lacking communicative value. Morse v. Frederick, 127 S. Ct. 2618, 2649 (2007) (Stevens, J., dissenting).

[199] Towne v. Eisner, 245 U.S. 418, 425 (1918).

[200] By this I mean that anti-identity speech cannot say what it says without also *doing* what it says – which is the coercive imposition of inferiority through words. As Catharine MacKinnon rightly notes, not all speech has this power to be both speech and action simultaneously, but anti-identity speech assuredly does. See CATHARINE A. MACKINNON, ONLY WORDS 12–13 (1993).

[201] Harper v. Poway Unified Sch. Dist., 445 F.3d 1166, 1178–1179 (9th Cir. 2006) vacated, 549 U.S. 1262 (2007).

[202] Nuxoll *ex rel.* Nuxoll v. Indian Prairie Sch. Dist. No. 204, 523 F.3d 668, 671–672 (7th Cir. 2008).

reasonable and natural – inevitable – if we are ever to reach this place where pulverization of the marginalized is not only condoned but encouraged, we must deal with the problem of anti-identity speech. The most reasonable way to do that is to admit that anti-identity expressions offend the equality norm and can thereby be restricted consistent with the First Amendment free speech norm. To put it another way – in the accepted parlance of the courts – dedication to equality and an understanding of how anti-identity speech obliterates hope of equality for people in the aforementioned ways create the compelling interest necessary to abridge the fundamental right of free speech (or to take discrimination in verbal form outside the expressive paradigm altogether).[203]

Of course, there is the problem of narrow tailoring. A case like *Harper*, which deals only with restrictions of anti-identity speech in public schools – realizing that young people are vulnerable and impressionable; still exploring their identities, they are at the greatest risk of destruction from attacks on their identity; and they are in this peculiar environment where they cannot escape attack – ought to satisfy this type of balancing quite easily. The resulting regulation is narrowly tailored to achieve the compelling interest in protecting the equality of identified, usual targets of anti-identity speech in a setting where they are perhaps most vulnerable to its effects. In other situations, less discrete, the balancing would still be performed. In some cases, bigoted speech might still prevail, but at least the constitutional balancing would be a fairer fight, including two recognized and legitimate constitutional rights – speech and equality – not merely the right of free speech juxtaposed against some vague notion of civility, "[m]utual respect and forbearance."[204] The operative difference in focus of current defamation theory and a substantive equality approach to the same is the all-important shift in focus from the *viewpoint expressed* to the *harm enacted* by that same expression – lived realities versus theoretical abstractions. When the problem is conceptualized this way – realistically – the constitutional balance shifts, and equality has a fighting chance.

A substantive equality approach does not require a total subversion of current First Amendment theory.[205] The theoretical underpinning of First

---

[203] It seems to me that sexual harassment law is an example of a category of speech being excepted from the usual First Amendment paradigm. So far as I know, no sexual harassment defendant has claimed successfully that his or her sexually charged expression is protected by the First Amendment.

[204] *Nuxoll*, 523 F.3d at 672.

[205] In fact, although he is not particularly sympathetic to the anti–hate speech movement, Professor Kenneth Karst's observation that "[t]he principal of equality ... is not just a peripheral support for the freedom of expression, but rather part of the 'central meaning of the First Amendment'" is salient. Kenneth L. Karst, *Equality as a Central Principle in the First*

Amendment theory, the principle that there is, under the First Amendment, no false idea,[206] is not jettisoned. Rather, a substantive equality approach to speech theory simply recognizes that there is another constitutional principle, that of equality under the Fourteenth Amendment, that has heretofore been absent from the analysis. The idea that some people are inherently inferior may be just fine under the First Amendment as a private opinion, but its authority as a privileged basis for public policy evaporates – is in fact rejected outright by the Constitution's espoused commitment to equality under the Fourteenth Amendment. This would not mean that ideas contrary to equality could not be expressed, only that their expression would not be effectively off-limits or out of the bounds of constitutional inquiry or regulation. An expressive means of practicing or effectuating inequality (enacting it) has never been recognized as an exception to the equality norm.[207]

In countries where atrocities are not consigned to a national amnesia, the words and symbols of subordination – the same words and symbols considered to be merely offensive viewpoints in the United States – are treated as acts and as instrumentalities of acts. They are held accountable for the realities they create.[208] In the international instruments that have emerged since World War II, subordinating prejudices are condemned as false.[209] The law does not ignore them; it confronts them. The law recognizes that subordination is an action, as well as a viewpoint, and that subordination accomplished through words is no less subordination. Take, for example, the International Convention on the Elimination of All Forms of Racial Discrimination, which requires all state parties to "declare an offence punishable by law

---

Amendment, 43 U. CHI. L. REV. 20, 21 (1975) (quoting N.Y. Times v. Sullivan, 376 U.S. 254, 273 [1964]).

[206] Gertz v. Robert Welch, Inc., 418 U.S. 323, 339–340 (1974).

[207] See Norwood v. Harrison, 413 U.S. 455, 470 (1973) ("Invidious private discrimination may be characterized as a form of exercising freedom of association protected by the First Amendment, but it has never been accorded affirmative constitutional protections"). My argument here and in the following paragraph is particularly indebted to Catharine MacKinnon. See MACKINNON, *supra* note 200, at 71–76.

[208] It is interesting to know that Telford Taylor, a U.S. prosecutor in the Nuremberg Trials, believed that Julius Streicher was wrongly sentenced to death: "There was no accusation that Streicher himself had participated in any violence against Jews, so the sole (and difficult) legal issue was whether or not 'incitement' was a sufficient basis for his conviction." TELFORD TAYLOR, THE ANATOMY OF THE NUREMBERG TRIALS: A PERSONAL MEMOIR 376 (1992). In fact, what Nuremberg showed emphatically was a connection between anti-identity saturation propaganda and genocide. Only the distinctly American hallucination that words have no meaning can explain Taylor's critique of Streicher's just deserts.

[209] See Stephanie Farrior, *Molding the Matrix: The Historical and Theoretical Foundations of International Law Concerning Hate Speech*, 14 BERKELEY J. INT'L L. 1, 3–4 (1996).

all dissemination of ideas based on racial superiority or hatred."[210] Also, an approach similar to the one I have outlined was adopted by the Supreme Court of Canada in upholding a provision of the Canadian criminal code that outlawed the dissemination of hate propaganda.[211]

Equality-based approaches to speech stand in stark contrast to the condition in the United States. But judicial understanding of equality and inequality from speech has not always been so stilted. The U.S. Supreme Court came closest to confronting that link in *Beauharnais v. Illinois*.[212] The majority opinion held that "a man's job and his educational opportunities and the dignity accorded him may depend as much on the reputation of the racial and religious group to which he willy-nilly belongs, as on his own merits."[213]

Even in dissent, Justice Douglas comprehended the basic relation between anti-identity speech and equality, writing:

> Hitler and his Nazis showed how evil a conspiracy could be which was aimed at destroying a race by exposing it to contempt, derision, and obloquy. I would be willing to concede that such conduct directed at a race or group in this country could be made an indictable offense. For such a project would be more than the exercise of free speech.[214]

Justice Douglas recognized that, in these situations, the pernicious speech is being restricted not for what it says, but for what it does. But neither majority nor dissent mentions the Fourteenth Amendment's guarantee of equality.

In fact, no speech case, before *Beauharnais* or since, has explicitly invoked an equality rationale as a basis for judicial decision making. It is no surprise that a Supreme Court intent on gender "blindness,"[215] and color "blindness,"[216] should also formulate a doctrinal edifice for speech that has as its foundation equality "blindness." The Court's intent to ignore inequalities and power structures reached dithering heights in *New York Times Co. v. Sullivan*, in which the Court brought the law of libel within the ambit of the First Amendment. Although it did not explicitly overrule *Beauharnais*, *Sullivan* is seen by many as the bullet to the head of group defamation law. But Professor Alexander Tsesis offers a particularly lucid explanation of how *Beauharnais* has survived

---

[210] International Convention on the Elimination of All Forms of Racial Discrimination art. 4, Mar. 12, 1969, 660 U.N.T.S. 195, 218–220.

[211] R. v. Keegstra, [1990] 3 S.C.R. 697 (Can.) (available in English at 1990 CarswellAlta 192).

[212] 343 U.S. 250, 262–263 (1952).

[213] Id. at 263.

[214] Id. at 284 (Douglas, J., dissenting).

[215] See, e.g., Miss. Univ. for Women v. Hogan, 458 U.S. 718 (1982).

[216] See, e.g., Parents Involved in Cmty. Sch. v. Seattle Sch. Dist., 127 S. Ct. 2738 (2007).

Sullivan – an explanation that I believe has not received enough scholarly attention. Tsesis observes:

> *New York Times* quotes *Beauharnais*, indicating its continuing precedential value. Moreover, even *R.A.V. v. St. Paul*, which was otherwise critical of a hate speech ordinance, quoted *Beauharnais* for the proposition that some categories of speech are "not within the area of constitutionally protected speech." 505 U.S. 377, 383 (1992). *New York Times's* effect on *Beauharnais* extends only to cases where group libels are directed at public personalities. New York v. Ferber, 458 U.S. 747, 763 (1982).[217]

Wherever one might come down on the vitality of *Beauharnais*, the truth is that the *Sullivan* Court had other options. The inaccuracies for which the racist police commissioner of Montgomery, Alabama, sued were extremely minor. To prevail in a libel suit, the plaintiff has to prove damage resulting from the untrue speech. The trivial inaccuracies in the *New York Times* ad criticizing racist police likely produced no such damage. Supporters of civil rights realized the police were racist; supporters of segregation refused to believe. Any discrepancies in the ad probably changed little. Moreover, the cause supported by the *New York Times* was of greatest constitutional import – it was the cause to advance racial equality, to destroy segregation. The Court just as easily could have concluded that the important, special nature of equality rendered the minor inaccuracies in the *New York Times* not actionable, instead of ruling that the special nature of public officials made them so. The *Sullivan* Court's refusal to even consider the equality implications of the case left the law of First Amendment speech and the law of Fourteenth Amendment equality entirely disintegrated.

Of course, speech authoritarians suggest that cases, like *Brandenburg*, in which the "ideas" of the Ku Klux Klan were protected,[218] naturally led to cases like *NAACP v. Claiborne Hardware*, in which the speech of Black civil rights agitators was protected.[219] In other words, we cannot protect the speech of those working for equality, like civil rights leaders of the 1960s, unless we also protect those who would threaten, terrorize, and incite the murder of those same leaders. But Catharine MacKinnon pulverizes this silly logic when she writes:

> Suppressed entirely in the piously evenhanded treatment of the Klan and the boycotters – the studied inability to tell the difference between oppressor

---

[217] Alexander Tsesis, *Regulating Intimidating Speech*, 41 HARV. J. ON LEGISLATION 389, 396–397 n. 57 (2004) (citation omitted).

[218] Brandenburg v. Ohio, 395 U.S. 444, 447–448 (1969).

[219] 458 U.S. 886, 915 (1982).

and oppressed that passes for principled neutrality in this area as well as others – was the fact that the Klan was promoting inequality and the civil rights leaders were resisting it, in a country that is supposedly not constitutionally neutral on the subject.[220]

Indeed, the Constitution does not require viewpoint neutrality in matters of equality. In fact, the Constitution requires that government not promote inequality. That guarantee does not require explication by way of an esoteric theory of interpretation of a "living" Constitution; it is textually explicit.[221] Any nation that has such a guarantee of equality has not only the ability but also the obligation to confront speech that creates and maintains a caste system among its citizens. The United States is no exception.

In the United States, however, the law of equality and the law of free speech are rarely seen as intersecting on the same plane – at least not by the courts or by those academics who believe in speech authoritarianism and who have come to monopolize free speech discourse. In most First Amendment speech jurisprudence, speech is treated not as an agent of equality, but rather as something detached and operating in some independent realm of existence. In this country, we will hear the Klansman speak because, as despicable as his message may be, we are told, he is engaging in sacrosanct "political speech." We will even allow him to goose-step through the neighborhoods predominantly inhabited by his targets because of his right to such free "speech."[222]

But no member of the Klan realistically believes that his marching and sheet wearing and cross burning will bring about a political shift in which African Americans are returned to shackles or even depart for Africa. In fact, dialogue between the oppressed and the oppressor cannot really exist in these circumstances. Those who create history and those who are dispersed outside of it simply do not speak the same language. No, the purpose of Klan activity is to send the haters' message to the hated: "Nigger, here is what we think of you; here is what we may do to you given the chance. We would replace this charred wood with your charred body. Live in fear!" This is no mere expression stopping in the abstract. It is quintessential anti-identity speech, and the anti-equality message it delivers is a real, palpable injury sustained by real, breathing human beings. Shielding this type of psychological battery as constitutionally protected speech makes the law of equality and the law of free speech as divorced, as disconnected, as disintegrated as they can possibly be.

---

[220] MacKinnon, *supra* note 200, at 86.
[221] U.S. Const. amend. XIV, § 1.
[222] See Collin v. Smith, 578 F.2d 1197 (7th Cir.) (holding that a Nazi party marching in the streets of a predominantly Jewish neighborhood is protected speech).

How did we get to this point? The modern law of free speech draws its essence from cases involving suppression of Communist speech during the McCarthy era.[223] The Supreme Court, in a vindication of free speech, ultimately ruled that Communists have the right to engage in anti-American government speech.[224] This conclusion, we are told, is supported by the history that shaped the free speech norm. And I believe that this is right. What does not follow as necessarily true is the conclusion that all speech must be constitutionally protected for the same reasons. For example, legal historian and free speech scholar Michael Kent Curtis has written a voluminous literature on the development of a robust free speech regime that should – and does – protect virtually all speech because all speech necessarily shelters an idea[225] and serve as a sort of insurance policy for "individual and political freedom."[226]

Curtis argues that a broad conception of free speech is absolutely necessary for the protection of minority interests and, a fortiori, that reconceptualizing free speech doctrine will destroy any hope for future progress. He cites his impressive historical scholarship as proof.[227] In his explication, there is compelling alarmist appeal. To the contrary, however, neither the history of the First Amendment nor its judicial development clearly points to that conclusion; and this is exactly what Professor Curtis's scholarship bears out (unintentionally). He writes:

> Many advocates of new restrictions on speech based on its ideas or point of view pay little attention to free speech history. As a result, while critics have

---

[223] Professor Michael Kent Curtis attributes this view to Catharine MacKinnon. MICHAEL KENT CURTIS, FREE SPEECH: THE PEOPLE'S DARLING PRIVILEGE 414 n. 1 (2000) (disagreeing with MacKinnon). Curtis has recently repeated this attribution in conversation with me. However, I arrive at this conclusion on the basis of an independent reading of the case law, with the understanding that *Yates v. United States*, 354 U.S. 298, 312–327 (1957), was the tipping point in the slide to *Brandenburg*. So far as I can tell, Professor MacKinnon does not cite *Yates* at all.

   Professor Alexander Tsesis also cites the debate over Communist speech as central to the development of modern First Amendment doctrine, but he makes no reference to the *Yates* decision. TSESIS, *supra* note 129, at 121.

[224] *Yates*, 354 U.S. at 318–321 (distinguishing *Dennis v. United States*, 341 U.S. 494 (1951) and holding that mere advocacy of belief was not enough for prosecution under the Smith Act).

[225] Michael Kent Curtis, *Critics of "Free Speech" and the Uses of the Past*, 12 CONST. COMMENT. 29, 64–65 (1995).

[226] Id. at 52.

[227] See generally, CURTIS FREE SPEECH, *supra* note 223, at 414–437; Curtis, *Uses of the Past*, *supra* note 225; Michael Kent Curtis, *Free Speech and Its Discontents: The Rebellion Against General Propositions and the Danger of Discretion*, 31 WAKE FOREST L. REV. 419 (1996). Professor Curtis wrote as a part of the symposium at which my ideas here were first presented, largely to refute the perspective I articulate in this chapter. See Curtis, *Be Careful*, *supra* note 34.

deepened our understanding by highlighting some of the costs of broad protection for speech that is evil, they have left the benefits of protection and costs of changing it in darkness.[228]

But Curtis's recitation of the past as though it were more than the past – as though it were preordained – obscures the ability of a different equality-based conception of free speech for the future to protect the free speech interests of the marginalized without doing the damage that is inherent in the current free speech framework. Gays should be suspicious of any approach, like Curtis's, that is backward-looking exclusively, requiring that the past take precedence over present, lived experience. Ordinarily, Gay people cannot afford to indulge in the luxury of asking the past to legitimate the present.

But in this particular instance, wiped clean of Curtis's postfigurative glosses, invocation of history actually proves my point. Consider the example of the plight of abolitionists in the antebellum South.[229] In the absence of a powerful free speech commitment grounded in equality, the South succeeded in suppressing the pro-equality speech of the abolitionists. Nobody, then or now, seriously contended that the abolitionists' speech was contrary to equality. The South understood why the speech suppression was necessary as surely as it understood, from the southern perspective of power, the necessity of the Civil War.

An equality-based speech system would have subjected suppression of abolitionist speech to the most stringent constitutional scrutiny. Through this lens, the justifications of the southern establishment collapse. The "emotional injury"[230] alleged by slaveholders because abolitionist theory was "offensive to their feelings"[231] is hardly compelling, especially when it is weighed against the equality interests of the voiceless slave, given voice by the abolitionists. So, under my system, we would have arrived at protection of the abolitionists without the supposedly necessary protection of the Klansmen. Why this would not be a preferable system is unfathomable to me. As for the fear that it will be impossible to tell the powerful from the powerless, Professor Curtis's scholarship also proves this false.

---

[228] Curtis, *Uses of the Past, supra* note 225, at 30.

[229] Id. at 35–40. Professor Alexander Tsesis explains (and I agree) that the suggestion that the abolition of slavery represents a historical triumph of the free speech system (the marketplace of ideas version, anyway) is a misinterpretation of history. See Alexander Tsesis, *Dignity and Speech: The Regulation of Hate Speech in a Democracy*, 44 Wake Forest L. Rev 497 n. 68 (2009).

[230] Curtis, *Uses of the Past, supra* note 225, at 36.

[231] Id.

Although the reasons given for silencing abolitionists were lofty – protecting the public peace and national unity – behind those reasons were the powerful economic interests of the slaveholders and the Northern mercantile classes who traded with them. In 1859, John Bingham, later the main author of section one of the Fourteenth Amendment, put it this way, "These gentlemen apprehend that if free speech is tolerated and free labor protected by law, free labor might attain … such dignity … as would bring into disrepute the system of slave labor, and bring about … gradual emancipation, thereby interfering with the profits of these gentlemen."[232]

Abraham Lincoln warned (more poignantly in my opinion) of the "proneness of prosperity to breed tyrants."[233] The difference in the condition of the tyrant and the slave (and those advocating for the dignity of Blacks) was apparent even then. As to the general fear that judges will not be able to distinguish adequately what is oppression in any given situation, I am drawn to Oliver Wendell Holmes's pithy observation that "even a dog distinguishes between being stumbled over and being kicked."[234] Is it too much to hope that judges are at least as discerning?

Consider, also, the comparatively recent example of suppressing the anti-war speech of Eugene Debs during World War I.[235] I support the notion that the free speech norm means that one may oppose wars; I have even written in opposition to war myself.[236] The rethinking of the free speech system in the way that I propose would not be a return to the "bad tendency" test that upheld Debs's jailing. This form of speech would still be governed by *Yates v. United States*[237] and contemporary precedent. It is outside the narrow realm of anti-identity, anti-equality speech as I have defined it. But even if we were to stretch, even if we were to force my round theory into a square hole, Debs might still win. He might win because my theory requires us to examine the power structure. Who has the power? Debs's speech is contrary to the government's own endorsement of the war. The government is the oppressor here; Debs is the oppressed. To suggest that protecting Gays from anti-identity, anti-equality speech means we must allow the government to suppress anti-war speech is to cast Gays on par with the power of the U.S. government. The assertion is ridiculous.

---

[232] Id. at 37 (quoting CONG. GLOBE, 36th Cong., 1st Sess. 1861 [1860]) (alteration in original).
[233] THE COLLECTED WORKS OF ABRAHAM LINCOLN 406 (Roy P. Basler, ed., 1953).
[234] OLIVER WENDELL HOLMES, JR., THE COMMON LAW 3 (1881).
[235] Debs v. United States, 249 U.S. 211 (1919).
[236] Shannon Gilreath, *Know Thine Enemy*, PRIDE AND EQUALITY, Jan./Feb. 2006, at 3 (discussing Gay servicemen and -women in the Iraq war effort).
[237] 354 U.S. 298 (1957).

Professor Curtis believes that suppression of speech based on injury that amounts to "hurt feelings, offense, or resentment"[238] will lead to the suppression of many types of speech that both of us would agree should be protected. He cites an impressive array of cases from First Amendment history. But this, again, is a reduction of anti-identity speech to mere "hurt feelings"[239]; it fails to distinguish between mere offense and real harm to the equality interests of the victim. The Court was confused about this (or obtuse) in *R.A.V.*, in *Texas v. Johnson*, in *Cohen v. California*, in *Terminiello v. Chicago*, and no doubt in other cases that Curtis would say were rightly decided. "[A]bolitionist criticism of slaveholders, jokes about political figures [assuming they were not also anti-identity speech], flag burning, wearing 'Fuck the Draft' on one's jacket"[240] are not imperiled by an equality-based speech perspective. People who may be "offended" by burned flags or the word "fuck" are not being attacked by such speech on the basis of a component of their core identity. To believe that they are is to see "identity" in the way that the powerful (whose identity is already protected) see identity: as an accumulation of entitlements to have things exactly the way they want them – pristine stars and bars, no expletives, or whatever the desire may be.

In conversation about my arguments here, a friend gave the following example in an effort to refute my theory:

> Any agitations against the status quo can be seen as an attack against the powerful. How is it that your rules won't end up protecting the powerful from merited attack? For example, what if unionists say, "CEO Smith is a capitalist pig and the blood of workers is on his hands?" Hasn't the CEO's identity been attacked?

This is an understandable reaction. It is understandable because it stems from the way the powerful have taught us to think about both free speech and identity. If we protect vulnerable minorities from anti-identity speech, surely this will mean that we will unintentionally insulate wrongdoers from justified impeachment. But this follows only if we fail to draw a principled distinction between speech used as a tool for democratic change and speech designed and utilized as verbal battery. The harm of anti-identity speech is different

---

[238] Specifically, Curtis writes: "The Court has refused broadly to find the fact that speech (not focused on a particular individual) that causes 'hurt feelings, offense, or resentment' is sufficient to strip the speech of constitutional protection. If such consequences were regarded as sufficient injury, much … expression … could be suppressed." Curtis, *Uses of the Past*, *supra* note 225, at 43 (quoting R.A.V. v. City of St. Paul, 505 U.S. 377, 414 [1992] [White, J., concurring]).

[239] This is a characterization of anti-identity speech that I have proved false in this chapter.

[240] Curtis, *Uses of the Past*, *supra* note 225, at 43.

in kind and degree from any harm inherent in general political unrest. For instance, if tomorrow an outcry against law professors arose – an outcry so resilient and prolonged that it became uncomfortable for me to be a law professor – I could renounce my profession; I could go to Tahiti and paint like Gauguin or assume whatever other profession struck my fancy. The same is true of the CEO in my friend's example. The CEO could change his anti-labor policies or just stop being CEO; there are a multitude of solutions for someone in that position.

But I cannot so easily relinquish my identity as a Gay man – in fact, it is impossible for me truly to relinquish it. I can pretend that I am other than what I am, but in the end I will simply be a Gay man closeting my true identity. Indeed, identity minorities are targeted precisely because of this inability to change identities. We are like the pariahs of the Indian caste system. It is impossible for us to transmute ourselves into a more acceptable caste, no matter what we do, no matter what we achieve, no matter how we pretend; that is exactly what makes us easy and comfortable targets. Therein lies the difference in speech targeting the CEO and speech targeting an identity group. The intentionality of anti-identity speech is not to get the target to change something about him- or herself. The intentionality is not social advocacy. The verbal predator knows that no meaningful change is really possible. Instead, the intention of anti-identity speech is to liquidate the target, to render him or her utterly powerless.

The failure to comprehend the difference is inherent in the power hierarchy itself. With power inevitably comes narcissism, and the invisibility of the victim in most First Amendment analyses of anti-identity speech is driven by a narcissism of which its perpetrators are mostly unaware. Maybe the vocabulary of vilification can really be understood, in an existential sense, only by its victims. This would explain why the defamation and discrimination accomplished through it are treated as if they don't matter by those who lack the experiences that animate the vocabulary. In this country, where the Holocaust is something that happened someplace else and where slavery and segregation of Blacks have been assigned to our peculiar brand of amnesiac history, the verbal and visual symbols that bring these traumas newly alive to their victims are considered perfectly legal – somebody else's civil liberty.[241]

---

[241] This, I think, explains why most academics who have written about speech from the pro-equality point of view have themselves been members of traditionally targeted minorities. See, e.g., DELGADO & STEFANCIC, WORDS THAT WOUND, *supra* note 71; DWORKIN, SCAPEGOAT, *supra* note 130; MACKINNON, *supra* note 200; Matsuda, *supra* note 69.

Because the speech authoritarians have dominated the debate, it is hard to believe that the absolutist view of free speech they advocate is wrong or that thoughtful departures from the absolutist norm are possible. But a free speech system that allows reasonable regulation of anti-identity, anti-equality speech aimed at people who face systematic and systemic powerlessness and subordination in contravention of their constitutionally guaranteed (and compelling) interest in equality is the *only* system that can lead to the vindication of that same interest. When the victims of anti-identity speech can finally assert human rights against devastating, victimizing speech, a rational understanding of the free speech norm will emerge, and Gays and Lesbians will finally have a shot at a dignified place in our country. We will be closer to an America where everyone matters – not just the powerful. Equality may mean something after all.

5

Pornography/Death

The Problem of Gay Pornography in a Straight Supremacist System

A weird life it is, indeed, to be living always in somebody else's imagination, as if that were the only place in which one could at last become real!

Thomas Merton, *The Seven Storey Mountain*

It was like life was a pornographic film.

Rodger McFarlane, *Gay Sex in the 70s*

Pornography, according to feminist theorist Jane Caputi, is "a worldview, a way of thinking and acting that sexualizes and genders domination and submission, from the bedroom to the war room, making domination masculine (even when a woman plays that role) and submission feminine (even when a man plays that role), and making both the essence of sex."[1] Professor Caputi may as well have been describing heterosexuality generally. As a political system, a system of governance, heterosexuality is as absolute as any monarchy, as dictatorial as any dictatorship, as fearsome as any terrorist regime; it is a system built upon the act of heterosexual sex, itself often explicitly violent, always implicitly so, constituted by aggressive intrusion, and constitutive of the philosophy of objectification through dominance and submission made sexual – experienced as sex – which is the ruling ethos of the world heterosexed. This philosophy of heterosexuality constitutive of and predicated on gender makes sexuality gendered, masculine over feminine (male over female in the heterosexual model), and gender – inequality – sexy.

The point of convergence of these two definitions in the analytic of gay pornography, specifically, reveals the paradox of "gay pornography": In gay

---

[1] Jane Caputi, Goddesses and Monsters: Women, Myth, Power, and Popular Culture 75 (2004).

pornography we see what heterosexuality is. A Gay liberationist critique of gay pornography claims the realization of this reality as its ground. From its perspective, that which is usually defended as liberation looks a lot like mimicry, cut from the same cloth as the argument for equality through assimilation, or for marriage, as such, as the vehicle for social acceptance. Gay pornography is predicated on the "truth," accepted as a priori good, that the heterosexual means of relation, always sexual by straight people's practice of objectification as sex, and objectivity as the mirror of this understanding of sexual relation, is the path to self-actualization. The Gay Self is replaced by this self, understood as the totality of Gay identity. In other words, *to be Gay is to be sex*, where sex is a practice of inequality.

The liberal defense of gay pornography, both social and legal, converges with this view of Gay identity. A career pornography lawyer once told me that Gays should be grateful that (heterosexual) pornography has removed some of the stigma from sex acts once deemed unnatural and deviant. In his view, pornography is a way that straights are educated about how pleasurable "sodomy" is, thus making straights less likely to support legal regimes that punish anal and oral sex. Gay pornography also, he said, is a way forward for Gay sexual liberation (especially for Gay men), normalizing for Gays the very sex acts about which we are taught to feel shame and guilt.[2] Finally, gay porn, by presenting enjoyable sex between people of the same gender, destabilizes conventional thinking about gender, which, admittedly, would be good for Gay liberation. In fact, gay pornography is said to be liberation, actualizing the sexual self that is the totality of Gay selfhood (from this more liberal heterosexual perspective).

Thus, gay pornography is defended even where heterosexual pornography is recognized as subordinating.[3] In 2000 the Supreme Court of Canada, which took Gay equality seriously, held that gay pornography could be legally prohibited in Canada under precisely the same-sex equality rationale it employed to uphold regulation of heterosexual pornography in 1992, in its decision in

---

[2]   This is not an unprecedented view. See Jeffrey G. Sherman, *Love Speech: The Social Utility of Pornography*, 47 STAN. L. REV. 661 (1995). See also the discussion of *Little Sisters Book and Art Emporium v. Canada* later in the chapter.

[3]   Pornography's most vociferous defenders, in my experience, are Gay men; the only men who seem to think pornography is more important than liberal male lawyers of the ACLU variety are Gay men. Put simply, Gay men love their pornography. It probably isn't surprising to many readers that pornography is a multibillion dollar per year business. It might surprise more readers to know that revenues from sales of gay male pornography constitute approximately half of that haul. See Mickey Skee, *Tricks of the Trade*, FRONTIERS MAGAZINE, Aug. 22, 1997, at 43. When you consider that Gay people (Gay men and Lesbians) are said to make up around 10% of the total population, that figure is even more astonishing.

Regina v. Butler,[4] namely that pornography harms the equality interests of its subjects/objects.[5] Some feminists, led by the Women's Legal Education and Action Fund (LEAF), the group that had successfully argued for the regulability of heterosexual pornography in *Butler*, argued that gay pornography should be excepted from the *Butler* equality standard. In a reversal of their articulation of the harm of gay pornography in *Butler*, in *Little Sisters Book and Art Emporium v. Canada*, LEAF argued that gay pornography produced no harms analogous to the harms inherent in heterosexual pornography. In fact, LEAF argued that gay pornography provided validation and affirmation for Gays, who otherwise had no voice.[6]

Similarly, "gay rights" organizations argued for a *Butler* exception because gay pornography allows Gays to feel good about ourselves. A brief for the appellant, Little Sisters Book and Art Emporium, argued:

> There is solid academic criticism of the equation of homosexual pornography with mainstream heterosexual pornography. Erotica produced for a homosexual audience does not and cannot cause the kind of anti-social behavior generally or through stereotyping and objectification of women and children that Parliament apprehended might be caused in heterosexual obscenity. While heterosexual obscenity is often misogynist, that cannot be said of homosexual pornography.[7]

And the following argument was made in a brief by Equality for Gays and Lesbians Everywhere (EGALE):

> Sexually explicit Lesbian, Gay, and bisexual materials challenge the dominant cultural discourse. They resist the enforced invisibility of our marginalized communities and thereby reassure us that we are not alone in the world, despite the apparent hegemony of heterosexuality. They reduce our sense of isolation. They provide affirmation and validation of our sexual identities which mainstream culture either ignores or condemns. In short, they help us feel good about ourselves in an otherwise hostile society.[8]

---

4 R. v. Butler, [1992] 1.S.C.R. 452 (Can.).

5 Little Sisters Book and Art Emporium v. Canada [2000] 2 S.C.R. 1120 (Can.). *Butler, supra* note 4, is by no means perfect. For a lucid analysis, see Ann Scales, *Avoiding Constitutional Depression: Bad Attitudes and the Fate of* Butler, 7 CAN. J. WOMEN & L. 349 (1994).

6 Factum of the Intervenor Women's Legal Education and Action Fund (LEAF), in the case of Little Sisters Book and Art Emporium v. Canada, S.C.C., File No. 26858, 27 September 1999, at 7.

7 Factum of Little Sisters Book and Art Emporium Factum, in the case of Little Sisters Book and Art Emporium v. Canada, S.C.C., 1999, at paras. 48 and 63.

8 Factum of EGALE, in the case of Little Sisters Book and Art Emporium v. Canada, S.C.C., 2000, at 7.

Like theorist-activist Christopher Kendall, I found myself wondering if any of these advocates had actually seen the pornography they were defending.[9] Kendall cites, as an example, readily available, "mainstream" gay pornography in which a straight man encourages another straight man to rape a Gay man.[10] Of course, the Gay man is depicted as enjoying the humiliation and pain.

If rape is now affirmation – if it looks, even from a "feminist" perspective, revolutionary – then the relevant query becomes: How can sex as violence – the graphic depiction of rape, or sex in the heterodominant model – be a "challenge [to] the dominant cultural discourse" when it *is* the dominant cultural discourse? Is the violence not violence, or not seen as violence, because it is experienced as (or seen as) pleasure? How does being raped by straight men comport with a liberation ethic? And does the analysis change if Gay men (as such, explicitly) are doing the dominating?[11]

An advertisement for the website straighthell.net shows a muscular young man stripped and hanging from handcuffs, obviously defenseless; he is grimacing, as if in pain. The caption reads, "Sexy Gullible Straight Lads: Stripped, Tied, Gagged, Spanked, and Fucked." Is this Gay liberation? As Susan Sontag asserted in the context of feminism:

[9]   See Christopher N. Kendall, Gay Male Pornography: An Issue of Sex Discrimination (2004). Kendall's brave book is the first serious look by a Gay male legal academic at the harms of gay pornography. Kendall's work is important because it creates a theoretical framework to apply sex equality to Gay men's lives. Kendall's work, and that of John Stoltenberg, on which it relies, along with that of Professor Robert Jensen, has, in multiple ways, made my work here possible.

[10] "Now, fuck that hard ass man.... Shove that big cock up there until he screams. Fuck him man, you know how bad he wants it. Just do it until he screams and you load him full of cream." Little Sisters Trial Exhibit 198, 1989:39. "The man's got a tight, tight pussy man," ... "Lean over and show this man your pussy ass" (1989:40).

[11] Professor Carl F. Stychin, for example, argues that, even when it reinforces ideas of male dominance, gay pornography does not have the same intent or effect as heterosexual pornography because of the context of stigma and social marginalization of same-sexuality and of Gays generally. See Carl F. Stychin, Law's Desire: Sexuality and the Limits of Justice 62–65 (1995). And although she reaches the conclusion that lesbian sadomasochism pornography at issue in the *Little Sisters* case did not merit an exception from the *Butler* standard, Professor Ann Scales argues:

> [L]esbian materials emphasize what I would call the "ethics" of lesbian sex. "Ethics" is a strange word to use, but I mean it in reference to the descriptive aspects of sexuality explicit in lesbian materials, wherein the authors go to some lengths to assure the reader that the participants are doing what they are doing because they really want to, because they are – dare I say it? – equals. Even in the S/M materials, there is an emphasis on negotiating for specific fantasies, for specific sexual practices, for specific endpoints of both fantasy and practice, and for subsequent return to equal status.

Scales, *supra* note 5, at 349.

The question is: what sexuality are women to be liberated to enjoy? Merely to remove the onus placed upon sexual expressiveness ... is hollow victory if the sexuality they become freer to enjoy remains the old one [based on objectification] ... the right of each person, briefly, to exploit and dehumanize someone else.[12]

Similarly, when Gays engage in or consume a mass-mediated version of sex that ritualizes dominance and submission, even when it is Gays who are doing the dominating, does that destabilize the Heteroarchy? Does it subvert heterosupremacy or reify it? Any defense of the use of the powerless by powerful people who would use them is a defense of tyranny. I'd like to say, here and now, that no defense of gay pornography is compatible with Gay liberation. No movement for real liberation can indulge in a double standard for human dignity; and any advocate who purports to defend gay pornography on liberationist grounds either does not understand what pornography is (or what is in it) or does not understand what liberation is. Objectifying sex, turning it into a thing, and then broadcasting it is a symptom of the social reality that fuses sex and objectification and that defines sex as a means to an end of social power. We call that reality, out of a need to differentiate it from homosexuality, heterosexuality. Wherever exploitation through enforced dominance, even when it is made to look like pleasure, is found, heterosexuality is found in operation.

THE MASCULINE ARCHETYPE

Dominance, as masculine identity, is celebrated in gay pornography in myriad ways. It is sometimes celebrated as the dominance by Gay men of straight men (the ultimate reclamation of masculine dominance denied Gay men by heterosexuality's gender hierarchy: man as fuck-er, never fucked). But it is more generally shown (and experienced) through the presence of the archetypal straight male image of the aggressive, dominant fuck-er.[13] Usually, this is no mere proxy or approximation; the protagonist of much gay pornography is understood as the straight man.[14] Visit any Internet site for gay porn and count

---

12 Susan Sontag, *The Third World of Women*, 40 PARTISAN REVIEW 180, 188 (1973).
13 The feminist philosopher Mary Daly explains that the word "archetype" is inherently contradictory. Archetype is derived from the Greek *archetypos*, which means "modeled first, as a model." Broken down into its component parts, *arche* and *typos*, "archetype" is exposed as a lexical contradiction meaning an "original replica." See MARY DALY, PURE LUST: ELEMENTAL FEMINIST PHILOSOPHY 78–79 (1984). Understanding this definitional contradiction sheds light on the sado-Self-annihilation performed through gay pornography. In other words, the straight man is *original*; the Gay man is but a faint impression.
14 Gay pornography exists in a context of social domination in which straights have unencumbered power over Gays. This power is pervasive political, social, economic, and physical

the titles that involve the word "straight."[15] They are legion because straight is the ideal; to be fucked by a straight man, understood as subordination to him, is taken as the apogee of Gay sexual experience.

Gay pornography is paradigmatically based on highly gendered concepts of male-over-female (and analogous male-over-subordinated-male) power. As Andrea Dworkin put it, "The excitement is supposed to come, in fact, from the visual reminder of male superiority to women in which homosexual men participate. Without that wider frame of reference, masculinity would be essentially meaningless."[16] In a 1979 interview with the *Gay Community News*, Gay writer Allen Young describes his resentment of this like-straight ideology of Gay pornography:

> For example, I've seen pictures of a guy jacking off to an issue of Playboy; in other words, a guy is looking at a naked woman and jacking off and I as a gay man am supposed to look at the picture and feel more excited looking at that boy because he's straight. The message is that a straight man is more desirable than a faggot. Obviously, this is a put down to gay men.[17]

Masculine identification is the principal theme of gay pornography in the same way that the masculine principle, which is the sexual superiority of men over women, is the principal theme of straight pornography. Gay pornography is the carnival house mirror reflection of straight male power found in the straight paradigm. Part of being a straight man in straight pornography, and in the coextensive heterosexual definition of what it means to be a man (gender's masculinity), is the ability to possess a woman sexually, to be the kind of man a woman wants (from the straight male perspective). It is this "man," this gender hyperbole, who is the hero of gay pornography too. The "feminine" – or non-hypermasculine – man is never celebrated. So even when no woman is present in gay pornography,[18] the straight man is celebrated in part for his relationship,

---

    power. Having the straight man inside Gay sex is a manifestation of this power and its incontrovertibility.

[15] Consider these titles from recent Gay porn releases: *Straight Men Fuck and Suck*; *How to Seduce a Straight Man*; *Straight Guys for Gay Eyes*; *Straight Men Taste Good*; *Gay 4 Pay*; *Straight Submission*; *Straight Guys Jerking*; *Bareback Married Men*; *Ream His Straight Throat*; *Almost Straight*; *Amateur Straight Guys*; *Straight to Bareback*; *Gag the Fag*.

[16] ANDREA DWORKIN, PORNOGRAPHY: MEN POSSESSING WOMEN 45 (1979).

[17] Id.

[18] Often, women are present. It is true in the case of pornography like that described by Young (id.), and it is especially true in the prolific college dorm/fraternity genre of gay pornography, in which "college girls" play the facilitators to get reluctant "frat boys" to "experiment" with same-sex sex. The ensuing sex between men is presented as serving the purpose of pleasing the women present; the Gay male consumers are simply the voyeurs in the room. A website, StraightGuysForGayEyes.com, markets straight men who fuck women "for gay men." This

socially, to her.[19] Other pornography presents straight men tricked into same-sex sex or driven to it by poverty. This is the cache of sites like Baitbus.com, which sells the fantasy of straight men cajoled into homosexuality in turn for promises of money or sex with women.[20] Gay men, clearly objects of straight derision and disgust, are shown to revel in sexual abjection, willingly participating in sex with straight men in spite of their obvious homophobia. One could also read such scenarios as instances in which Gays are again emulating the straight male practice of sex as inequality – as subordination. On sites like Baitbus.com, straight men are successfully "bought," thus prostituted and made abject in ways usually practiced on women by straight men. Because the Gay man is getting off in a way that is paradigmatically straight in such scenarios, one could say that there is a reversal of who the homosexual is.

Thus, pornography sexualizes every facet of Gay subordination. If you have a hierarchy of straights on top and Gays on the bottom socially/politically/legally, then that is what you get in gay pornography, literally: straight men on top and Gay men on the bottom, straight men fucking Gay men. The hierarchy is sexualized, so that the Gay man is shown to get pleasure from the power the straight man has over him. We're getting pleasure from the fact that they view us as lower and less human than they are. In this way, pornography, itself inequality, is the antithesis of liberation: It helps to create our civil inferiority.

The physicality of the men portrayed also reaffirms traditional notions of masculinity. Gay pornography tells us, as Jeffrey Escoffier explains, what desirable Gay men look like: They look straight.[21] They are macho, young, muscular, and, generally, have hairless bodies.[22] Gay pornography's vision of

kind of site is basically the Internet version of the kind of magazine Young was describing in the 1970s.

[19] Consider an online advertisement for the gay pornography website Suite703.com: "He's married to a woman, but that doesn't mean he won't fuck you in the ass." Also, bottoms (the receptive partners) in gay pornography are often referred to as "bitch" or "cunt" or "pussy." The obvious message is that the top would prefer to be fucking a woman, but that a Gay man is an acceptable substitution.

[20] All video available from Baitbus.com features the same theme: a "straight" man, conveniently walking by, is approached and invited into a waiting van, where a cameraman and a woman are waiting. The cameraman asks the "straight" man to submit to a blindfolded blow job from the woman. A Gay man is then substituted for the woman. When the "straight" man removes the blindfold at just the right moment, he responds with anger or disgust. But he is coaxed back into sex with the Gay man (always the bottom) by the promise of money.

[21] Jeffrey Escoffier, Bigger Than Life: The History of Gay Porn Cinema From Beefcake to Hardcore 144 (2009).

[22] Id. In fact, Escoffier hits only the tip of an iceberg here. Virtually every straight male power ideal is represented in Gay pornography. Certainly, there is the college jock or corn-fed American boy next door. But there is also the fetishized blue collar worker, the hairy muscle-daddy, and even the "fat" daddy.

the male ideal thus follows from the hetero-ideal of masculinity, but adds an important twist: In gay pornography the ideal Gay man, the Gay man understood and accepted as masculine (the only way in which Gay men, as such, can be acceptable), is "the boy next door who looked like they [*sic*] wouldn't ever do anything but be the best little fellows – the little businessmen, the good members of their community – and all of a sudden they'd just kiss each other, and all hell would break loose, and they'd just try to fuck one another to death."[23] This desperation for the fuck and the equation of fucking with Self-annihilation is what separates the Gay man from his straight idol, for whom sex is not Self-annihilation but actualization – an actualizing of the purpose for which he is born. And while I believe this observation to be entirely accurate, one should not overlook the actual grammatical construction of the quoted material. The actual quotation is "try to fuck *one another* to death." This assumes that Gay sex is not only suicidal, but also homicidal, as a means to *mutual* annihilation.

Whereas the straight man controls the fuck and exerts control through the fuck, Gay men are presented as controlled by the fuck, as being somehow desperate for it.[24] They fuck men they meet in the gym, the garage, the shopping mall, the classroom, even the doctor's office. This need for the fuck defines them, wildness incarnate, restlessness personified in the world. Nothing else is gratifying, not being a doctor, or lawyer, or stockbroker on Wall Street (see the Gay porn film *Wall Street*)[25]; nothing satiates but the fuck. This is the usefulness of gay pornography to straight supremacy. The stigma of Gay sex and Gay personhood as reducible only to sex – and the definition of that sex as antithetical to human becoming – once imposed from the outside, is now internecine. And as Andrea Dworkin observed, "When those who dominate you get you to take the initiative in your own human destruction, you have lost more than any oppressed people yet has ever gotten back."[26]

ARCHETYPAL OPPRESSION

The invidious system of dominance at work in gay pornography, capturing Gay political imagination and subverting Gay political energy, is not new. In heteroarchal societies, homophobia, the fear of homosexuality, has proved an

[23] Id. at 135.
[24] As Gay porn mogul Chuck Holmes, head of Falcon Studios, said, the sex is "fast, urgent, desperate sexual contact between two or more persons, as desperate as we can capture on film or video." Id. at 134.
[25] WALL STREET (Lucas Entertainment, 2009).
[26] ANDREA DWORKIN, INTERCOURSE 181 (1987).

incredibly effective tool for powerful men to use in the control of less powerful men, encouraging male-on-male group conflict in the name of masculinity.[27] In the Jim Crow South, for example, anti-Black racism was sexualized as a tool to encourage the terrorization and murder of Black men by white men. The terrifically successful propaganda film *Birth of a Nation* depicted Black men as rapists, transgressing the unquestioned property right white men had in all white women. The explicit transformation of the Black man, hypermasculinized as the rapist, pitted white men against Black men through the tacit implication of white men's effeminacy in the face of the Black man's new masculinity, understood as the capacity for sexual conquest by force. This challenge to white masculinity was met by anti-Black violence and death.[28]

In contrast to Jim Crow's manufactured rapists, Black men as slaves were, as Black radical writer Eldridge Cleaver acknowledges, emasculated.[29] This was, apparently for Cleaver, the worst possible fate; surely, loss of gender identity is the worst blow to the straight male self.[30] Cleaver's response to racist ambiguation of gender norms reveals the total brilliance of the system of straight, white male supremacy and of homophobia. The quest for a stake in the gendered power hierarchy controlled by straight, white men turned Cleaver into exactly what he was propagandized to be, a rapist. It was his status as rapist that sent him to prison, the ultimate ghetto to which Black men are still disproportionately assigned.

In 1968 Cleaver published *Soul on Ice*, a collection of essays he wrote while in prison. The book was quickly heralded as a masterpiece by literary critics. These mostly male, ostensibly straight critics, who had made of Norman Mailer a patriarchal poet laureate, were likely taken by Cleaver's self-conscious

---

[27] On homophobia in pornography see John Stoltenberg, *Pornography and Freedom*, in REFUSING TO BE A MAN: ESSAYS ON SEX AND JUSTICE (1989).

[28] Jim Crow violence certainly isn't the only example of sexualizing despised minorities through explicit hypermasculinization and implicit homophobia. Nazis, for example, propagandized male Jews in the same ways as partial justification for the Holocaust.

[29] ELDRIDGE CLEAVER, SOUL ON ICE 103 (1968).

[30] This is a dogma of heterosexual maleness not to be disputed. Its incontrovertibility was brought home to be in a recent conversation about Thomas Jefferson with a well-known Jefferson scholar. Even though this scholar has himself been acutely critical of Jefferson on slavery and other issues, my suggestion that Jefferson's sexual relationship with Sally Hemmings was the result of rape instead of successful seduction was too much for even an outspoken critic to bear. My argument that an enslaved woman, by definition lacking the legal capacity to consent, could never "consent" and that, in the absence of that consent, sex between white masters and Black slaves was nonconsensual was simply talked over, drowned out by increasingly indignant protests. Jefferson could be fallible in virtually everything else, but not in this most masculine realm of seduction. The brilliance of the patriarchal system of oppression through sex is that sexual coercion of women is romanticized as seduction, celebrated as an art.

fixation on and celebration of masculinity: Mailer in black face. Like Mailer, who once said that a great writer writes with his balls,[31] Cleaver is obsessed with his balls, seeing them as a symbol of the Black man's emergence from a long, imposed alienation from the gendered power structure of white privilege, lamenting, for example, "the naked abyss of negated masculinity, of four hundred years minus my Balls," which had been Black men's fate.[32] This feeling of alienation from the masculine power structure motivated not only Cleaver's rapism but also his rejection of and utterly homophobic attack on the Black civil rights advocate and Gay writer James Baldwin. It was Baldwin's gender transgression, his willful alienation from gendered power – the act of becoming rapable inherent in the straight man's understanding of homosexuality – that made Baldwin Cleaver's anathema.

Cleaver repudiates Baldwin in favor of more ideally masculine writers, like Mailer[33] and Richard Wright, describing Baldwin, and by extension all Gay men, as "deprived ... of ... masculinity" and "castrated."[34] Even Baldwin's prose is feminized as "perfumed," and in contrast to Mailer, a "tiger," Baldwin is a "pussy cat."[35] Richard Wright, whom Baldwin famously critiqued in *Notes of a Native Son*, is better than Baldwin for no other reason than that he was heterosexual and that his characters were thoroughly heterosexual[36] and that no "homosexual bisexual ... had fucked him in the ass."[37] Baldwin's criticisms of Wright are reduced to a jealousy of Wright's masculinity.[38] Baldwin, specifically, and all Gay men, generally, are thoroughly sexualized and overtly feminized in an effort to discredit them by suggesting that Gays want to be women:

> The case of James Baldwin aside for a moment, it seems that many Negro homosexuals, acquiescing in this racial death-wish, are outraged and frustrated because in their sickness they are unable to have a baby by a white man. The cross they have to bear is that, already bending over and touching

---

[31] Andrea Dworkin, Right-wing Women 41 (1978).

[32] Cleaver, *supra* note 29, at 206.

[33] Mailer unquestionably understands gender power in heterosexual terms. "I think one of the reasons that homosexuals go through such agony when they're around 40 or 50 is that their lives have nothing to do with procreation. They realize with great horror that all that wonderful sex they had in the past is gone – where is it now? They've used up their being." Norman Mailer, The Presidential Papers 144 (1964). Not surprisingly, then, Mailer also believes "[i]t's better to commit rape than masturbate." Id. at 140.

[34] Cleaver, *supra* note 29, at 103.

[35] Id. at 100.

[36] Id. at 106–107.

[37] Id. at 107.

[38] Id. at 109.

their toes for a white man, the fruit of their miscegenation is not the little half-white offspring of their dreams but an increase in the unwinding of their nerves – though they redouble their efforts and intake of the white man's sperm.[39]

At the same time, power is sexualized and gendered masculine.[40] Cleaver, the admitted rapist, exalts rape as an "insurrectionary act."[41] Indeed, Cleaver's "pride as a man dissolved" at about the same time that he, conveniently in prison, could no longer "approve the act of rape."[42] Cleaver's missive, clearly intended to be radical and proudly marginal, is instead a total buy-in to the patriarchal conceptions of power and justice, in which sexuality is political and sex is a weapon. It is his alienation from this system – forced by whites, as Cleaver sees it – that makes it difficult for the Black man to triumph over whites. Claiming the system, not destroying it, is therefore as essential to survival as repudiating homosexuality is.

In similar ways, Gay men, presumptively alienated from the gender power hierarchy, attempt to claim it as a method of empowerment, in pornography and in political activism that follows pornography's explicitly gendered understanding of power. As politics, this ideology is best represented in Bruce Bawer's book, A *Place at the Table*, heralded by liberals and conservatives alike as representing a responsible Gay politics.[43] Bawer tells his straight readers what they want to hear: Gays are most deserving of respect and dignity when we most closely approximate the straight ideal – when we look most like straight people.[44] Much in the same way that homosexuality became the

---

[39] Id. at 102.

[40] And allusions to the phallus as the central fixture of male power are only thinly veiled in his criticism of Baldwin: "Baldwin felt called upon to pop his cap pistol in a duel with Aime Cesaire, the big gun from Martinique." Id. at 99.

[41] Id. at 14.

[42] Id. at 15.

[43] See Bruce Bawer, A Place at the Table: The Gay Individual in American Society (1993).

[44] Id. at 51. ("If the heterosexual majority ever comes to accept homosexuality, it will do so because it has seen homosexuals in suits and ties, not nipple clamps and bike pants; it will do so because it has seen homosexuals showing respect for civilization, not attempting to subvert it"). Talk about unreal loyalties.

Bawer also criticized ACT UP for not being "clean-cut and wholesome" enough and attacked Gay studies programs as instruments of a subversive subculture. But his philosophy of unquestioning assimilation is perhaps best summed up in his admonition (again in reference to ACT UP) that Gays "should [be] *waving* American flags, not burning them." Id. at 39, emphasis in original. It's a directive that rings even emptier when you discover that it was made by a Gay man with the means to expatriate when the going got too rough; Bawer now lives in Norway. See www.brucebawer.com.

target of Cleaver's frustrated liberatory impulses, gay assimilationist politics says that the focus of anti-Gay animus should be on (and its existence blamed on) non-straight-acting Gays.

Gay pornography is less pretentious about this, but, tellingly, it makes essentially the same argument: You are powerful when you act like the oppressor.[45] The oppressor in the heteroarchal system is first and foremost the straight man. It is his power that is both feared and desired. Andrea Dworkin described this power as the combined power of self-possession, physical strength, terror, naming, owning, money, and sex.[46] This formula distinguishes the *real* (read: straight) men from the Gay men in gay pornography and in life.

Consider the following scene from the gay pornographic website rawrods. com. The scene opens with the protagonist, "Rock" (of the three men in the film, his is the only name we know), working on his laptop. Rock represents all that is most desirable about the pornographed male ideal, principally that he is not Gay at all – not really. He is bisexual, which means that, like a real man, he also fucks women. He is also the flick's straight man because he is a capitalist. Rock has the power of money. The two other men in the scene come to Rock because they need financial help. Rock makes his money by making pornography; so he is paradigmatically straight in that he has commodified sex and profits from it. On this point, though, the script is interesting, because Rock is not the character who proposes the exchange of sex for money. He hints at it, hesitantly. It is left to the Gay figures to offer themselves, underscoring that that is their purpose and casting the Gay men unequivocally as the "whores."[47]

---

[45] Consider recent films like *Revenge*, about the vengeful rape by a man of his lover's paramour, or *Men of Israel,* glorifying colonialism and militarism. Both films are from gay porn giant Lucas Entertainment. REVENGE (Lucas Entertainment, 2009); MEN OF ISRAEL (Lucas Entertainment, 2009).

[46] See Andrea Dworkin, *Power,* in PORNOGRAPHY: MEN POSSESSING WOMEN, *supra* note 16.

[47] I should acknowledge that "gay pornography" is something of a misnomer. The word "pornography" does not mean "writing about sex" or "depictions of the erotic" or "depictions of sexual acts" or "depictions of nude bodies" or "sexual representations" or any other such euphemism. It is derived from the ancient Greek words *pornē* and *graphos,* literally "writing about whores" (see DWORKIN, PORNOGRAPHY: MEN POSSESSING WOMEN, *supra* note 16, at 199–200). *Pornē* was the designation for the lowest of the sexual low: the brothel whore, freely available to all male citizens. The *pornē* were sex slaves. *Graphos* means "writing or drawing." So we get pornography: the graphic depiction of whores. I say "gay pornography" is a misnomer because originally, of course, pornography was the graphic depiction of women as whores (the *pornē*). Gay pornography must have come later. But it is still the graphic depiction of whores – male whores. That use of the adjective "male" is necessary to distinguish from those people defined as whores by birth (as Kate Millet observed: women). In gay pornography, a man takes the place of a woman. So perhaps there is no misnomer at all. This is made plain by the ubiquitous presence of the straight man (or his proxy the "straight-acting" Gay male) even in gay pornography. Whores exist to serve a man – all men – sexually.

As the scene progresses to sex, Rock disrobes to reveal his enormous cock, 10.5 inches and extremely thick.[48] Both of the other men begin to lick it and suck it. Rock starts to put on a condom, at which point the other men protest, "Raw ridin'only." That the sex is bareback (the subculture euphemism for anal sex without a condom) is important to the pornographic image.[49] It valorizes real men as those who fuck "raw."

A useful way of understanding the raw fuck, following on Dworkin's explication of the male power to terrorize, is to see the real threat of HIV to be one that is understood but, nevertheless, sought after. The terror of HIV exposure is transmuted by Gay men, alienated from the masculine power structure, into a kind of talisman of male power in reverse – a willing assumption by bottoms, who are at the greatest risk of being infected, of the top's ability to terrorize in this uniquely masculine, insertive way. The Gay bottoms claim some return to the gender system from which they have been alienated by claiming the possibility of HIV infection as a gendered gift.[50] It is also an element of the overt sexualization of racist stereotypes present in much pornography (the Black man as breed stud)[51] and amplified in this flick, in which all three men are Black (and in which the fraternal "nigga" is peppered throughout), and of the overt sexualization of careless masculinity. For example, Rock, the principal character, proudly identifies as "gangsta." The unprotected sex thus underlines what makes a man a man, a gangsta – taking risks, heedless of consequences, and breeding men in the way that women are bred, when men take the place of women.

The sex that follows is very rough. Rock pounds the smaller of the two visitors. The larger visitor then takes over – but only when Rock indicates that it is

---

A material difference in gay pornography and straight pornography is that in gay pornography the definition of "man" is up for grabs. The definition of "whore" remains quite constant.

[48] DWORKIN, PORNOGRAPHY: MEN POSSESSING WOMEN, *supra* note 16, at 15. Dworkin explains that the penis is a "symbol of terror." Id. at 15. The bigger the penis, the more damage it can do; perversely, in gay pornography, the more desirable it is.

[49] Barebacking conjures images of the North American cowboy and his quintessential masculinity so important to the iconography of American male power and to those who want to claim its legitimacy.

[50] For an illuminating look at the psychology of "bareback" culture, see TIM DEAN, UNLIMITED INTIMACY: REFLECTIONS ON THE SUBCULTURE OF BAREBACKING (2009).

[51] The myth of the Black man's big, black cock is exalted. Black men are routinely represented as thugs or as studs reminiscent of slavery propaganda. Latino men are routinely exoticized. Black and Latino men are shown more often than white men in bareback films. Even overt racism, as in the gay pornography of *Niggas' Revenge* (Dick Wadd Fetish Productions, 2001) is apologized for, as in the analysis of that film by Professor Tim Dean, who finds the "repathologiz[ing] of [racial] fetishism ... troubling" and wonders why, "the shift from a heterosexual to a gay context [doesn't] mitigate [the] sweeping critique of racial fetishism." See DEAN, *supra* note 50, at 158–159.

okay for him to do so. Rock, as the straight man, owns the Gay body he is using, and only he can grant access to it. Rock controls the action, directing how fast or slow the two men are to fuck as he watches. Rock then has one man lie on top of the other and proceeds to take turns fucking both of them. Rock then has the smaller man sit down on the other man's cock. Rock then proceeds to fuck the fucker. Rock fucks this bigger of the two men hard, telling him not to "bitch out" on him when the man begins to cry out in pain. The smaller man, while sucking Rock's dick, then fucks the bigger man, with Rock continuing to direct the action. Rock spits on his cock and tells the smaller man to lick it off. He makes him say, "I want that dick, Rock." Rock then fucks him again, while he is still inside the other man. Rock then fucks the other man again. Each time Rock pulls out, the men immediately start sucking him. The scene ends when the smaller man comes while Rock is fucking him. Rock and the other man then jerk off on the smaller man. The smaller man then licks the semen from their cocks. As the scene ends, one of the men asks Rock, "What about that money?" Rock responds, "Access granted." Rock, as bisexual, as capitalist, exacts sex as payment, and does it raw.

This claim to masculine power through celebration of the straight masculine ideal – either as celebration of the subordinating power of straight masculinity or denigration of Gay submission to it – is the predominating theme of gay pornography. It is also the currency of popular pornography websites. Sites like hazehim.com reinforce the idea that the man who does the fucking isn't Gay. The man who gets fucked or "owned" or "hazed" is treated like property. In an advertisement for the gay porn site hazehim.com, a clothed young man in a football jersey, his erection visibly protruding from the fly of his jeans, approaches another young man, stripped and on all fours, from behind. The caption over the head of the clothed man reads, "Your ass is mine freshman." The caption next to the stripped man reads, "Oh No!!! Here Comes the Quarterback." The college quarterback is, quite clearly, taken as the masculine, straight ideal. The hazing context allows for the fullness of masculinity's mystique. The quarterback might be homosexual, but it is more likely that he will fuck the other man in the context of hazing, as a form of degradation and punishment, not for his own sexual gratification per se. The fact that the fucker does not enjoy the fucking as sex, existentially, makes him more believably straight; and it makes the sex somehow sexier. Indeed, the fact that the sex is intended as violation makes it sexier, the stripped man's protest belied by his faintly visible smile.

As with the pornography from rawrods.com, the message in this pornography is clear: To be straight is to be in control. Since we don't actually know the sexuality of the fucker, he may be Gay, but nevertheless dominant, as the archetypal straight jock. The politics of assimilation is thus represented in the pornography, the pornography reified in the politics: Assimilation into the straight, masculine model is power. This politics may have found its pseudo-intellectual voice in the likes of Bawer, but it emerged as the dominant discourse on domination long before the advent of the gay neo-con. Jeffrey Escoffier explains that the rise of gay pornography in the hetero-model coincided with (if it didn't operate as a direct cause of) the "new masculine style" embraced by Gay men in the 1970s.[52] He observes:

> Rejecting the traditional idea that male homosexual desire implied the desire to be female, gay men turned to a traditionally masculine or working-class style of acting out sexually. Camp as an effeminized gay sensibility was out. The new style of gay men was almost macho – but macho with a twist. Macho and sexually provocative, the new style included denim pants, black combat boots, a tight t-shirt (if it was warm), covered by a plaid flannel shirt (if it was not), pierced ears or nipples, tattoos, and beard or moustache.... The Marlboro man, a cowboy, was the iconic masculine model.[53]

Escoffier opines that the sex Gay men were having in the seventies "eventually did make its way into video pornography."[54] But since gay pornography was around through the decade of the seventies, there is good reason to wonder whether the pornography dialogue didn't become the reality of sex, not the other way around. Escoffier quotes a conversation between Gay men in a bathhouse in the late seventies, reported by Martin Levine in his book *Gay Macho: The Life and Death of the Homosexual Clone*:

> "Yeah take a good look at that big fucking dick. Uh huh. Look at how big, long, and hard that fucker is. Yeah. That fucker is going to go up your fucking asshole. Uh huh. That big fucking cock is going to be plowing your ass, ramming and ramming your manhole. Shit you're going to be begging for more. Yeah. You want dick, fucker you want it?" At this point, a second voice chimed in, rasping hungrily, "Give me that dick, man. Yeah. Give it to me. Give me all of that man meat. Shove it down my hot throat. Yeah. Gag me with that huge tool."[55]

For Escoffier, this is the real-life sexual dynamic that became porn fantasy. But accurately, it is the pornographic reality that became all of gay reality, sexually speaking.

---

[52] ESCOFFIER, *supra* note 21, at 136.
[53] Id.
[54] Id. at 137.
[55] Id. at 137–138.

The autobiography of the noted Gay writer Edmund White makes this plain. In his *My Lives*, White gives an account of his life that follows from (and follows) his sexual relationships.[56] In fact, his life is related *as if it were sex*. The other things – his numerous and celebrated books, his friendships with famous people, his professorship at Princeton – are there, but they take a backseat to White's sex life. Most of the sexual relationships he documents are narrated as if they were scripted out of any gay porno. White experiences sex as a masochist and masochism as sex; submission to dominance is sexually arousing for him. Sometimes his sexual relationships are based explicitly on pornography, which is to say that pornography, usually in the form of video, plays a facilitating role. For example, White meets a twenty-year-old on the Internet and establishes a relationship with him through money and pornography: "I quickly discovered I could please him if I brought him a new porno video every week, which he'd fast-forward and freeze-frame at strategic places as I knelt on the floor between his legs."[57] But more often, the pornography was implicit, so hardwired into White's and his partners' understanding of what sex between Gay men is that its script was always running in their minds[58]:

> T invited me over to his place the first evening he was alone. When he opened the door the lights were off.... T was wearing nothing but his metal-cupped karate jockstrap and once he'd closed the door he instructed me to get on my knees and to lick around the edges.... He had me strip and then he pulled me down the metal stairs [to the basement], which were painful on my bare feet. No sooner were we downstairs than he ordered me back up to fetch my own belt.... I felt stupid (slavery made me stupid); only later did I realize that that was the point. The slave was a fuckup so he could be punished. The boutique website on slaves4masters.com was called "Stupidboy. com." There the confused boy, whose judgment was undermined and self-esteem was eroded by servitude, could spend his dollars on products (a genital cage, a locked-on butt plug, all the plastic wrap necessary for total mummification) which would render him all the more non-functioning in the real world, though more and more useful as a fool in constant need of correction. Because I took so long locating the belt I needed to be whipped with it right away.... T ordered me to kneel on all fours facing the wall.

---

[56] EDMUND WHITE, MY LIVES: AN AUTOBIOGRAPHY (2005).

[57] Id. at 134–135.

[58] Pornography seems to have this effect on straight men too. Pop singer John Mayer made the astonishing claim that he wasn't able to have sex with Jessica Simpson, something of the Marilyn Monroe of pop starlets, without having porn running in his head. See Playboy Interview: John Mayer, PLAYBOY.COM, http://www.playboy.com/articles/john-mayer-playboy-interview/index.html?page=2.

When I heard him rooting around looking for a rubber and lubricant in the stash beside the marriage bed, I glanced back over my shoulder. Furious, he sprang forward and beat my ass with my belt: "I told you to fuckin' stare at the wall, shithead!" A minute later he'd unrolled the rubber and was slamming his way inside me. He reached around to pinch my nipples. I felt so happy.[59]

White obviously feels safe in this world. His insecurity about his own body and sexual prowess[60] is obviated by the pseudo-safety pornography gives to push boundaries of sexual exploration while simultaneously providing avenues to live out internalized shame in self-flagellating ways. White's chronicle reveals the destruction of the authentic Self and the resulting captured consciousness that remains under pornography's aegis through the perpetuation and internalization of Gay-hating, the indoctrinization of which is a major heteronormative social project.[61] The straight hatred of Gays is internalized through and institutionalized in gay pornography via pornography's repetitive, catatonia-inducing script of Self-loathing, and it is reified in pornographic imitations in everyday life. Pornography creates the reality in which fucking is the where, how, why, and when of being Gay. And most of us die the way we fuck – in the Self-hate that pornography tells us to embrace. We do not belong to ourselves; we abandon our identity. This is the determinative reality of the ubiquity of the straight man in gay pornography. *His is the identity we want.* And the more violent and dominating it is – the straight-er it looks – the more we want it.

---

[59] WHITE, *supra* note 56, at 248.

[60] Id. at 56, at 227.

[61] At a lecture on this book, while it was still being written, I opined that the widespread dependence on pornography – its utter ubiquity – and its reiteration of the heterosexual paradigm prevented Gays from discerning that which might be authentically Gay. A young woman in the audience then asked me what Gay authenticity looks like. It is a fair question, or at least it seems that it should be; but I cannot be expected to know the answer. How could I know? I have never lived in a world where imagination is free of pornography's gruesome grasp. I want the transformative power of the porn-free imagination for Gay people – this imagination that can uncover the hidden meanings, hidden from us by the Heteroarchy, that can shape tomorrow in new and meaningful ways – that can uncover for us the authentic. This imagination could reveal a Gay life full and complex in the richness of its empathy. But instead of this richness we are impoverished by the fuck. And this poverty of the fuck leaves us with nothing of our own. We are left bereft of even a language to describe ourselves, relying instead on a straight vocabulary of subordination, calling each other "fag," supposedly as a term of endearment, but with an undeniably biting edge; or describing things that are worthless or stupid or banal as "gay" – "That's so gay." The key to uncovering Radical authenticity lies, I think, in the reality of Meta-Memory," explained in Chapter 6, this volume. Escaping pornification as a tool of the heteroarchal everyday will, however, be necessary to unlock Meta-Memory in its fullness.

Siding with the straight man, either by acting as his proxy or by being possessed by him outright, through the fuck, is a way of claiming a measure of the straight male dominance that is usually used to crush us. We see that in White's idealization of the aggressive straight male – his jock fetish. In pornography's twisted reality, to side with the abuser is to be less abused; it is a sexual Stockholm syndrome. Moreover, pornography's scenarios of loveless fucking underscore and validate the straight lie that Gays are not capable of love or worthy of it. This is *the* Lie that defines us. Trapped in this cycle, where utter dehumanization looks like empyrean, White explains how he was genuinely tempted by an offer to relocate to Amsterdam to become a man's human dog, to eat dog food and "to have a dog tail permanently attached some five inches into my asshole."[62]

White gets pleasure from playing out various pornographic degradation scenarios. He likes being urinated on and drinking the urine of a man he calls "master."[63] And he is enamored of the increasingly popular pornographic genre centered on shit. "Three times I got him to shit while I knelt beside him. He'd use the slave collar I'd just bought at the corner leather store to pull my mouth down onto his rock-hard dick while a rich, barnyard stink rose up around us."[64] And while reveling in total subjection, White also objectifies the body of his partner: "I loved the look of his penis, heavy, drooping. I never wanted to anthropomorphize it or turn it in to a one-eyed puppet or little fellow or fondle it idly. In this regard I truly was an idolater who looked with respect at its ancient repose on its sac like a water god splayed on a shaded rock. Or I bowed before its erections, as if it were a numinous presence separate from me and from T."[65]

Jane Caputi explains how this kind of phallus worship is a central part of the pornographic worldview:

> The always hard, sterile and detached phallus identifies power not with capacity or creativity but with domination and violence, and is symbolized characteristically by weaponry. The phallus is not a true representative of the penis, which is definitely attached, sometimes hard, but more often soft, not eternal but changeable, not a weapon but a flower (Dyer 1993, 112), not an artifact, but a body – but alive, responsive, and fertile. The phallus, Susan Bordo (1999, 89) argues, stands for "a superiority that is distinctively connected with ... *generic* male superiority – not only over females but also

---

[62] WHITE, *supra* note 56, at 231.

[63] Id. at 234 ("Once he came over with a full bladder but both bathrooms were occupied so I led him to the little study and drank every drop with his penis in my mouth").

[64] Id. at 231.

[65] Id. at 232.

over other species . . [associated] with higher values – with the values of 'civilization' rather than 'nature,' with the *Man who is made in God's image"* [emphasis Caputi's]. The phallus, then, is the emblem of the rejection of sexuality and the body and ultimately of the dirt, the animal, and the Earth cultivated by patriarchal religion.[66]

Caputi goes on to explain that this rejection of the Earth, of the "dirti-ness" of sex, so described, amounts to a rejection of the Self (we get the word "human" from *humus,* Latin for "dirt"), a rejection cultivated by patriarchal religious morality as a way of keeping its subjects devoid of the power of Self-determination that comes from Self-possession. Patriarchy/ Heteroarchy depends upon this imposed emptiness, this renunciation of any claim to our very humanity. In White's memoir and in Caputi's theory, pornography is exposed as an important weapon in the heteroarchal war on the Gay Self.

White does not seem conscious of any of this, although he is conscious of the pornographic influence:

> We never looked at porno films because we were the stars of our own fan-tasy....[67] "[H]e'd lie on his back and I'd place the money on his hairless, smooth stomach while I knelt between his knees. He was good, very good – he counted the money, bill by bill, and muttered, 'Goddam faggot, you like paying for this hot jock dick.' We lived in this low-level world of industrial-ized porn dialogue, but we were always refining it. I was the bespectacled, nerdy high school math teacher; T was the greaser who kept flunking and Teach was always lurking around the station where T pumped gas. One day T burst into the filthy, shit-streaked, fly-buzzing toilet and started fucking Teach's face. Now he was getting A's and money.[68]

Ultimately, White is taken in by the only real "fantasy" involved in por-nography: that subordination through sex equals Self-actualization and happiness for Gay men. The masochist, strangely surprised when the sadist actually hurts him, is stunned when the relationship ends. White is left feel-ing desperate and alone. And his readers are left with the truth pornography has to tell: the Gay man – the Princeton man of letters, no less – dominated, subjected, shit on, and ultimately alone – unlovable. Pornography tells us who we are.

[66] Jane Caputi, *Recreating Patriarchy: Connecting Patriarchal Religion and Pornography,* 1 WAKE FOREST J. OF LAW AND SOC. POL'Y (forthcoming) (I read Professor Caputi's article in manuscript form).

[67] WHITE, *supra* note 56, at 235.

[68] Id.

SACRIFICIAL VICTIM

What makes White's pornographic account of his own life so unusual – and it is not the narcissistic frankness with which it is narrated – is his realization, however much obfuscated by his literary pretentiousness, that pornography is not entirely harmless. Gay men used to create his "fantasies" were actually harmed. After making his boyfriend enact a pornographic scene with a male prostitute, with White as the voyeur, White realized, "the guy was hurting him; [so] we all called it a day."[69]

Jeffrey Escoffier's misunderstanding of the reality of the lives of people used to make pornography, on the other hand, makes it unsurprising that he would link the early, and incredibly economically successful, gay film *Boys in the Sand* (1971) with the heterosexual film *Deep Throat* (1972) as watersheds in the "sexual revolution" toward individual expressiveness.[70] The reality of life for Linda Boreman, coerced as Linda Lovelace into the making of *Deep Throat*, was one of torture.[71] Both gay pornography and straight pornography are exercises in the sadism they represent/perpetuate in the wider world and of the politics constituted by this sadism. But neither the reality of Boreman's life nor the reality of the lives of gay porn "performers" is given attention in Escoffier's treatment of gay pornography.[72] This unattended reality is grim.

In *Gay Male Pornography*, Christopher Kendall makes a compelling case that the "actors" in gay pornography aren't much different, in terms of social circumstances, than the women used to make straight porn. Kendall documents a history of social and familial ostracism, addiction, and poverty that drives many Gay youth to the pornography industry.[73] Moreover, the "body fascism"[74] that demands the perfect masculine body, with focus on the cock

---

[69] Id. at 233.

[70] ESCOFFIER, *supra* note 21, at 1.

[71] See LINDA BOREMAN, ORDEAL (2006). Linda Boreman encouraged Catharine MacKinnon to theorize legal redress for women harmed in/through/by pornography. She testified in support of the first go at enacting the ordinance in Minneapolis in 1983. She continued to be an outspoken advocate for the victims of pornography until her death in 2002.

[72] Interestingly, Boreman's "autobiography" is mentioned in *Bigger Than Life* (ESCOFFIER, *supra* note 21), but only as the inspiration for fluffers on gay porn sets. A fluffer, already in use in hetero-porn, like *Deep Throat*, is an employee whose sole purpose is to be on a porn set to suck dick before and between takes to facilitate constant erections for the male "performers."

[73] See CHRISTOPHER N. KENDALL, GAY MALE PORNOGRAPHY: AN ISSUE OF SEX DISCRIMINATION, ch. 4 (2004). Kendall does strong work utilizing the studies available. Obviously, more work on this issue must be done.

[74] MICHELANGELO SIGNORILE, LIFE OUTSIDE: THE SIGNORILE REPORT ON GAY MEN: SEX, DRUGS, MUSCLES, AND THE PASSAGES OF LIFE (1997).

and ass, has created a culture of damaging physical choices. Whether for the "real" straight man in gay porn or the "straight-acting" masculine Gay man, big pecs, bigger dicks, and testosterone-fueled aggression are the measure of manhood for Gay men in the pornographer's manufactured reality: *Big Dicks; Big Poles; Hung Riders; Muscle Gods; Men at Work; Cockaholic; Dorm Life Dick Addiction; Teen Muscle; Young and Hard; Monster Cock; Bareback Big Uncut Dicks; Now Serving 13 Inches; The Bigger the Better; Bubble Butt Boys; Super Jocks, Manplay: Size is Everything* are representative video titles. This pornographic ideal is conducive to the development of harmful relationships with one's body and, consequently, with one's Self. This is so not only for Gays who are used to make gay pornography, but also for gay pornography consumers who want to emulate what they see.

Douglas Sadownick explains the relationship between pornography and body image (first quoting from William Mann's article, "Perfect Bound," published in *Frontiers*, January 13, 1994):

> "Think for a moment," challenged William J. Mann, "of the images of gay men in the '90s. What comes to mind? The hunky boys tossing streamers from the deck of the RSVP cruise ship. Ryan Idol. Bob and Rod. Big, buff, young, white. So perfect that their sexiness … becomes muted." He argued that in fifteen years the image had not predominated over the human. "The image of a gay man was overtly sexual: the Village People, in all their assorted sexual stereotypes; the Castro clone, with his over-emphasized basket and buns; the phallic supermen of Tom of Finland. It was a radical revolution from the limp-wristed pansies of the '50s and the androgynous flower children of the '60s."
>
> The '90s saw the triumph of the image – it had almost been raised to the level of pagan worship. This "symbol" of homo eros – this buff dude one sees on every porn magazine and every gay advertisement – confused gay men who naturally felt they could never measure up to these standards. It did not ease anyone's minds to suggest that these porn-perfect images were reflections of the archetypal: the gay version of graven images – gods. In our antimyth culture, people lacked the conceptual tools to differentiate the archetypal from the personal. All men could do was shake their heads at the primacy of the Marky Mark images and feel oppressed by it or enslaved to it.… To make matters more complex, the rigid roles of gay looks encourage straight-acting behavior. Psychologists say that there is both a personal and archetypal way of looking at this problem as well. On one hand, it refers to feelings of internalized homophobia by valorizing straight-acting over "gay-acting." … But on an archetypal level, it calls up what Jack Fritscher calls the image of the "masculine homosexual," which, like it or not, seems at the core of many gay men's fantasies.…

But because *few* gay men were taught that the doll-faced pinup boy was an inner symbol of something that is not yet conscious *in them*, men looked for this replica in the outside world, disappointing everyone, including themselves.[75] Few made distinctions between the transpersonal, with its grandiosities, and the personal with its inferiorities. Contaminating each with the other, one appreciates neither.[76]

This is why the marketplace remains successful. Sellers know how to go to the most private and vulnerable places in the imagination for the purpose of cajoling people into buying.[77]

Sellers know how to take our sexuality, damaged and alienated by heteroarchal oppression, repackage it, and sell it back to us. One would hope that Gay men would resent this, but as Sadownick explains, "The man who is too cowardly to wrestle his morally problematic archetypes will be less inclined to admit that he has them."[78] Less likely still is a rebellion against "problematic archetypes" when those enslaved by them are not allowed the consciousness necessary to engage them. The realities of heteroarchal oppression make cowardice too simple an answer.

Aside from steroid abuse to gain the mounds of muscle showcased in gay pornography, there is a thriving industry of gadgets and pills and potions, many with harmful side effects, to cater to a Gay man's worry that his penis is too small. In the course of trying to find out everything I can about gay pornography, the people who are used in its creation and the people who consume it, I have met young men in their twenties who routinely have silicone injected directly in their penises and buttocks, not by doctors, because injections of medical-grade silicone would be prohibitively expensive in the United States, but by black market hacks for lots of money. I had no idea of the pervasiveness of this practice until I started investigating gay pornography. I've met young men in my conservative home state of North Carolina who do this. Silicone injections, especially when the purity of black market silicone is in question, carry a high risk of deformity and/or death. But the relentless pursuit of the body as pornographed ideal renders these facts mere afterthoughts, if they are

---

[75] DOUGLAS SADOWNICK, SEX BETWEEN MEN: AN INTIMATE HISTORY OF THE SEX LIVES OF GAY MEN POSTWAR TO PRESENT 214–217 (1996). Sadownick would have been more accurate had he recognized that this image simply colonizes other Self-images, blotting them out, by obscuring all else as the Big Cock takes up all the imaginative space.

[76] Id. I find Sadownick's observations here illuminating and fascinating. Still, I wonder if the authentic Self, if we were to know it, would fantasize thus grandiosely. I tend to think we would recognize and affirm strength and fragility coexisting.

[77] Id.

[78] Id. at 217.

thought of at all. The pornography we make commonplace in our lives leaves many to conclude that such practices are worth the risk.

I have met young men used in porn, many of whom also prostitute (they call it "escorting"),[79] who were perfectly attractive (in the conventional sense) before they entered what they call the "industry." Since their involvement in this "industry" began, many of them have engaged in serious self-mutilation in pursuit of the pornographic ideal, including getting pectoral implants, buttock implants, calf implants, injections, and fat suctioned from their stomachs to make their abs more prominent. Once, in Miami, I met a porn-"star"-hopeful who told me he spent approximately five hours per day in the gym and that he spent the rest of the time trying to consume a 5,000 calorie per day diet. Because he had no time for much of a job (other than sporadic "escorting"), he moved from one friend or acquaintance to the next and sometimes, when no one would give him a place to stay, slept on the beach.

Another manifestation of the like-straight ideology of gay pornography may be its most dangerous for performers and consumers. Laramie, Wyoming, is infamous as the site of the torture-murder of twenty-one-year-old Matthew Shepard, in 1998. But a little more than a decade later, the death of another former Laramie resident did not garner headlines. On March 17, 2010, twenty-five-year-old Chad Noel died in New York City from complications of HIV. Noel had been used to make bareback "twink"[80] genre pornography since he was eighteen, under the aliases of Donny Price and Craven Cox. His life and death are reflective of the resurgence of bareback gay pornography glorifying unsafe sex and the corresponding spike in HIV infections among Gay men.[81]

---

[79] Pornography is prostitution captured on film; it is sex in exchange for money filmed. Many (if not most) Gay men prostituted in porn also prostitute outside of porn. Even "stars" find it hard to make a living without resorting to prostitution. Ronnie Larsen, director of the documentary from inside the porn industry, *Shooting Making Porn*, reported:

> Ryan Idol [a huge name in Gay porn in the 1990s] has cried on my couch that he didn't ever want to make another porn video or turn another trick. Well, he's still advertising in *Frontiers* as an "escort"! Everyone pretends the Industry is such a big happy family – bullshit! They're miserable, unhappy people. So many of the models say they don't like turning tricks, but they continue to do it because they cannot see any other way to make a living – they can't act and most come and go so quickly.... They aren't paid all that well and what they make they blow on drugs.

Reported in KENDALL, *supra* note 9, at 80. Kendall's research comports with my own experiences meeting and talking with performers in the gay porn industry.

[80] Twink is a subculture referent for a young (or young-looking) man, usually with a thin, hairless body.

[81] See Joe Mirabella, *Bareback Porn Is Killing Our Community and You're to Blame*, THE BILERICO PROJECT (Apr. 9, 2010), http://www.bilerico.com/2010/04/is_bareback_porn_killing_our_community.php (last visited Nov. 4, 2010).

For a while, because of AIDS, these films went underground; now, they are once again out in the open. A recent look at the website of the largest Internet streamer of gay porn in the country revealed that bareback movies constituted the largest segment of the "most watched" list.[82] *Raw Ass Fuckers, Cum in My Hole, Wild West Raw, Bareback Neighborhood, Bareback Boners, Young Barebackers, A Decade of Cum, Cream Pie Surprise, Cum Fucking Skinheads, Cum Filled Man Holes, Bareback Breeding, Holes 4 Seed, Cum Gushers, Breeding Virgins, Barebacking Across America, Hook'n Up Bareback, Filthy Fuckers,* and *Raw Boys* are merely examples of the recent proliferation of Gay films focusing on unprotected sexual contact.

HIV infection rates have been on the rise among "performers" in the California porn industry since 1998,[83] and performers in hard-core pornography are ten times more likely to contract a sexually transmitted infection than are people in the general population.[84] In *Gay Male Pornography*, Christopher Kendall asks a salient question: "'Gay rights': Doesn't Joey Stefano have any?"[85] Joey Stefano, whose real name was Nicholas Iacona, "was something of the Marilyn Monroe of the gay-underground-porn-glam crowd: a manufactured porn icon whose career was masterminded by Chi Chi La Rue [the pornographer/pimp who still produces porn and has a "mainstream" career as a drag queen mc for gay events, white parties, and the like]."[86] Stefano was, as Douglas Sadownick explains, the first bottom to become really famous. Sadownick observes obliquely that this "rise to stardom ... may have been too much for the once-awkward, always-needy young man."[87] (Yes, it was the "stardom" that did it.) Stefano's career as a bareback bottom ultimately cost him his life. Pornography took his life. Although Stefano made unsuccessful attempts to leave the porn industry, by that time HIV positive, he sank deeper into depression and drugs, dying of an overdose that many considered suicide.[88] Just before his death he penned this poetic lament:

---

[82] This information was gathered for me from www.aebn.net by my research assistants in 2008.

[83] See Clarence A. Haynes, *Does Watching Bareback Porn Increase Your HIV Risk?* BODY (Aug. 2, 2010), http://www.thebody.com/content/art57955.html?ts=pf (last visited Nov. 4, 2010).

[84] See Xavier van Beesd, *Judge Rules Bareback Porn Should Be Allowed*, GAY NEWS (Mar. 20, 2010), http://www.gay-news.com/article04.php?sid=2792 (last visited Nov. 4, 2010).

[85] KENDALL, *supra* note 9, at 76.

[86] SADOWNICK, *supra* note 75, at 190. Sadownick's analogy to Monroe reminded me of Catharine MacKinnon's feminist analysis of Norman Mailer's remark about Monroe, "She is a mirror of the pleasure of those who stare at her." MacKinnon says: "Suppose this is true and she knew it and killed herself. A feminism that does nothing about that, does nothing for her, does nothing." CATHARINE A. MACKINNON, FEMINISM UNMODIFIED: DISCOURSES ON LIFE AND LAW 16 (1988). So it is for Joey Stefano. So it is for Gay liberation.

[87] SADOWNICK, *supra* note 75, at 190.

[88] Id.

No job
No money
No self-esteem
No confidence
All I have is my looks and body,
And that's not working anymore.
I feel washed up.
Drug problem.
Hate life.
HIV-positive.[89]

Former ACLU president Professor Nadine Strossen[90] ridiculed Linda Boreman by asserting, "[Boreman's] experience does not provide proof of abusive working conditions within the porn industry [because] she speaks only for herself."[91] I guess Joey Stefano was speaking only for himself too. No one was listening then, before he killed himself. Is anyone listening now? Strossen and the ACLU party line are all about "free" speech. But they don't seem to care about those people who are so submerged in pornography that they can't speak or those whom, when they do speak, no one hears.[92]

Since the Internet ensures many Gay men, from childhood to old age, access to imagery of bareback sex without consequences, the spike in HIV infections correlating with the resurgence of bareback films is not surprising.[93] HIV infection rates for Gay and bisexual men thirteen to twenty-four years old declined from 1994 to 1998 but rose sharply from 1999 to 2003.[94] The correlation between HIV infection rates and the surge in bareback gay pornography

---

[89] As quoted in CHARLES ISHERWOOD, WONDER BREAD AND ECSTASY: THE LIFE AND DEATH OF JOEY STEFANO (1996), reprinted in KENDALL, *supra* note 9, at 69.

[90] Cf. Pauline Bart, *The Banned Professor: or How Radical Feminism Saved Me from Men Trapped in Men's Bodies and Female Impersonators, with a Little Help from My Friends,* in RADICALLY SPEAKING: FEMINISM RECLAIMED 273 (Diane Bell & Renate Klein, eds., 1996).

[91] NADINE STROSSEN, DEFENDING PORNOGRAPHY: FREE SPEECH, SEX AND THE FIGHT FOR WOMEN'S RIGHTS 183 (1995).

[92] In 2010 the Aids Healthcare Foundation (AHF) filed suit against the California Occupational Safety and Health Standards Board challenging the lack of condom use on porn sets. A judge ruled against AHF, holding that LA County has discretion in how it oversees health.

[93] A May 2006 study by Emory University and the Georgia Department of Human Resources reported that 25% of the 1,000 Gay men surveyed reported having unprotected anal intercourse with their most recent casual sex partner. David R. Holtgrave et al., *Correlates of Unprotected Anal Sex with Casual Partners: A Study of Gay Men Living in the Southern United States,* 10 AIDS AND BEHAVIOR 575 (May 2006).

[94] See data available at http://www.cdc.gov/hiv/resources/reports/hiv3rddecade/chapter4.htm#MSM.

during this period is more than coincidental.[95] As Richard Mohr once wrote, Gay people in the United States "have fewer rights than do barnyard animals in Sweden."[96] Dead Gay people have fewer rights still. But pornography truncates our senses and ensures that those who view it are increasingly indifferent to what amounts to real human suffering, ambivalent to the realities of disease and death. Pornography makes us numb to violence and dehumanization.[97]

One man who participates in the making of bareback porn told me quite coolly that nothing he did contributed to the destruction of Gay people. Gay people, he said, ought to be able to distinguish fantasy from reality. They ought to educate themselves about the dangers of barebacking and not do it. Pornography is fantasy, he said. In this, the porn "star" and the free speech lawyer are one. Degradation and humiliation are reconstituted as pleasure, and no consequence, however concrete, outweighs in importance the pornographer's "fantasy" or the lawyer's "idea."[98]

LAW

Women used and abused in/by heterosexual pornography have been told that pornography must be protected because it is an idea, art, fantasy.[99] Usually, Gay defenders of pornography also believe that protecting pornography is integral to protecting freedom of speech. But whose speech exactly? If they mean free speech for Gay people, then it should be known to them that Gay speech is not free. Gay people are largely, historically and one suspects contemporaneously, a silent people. Heteroarchal terror campaigns ensure that Gays rarely exercise even the most existential speech – the speech of "coming out" and identifying as Gay. Those of us who do speak in a climate of

---

95 See Lou Chibbaro Jr., *Bareback Sales Booming: Some Video Stores, Porn Producers Ignore Pleas of AIDS Activists*, WASHINGTON BLADE, June 2, 2006. This article also reports that "major" porn studios, which claim to be taking the moral high road and requiring condom usage on their sets, are releasing their pre-AIDS, condomless films as a new "pre-condom" genre.

96 RICHARD D. MOHR, GAY IDEAS: OUTING AND OTHER CONTROVERSIES 5 (1992).

97 This is reflected in the attitudes about gay pornography "performers" reflected in posts to the *Advocate* website forum regarding the AHF lawsuit. The discussion tended toward anger about too much regulation of pornography and blame of porn "actors" who "consent" to barebacking.

98 American Booksellers, Inc. v. Hudnut, 771 F.2d 323 (1985), Aff'd Mem., 475 U.S. 1001 (1986) (summary affirmance).

99 Obscenity law, the regulatory apparatus purportedly directed at pornography, is not about pornography at all, at least not when pornography is rightly understood "as a way of ... *acting* that sexualizes and genders domination and submission." See CAPUTI, *supra* note 1, at 75 (emphasis mine). Pornography is a practice. Obscenity is an idea.

anti-Gay violence do so at great personal risk. Pornography is part of what keeps us silent and invisible.

Gay pornography both constitutes and perpetuates Gay silence born from Self-alienation. No one looks at the pornographed men of "Anal Warriors" or "Cum-Filled Holes" and says, "Now, he has something to say that is worth hearing." Therefore, even if a Gay man were to speak, no one would hear. The Gay man says, "I am human!" Pornography replies, "Shut up, and bend over!" In gay porn, we literally see Gay men as straight people experience us – as categorically *nothing*, with our very *being* (or nonbeing) rendered coextensive with how categorically meaningless they imagine Gay sex to be. The message is not we have rights, we have choices, we are citizens – we are humans; rather, it is we *are* sex. We are cocks, asses, throats, tongues, lips, and we are our happiest when we are being used by a straight man or in the way that a straight man would use a woman. For these reasons, gay porn has nothing to do with "free" speech. It is not speech, and it assuredly is not free. Any question of freedom is rendered ridiculous in the pornographic context. The question of a right to speech – of any right, for that matter – is alien to the frame. But free speech lawyers, who are mostly straight men, normalize our dehumanization by sexualizing our humiliation and then telling us that it is *our* speech. When Gay people who object to pornography refuse to buy that lie, we are told that our dehumanization is someone else's speech: the pimp's, the pornographer's, or that of anyone who gets off on Gay subjection. The pimp and the pornographer are often the same person in the Gay pornography industry. The heads of studios, so-called porn executives, often hold exclusive "rights" to their "stars." So if a man "performing" for Lucas Entertainment wants to do a film with another studio, Michael Lucas must grant permission. A man who controls access to the body of another for sex is a pimp, and his is the speech that matters. From this standpoint, no less liberal than conservative, sex is as sex does; power is as power says. So even to Gay people, our degradation and sexual reducibility tend to look inevitable – beyond law.

Thus positioned, pornography, the practice, constitutes and perpetuates "the worldview" (the "way of thinking")[100] that shapes the law and Gays' access to it in virtually every other respect. In the same way that women are reduced to and defined as the "cunt" in heterosexual pornography and in extended heterosexual reality, Gay men are reduced, utterly, to "dicks" and "asses" in pornography and in everyday life. Pornography becomes, literally, everyday life.

While sexual harassment law has had some success in mitigating the effect of the pornographic script in the everyday work life of women, because sexual

---

[100] Id.

harassment law in the hands of heterocrats is, like all law, concerned primarily with heterosexuality only, it has not produced similar results in Gay life, professional or otherwise.[101] Gay men relate to each other, acceptably, through sex in virtually every facet of interrelation. What does work look like for Gay men? In an episode of the popular television series *Queer as Folk*, the definitively masculine Gay male character, Brian, seduces a client (ambiguously Gay, but obviously married – he wore a ring) of his marketing firm, who is reluctant to accept the firm's ideas. Brian fucks him in a bathroom stall and, incredibly, he is then onboard with the firm's agenda. The clear message is that sex is acceptable professional currency for Gays.

When I recently spoke at a national Gay law conference, where firms send recruiters to interview Gay law students, I attended a mixer held the night after the conference. Shortly after I arrived, a lawyer from one of the hiring firms, who obviously mistook me for a student, said to me, "Damn, you have a big ass; I could eat that thing for hours." All around the party, students and prospective employers were unashamedly making out with each other. A student confirmed for me that this was not unusual behavior at this annual event. Another student told me, candidly, "A few of the lawyers from Firm X want me to go back to their hotel with them. I think if I don't do it I may not get a job." He then added, almost as a corrective to himself, "Not that I mind going back with them." In light of this reality, the question of sexualized violence in pornography becomes a query as to whether there can be sexual harassment when the inevitability of sex is wholly accepted.[102] Moreover, can sexual harassment law be operative for a people understood as sex in a way no other people, perhaps not even women, are currently understood?

When the sexual terrorization of an oil rig worker, Joseph Oncale (ostensibly straight), degraded by his male co-workers (again, ostensibly straight) as Gay, made it to the U.S. Supreme Court, the Court held that instances of same-sex sexual harassment were actionable as sex discrimination in limited factual circumstances.[103] But even this meager understanding of Gay male humanity was apparently unsettling for Professor Janet Halley, who opined that the approach to the case left out the possibility (apparently probable in her mind) that Gay men experience sexual degradation and subjection as

---

[101] Oncale v. Sundowner Offshore Services, Inc., 523 U.S. 75 (1998) (Recognizing the actionability of same-sex sexual harassment until Title VII in limited factual circumstances).

[102] This observation should not be taken to reinforce Janet Halley's incredible assertion that the sex discrimination analysis in *Oncale* left out the possibility/probability that Gay men want to be sexually harassed. Joseph Oncale (we don't know whether he was Gay, and it makes no difference) clearly did not want the sexual torture he was subjected to.

[103] *Oncale, supra* note 101.

desirable: "We can imagine that a [Gay] plaintiff with these facts willingly engaged in erotic conduct of precisely the kinds described in Oncale's complaint, or that he engaged in some of that conduct and fantasized about the rest, or indeed fantasized all of it – and then was struck with a profound desire to refuse the homosexual potential those experiences revealed in him."[104] As Christopher Kendall explains, Halley implies "that the facts in *Oncale* can be seen as indicative of what gay sex is today and, as such, harmful to Oncale and others only because they are not yet prepared to deal with the apparently liberatory potential of homoerotic desire. In other words, if Oncale were more comfortable with gay sex, then what happened to him, because it *is* gay sex, would not have "upset" him." From Halley's perspective, then, performance of the condition that defines Gay men is, legally speaking, unproblematic.[105] This is not to suggest that Halley, an out Lesbian, watches gay male pornography; rather it is proof positive that pornography constitutes the reality of Gay life, glimpsed, however briefly by the law, in the reality of Oncale's experiences and in the brutality of Halley's theory.

Rape, sex as dominance, is a common theme in straight pornography. Because of the power differential between men and women, heterosexual sex, the gendered realities of which are claimed and reinforced in gay pornography, is inherently nonconsensual.[106] This same lack of consent must, therefore, be mirrored in gay pornography and in Gay relationships for which pornography is the principal script. When Falcon Studios pornographer Chuck Holmes started his now legendary studio, his choice of names was deliberately evocative of the Gay sex his studio mass-markets, that is, heterosexual, sadistic dominance/submission sex, with only men used in filming:

> I wanted ... something that had an image of fierceness and power and grace and was natural.... I thought a falcon represented that. It was a bird of prey.

---

[104] Janet Halley, *Sexuality Harassment*, in DIRECTIONS IN SEXUAL HARASSMENT LAW 192 (Reva B. Siegel & Catharine A. MacKinnon, eds., 2004).

[105] KENDALL, *supra* note 9, at 38–39. Halley's argument also precludes any possibility of sexual relating for Gay men other than the violent, degrading model presented in *Oncale*, underscoring that Gay men are this sex, existentially. Kendall observes of Halley's *Oncale* thesis: "Given what we know about what did happen to Joseph Oncale, it would appear that what we have here (perhaps for the first time) is a feminist writer asserting that within a same-sex context, rape *is* sex and, as such, non-harmful once accepted as something uniquely gay male." Id. at 39.

[106] Because of the gender inequity between men and women, heterosexual sex rarely takes place under conditions of social equality. In heterosexuality, force is experienced as sexually arousing; thus, the paradigm for heterosexual sexual intercourse is rape. The brilliance of the patriarchal system of oppression through sex is that sexual coercion of women is romanticized as seduction, celebrated as an art.

> With sexual acts – at least the way we make 'em here at Falcon – there is generally someone who is the predator and someone who's the prey ... by the end of a Falcon film, somebody has snatched someone and given it to 'em good.[107]

Again, the socially despised, always in relation to the heterosexual male ideal, misdirects the impulse toward liberation back into the destructive reality that is the actuality of the hierarchy from which he desires escape.

Recall Eldridge Cleaver's revelation on rape in *Soul on Ice*. The corollary between rape and masculine esteem that Cleaver illuminates, which is a corollary between masculinity as a gender norm and sexuality – which is to say that masculinity as a gender construct follows from heterosexuality and is understood as such – is important for understanding gay pornography too. Cleaver reports an increase in self-esteem corresponding to an increase in masculine feeling directly resulting from his success in raping women.[108] This anecdotal evidence of the relation between gender hierarchy sexualized and masculine self-worth is supported by formal data on men and pornography and men and rape. Men viewing straight pornography in laboratory settings showed increased levels of arousal from rape scenes.[109] A staggering one-third

---

[107] ESCOFFIER, *supra* note 21, at 132.

[108] CLEAVER, *supra* note 29, at 14.

[109] See Dr. Edward Donnerstein's illuminating testimony at the Minneapolis pornography ordinance hearings, collected in IN HARM'S WAY: THE PORNOGRAPHY CIVIL RIGHTS HEARINGS 44 et seq. (Catharine A. MacKinnon & Andrea Dworkin, eds., 1997).

    For correlating data see Edward Donnerstein, *Pornography: Its Effect on Violence Against Women*, in PORNOGRAPHY AND SEXUAL AGGRESSION 53 (Neil Malamuth & Edward Donnerstein, eds., 1984); Larry Baron & Murray A. Straus, *Sexual Stratification, Pornography, and Rape in the United States*, in id. at 185; Dolf Zillmann & Jennings Bryant, *Effects of Massive Exposure to Pornography*, in id. at 115; Neil Malamuth & James V. P. Check, *The Effects of Mass Media Exposure on Acceptance of Violence Against Women: A Field Experiment*, J. RES. IN PERSONALITY 436 (1981); Edward Donnerstein & Leonard Berkowitz, *Victim Reaction in Aggressive Erotic Films as a Factor in Violence Against Women*, 41 J. OF PERSONALITY & SOC. PSYCHOL. 710 (1981); Neil Malamuth, *Factors Associated with Rape as Predictors of Laboratory Aggression Against Women*, 50 J. PERSONALITY & SOC. PSYCHOL. 953 (1986); Neil Malamuth & James V. P. Check, *Aggressive Pornography and Beliefs in Rape Myths: Individual Differences*, 19 J. OF RES. IN PERSONALITY 299 (1985); James V. P. Check & Ted H. Guloien, *Reported Proclivity for Coercive Sex Following Repeated Exposure to Sexually Violent Pornography, Nonviolent Dehumanizing Pornography, and Erotica*, in PORNOGRAPHY: RESEARCH ADVANCES AND POLICY CONSIDERATIONS 159 (Dolf Zillman & Jennings Bryant, eds., 1989); James V. P. Check & Neil Malamuth, *Pornography and Sexual Aggression: A Social Learning Theory Analysis*, 9 COMM. YEARBOOK 181 (1986); Dolf Zillman and James B. Weaver, *Pornography and Men's Sexual Callousness Toward Women* in PORNOGRAPHY: RESEARCH ADVANCES AND POLICY CONSIDERATIONS 159 (Dolf Zillman & Jennings Bryant, eds., 1989); Diana E. H. Russell, *Pornography and Rape: A Causal Model* 9 POL. PSYCHOL. 41 (1988).

of men say they would rape a woman if they knew they would not get caught.[110] And rapists understand rape, as Cleaver did, to be a necessary component of masculine self-esteem.[111]

Feminists have persuasively shown the connection between sexualized violence, which, if we are being generous, might be the kind of "ideas" First Amendment mucks are apparently concerned about (violence in the head), and real violence, inflicted through sex in the home or in the street, against women.[112] Despite the assumption that violence cannot exist or exists only rarely in same-sex relationships, sexual violence between Gay men, at least, may occur at rates equal to those of violence by men against women in the straight community. More than 23 percent of cohabiting Gay men say they have been raped and/or physically battered by a spouse or cohabiting partner at some time in their lives, compared with 7.7 percent of men cohabiting with opposite-sex partners.[113] And men who have sex with men are six times more likely to suffer an assault as an adult.[114] As with heterosexual pornography,

---

One particularly interesting study shows that simulated juries exposed to pornography were less capable than real juries of perceiving an account of a rape as an account of a rape. See Neil Malamuth and James V. P. Check, *Penile Tumescence and Perceptual Responses to Rape as a Function of the Victim's Perceived Reactions*, 10 J. APPLIED SOC. PSYCHOL. 528 (1980); Daniel Linz et al., *The Effects of Multiple Exposures to Filmed Violence Against Women*, 34 J. COMM. 130 (1984).

For more data on the correlation between pornography consumption and sexual aggression, see Mike Allen et al., *Exposure to Pornography and the Acceptance of Rape Myths*, 45 J. COMM. 5 (1995); Fena Attwood, *What Do People Do with Porn? Qualitative Research into the Consumption, Use, and Experience of Pornography and Other Sexually Explicit Media*, 9 SEXUALITY AND CULTURE 65 (2005); Kimberly A. Davies, *Voluntary Exposure to Pornography and Men's Attitudes Toward Feminism and Rape*, 34 J. SEX RES. 131 (1997); William A. Fisher & Guy Grenier, *Violent Pornography, Antiwoman Thoughts, and Antiwoman Acts: In Search of Reliable Effects*, 31 J. SEX RES. 23 (1994); Susan H. Gray, *Exposure to Pornography and Aggression Towards Women: The Case of the Angry Male*, 29 SOC. PROBLEMS 387 (1982); Laura L. Jansma et al., *Men's Interactions with Women after Viewing Sexually Explicit Films: Does Degradation Make a Difference?* 64 COMM. MONOGRAPHS 1 (1997); Neil Malamuth, *Sexually Violent Media, Thought Patterns, and Antisocial Behavior*, 2 PUBLIC COMM. & BEHAVIOR 159 (1989).

There is evidence that exposure to pornography affects women in similar ways. Women have been found to be less likely to see rape as rape after exposure to violent, sexually explicit material; see Carol Krafka et al., *Women's Reactions to Sexually Aggressive Mass Media Depictions*, 3 VIOLENCE AGAINST WOMEN 149 (1997).

This note is not exhaustive; it references studies I have read.

[110] CATHARINE A. MACKINNON, TOWARD A FEMINIST THEORY OF THE STATE 145 (1989) (and sources cited).

[111] Id.

[112] See generally JANE CAPUTI, THE AGE OF SEX CRIME (1987).

[113] L. KEVIN HAMBERGER & MARY BETH PHELAN, DOMESTIC VIOLENCE SCREENING AND INTERVENTION IN MEDICAL HEATHCARE SETTINGS 301 (2004).

[114] National Coalition of Anti-violence Programs, *Lesbian, Gay, Bisexual, and Transgender Domestic Violence in 2000* 4 (2001).

the rapist reality of sex steeped in the heterosexual model of domination and submission is glamorized in gay porn.

Snuff films, which show a woman tortured to death, exist.[115] Torture, terrorization, and murder are experienced as sex for men who seek out snuff films. Under the predominating understanding of freedom of speech, there is no reason to think that the First Amendment wouldn't shelter these films too.[116] Similarly, torture is accepted as unproblematic when it is presented as Gay sexuality – in the reality of pornography or in the pornographic reality of everyday. In 1991 police received a 911 call from two women who said they witnessed a young Asian male running from an apartment and being followed into the street by a white man. The boy was bleeding and disoriented. The officers who responded returned this victim, Konerak Sinthasomphone, a fourteen-year-old Laotian boy, obviously bleeding from the holes Jeffrey Dahmer had drilled into his skull with a power drill, to the mass murderer, who convinced them that they had merely encountered some rough love – a lover's quarrel. The police officers did not bother to check Dahmer's identification; if they had they would have realized he was a registered sex offender. They did not bother to ascertain the age of Konerak Sinthasomphone. Would they have reacted the same way had the scene they encountered been heterosexual? We cannot know for sure. But we do know that the officers, after leaving this boy to be tortured to death, joked about "homosexual lovers" and being "deloused."[117]

The reality of Gay life and the ceaselessly inventive pornographic imagination converge in Konerak Sinthasomphone's experience of reality as Jeffrey Dahmer's victim and in Janet Halley's theory of the reality of Gay sexual violence, exposing the limitlessness of both. The reality of Joseph Oncale, isolated for long periods on an oil rig in the Gulf of Mexico, unable to escape from constant assault and sexual battery, was one of torture, and not unlike so much gay pornography. Halley says, effectively, "Embrace it." Konerak Sinthasomphone's reality as Dahmer's victim was one of torture to the point of death. Should he have embraced the liberatory promise of death that sexual torture, experienced as sexually arousing, thus as sex, by Dahmer promised? This is not a rhetorical question. It also points to why a Gay liberationist analysis of gay pornography and the reality of life on account of it is met with so much resistance. The violation that people see happening in front of them is said not to have happened because it happened to Gay people, for whom its happening is natural and normal. The desire to cling to some small share

---

[115] Dworkin, Intercourse, *supra* note 26, at 240.
[116] Cf. *United States v. Stevens*, 130 S. Ct. 1577 (2010).
[117] See *Milwaukee Panel Finds Discrimination by Police*, N.Y. Times, Oct. 16, 1991.

of the power structure, even when you are always already excluded from it, makes even many liberation-minded Gay people think that the people in the pornography can't be them. But if you identify with victims because you realize that, no matter what you'd like to call yourself, you are a victim, you identify with the people in the pornography. You can't identify with the liberal position that they consented because they "got paid." Anybody who has lived a Gay person's life understands that coercion is subtle, except when it isn't. If I find a desperate, hungry man on the street and promise to feed him or to give him money to buy food only if I can fuck him and film the fucking, is that not torture? Am I not a torturer? Then again, maybe I'm not exactly right on that point. Maybe if I do these things I'm merely liberated sexually or merely exercising my right to free speech.

There has been only one attempt in the United States to take pornography seriously as a legal matter. In 1983 Andrea Dworkin and Catharine MacKinnon were hired to draft an amendment to the Minneapolis civil rights code to recognize pornography as a civil rights violation.[118] Their ordinance targeted the harm and subordination pornography is/does, rather than the "ideas" supposedly expressed by it. Some in the Gay community opposed the law. Some Gay advocates worried, unfoundedly, that the ordinance might give homophobic police more excuse to harass Gays and target Gay establishments.[119] But the genius of the Dworkin/MacKinnon approach was that it provided a tort remedy for victims of subordination accomplished through pornography, not a new criminal prosecution mechanism. Obscenity laws already provide police all the means necessary to unfairly target Gay bookstores. Perhaps the publicity whipped up by the ordinance may have encouraged increased police harassment, but the ordinance itself did not involve the police power. Other Gays, those who had been abused through pornography, understood the ordinance's importance; testimony at the Minneapolis hearings on the ordinance revealed Gay men forced into pornography, violent relationships based on pornographic scripts, and esteem destroyed by unrealistic body expectations.[120]

But what was most striking about the civil rights hearings on pornography, from the perspective of a Gay liberation analysis, was that gay pornography was discussed and defended as though it were the totality of the Gay creative impulse. The possibility of the availability of civil damages to pornography's victims looked like open season on Gays to some opponents who talked about

[118] Catharine A. MacKinnon, *The Roar on the Other Side of Silence*, in In Harm's Way, *supra* note 109, at 4.

[119] See testimony of Robert Halfhill, in In Harm's Way, *supra* note 109, at 95.

[120] In Harm's Way, *supra* note 109, at 107 et seq.

the ordinance as if it would take away Gays' ability to read and write.[121] For example, Carol Soble, from the American Civil Liberties Union, talked about pornography and "gay and lesbian *literature*" as if they were the same thing.[122] Nobody equated pornography with the totality of straight male "literature." Straight bookstores were not discussed as if the totality of their contents were pornography, as Gay bookstores were. Just as troubling, the Gay advocates did not ask why the shelves of Gay bookstores or the Gay/Lesbian sections of mainstream bookstores are freighted with sexually explicit material, while hardly anything else is available. Pornography is a supply-driven business, and the supply has so overwhelmed the Gay community that either it seems integral to the politics of those Gays still left with a political consciousness, or, more likely, it has completely supplanted that political consciousness with the propaganda that Gay *is* sex; therefore, pornography is Gay literature – all of it, period.

Gays are perhaps the pornography industry's most susceptible consumer audience. We are conditioned from birth (or at least as soon as the heteros in our lives discover we are Gay) to think of ourselves sexually – as the sex acts we do, not as complete, moral beings. Straight people's unrelenting need to convince us to reject our sexuality makes sexuality the sole focus of our lives. This heteroreductive project leaves us with a subjectivity that is only sex/ual. Pornography, then, reinforces this imposed mental state – this brainwashing – and amplifies it. To the Gay conscience thus warped by heterosexism and heteronormativity, pornography feels like home.

Understandably, therefore, Gay people fear talking about sex as exploitation. And mainstream anti-porn organizations, Stop Porn Culture, for example, seem to prefer to pretend gay porn doesn't exist.[123] Even allies with the best of intentions, understanding that Gay sexuality has been the means of our exploitation through criminal sanction and social and religious stigma, are reluctant to condemn it. For example, Professor Jane Caputi, whose work exposing the parallels between the pornographic worldview and patriarchal religious myth is a project of brilliance, has written that "[g]ay and lesbian pornographies frequently differ from heterosexist pornography in that they affirm the beauty, dignity, and exuberance of sexualities that mainstream religions and moralities condemn."[124] I can't say that I agree with her on this, since most

---

[121] See testimony of Sally Fisk, in IN HARM'S WAY, *supra* note 109, at 348.

[122] IN HARM'S WAY, *supra* note 109, at 350.

[123] When I protested this to one of its principals, I first got the "gay pornography is problematic to engage because engagement looks like attacking Gay people" defense of inaction and, finally, I was told that I "should do something about it." This should be sufficient explanation for why I prefer to keep my independence from "organizations."

[124] CAPUTI, GODDESSES AND MONSTERS, *supra* note 1, at 417 n. 1.

gay pornography is the kind of blatant celebration of the heterosexual, rapist model of sexuality already presented. Still, because Caputi has the depth of insight to understand what pornography is all about, she continues:

> Yet questions remain. Do the gay and lesbian pornographies … participate in the same habit of thought as regular pornography? Do they have objectifying, voyeuristic, and other-subordinating structures? Are viewers getting off (deliberately or inadvertently) on someone else's prostitution or oppression?[125]

Affirmative answers to all of these questions are found in gay pornography, and then some, for as a point of clarification, in gay pornography Gay people are getting off, however vicariously, to *our own* oppression. The Gay liberationist critique of gay pornography thus clarifies what is at stake in gay pornography: not sex, not speech, but Gay people's lives. It is up to us to decide, again, which is more important.

[125] Id.

PART III

Millennial Equality: A Primer on Gay Liberation in the Twenty-First Century

6

Gay/Straight

The Binary Ontology of the Gay Marriage Debate

The civilizing influence of family values, with or without children, ultimately may be the best argument for same-sex marriage.

William Eskridge, *The Case for Same-Sex Marriage*

True rebels, after all, are as rare as true lovers, and, in both cases, to mistake a fever for a passion can destroy one's life.

James Baldwin, *No Name in the Street*

If the imitation is always trying to be something, and cares desperately for its status, the original is really something, but does not care.

Teresa Brennan, *History after Lacan*

The marriage issue ... is a great boon for homophobes because it lets them side-step all the things that should be set right, from sodomy laws in various states, to discrimination in the workplace. Also marriage makes people think of God, who is so very important to our poor, bamboozled folks. The founders (and I) wanted God thrown out the window at Philadelphia, but the crazies breed like chiggers and he keeps slithering back in. He now dominates so much of radio and TV. Until a stake has been driven through the heart of monotheism, the U.S. will never come within a continuum of civilization. That suits them chiggers real fine.

Gore Vidal, *Southern Voice* (January 13, 2000)

When you are criticizing the philosophy of an epoch, do not chiefly direct your attention to those intellectual positions which its exponents feel it necessary explicitly to defend. There will be some fundamental assumptions which adherents of all the various systems unconsciously presuppose. Such assumptions appear so obvious that people do not know what they are assuming because no other way of putting things has ever occurred to them.

Alfred North Whitehead, *Science in the Modern World*

On November 17, 2008, a positively giggling Robin Young, of National Public Radio's *Here and Now*, interviewed Texas megachurch evangelist Ed Young.[1] Young gained considerable notoriety and media airtime in 2008 when he preached a sermon encouraging his megachurch flock to have more sex. Of course, this admonition was for married church members only, a subsequent clarification that underscored the presumptive place of marriage as the standard for both Christian and citizen, which, from the evangelical perspective, are the same things. Young's original message for "seven days of sex" was complete with the drama and optimism (albeit the hellfire-and-damnation variety) evangelicalism brings to every topic, delivered as Young paced in front of a huge bed, set up in the church of his flock of twenty thousand. Young occasionally reclined on the bed during this most unusual sermon, flipping through a copy of the Bible and emphasizing, as the *New York Times* put it, the need to "put God back in the bed."[2]

Once this original sexperiment came to an end, the pastor, apparently having a high old time, admonished his flock to keep it going. Parishioners at a Grapevine, Texas, satellite branch of the church were treated to a prerecorded message from Pastor Young, broadcast on jumbo screens, encouraging them to press on. Of course, Mrs. Young was on the recording, too, a mix of submissive wife/Virgin Mary – "[Do] unto me according to thy word" – and pornographic sex goddess (in jeans and knee-high black boots). "Some of us are smiling," she said, playfully. The pastor, for his part, made crystal clear how important *real* sex is. "We should try to double up the amount of intimacy we have in marriage," he said. "And when I say intimacy, I don't mean holding hands in the park or a back rub." Why not, you ask? (at least, I did). Well, we don't get the answer from him. What he does give us is a direct link between sex, marriage, and patriarchal theology.

> Just look at the sensuousness of the Song of Solomon, or Genesis: "two shall become one flesh," or Corinthians: "do not deprive each other of sexual relations. For some reason the church has not talked about it, but we need to," he said.... There is no shame in marital sex, he added, "God thought it up, it was his idea."[3]

I can't disagree with the connections he draws; the Bible seems to be a compilation of three-thousand-year-old rules about who can fuck whom,

---

[1] *Here and Now: Interview with Ed Young* (NPR broadcast Nov. 17, 2008), http://www.hereandnow.org/2008/11/17/show-rundown-for-11172008.

[2] Gretel C. Kovach, *Texas Pastor's Advice for Better Marriage: More Sex, More Often*, N.Y. TIMES, Nov. 24, 2008.

[3] Id.

when, and how; yet nowhere does it dispute that fucking (the holy kind) is good. "'In other words', writes Marabel Morgan, interpreting Scripture no less, 'sex is for the marriage relationship only, but within those bounds, anything goes. Sex is as clean and as pure as eating cottage cheese'. '4

The publicity surrounding the megachurch's "seven days of sex" highlights that the debate about sex between Right and Left is principally about the artificial distinction between sex, that which is sanctified, morally right, natural, healthy, et cetera, and "fucking," that which is the antithesis of all those things from the perspective of the Right. The Left doesn't debate that sex is morally right, natural, and healthy; it simply sees as sex more of what the Right sees as fucking. Marriage is an important litmus test in this.5 The Right agrees that

4 ANDREA DWORKIN, INTERCOURSE 59 (1987) (quoting Marabel Morgan). Dworkin goes on to describe Morgan's book *The Total Woman* (1975) as "a manual for wives who want to get their husbands to fuck them and maintain a cheerful attitude and a belief in God all at the same time." Id. at 59–60. Personally, I think Morgan's *Total* title is evocative of the totality of woman, as the social creation of patriarchy, which is that woman is for fucking, a message enforced through the Right's Bible and the Left's pornography, which proceed from a strikingly similar central story line. The story of the Virgin Birth of Christ, for example, has all of the hallmarks of the pornographic script. Father-god approaches *his woman*, of course a virgin (since virgins are part of the weird virgin/whore fantasy of straight men; just count sometime the number of straight porn titles involving the word "virgin"), and essentially rapes her. My analysis, of course, supposes that rape happens when meaningful consent is not given or cannot be given (for a host of reasons involving power imbalance). Feminists have long understood that pornography consumers are watching a rape; rarely has anyone understood that Bible readers are reading about one. In any event, the focus of the dynamic of the Virgin Birth rape myth is on the Holy Ghost, which "came upon" Mary and left her pregnant. The focus on the Holy Ghost in this respect is equivalent to the focus of most porn on the thrusting penis. The Holy Ghost is the god-phallus. Mary's "[Do] unto me according to thy word" is taken as consent, making the parallel I draw here to rape as incredible as it is (needless to say) offensive. But that is not so different from the pornographic world either, where rape is obfuscated by the "fact" that the woman is ostensibly being paid or that she smiles or verbally affirms that she enjoys what is done to her.

5 This is especially true in arguments from "natural law jurisprudence." See, e.g., Sherif Girgis, Robert P. George, & Ryan T. Anderson, *What Is Marriage?* 34 HARVARD J. L. & PUB. POL'Y 245–287 (2010). This example contains the typical vermicular definitional imprecision presented as precision. "Nature" is what the writers say nature is in the context of circuitous argumentation designed to mask apartheid in operation. George's argument about "real" marriage, as opposed to any Gay imitation of it, is contrived in terms of "nature" and "naturalness" but is, of course, really an argument that, stripped of its philosophical pretenses, would read something like this: "Marriage is a sacrament reserved for holy people; the church says gays (obviously, if George were writing, to be rendered in the lowercase) are not holy people; therefore, marriage and the holy, heterosexual way of life, ordained by God and sanctioned by the church, must be maintained by excluding gays from marriage and keeping the distinctions between the holy and unholy crisp and easily discernible." The argument can be dressed up as one about the naturalness of heterosexuality based on observations about procreation, but missing, of course, is the admission that heterosexuality and procreation are, in fact, religious imperatives and are being valued in this context solely because of

sex is wholesome and healthy when it takes place between married people (specifically between two people of opposite sexes married to each other); all other intercourse is fucking, unwholesome and unhealthy. The (liberal) Left agrees that sex is better morally (and allegedly physically and qualitatively) if it takes place within marriage (understood to mean between two people who love each other).[6] Thus, marriage is celebrated by Left and Right. Like its counterpart, heterosexuality, marriage is in many ways compulsory.

In this chapter, I dispute marriage and the Left-liberalism that is really Right-conservatism demanding it and reinforcing the patriarchal/heteroarchal notions of morality, monogamy, and, in the end, reproduction as definitions of citizenship. The convergence of Left politics with Right moralism in the marriage context constitutes a new hierarchy in which to be a like-straight, monogamously coupled, ideally married, Gay unit defines responsible Gay citizenship and good living, leaving Radical Resisters of the Heteroarchy with a searing brand of civic irresponsibility where the pink triangle might once have been. In order to avoid misunderstanding, it is necessary to bracket what this argument is not about. This is a criticism of the "gay rights" movement's current obsessive focus on marriage as a status; it is *not* a criticism of the pursuit of equal rights. Gays are entitled to the same rights as straights when it comes to tax treatment, rights of access to children or to one's partner in times of ill health or other crises, et cetera. The impulse toward these legal rights is completely understandable. This is also not an attack on the argument that the Constitution guarantees marriage for Gays in every sense, including, probably, the word "marriage." Nevertheless, I think the millions of dollars invested (not to mention the emotional investment) in the ongoing fight over the word "marriage," as distinguished from the bundle of rights concomitant with state-sanctioned coupling, is not only tragically wasteful but also dangerous.[7]

---

this fact, and not for the (convenient) fact that they can be observed in the natural world. In new natural law jurisprudence, "nature" is merely a *motif* for manipulation. The academic pretentiousness of presenting the argument in any other terms is enviable in degree of chutzpah and, certainly, career-making.

6 Except, of course, when it takes place in the other great fetish of the liberal Left – pornography – where neither lack of love nor limitless partners seems to dim the glow-in-the-dark "goodness" of sex (in this context understood even by liberals as "fucking").

7 It is important to understand that the label "marriage" is all that is involved in the marriage drama unfolding in California (and elsewhere). California already had a system of domestic partnerships that afford Gay couples all the rights and imposed all of the burdens of state-sanctioned coupling. See In Re Marriage Cases, 183 P.3d 384, 298 (2008). *In Re Marriage Cases* (the California Supreme Court decision finding that the bifurcated naming system violated state equality guarantees), Proposition 8 (the religionist-funded amendment to the California Constitution overturning *In Re Marriage Cases* and reinstating the bifurcated

I should note upfront that the internal debate about the good or ill of marriage for Gay people has been going on for some time, waning as the movement became increasingly conservative and assimilationist. In this context, many scholars and activists have presented lucid arguments against marriage.[8] And, of course, many intelligent, well-meaning advocates have supported marriage as central to full citizenship for Gays.[9] The significance of Radical critique now, in the second decade of the twenty-first century, arises from the nearly total capture of the debate by the liberal individualism inherent in the advent of a gay rights movement that defines progress in terms of individual exceptionality and, increasingly it seems, overlooks anyone unable or unwilling to assimilate on straight people's terms. Basically, popularly at least, in the famous debate between Andrew Sullivan and Michael Warner on the efficacy of normalcy, Sullivan has won. From all appearances, there is only one debate about Gay marriage going on today, in the popular press, in most classrooms I know of, and within "mainstream" gay rights organizations – the debate between gay rights and the religious Right.[10] When I speak to undergraduate students in my introductory Gay

---

naming system – domestic partnerships for Gays and marriage for straights), *Perry v. Schwarzenegger* (overturning Prop 8 on federal constitutional grounds), and ongoing appeals have all been about the "right" of Gays to refer to their couplings officially as marriages. In Re Marriage Cases, 183 P.3d at 384; CAL. CONST. art.I, § 7.5; Perry v. Schwarzenegger, 704 F. Supp. 2d 921, 1003 (N.D. Cal. 2010).

It seems to me, in light of the argument about marriage that follows, that Gays are missing an important opportunity to renounce patriarchal/heteroarchal marriage and to create something better (call it domestic partnerships or civil unions or what you will) and, perhaps, to bring progressive straights along to a more evolved model of human relating.

[8] For a concise discussion of the internal debate, see the observations of Israeli scholar Zvi Triger (and scholars referenced) in *Fear of the Wandering Gay: Some Reflections on Citizenship, Nationalism, and Recognition of Same-Sex Relationships* (2011), http://ssrn.com/abstract =1731519. For those anti-marriage scholars I find particularly influential, see *infra*, note 20.

Early arguments began as a call to renounce even the bundle of rights associated with state-subsidized coupling (see, e.g., Ettelbrick, *infra* note 20). While I think the heteromajoritarian decision to incentivize coupling is irrational, the tremendous financial and legal handicaps arising from coupled Gays who are "legal strangers," as Professor Art Leonard put it in conversation with me, is a sacrifice I'm not willing to ask Gays to make – although I do think Gays choosing state recognition should be cognizant of its inherent detriment, namely that state-encumbered relationships are harder to exit.

[9] In addition to those I engage and refute in this chapter, I should mention David A. J. Richards, e.g., *Introduction: Theoretical Perspectives*, in LEGAL RECOGNITION OF SAME-SEX PARTNERSHIPS: A STUDY OF NATIONAL, EUROPEAN AND INTERNATIONAL LAW 25–29 (Richard Wintemute & Mads Andenaes, eds., 2001); and Marc R. Poirier, e.g., *The Cultural Property Claim Within the Same Sex Marriage Controversy*, 17 COLUMBIA J. GENDER & L. 343 (2008). I also wrote approvingly of marriage in *Sexual Politics: The Gay Person in America Today* (2006). Obviously, I have changed my mind.

[10] Religionist arguments are engaged and refuted in the following chapter.

studies course, I routinely ask why they have decided to take the course. And, just as routinely, a majority of them reply with some variation on the theme of the importance of learning about Gay marriage, as if that were the totality of the subject matter at hand.[11] Most of them believe that Gays should have the right to marry (and I am usually left with the impression through class discourse that they also believe Gays *should* marry). Now, certainly, I am aware that my critique of marriage here, as well as my assertion of a Gay community and identity, will be labeled "essentialist." That label is a favorite attack/dismissal occasioned by the spuriousness of Self that is central to the postmodern (non)view of the world. Missing from the usual analysis, however, is the fact that the marriage wars are also essentializing us (in ways I find problematic) by setting up an undeniably heteroarchal goal as our raison d'être.

I also want to say here that nothing in the following critique is meant to be a moral judgment about any Gay persons desiring marriage for reasons of personal importance to them[12] (although my critique may explain why the desire for marriage *is* important to them in ways they do not fully understand because the power that constructs desire in the straight model has been invisibilized). My project is not to pass judgment on my Gay sisters and brothers, but to comment on an institution in/through which our subordination is (or is to be) accomplished. But it must also be said that any personal claim to a priority for relating in the heteroarchal model has nothing to do with Gay liberation, and I object to the claim that it does. Such claims mark the stark contrast between the communitarian philosophy of Gay liberation (outlined in Chapter 1) and the liberal individualism that defines the gay rights movement.[13] As much as any other dilemma, the marriage question calls for an accounting by those who would prioritize personal gain over real Gay liberation.

---

[11] A scarier manifestation of this phenomenon is occurring within the legal community, with marriage eclipsing any substantive equality perspective altogether. The best and worst example of this, I think, is the "equal access" strategy for litigating marriage proposed by Professors Nelson Tebbe and Deborah Widiss. See Nelson Tebbe & Deborah Widiss, *Equal Access and the Right to Marry*, 158 U. Pa. L. Rev. 1375 (2010). Tebbe and Widdis call Gay advocates to abandon the equality conversation in toto. This kind of blinkered vision, concentrating only on the gain of individual litigants is, perhaps, liberalism carried to its natural end. For my reply to Tebbe and Widiss, see Nelson Tebbe, Deborah Widiss, & Shannon Gilreath, Debate, *The Argument for Same-Sex Marriage*, 159 U. Pa. L. Rev. PENNumbra 21 (2010), http://www. pennumbra.com/debates/pdfs/Marriage.pdf.

[12] Certainly, I have Gay friends who want to marry.

[13] Perhaps marriage could be of some value to a people already imbedded in a community, but Gay people are not yet at that place; and marriage is a serious impediment to achieving community.

MARRIAGE AND HETERONORMATIVITY AS ERASURE (CONCEPTUAL/EXISTENTIAL VIOLENCE)

In 2004 Professor Katherine Franke presciently warned of an increasing domestication of Gay rights in the wake of *Lawrence v. Texas*,[14] with a view toward the normative project *Lawrence* galvanized, namely marriage.[15] Like Franke, I am alarmed by the *Lawrence* opinion's removal of the Gay litigants into the heteronormative project of monogamous, familial coupling. This follows the like-straight logic of the Gay groups that intervened in the case as amici, principally asking the Court to extend the presumptive value of heterosexual sexual relationships to Gay sexual relationships that, according to the Gay amici, are like straight relationships in every way.[16]

The *Lawrence* majority thus transformed what for all we really know was sex between friends or simply no-strings-tricking into a relationship in the romanticized, straight tradition, which made the sex acceptable. In other words, the domesticity of the sex involved – indeed, the *Lawrence* majority's compulsory domestication of Lawrence and Garner – sufficiently inoculated the Gayness of Lawrence and Garner's claim to sexual liberty by replacing it with a claim for relationship-based intimacy. What is most important here is that by domesticating the sex in *Lawrence*, indeed one might say by disappearing it, the majority accomplished the domestication and disappearance of the Gay men involved, assimilating them into the relationship-oriented model on which patriarchy/Heteroarchy rests. Having established this as the normative framework for arguing for Gay equality, *Lawrence* thus catalyzed the marriage craze. *Lawrence* dangled the bait, signaling that marriage was the door to acceptance and legal protection through heteronormative assimilation (while explicitly disavowing it as such), and Gays swallowed it. *Goodridge v. Department of Public Health*[17] followed and, ultimately, so did *In re Marriage Cases* and *Perry v. Schwarzenegger*.

The result of *Lawrence* and the marriage model has been the transfiguration of Gay liberation into the universalities of "gay rights." The metaphysics of formal equality transfigures marriage, the institution, into the gateway to

---

[14] Lawrence v. Texas, 539 U.S. 558 (2003).

[15] Katherine M. Franke, *The Domesticated Liberty of Lawrence v. Texas*, 104 COLUM. L. REV. 1399, 1407–1409 (2004). Given the current state of things, if Professor Franke wanted to write the shortest (and perhaps most poignant) law review article in history, she might simply write, "I told you so."

[16] See Chapter 3, this volume, for elaboration.

[17] Goodridge v. Dep't of Public Health, 798 N.E.2d 941 (Mass. 2003). *Goodridge* was the first case to open marriage, in name, to Gay couples.

ontic happiness and freedom. I find this paradoxical, considering that the history of Gay identity is one of institutionalization as a means to essentialize and ultimately erase us. Our first institution was the prison. Then there was the psychiatric ward, where we, medicalized as psychotics, were electroshocked, lobotomized, and murdered.[18] Having only recently emerged from this history, some Gays rush to marriage for its value *as an institution*. It is a reversal that perhaps only Foucault could really appreciate.

Consider the institutional politics of marriage expounded by Marriage Equality California and Lambda Legal:

> [There] is no other way for gay people to be fully equal to non-gay people – both in the eyes of the law, and in the eyes of the larger community – than to participate in the same legal institution using the same language.... Any alternative to marriage is not marriage. *Anything less, is less than equal!*[19]

The important revelation here is that, unlike the situation in the first two phases of institutionalization, in which Gays who were demonstratively non-normative (because they were caught, self-identified, or could not otherwise hide their sexual orientation) were medicalized and criminalized, it is now non-normative Gays – those who do not acquiesce in patriarchal notions of monogamous coupling and child rearing – who are said to fail to appreciate the good of institutionalization in the form of marriage. It is also the non-normative Gays who, by virtue of our dissent, are pushed outside the ever-shrinking Gay political universe.[20] This is the political project that finds its voice in cultural criticism from the likes of Bruce Bawer in *A Place at the Table: The Gay Individual in American Society* (1993) and Andrew Sullivan in *Virtually Normal: An Argument about Homosexuality* (1995) and in law from neo-con-liberals like William N. Eskridge in *The Case for Same-Sex Marriage: From Sexual Liberty to Civilized Commitment* (1996).

---

[18] See generally Shannon Gilreath, Sexual Identity Law in Context: Cases and Materials 141–148 (2007).

[19] Franke, *supra* note 15, at 1415 (quoting *Roadmap to Equality: A Freedom to Marry Educational Guide* [Marriage Equality California & Lambda Legal Defense and Education Fund, 2002]) (emphasis in original).

[20] Nonetheless, courageous resisters do continue to write Radical critiques of marriage. Notable examples are Paula Ettelbrick, e.g., *Since When Is Marriage the Path to Liberation?* Out/Look National Gay and Lesbian Quarterly, Fall 1989, at 14; Michael Warner, The Trouble with Normal (1999); Nancy Polikoff, e.g., *Ending Marriage as We Know It*, 32 Hofstra L. Rev. 201 (2003); Ruthann Robson, *Compulsory Matrimony*, in Feminist and Queer Legal Theory: Intimate Encounters, Uncomfortable Conversations (M. A. Fineman, J. E. Jackson, & A. P. Romero, eds., 2009); and Katherine Franke, e.g., *The Politics of Same-Sex Marriage Politics*, 15 Colum. J. Gender & L. 236 (2006).

Indeed, the politics and law of the gay rights movement have become uni-vocal in their supplication to straight power: *Look at me! I'm like you!* Having thus set the parameters of political organizing, the leadership has narrowed the focus of community resources nearly exclusively to marriage. A Radical, revolutionary stance, one that critiques patriarchy and militarism, is less often heard. Aggressive calls for assimilation into the very institutions that define those evils – marriage and military – have replaced it. The Gay "masses" see the liberal leadership of the gay rights movement and, realizing that these leaders are the only Gay people they know who are not being denied employ-ment or status simply because they are Gay-identified, believe the leadership must be on the right road. What they fail to see is that this same leadership has co-opted the Gay Movement for their own ends, focusing on only those goals (usually marriage) that are central to their comfortable (and total) middle-class assimilation. One wonders what, if marriage did open up nationally, this leadership would do – retire, perhaps. After all, what more would be left for them to accomplish from their perspective? Until Gay people begin to cri-tique the politics of representation that values only that which is paradigmati-cally straight, then liberal opportunism in the name of individual progress is about the most we can hope for. And until we embrace seriously the shift from reformism to Radicalism inherent in this critique, we will not be free from the endemic Self-hate that consumes us and drives assimilation.

Relatedly, there is something even more disturbing about the case for marriage reflected in its propaganda. Consider, again, the admonition that "[there] is no other way for gay people to be fully equal to non-gay people ... than to participate in the same legal institution."[21] This reveals marriage to be a safety strategy. In other words, marriage is a way of legitimating behaviors other-wise illegitimate, a way of avoiding discrimination and second-class citizenship and of achieving civic safety. If Gay marriage boils down to a desperate attempt at assimilation in an effort to avoid the lethal attentions of heterosexuals, can we honestly talk about Gays entering marriage in anything resembling a condi-tion of freedom? In this realization, same-sex marriage – supposedly this new and game-changing thing – looks a lot like old patriarchal marriage, in which women "consented" to marriage as a way to achieve safety in a world that was nothing short of murderous for a woman without the "bonds of matrimony" as her shield. When William Eskridge argues that marriage is a way for Gays to become "civilized," I wonder if he wants Gays to be "civilized" in the same ways that women have been "civilized" by marriage.[22] Institutionalization out

---

[21] Franke, *supra* note 15, at 1415.
[22] WILLIAM N. ESKRIDGE, JR., THE CASE FOR SAME-SEX MARRIAGE: FROM SEXUAL LIBERTY TO CIVILIZED COMMITMENT (1996).

of desperation hardly seems much like freedom to me. Neither does becoming heterosexualized ghosts of ourSelves.

Of course, marriage is generally presented as an issue of personal choice and freedom.[23] Returning for a moment to the initial narrative of this chapter, that of the evangelist's sexperiment, one sees that the appearance of choice is cleverly maintained through appeals to nature (for evangelicals and so-called natural law adherents in the Catholic tradition, nature is merely a reflection of the Divine),[24] thereby masking the reality of force actually rendering marriage compulsory. Under patriarchy, society and law work *in tandem* to force women into marriage – socially, (apparently) monogamous, state-sanctioned relationships are favored, and legally these relationships are rewarded with a host of advantages. Only rhetorically is choice a factor, although the concept has certainly been effectively co-opted. Currently, I think, a discernible reverse feminism is at work, in which women "choose" to have children at the expense of career or other goals and attribute "failure" or "selfishness" to women who do not have children or who procreate but continue to work. How many times must one hear that "the most important job is being a mother?" This is to say nothing of the failure to see women's work, that work which has been allowed women historically, as valuable, but rather to gesture toward the retrenched position that marriage and child obligation are women's work because they are naturally fulfilling for women, not because they are what women have been valued for in a system of value defined by men.

What social pressure could not accomplish, legal and economic pressures often have, with feminist marriage resisters being coerced into marriage by the state. I was struck recently by an email I received from a woman I consider to be a serious feminist. She wrote in relevant part:

> I speak, by the way, as a once-radical feminist who reluctantly "caved" 18 years ago on my own long-held anti-marriage position during a bitter custody dispute over my partner's young sons when it became clear that in S. Carolina he and I would risk losing equal access to them if we "lived in sin." Although I enjoyed making a public commitment, as it turned out, and I've appreciated the comforts of long-term intimacy, I recognize that the economic and social privileges I receive as a married woman render me a tacit supporter of patriarchy in ways I find unsettling.[25]

[23] See Evan Wolfson, *Crossing the Threshold: Equal Marriage Rights for Lesbians and Gay Men and the Intra-Community Critique*, 21 N.Y.U. Rev. L. & Soc. Change 567 (1993) (esp. part IIA).

[24] Specifically in regard to the naturalness of heterosexual marriage (and the unnaturalness of Gay marriage), see the sado-scholarship of the Ramsey Colloquium, *The Homosexual Movement: A Response by the Ramsey Colloquium*, First Things 15–20 (Mar. 1994).

[25] Personal email correspondence with the author. Used with permission.

Her story is not unique (although her own analysis of her status is unusual). I hear from other feminist marriage resisters who feel compelled to marry because they need health insurance, for example. Women, not unlike Gays, are compelled into marriage in a system of patriarchal Hobson's choices that render real choice or consent virtually impossible.

And to those few resisters whom economic and social pressures could not break, the cult of romance turns full force. The heterosexualized ideal of *love*, with which we are bombarded ceaselessly, works to alter desire, in fact to supplant it completely with the romanticized ideal of monogamous, familial coupling in the heterosexual model. Romance, of course, has always been a serious weapon in the war to keep the dynamic of compulsion inherent in the marriage model for women hidden, in which every violation is variously deemed love, or sex, or consent, concealing the compulsion on which the system is based – that which Andrea Dworkin named when she wrote that "romance … is rape embellished with meaningful looks."[26] But what is most curious about the heteronormative romantic project from the perspective of Gay liberation is that it exists and works in essentially unaltered form even in same-sex relationships, in which pro-marriage advocates claim traditional gender dynamics have been disrupted. For example, the named plaintiff in *Perry v. Schwarzenneger*, Kristin Perry, testified in district court that "marriage would provide her what she wants most in life: a stable relationship with Stier [her partner], the woman she loves and with whom she has built a life and a family. To Perry, marriage would provide access to the language to describe her relationship with Stier: 'I'm a 45-year-old woman. I have been in love with a woman for 10 years and I don't have a word to tell anybody about that'."[27] Perry's testimony reveals that her idea of love is essentially that which the Heterarchy has prescribed, necessarily encapsulated in the heterarchal-family construct. It is also (should be, at least) unsettling that Perry believed that the inaccessibility of "marriage" as a label deprived her totally of the ability to name her relationship with Stier, bringing us again to Monique Wittig's observation on the "discourses of heterosexuality" that "prevent us from speaking unless we speak in their terms."[28] Gay liberation understands that the problem with appropriating marriage is that access to marriage in its unaltered heteronormativity does not signal a coming to speech for Gay

[26] See Andrea Dworkin, *The Night and Danger*, in LETTERS FROM A WAR ZONE: WRITINGS, 1976–1989 14 (1993).

[27] *Perry*, 704 F. Supp.2d at 933.

[28] See Chapter 1, this volume, for a discussion of Wittig's ideas.

people; rather it signals a subsuming of the Gay consciousness into a thoroughly heterosexual discourse.[29]

This failure to situate marriage in heteroarchal social reality is one of the great failures of the gay rights movement. Thus, when marriage advocate Evan Wolfson points to polling showing that 85 percent of Gay male respondents would marry if they could do so legally,[30] I am persuaded of little more than the fact that the discourses of heterosexuality are totalizing. Wouldn't one expect this kind of result when from birth we are socialized to believe that marriage is the path to both personal fulfillment and civic responsibility? Valuing such statistics as evaluative of homosexual desire is to revalue that which has been established and enforced as compulsory by heterosexuals as a "genuine expression of [*a homosexual's*] desires."[31] How can such scholarship be taken seriously? If Gay reality under straight supremacy has meant anything, it has meant that what Gays have been and thought has largely been limited to what straights have permitted us to be and to think. As an answer to this kind of criticism, Wolfson paradoxically cites Adrienne Rich's idea of a "lesbian continuum" as proof that some Gays could desire marriage as an authentic expression of Self.[32] To use Rich in this way is not only to misunderstand her, but to give too little attention to the ways that straight supremacist power operates in material reality. Wolfson's position is revealing and useful, however, to the extent that it illuminates the degree to which the gay rights movement treats acceptance of compulsory heterosexual forms and patterns of relating as real progress toward Gay equality. This movement essentially takes straight supremacy as a myth to be debunked rather than as a totalizing political and legal discourse limiting Gay possibilities. By contrast, Gay liberation understands that equality, no less freedom, for Gays will require real change in thought and action, not mere reconceptualization of old ways of thinking. It understands that Gay "desire" is not merely an outgrowth or echo of some underlying fixed set of essential desires shared by all (hetero and homo).

---

[29] Real political revolution comes with a revolution of concepts, linguistically and institutionally. By adopting marriage, we are leaving within the power of the straight mind the definition of what constitutes a respectable relationship. The networking of our relationship as Gay people to society at large is thus negotiated through the adaptation of an institution and a lexicon that is statically patriarchal and heteroarchal and that is presented as a logical necessity. Most Gay people I talk to who insist on legal access to the word "marriage" (again as opposed to the bundle of rights currently triggered by the word in statutes) insist that access is necessary because marriage signals to society that their relationships are valuable.

[30] Wolfson, *supra* note 23, at 583.

[31] Id. at 582.

[32] Id. at 586, n. 82.

From its essentially heteroarchal frame of reference, the pro-marriage, gay rights movement asks us to accept an essentially reformist philosophy. This philosophy exposes acutely the individualism and idealism that are the gay rights movement's central tenets, asking us to accept that marriage is what an individual (or individual couple) makes of it and asking us to ignore the reality of Gay lives when those lives are not comfortably middle-class. When liberal individualism and idealism are mixed with conservative moralism, in calls for Gay domesticity as a means toward civilization, from radicals like Larry Kramer to neo-cons like William Eskridge, marriage is categorical in the liberal tradition – long on universality but short on social reality. The gay rights movement has fetishized marriage by focusing on access to the category at the expense of a principled analysis of the social reality that produced the category and that operates through it. In virtually every instantiation of the liberal argument for marriage, the patriarchal category of marriage has been accepted as a social good and, since it is supposedly reformed because gender inequality is not apparent when marital partners are of the same sex, taken as the only validation of a sexual/emotional relationship that is meaningful/authentic.

For example, when Professor William Eskridge criticized Professor Nancy Polikoff's lucid critique of marriage,[33] he asserted that

> Polikoff comes perilously close to essentializing marriage as an inherently regressive institution.... That Western marriage has traditionally been the social instrument by which women have been subordinated does not mean that marriage "causes" that subordination. Women's subordination may be more deeply related to social attitudes about gender differences than to the formal construct of marriage per se. If that is true, same-sex marriage does not buy into a rotten institution; it only buys into an institution that is changing as women's roles and status are changing in our society.[34]

Eskridge's reformist, revisionist position is contra-historical, to say the least. Historically, marriage encoded in law the social inequality between men and women, institutionalizing sex inequality socially by drawing circles around women legally. Women became, literally, the property of their husbands, ceasing to exist as persons legally under a system of coverture,[35] with men's access to women's bodies as the system's central tenet. In marriage, being gendered female, which had meant being rapable socially, was redefined to mean

[33] Nancy D. Polikoff, *We Will Get What We Ask For: Why Legalizing Gay and Lesbian Marriage Will Not "Dismantle the Legal Structure of Gender in Every Marriage,"* 79 VA. L. REV. 1535 (1993).

[34] William N. Eskridge, Jr., *A History of Same-Sex Marriage*, 79 VA. L. REV. 1419, 1488 (1993).

[35] For a discussion of coverture, see SUZANNE REYNOLDS, 1 LEE'S NORTH CAROLINA FAMILY LAW § 5.1 (5th ed., 2010).

the impossibility of being raped legally, as the marital rape exception gave husbands license to exact sex from their wives, who were said to have given unlimited consent by virtue of marrying.[36] And the marriage model meant silence for women, circumlocution of speech, because women could not enter into contracts on their own or give testimony against their husbands and could be battered with impunity simply for talking too much.[37]

If Professor Eskridge believes that Professor Polikoff came only "perilously close" to essentializing marriage as inherently bad, let me make it plain for him: Marriage *is* inherently "regressive" and "rotten." How perverse would Eskridge's argument be if it were applied to any other institution through which so many atrocities against body and mind have been accomplished? How laughable would such a reformist argument appear when applied to slavery, for example?[38] Can slavery be reformed? Is the historical subjugation of Blacks more closely related to attitudes about race than to the formal construct of slavery per se?[39] And Professor Polikoff and I are not alone in thinking so. John Stuart Mill asserted that marriage is "wrong in itself" as the principal source of the subjection of women to men.[40] Before Mill, Engels observed that "[m]onogamous marriage was a great historical step forward [economically]; nevertheless, together with slavery and private wealth it opens the period that has lasted until today in which every step forward is also relatively a step backward, in which prosperity and development for some are won through the misery and frustration of others."[41] Marriage was also explicitly recognized as inherently flawed and destructive by early Gay liberation, as in *The Gay Liberation Manifesto*.[42] It is perhaps this incompatibility of the movement's new, warm relationship with marriage and the origins of Gay liberation that causes Eskridge to paint such a one-sided portrait of Gay American history

---

[36] See, e.g., Act of May 29, 1979, ch. 682, §1, 1979 N.C. Sess. Laws 725, 726–727 (codified as amended at N.C. Gen. Stat. §14-27.8 [2001]) (A person *may not be prosecuted* under this Article *if* the victim is the person's legal spouse at the time of the commission of the alleged rape or sexual offense, unless the parties are living separately and apart pursuant to a written agreement or a judicial degree).

[37] See, e.g., Joyner v. Joyner, 59 N.C. (6 Jones Eq.) 322, 325 (1862).

[38] This analogy is not hyperbole. Marriage under patriarchy has been a system of sexual slavery. John Stuart Mill's observation that "there remain no legal slaves, except the mistress of every house" is especially poignant. John Stuart Mill, *The Subjection of Women*, in Essays on Sex Equality 217 (Alice S. Rossi, ed., 1970).

[39] Many abolitionists, at any rate, understood the relationship in the inverse. Lydia Maria Child, for example, wrote in *An Appeal in Favor of Americans Called Africans* (1833), "We made slavery, and slavery makes the prejudice."

[40] Mill, *supra* note 38, at 125.

[41] Frederick Engels, Origins of the Family, Private Property, and State 129 (1884).

[42] Gay Liberation Front, Gay Liberation Manifesto (1971, rev. 1978).

as one in which Radical liberationist kooks were naturally replaced by the monogamy-minded, AIDS-phobic, propertied – in a word, acceptable – Gays of the modern gay rights movement.[43]

Nevertheless, Eskridge's retort to Polikoff invites us to look more closely at the relationship between gender hierarchy and marriage. Eskridge claims that "[w]omen's subordination may be more deeply related to social attitudes about gender differences than to the formal construct of marriage per se." Since Lacan, especially since Foucault, it has generally been acceptable to see practically everything as socially constructed to one degree or another. It thus strikes me as odd (dare I say convenient) that Eskridge would separate "social attitudes about gender differences" from the "construct of marriage per se." If we are to accept, after Foucault, that sexuality is socially constructed, can we really say that marriage is not? Can an institution that *is* the institutionalization of social mores of inequality through the legalization of inequality be so easily separated from those original and motivating social impulses? Is the formal construct of marriage not one of hierarchy based on gender difference? If it isn't, perhaps Professor Eskridge should have filled in the blanks for us. What "there," exactly, is there in marriage? If heterosexuality is masculine power in its social form, marriage is masculine power (heterosexuality) in its legal form. And since, as we have seen, heterosexuality cannot exist without gender, the germane question becomes whether marriage can exist without gender in the ways its advocates claim. In fact, in her analysis of Professor Eskridge's survey of same-sex marriages,[44] Professor Polikoff notes that

> most of the marriages Eskridge uncovered support rather than subvert hierarchy based upon gender. His historical and anthropological evidence contradicts any assumption that "gender dissent" is inherent between two men or two women. Rather, most of the unions reported were in fact gendered ... one partner tended to assume the characteristics and responsibilities of the opposite gender, with both partners then acting out their traditional gender roles.[45]

In theory, and perhaps to some degree in reality, allowing marriage by partners of the same sex could disrupt a still powerful and obvious institution of sex discrimination, and it has the potential to disrupt gender roles to the extent that marriage is a powerful vehicle by which the gender binary is communicated and reified. Some feminists have made this argument. Professor

---

[43] ESKRIDGE, THE CASE FOR SAME-SEX MARRIAGE, *supra* note 22. For a similar critique, see Walters, *infra* note 47.

[44] See Eskridge, *A History of Same-Sex Marriage*, *supra* note 34, at 1487–1488.

[45] Polikoff, *supra* note 33, at 1535, 1538.

Mary Anne Case, for example, wrote recently of these potentialities and of the need to pursue them through adherence to what she calls a "thin definition of marriage."[46] But the urgent question here is whether marriage can in fact be disrupted to any appreciable degree or whether the incredible resilience of heteroarchal/patriarchal institutions will simply metastasize to absorb, corrupt, and undo any change accomplished in time. To use Professor Case's vocabulary, can marriage be made "thin" enough? Perhaps the more useful project – one of providing a coherent alternative to marriage altogether – could accomplish the laudable, fundamentally feminist goal articulated by Case as well as obviate (or at least slow) the regrettable like-straight normative engine driving the marriage obsession in the first place.

The social, legal, and political changes that Professor Eskridge and others see as the key to marriage reformism are not substantive when one understands the central tenets of marriage to be those of compulsion, hierarchy, and regulation. The overlay of a gay politics of individualism and choice on this traditional structure has not really altered the rules beyond the surface transformation of the sex of the partners involved; the politics of marriage, as an engine of conformity and regulation, have changed little. The lack of change reveals the cognitive dissonance between marriage and Gay liberation, and Gay liberation and "gay rights." In her profound essay on the marriage question, Professor Suzanna Danuta Walters notes that in the dominant like-straight discourse of both heterosexuals and assimilationist Gays, "[o]ur relationships, our desires, our parenting styles are again and again presented as replicas of heterosexual patterns, as if gay families exist in a sort of alternate universe that isn't really alternate at all. While odes to family *diversity* abound, real invocations of family *difference* are muted."[47] Walters's assessment of assimilationist discourse in the marriage context sounds a lot like a description of liberal religious ecumenism, which generally holds that the god-father religions should respect each other but says little about reconceptualizing god as goddess or in dis-anthropomorphized terms. Religious diversity in the liberal model is simultaneously acknowledged *and* erased in a disingenuous nod to change, all the while understanding that no real change is promoted that might threaten patriarchal religious hegemony.

---

[46] Mary Anne Case, *What Feminists Have to Lose in Same-Sex Marriage Litigation* (July 2010), http://ssrn.com/abstract=1639182.

[47] Suzanna D. Walters, *Wedding Bells and Baby Carriages: Heterosexuals Imagine Gay Families, Gay Families Imagine Themselves*, in The Uses of Narrative: Explorations in Sociology, Psychology, and Cultural Studies 49 (Molly Andrews et al., eds., 2004) (emphasis in original).

Similarly, marriage, as assimilationist catalyst, allows the liberal Left to say that Gays are "different," to the extent that we want to fuck people of the same sex, while grandly proclaiming that we are all the same – that Gays, naturally, want fucking and *love* to occur in a marriage, that we want children, et cetera. Gays' Gayness is erased entirely, and we are reconstituted into something that sounds a lot like the Vatican's pronouncement that we are simply disordered straight people in need of reordering. Marriage becomes the tool used to civilize us; in William Eskridge's words:

> The civilizing influence of family values, with or without children, ultimately may be the best argument for same-sex marriage.[48]

Here it is, then, plainly: We, the Wild Gay Ones, are in need of civilization. Marriage, apparently because it is heterosexuality at its apogee – legalistic and confining – is taken as both the indicator and means of civilization: as civilization itself. Getting Gays into marriage will therefore transform us into civilized beings. Eskridge's syllogism gives Adrienne Rich's idea of compulsory heterosexuality new meaning. Rich understood heterosexuality as a ruling institution. I understand marriage as a heterosexual conspiracy – a way to consolidate power and to erase the threat that Gay liberation poses. The essential argument, à la Eskridge, Bruce Bawer, Andrew Sullivan, and other purveyors of hetero-speak, is that marriage is pro-family, pro-monogamy, et cetera – in a word, pro-heterosexuality. A principle of Eskridge's argument, for example, is that, in our married, civilized reformulation, Gays will be more "acceptable" to straights.[49] In this neo-con philosophy (what passes for liberalism in a supposedly Left academy), the definition of citizenship is totally surrendered, and the capitulation is on straight terms alone. Marriage remains compulsory – an extension of the compulsory ethic of compulsory heterosexuality – and regulatory, in that Gay relationships are regulated by the marriage framework in which some Gays – the "good" or "civilized" Gays – conform to the time-honored marriage model. Nonconformists are adjudged civically irresponsible and destructive.

Through this Self-inflicted reversal, the pro-marriage, gay rights movement is complicit in the erasure of the Radical Gay Self. Gay marriage is a strategy for Gay assimilation into pop-culture reiterations of the heteroarchal/patriarchal romantic myth. In her essay, Professor Walters insightfully elucidates this point by analyzing the central theme of popular television depictions of "the gay wedding" (the *only* issue Gays are

---

[48] Eskridge, The Case for Same-Sex Marriage, *supra* note 22.
[49] Id. at 9.

presented as caring much about [unless it's children] in the mainstream media). Walters writes:

> Nowhere is this new gay visibility more pronounced – and more prob-lematic – than in television. Gay weddings appeared in numerous series, including Friends ... Northern Exposure, and Roseanne. For all the obvious newness of these representations, most have forgone the taboo gay kiss and presented gay marriage ceremonies as cuddly, desexualized mirrors of the more familiar heterosexual ritual. Notably absent are the odes to same-sex love and the revisions of traditional vows that most assuredly accompany many gay commitment ceremonies. The Friends wedding – while carefully sensitive – went out of its way to portray the gay wedding as an exact replica of its heterosexual counterpart, only with two bridal gowns. The episode focused more on the heterosexual response to the gay environment than on the gay participants themselves. Indeed, the gay wedding was framed by a secondary plotline concerning the impending divorce of a character's traditional mom, implicitly linking heterosexuality and homosexuality in a liberal scenario of sameness.[50]

Walters goes on to note that in these "major 'gay weddings' ... on TV, it is a heterosexual character who brings the nervous and fighting homosexual cou-ple together when the nuptials are threatened."[51] The fact that it is often the most homophobic of characters who "saves" the day is of no small significance and continues the theme of pro-marriage advocates that if straights could just realize that Gays are like them homophobia would be undone. Walters writes that "[t]he straight character gets reformed and redeemed through a demon-strated expertise in pre-wedding cold feet, thereby avoiding reckoning with a previously impregnable homophobia."[52] The salient point here is that the purported key for straights to overcome their homophobia is an understand-ing of Gay/straight sameness. The liberal media, like the rest of the liberal establishment, has its *focus on straights and their capacities*. But there is a mes-sage, not entirely subtle either, sent to Gays from this scenario too: If you want to be accepted, get with the program and assimilate. In this light, Walters's point on straight characters bringing nervous Gays to the altar has other, per-haps more important and ominous implications on which she does not focus, namely that in leading Gays to the altar, liberal straights are leading the way to Gay erasure and congratulating themselves on it. But it also gestures to the possibility of Radical Resistance. What if, instead of following straights

[50] Walters, *supra* note 47, at 50.
[51] Id.
[52] Id.

down the aisle, Gays followed our instincts? Perhaps the Gay nervousness Walters notes, quickly assuaged by eager hetero-do-gooders, was actually a rare Meta-Memory,[53] a brief clarity of insight cutting through the heteroarchal everyday[54] – what Walt Whitman called "a glimpse through an interstice

---

[53] "Meta-Memory" is my way of conceptualizing the idea of a Memory that creates insight from a deeper consciousness and breaks through the heteroarchal false possibilities of everyday that are designed to capture Gay consciousness and thwart authentic Radicalism. In a sense, this kind of Meta-Memory is the act of un-remembering the false memories prescribed for us by our heteroarchal rulers, both civil and religious. Again, noting that the prefix "meta" means "beyond," I mean to signal here a transcendence of known possibilities by tapping into Gay creativity and imagining new ways of being – with the purpose of actualizing a new reality. Part of such a process must be drawn from our past experiences, but much of it will have to come from the courage to imagine possibilities that we may not be able to envision clearly because we have never been allowed under Heterarchy to control our own destinies. The idea of such a Memory can be directly traced to the philosophy of Virginia Woolf, who wrote of "memories – what one has forgotten – [that] come to the top.... I feel that strong emotion must leave its trace; and it is only a question of discovering how we can get ourselves again attached to it, so that we shall be able to live our lives through from the start" (V. WOOLF, MOMENTS OF BEING: UNPUBLISHED AUTOBIOGRAPHICAL WRITINGS [ed. and with an introduction and notes by Jeanne Schulkind, 1976]). It is worth noting, since this concept surfaces in the context of the marriage discussion, that Woolf was a Gay woman who, despite having genuine goodwill toward her husband, was captured by compulsory heterosexuality's compulsory marriage. She sought a return to Meta-Memory and authentic Radicalism through her writing and through empowering relationships, outside of compulsory heterosexuality, with other Gay women. Of course, the other two intellectuals, Whitman and Dworkin, integral to the discussion of Meta-Memory and Radical Resistance here were also Gay. Whitman certainly recognizes Meta-Memory in his writing, but does not name it. Radical Gay prophet Harry Hay also wrote of it, although not by name, when he observed "reunion with that long-ago-cast-out shadow-self so long suppressed and denied, the explosive energies released by the jubilations of those reunions were ecstatic beyond belief" (quoted in RADICALLY GAY: GAY LIBERATION IN THE WORDS OF ITS FOUNDER HARRY HAY 255 (Will Roscoe, ed., 1996)).

Radical Lesbian philosopher and theologian Mary Daly drew on Woolf for her concept of "Original Memory" or "E-motional Memory" in her *Pure Lust: Elemental Feminist Philosophy* (1984). In a later work, she and Jane Caputi defined *Metamemory* as "Deep, Ecstatic Memory of participation in Be-ing that eludes the categories and grids of patriarchal consciousness, Spiraling into the Past, carrying Vision forward ... Memory beyond civilization" (see M. DALY AND J. CAPUTI, WEBSTERS' FIRST NEW INTERGALACTIC WICKEDARY OF THE ENGLISH LANGUAGE 81 [1987]). I developed my concept of Meta-Memory, substantially as it reads here, from Woolf, Whitman, and Dworkin, without consciously relying on Daly, although I was familiar with her major, early works, *Beyond God the Father* (1973) and *Gyn/Ecology* (1978), which I read in college and the latter of which I found extremely influential and useful as a springboard to new analyses. It was not until I was sharing drafts of chapters of *The End of Straight Supremacy* with Daly's and my mutual friend (and co-author with Daly of the *Wickedary*) Professor Jane Caputi that Jane directed me to Daly's work on Memory in *Pure Lust* and simultaneously sent me an autographed copy of the *Wickedary*. It was then that I realized the close connectedness of our ideas/ideals. I think the relationship is proof that Meta-Memory (as I've chosen to call it) exists and that it connects Radical Consciousnesses, past, present, *and* future.

[54] See the discussion of the heteroarchal everyday in Chapter 1, this volume.

caught."[55] In that glimpse, Gays see compulsory heterosexuality's compulsory marriage project as real violence to our Gay Selves and to our relationships with other Gay Selves. The overwhelming crush of the Heteroarchy's everyday makes such moments of clarity and Meta-Remembering come only infrequently. Gays need to Meta-Remember our Radicalism and to engage in Radical Resistance to the everyday and its traps, including compulsory marriage, if we are to survive as authentic Beings. In Andrea Dworkin's words, *Remember, Resist, Do Not Comply.*

MARRIAGE AND PHYSICAL VIOLENCE

It is often noted that approximately 50 percent of heterosexual marriages end in divorce.[56] It is less frequently remarked, as Claudia Card once quipped, that the other 50 percent probably should. But the legal entanglement that is marriage is, despite the existence of no-fault divorce, still difficult to get loose from. Economic dependence (which marriage encourages on the part of one spouse – most often the woman) and the presence of children, coupled with legal strictures that make exit difficult, often keep bad marriages intact. This has been most alarming because, for women, the marital home is often violent.[57]

There is strong evidence that Gay relationships mirror the violence of their heterosexual counterparts. Gay relationships are violent precisely because the only model Gays have for what a relationship should look like is the straight model. The dominant structure of sexual inequality inherent in heterosexual marriages bleeds over into the Gay model, so that Gay relationships reaffirm those social conditions to the detriment of the people involved. Some reports speculate that domestic violence among Gay men may occur at rates greater than domestic violence in the straight community. One study indicated that 23.1 percent of cohabiting Gay men said they were raped and/or physically battered by a spouse or cohabiting partner at some time in their lives, compared with 7.7 percent of men cohabiting with opposite-sex partners.[58] Another

---

[55] Walt Whitman, Leaves of Grass 138 (1867).

[56] The Nat'l Marriage Project at the Univ. of Va. & the Inst. For Am. Values, The State of Our Unions, Marriage in America, 2009: Money & Marriage 77 (2009), http://www.virginia.edu/marriageproject/annual reports.html.

[57] See Patricia Tjaden & Nancy Thoennes, U.S. Dep't of Just., NCJ 181867, Extent, Nature, and Consequences of Intimate Partner Violence, iii (2000), http://www.ojp.usdog.gov/nij/pubs-sum/181867.htm (noting that 25% of women were raped or physically assaulted by a current or former spouse or cohabiting partner).

[58] L. Kevin Hamberger & Mary Beth Phelan, Domestic Violence Screening and Intervention in Medical and Mental Healthcare Settings 301 (2004).

study showed that men who have sex with men are six times more likely than straight men to suffer an assault as an adult.[59] I think there are very important sociological reasons for this. We inevitably strike out against the thing we are conditioned to hate. In the case of cohabiting Gays, that target is readily accessible in the home. It is a form of internalized and then externalized queer bashing in the most intimate dimensions of the Gay community itself.

Knowing what we know, do we really want to make our relationships harder to get out of than we need to? There is certainly no reason to believe that the legal entanglements of marriage would affect battered Gays differently than they have battered women. Recall that when one of Jeffery Dahmer's victims escaped – dazed, nearly naked, and understanding nearly no English – and made it to the police, those police returned him to Dahmer, despite the fact that his head was obviously bleeding from Dahmer's attempts to drill holes in his skull. Reportedly, the officers joked that it was a lover's spat.[60] The obvious violence was somehow rendered consensual in the minds of these (ostensibly heterosexual) officers because it took place within the parameters of an assumed romantic relationship. Interesting how the officers made basically the same reductionistic assumptions about Gay men that the majority did in *Lawrence.*

The anticommunitarian nature of marriage puts Gays at risk of violence from outside of our relationships, too. One of the preconditions to violence is that the victim is usually alone and cut off from systems of support. This is one reason that marriage has been so dangerous for women. But the anticommunitarian nature of marriage may be even more dangerous for Gays, because historically a woman has traded (sometimes violent) bondage to one man in marriage for safety from the danger of violence from many men if she were not married. The respect of patriarchs for one another has generally meant some safety for women in marriage relative to the rest of the patriarchal world. Not so for Gays. Marriage, because it privatizes energies into the family unit, results in the dismantling of support systems found in the community. When Gays recognize other Gays, we often say they are "family." The gay rights movement has abandoned this communitarian conception of family in favor of the heterosexualized, privatized, monogamous family model found in marriage.

The marriage craze is also driven by an emerging obsession by Gays with procreation – an enterprise that further privatizes energies. Arguably, this

---

[59] GILLIAN C. MEZEY & MICHAEL B. KING, MALE VICTIMS OF SEXUAL ASSAULT 9 (2d ed., 2000).

[60] *Milwaukee Panel Finds Discrimination by Police*, N.Y. TIMES, Oct. 16, 1991.

retreat into the nuclear family unit leaves us even more vulnerable to out-side attack, as political consciousness recedes in favor of the romanticized family ideal. Monogamy, definitionally, is the anticommunitarian privatiza-tion of sexual energies, and with those energies comes the privatization of the very sexual politics of community building. Philosopher Richard Mohr, notably, has argued that marriage ought to be reformed to allow for the often open, communitarian nature of Gay multi-partner relationships.[61] But there seems to be no interest on the part of the Gay leadership in pursuing this path instead of the fetishized, heterosexual ideal. In the closed, like-straight liberal universe, anything not approximating the (fictionally) monogamous hetero-sexual union is valueless. Consequently, since there is no special safety in Gay marriage in the same way that it is built into the heterosexual marriage racket for the preservation of patriarchy, marriage may leave Gays more vulnerable to outside violence.

THE AIM OF RADICAL CRITIQUE

A critique of reformism is serious business, and it can be seriously misunder-stood. There is nothing qualitatively revolutionary about wanting to sit at a dirty lunch counter in some dead-end Southern hamlet or about giving your lunch money to the white supremacist who wants to exclude you from his or her restaurant, but we have understood the basic indignity of a caste-based denial of access and, accordingly, Blacks' right to be there. Similarly, there is nothing remotely revolutionary about wanting to join the ranks of America's military–industrial complex or about the weird desire to be shot at in "defense" of a country that routinely denies you political rights and basic human dignity, and yet we have understood the pathological sexism and heterosexism that barred women and Gays from military service, and we have understood that a basic commitment to equality gave women and Gays the right to be included. We understood the caste ramifications of allowing only whites or only men or only straights to control all of anything at any time. In light of this recognition, we did not ask Blacks why they wanted to eat at the bigot's lunch counter or women why they wanted to enroll at VMI.[62] Radicalism is not always synony-mous with separatism.

---

[61] Richard D. Mohr, *The Case for Gay Marriage*, 9 NOTRE DAME J. L. ETHICS & PUB. POL'Y 215, 233 (1995).

[62] See United States v. Virginia, 518 U.S. 515 (1996). See also Chapter 2, this volume, discussing the VMI case. Women, it should be noted, *were* asked the question for a very long time. See Andrea Dworkin, *Redefining Nonviolence*, in OUR BLOOD: PROPHESIES AND DISCOURSES ON SEXUAL POLITICS (1976).

For many who identify with the gay rights movement, the inability of Gays to marry in most states is simply another example of caste-based exclusion. Clearly-caste-based reactions to the small number of jurisdictions where Gays have won the right to marry, like efforts to amend the federal Constitution to take away states' rights to define marriage, certainly lend credence to that view. Thus, for many Gay advocates, marriage – called marriage – is necessary to vindicate equality, and anything short of marriage by name would be unequal. The focus of such arguments is on the exclusionary properties of having a dual lexicographical system for state-sanctioned coupling based on the sexual orientation of the couple involved. I understand the argument; I have some sympathy for it; and I don't believe it should be sneered at or dismissed offhandedly in the name of Radicalism. But I do think that the marriage obsession that has gripped the gay rights movement, the frenetic, messianic character of its arguments, requires us to look more carefully at why the label of marriage is valued, at why equal rights for Gays who choose state-regulated coupling are not enough – are in fact derided – by a gay rights movement that spends millions litigating over the right to a word, when far more basic, far more important (from the aspect of general safety) measures have languished.[63]

If, at bottom, the marriage craze is fueled by a gay politics that values only that which is paradigmatically straight – that recognizes value in only those things that are most cognizably heterosexual in form and function – then a Radical reply is necessary. I believe the marriage project (here to be distinguished from the demand for equal rights in state-sanctioned coupling) is the product of such a like-straight politics, and is therefore dangerous. It should be Radically Resisted.[64]

This conclusion having been reached, one important, clarifying question is left begging, namely: Why, if Gays are making essentially patriarchal/heteroarchal arguments for Gay marriage, are patriarchal religionists so threatened?[65]

---

[63] The continuing lack of federal employment nondiscrimination protection means that the most vulnerable Gays, poor and working-class Gays, will continue to be the most vulnerable. The emergent centrality of marriage to the gay rights movement exposes the movement as one centered on the assimilationist desires of a middle-class, predominantly white interest group at the expense of lower-income Gays, making them a caste within a caste. This is a movement most aptly described by David Valentine's brilliant paraphrase of Eve Sedgwick: as an "epistemology of the walk-in closet." See DAVID VALENTINE, IMAGINING TRANSGENDER: AN ETHNOGRAPHY OF A CATEGORY 242 (2007).

[64] Of course, civil marriage is open to Gays in six states now and the District of Columbia. This raises the question of the appropriate ethic in that particular situation. I think the proper focus from the perspective of Gay liberation is what Gays will do with marriage as a form of power when we have it; that is, will we use it differently than straight men have used it?

[65] This is exactly the clarifying way in which David A. J. Richards put it in a conversation with me about this chapter.

In other words, isn't fundamentalist outrage at Gay marriage driven by the belief that patriarchal marriage is, in fact, threatened by gay rights arguments for inclusion?[66] And if that is the case, as I believe it to be, might it not be that making the argument for Gay marriage is the best way to challenge American patriarchy? As usual in a system of heteroarchal reversals, getting to the real answer to this apparent paradox requires unthinking heteroarchal thinking and realizing that patriarchal/heteroarchal supremacy is more ingeniously designed for self-preservation than would be the case if its only defenses were in blatant religiously motivated obstructionism.

The most desperate reason some Gays want inclusion in marriage is a question of caste – they see exclusion (as opposed to the renunciation that I call for) as imposed caste status. It's also true, I think, that from the Bawer/Sullivan/ Eskridge perspective, getting "in" will cure the caste deficit, will make Gays equal and, over time, socially acceptable to the conservative establishment. So they make patriarchal arguments for two principal reasons: (1) They think that patriarchal argument is what patriarchy understands; and (more disturbingly) (2) they actually believe what they say. As to reason (2) we are back to Wittig's observations on the totality/totalitarianism of heterosexual discourse and resulting captured consciousnesses.

For their part, religionists reject the gay patriarchal argument because it doesn't fit their definition of what patriarchy is – namely compulsory heterosexuality in form *and function*. Allowing Gays to assimilate into the bedrock patriarchal institution and still keep fucking as Gays is unacceptable because it blurs the caste lines between the "good" people and the "bad" people – lines along which power is distributed and stabilized.[67] The real tragedy of all this is that Gays' mad rush to marriage will never, from the perspective of hardliner patriarchs, turn "us" (Gays) into them; so, in the end, it simply makes us less ourSelves – it stunts the Gay creative capacity. Of course, there is some satisfaction in forcing our way in and putting a collective Gay thumb in their

---

[66]   See Chapter 7, this volume, for the presentation of some patriarchal arguments about Gay exclusion (dressed up as inclusion) and my refutation.

[67]   On this point, I need to comment on a typical attack on Radical Gay critiques of marriage, namely that those of us making such arguments are somehow doing the right wing a favor by arguing that Gays should not marry. Actually, the argument I am making here, that marriage should be resisted because it is a vehicle of patriarchal violence and of a compulsory heterosexuality that is inherently harmful, is not the sort of argument that right wingers care to hear. My argument against marriage for Gays is distinctly an argument from Gay liberation, thus from Gayness. In the Heteroarchy, everything perceived to be Gay must be pushed away: The gay rights movement's argument for marriage and its opposite, the Gay liberation argument for resistance, are equally reprehensible.

collective patriarchal eye, but the satisfaction is likely not worth the end-loss in Gay community and purpose.

If the incompatibility of Gay marriage advocacy and patriarchal religion (from the perspective of patriarchs) was the only component with which to contend, the deception would be much easier to reveal. But the Heteroarchy has a beguiling Janus-identified political system that seems to offer magnanimity through liberal encouragement for assimilation through marriage. Liberals, who in most cases are still patriarchal,[68] are really no less anti-Gay than are conservative religionists (except that being conceptually erased for Gay people is more than a little better than being dead). So liberals decide to turn Gays into their liberal image of evolutionized heterosexuality, making Gays, through marriage and other assimilationist traps, into heteros in form *if not in function*. In this case, the inclusion is a reductionistic inclusion, which is to say erasure by inclusion.

You can fight religious conservatives in the open (their enviable ability to propagandize themselves into the endangered minority notwithstanding). Liberals are slipperier. Patriarchy/Heteroarchy is maintained through the liberal tradition by the willingness of liberalism simply to absorb what it cannot combat. Pushing Gays into marriage (despite whatever minor gender role disturbance that might come through marriage by gender equals) thwarts the development of a meaningful alternative that might *actually* be antipatriarchal. If liberal politics gets its way, the status of the feminine as a political stigma remains relatively unchanged; Gays are simply invisibilized. Straight liberals are like the alien invaders in so many sci-fi horror flicks – when you let your guard down, they take over your body. Those of us who refuse are in for one hell of a time.

CONCLUSION

As I thought through this chapter, I reread "The Speech of Aristophanes" from Plato's *Symposium*, that antique defense of same-sex love still widely regarded as the best exposition of the Self-actualizing and legitimating power of Gay relationships, and was struck again by the realization that marriage nowhere figured.[69] Maybe the gay rights movement's leadership and the

---

[68] If they weren't, could Catharine MacKinnon seriously ask in the twenty-first century, "Are women human?" and be met with such a calculated, straight-faced (pun intended) academic dead silence? See CATHARINE A. MACKINNON, ARE WOMEN HUMAN? AND OTHER INTERNATIONAL DIALOGUES (2006).

[69] PLATO, THE SYMPOSIUM 22–27 (M. C. Howaston & Frisbee C. C. Sheffield, eds.; M. C. Howaston, trans., 2008).

lawyers who theorize to support them could use a refresher course in the classics. Otherwise, I fear that when the history of the Gay Movement itself is written, it may read more as epitaph than epilogue: "Once upon a time there was a movement ... then there was marriage." And one of the few ways of life in our culture that flourishes outside patriarchy and resists many of its demands will have uncritically compromised its moral independence.

7

Knowledge/Power

Reversing the Heteroarchal Reversals of Religion, Marriage, and Caste

Surely it was time someone invented a new plot, or that the author came out from the bushes.

Virginia Woolf, *Between the Acts*

The issue of same-sex marriage, newly illuminating Gay lives for people who long preferred to see us only dimly, has focused the disparity between Gay and straight America in bold relief. Recently, an influential cadre of law professors has used this disparity in status and understanding to mount a full-scale attack on emergent marriage equality laws and state antidiscrimination paradigms generally – at least insofar as such antidiscrimination paradigms are applied to Gays. What is most alarming is that these privileged law professors, ostensibly straight and typically unable to absent themselves from the attendant privileged status of that condition, peddle their sweeping attack on Gay equality as a gift. They insist that their proposals to give religionists special rights to discriminate against Gays, by allowing state actors and private citizens in the general stream of commerce to refuse on "religious conscience" grounds to facilitate same-sex marriages in defiance of state or local antidiscrimination laws, will make Gays' precarious citizenship somehow less so.[1]

In this chapter, I engage their arguments, expose them for what they are (heteroarchal reversals), and refute them. Fortunately for someone in my position, the most elaborate explications of these arguments have been published

---

[1] Such proposals, aside from being intellectually vulnerable and at times downright dishonest, also, to quote Justice Scalia in a moment of uncharacteristic understatement, "contradict[] ... common sense" (Employment Division v. Smith, 494 U.S. 872 [1990]). The *Smith* decision, upholding the validity of generally applicable laws against attacks on the Free Exercise Clause, is surely one of the reasons that the law professors have lobbied with such urgency for *explicit* statutory opt-out rights for religionists.

in one place, *Same-Sex Marriage and Religious Liberty: Emerging Conflicts*, the recent book of essays edited by Douglas Laycock, Anthony R. Picarello, Jr., and Robin Fretwell Wilson, which purports to offer compromise solutions that will allow Gay people access to the civil status of marriage while allowing religious objectors to exercise unfettered religious conscience. Unfortunately, despite these stated aspirations, the work represents the rampant structural liberalism[2] currently eroding equality at every turn.

I should note now that any perceived tension between the following argument and the discussion in the preceding chapter, in which I critically evaluate – and reject – marriage as a goal of Gay liberation, is more apparent than real. Chapter 6 argues against Gay marriage – which is to say it argues that Gay liberationists should voluntarily renounce marriage for a variety of reasons the chapter explains. The present chapter rejects recent inroads into emergent marriage laws in the name of religious freedom, not because marriage is normatively good, but rather because of what this means for Gay people in states where same-sex marriage is possible and the possible extension of the rationale of those same "religious conscience exceptions" to other areas of antidiscrimination law necessary to Gay liberation. Marriage is simply the conveniently divisive wedge in the door. This should be resisted. In fact, the well-organized special interests backing the conscience clause movement are already taking aim at more general antidiscrimination provisions protecting Gays and Lesbians. Moreover, rejecting marriage on liberationist grounds to avoid uncritical identification with the oppressor and being subsumed into a largely unexamined and deceptively comfortable heteronormative/patriarchal institution is something quite different from having inferiority imposed (or reimposed) by the already dominant through a morally rationalized caste system, even if I think the "prize" in the tug of war needs more thorough examination by the Movement.

This same lack of thorough examination characterizes the arguments in *Same-Sex Marriage and Religious Liberty*, making the book most remarkable for what it *does not* contain. It does not contain a serious, substantive discussion of the real equality dimensions of the same-sex marriage question.

---

[2] I employ the term "structural liberalism" to describe a perspective that proceeds from the faulty premise that members of society are already basically equal. It is a perspective that is ecumenical for ecumenism's sake. It fails to take account of power realities. It supposes social progressivism, but then turns on the socially and legally subordinated when they dare demand equality over tolerance. It defines progress in terms of what subordinated people can work out with the dominant in society on the oppressors' terms. And it faults disempowered people for failing gratefully to assimilate into this paradigm from which they are always already excluded.

Because this is a complex book, with contributions by six writers, I will focus on what I consider to be the book's intellectual epicenter,[3] the contribution entitled "Matters of Conscience: Lessons for Same-Sex Marriage from the Healthcare Context," by Professor Robin Fretwell Wilson,[4] in which she challenges the appropriateness of analogizing same-sex marriage to interracial marriage and proposes analogizing it to abortion instead, as well as the Afterword by Professor Douglas Laycock,[5] which offers a summary and scaffolding for Professor Wilson's claims, as well as his own claim that the religious and civil components of marriage should be dissociated entirely in order to preserve marriage in its traditionalist form.

Shortly after I finished reading *Same-Sex Marriage and Religious Liberty*, I attended a panel discussion on marriage equality organized by student

---

[3] I say this because the argument it represents is already becoming quite influential. The authors have been well represented in the popular press of late, especially Professor Wilson, whose op-ed in the *Los Angeles Times* (Robin Wilson, *Protection for All in Same-Sex Marriage*, L.A. TIMES, May 3, 2009) states her case to a general audience. Another piece by Wilson in the *Hartford Courant* (Robin Fretwell Wilson, *Will Law Demand We Support Gay Marriage?* HARTFORD COURANT, Mar. 6, 2009) lobbied for religious conscience exemptions in the state's new marriage law, which passed in Connecticut with three conscience exceptions. Professors Laycock and Wilson, joined by several law professors, sent lobbying letters to the governor of Maine arguing for religious exceptions to that law as well. Professor Laycock wrote separately on April 30, 2009, but endorsed the suggestions made by Professor Wilson and others in their May 1, 2009, letter. Letter from Robin Fretwell Wilson et al., Professors, to John Baldacci, Governor of Me. (May 1, 2009) (on file with author) [hereinafter *Wilson Letter*]; Letter from Douglas Laycock, Professor, Univ. of Mich. Law Sch., to John Baldacci, Governor of Me. (Apr. 30, 2009) (on file with author) [hereinafter *Laycock Letter*]. These letters are reprinted in full (without internal citation) in the chapter appendix on page 253.

The Maine marriage law passed with an exemption for anyone with a conscience objection to refuse to perform any marriage they want. Emily Sherman, *Same-Sex Marriage Battle Moves to Maine*, CNN, Oct. 26, 2009, http://www.cnn.com/2009/POLITICS/10/25/maine. same.sex/. In New Hampshire, the governor decided to send his state's marriage bill back to the legislature for additional "religious liberty" protection, along the lines proposed by Wilson et al. in their model provision. Abby Goodnough, *New Hampshire Pact Near on Same Sex Marriage*, N.Y. TIMES, May 14, 2009.

Wilson's campaigning on the issue has been especially prolific, with numerous op-eds on the subject: *Same-Sex Marriage: How Will It Impact Marriage and Family Therapists and Other Family Professionals*, THERAPIST (magazine of the California Assoc. of Marriage and Family Therapists) (May/June 2009); *A Marriage Equality Bill That Respects Religious Objectors*, WASHINGTON POST, Nov. 1, 2009; *Same-Sex Marriage Law Lacks Religious Protection*, BANGOR DAILY NEWS, Oct. 17, 2009; *NH's Same-Sex Marriage Bill Is Needlessly Discriminatory*, NEW HAMPSHIRE UNION LEADER, May 6, 2009.

[4] Robin Fretwell Wilson, *Matters of Conscience: Lessons for Same-Sex Marriage from the Healthcare Context*, in SAME-SEX MARRIAGE AND RELIGIOUS LIBERTY: EMERGING CONFLICTS 77, 77–102 (Douglas Laycock et al., eds., 2008).

[5] Douglas Laycock, Afterword to SAME-SEX MARRIAGE AND RELIGIOUS LIBERTY, *supra* note 4, at 189–207.

members of the newly formed Gay/Straight Student Alliance at Winston-Salem State University.[6] The effort of these students, one hundred strong, to broach this topic at a historically Black university was a particular act of bravery. What was most interesting to me about the ensuing discussion was that none of the three Gay couples or the straight minister (supportive of marriage equality) on the panel could answer the question "What is at stake for people who oppose Gay marriage?" It was a fair question raised by a student-activist. The panelists, who sincerely wanted to believe their answer, I'm sure, responded that Gay marriage costs its opponents nothing. Of course, nothing could be further from the truth. At the center of the crossroads of the substance (as opposed to the rhetoric) of the Gay marriage debate is the question of power: who has it, who wants it, and what those who already have it will do to keep it.

Equality questions – and the question of same-sex marriage is undeniably one (up to a point) – are acme examples of cases affecting (and effecting) the distribution of power. The two groups, the marriage equality panelists (from the perspective of the law, laypeople) and Professors Wilson and Laycock (from the perspective of the law, experts), both misstate the true nature of the question in curiously similar ways. Both groups proceed from a formalistic approach to equality, which particularizes inequalities and focuses on the individuals involved in a particular legal dispute. Of course, there is some truth in this, because all law is someone's story in the individual sense. But few cases, and certainly no equality cases, really stop with the individual litigants – parties named and usually forgotten in all but the opinion's caption. A case's greater importance lies not in what it does in the confines of these individualized disputes, but in what it does in the wider world. This is what a case is really about, what it really means.

Wilson and Laycock understand that equality claims and equality-based decisions reach beyond individual disputes. That is what makes equality decisions dangerous to the power hierarchies they theorize to support. So they use individual rights as a bulwark against equality, in an attempt to make what is generally substantive – that is, equality – into that which is particularly abstract – that is, amorphous claims of individual moral conscience. Wilson and Laycock may have bad arguments (in the sense that they are terribly undertheorized), but they are clever lawyers. They know that what a thing is called in the law can make a lot of difference. When cases centered on the question of distribution of power are litigated (or commented on) as purely

---

[6] The panel discussion was held April 14, 2009, on the campus of Winston-Salem State University, Winston-Salem, North Carolina.

individuated, person-to-person conflicts, their true substance – equality – is evaded.

Reading Professor Wilson's argument, one gets the impression that it aspires to be something more than it turns out to be. Her points are thoughtful and they are rigorously argued, making the lack of a serious equality analysis all the more startling. Throughout her substantial chapter, Professor Wilson speaks consistently of the "dignitary rights of gays and lesbians,"[7] which she defines as "the right not to be embarrassed, not to be inconvenienced, not to have their choices questioned."[8] The word "equality" does not appear once.[9] The rights of Gays and Lesbians as a class of people, located most sensibly at the core of the equality norm, are reduced to hurt feelings or inconvenience.[10] This seems rather perverse, particularly given that we live in a system of government supposedly not constitutionally neutral on the subject of equality.

Equally perverse is how purposefully she elides the obvious analogy for same-sex marriage, which is interracial marriage.[11] Why wouldn't we analogize marriage to marriage? It's what might be called the "duh" analogy.[12] *Loving v. Virginia* was an equality decision,[13] perhaps our best example – far better than *Brown v. Board of Education of Topeka*[14] – in which the Court actually named the real evil at issue. In striking down Virginia's antimiscegenation law, the Court recognized that the law was a tool for the maintenance of "White Supremacy,"[15] which struck at the core of the Fourteenth

---

[7] Wilson, *supra* note 4, at 94.

[8] Id.

[9] It is unclear whether this is because Professor Wilson agrees with co-contributor Marc D. Stern when he asserts, approvingly it seems, that "[e]quality is less central to the American constitutional universe than it is in Canada or Europe." Marc D. Stern, *Same-Sex Marriage and the Churches*, in SAME-SEX MARRIAGE AND RELIGIOUS LIBERTY, *supra* note 4, at 1, 6.

[10] Wilson, *supra* note 4, at 94.

[11] Analogy, because it is the methodology of the law, cannot be ignored, but neither can one afford to be ensnared by it. One of the challenges of Gay liberation is to highlight how much "like" racial discrimination Gay subordination actually is while insisting that it need not be "like" racial discrimination to constitute a real, systematic and systemic form of invidious discrimination.

[12] Professor Andrew Koppelman, whose theories about religious exemptions to generally applicable antidiscrimination laws are favored by the authors, has made this analogy. See Andrew Koppelman, Note, *The Miscegenation Analogy: Sodomy Law as Sex Discrimination*, 98 YALE L. J. 145, 161 (1988). I explore it fully in Chapters 2 and 3, this volume.

[13] 388 U.S. 1, 11 (1967).

[14] 347 U.S. 483 (1954).

[15] *Loving*, 388 U.S. at 7. I have always believed that the Court's capitalization of "White Supremacy," to recognize the institution of it, was no mere stylistic accident. Any substantive equality decision must necessarily deal with the epistemological basis of inequality, which is the systemic institutionalization of social distinctions into legal castes. Of course, this connection between epistemology, as a method of knowing and thinking, with politics and

Amendment. But Professor Wilson does not make this analogy, writing instead that

> [w]hile the parallels between racial discrimination and discrimination on the basis of sexual orientation should not be dismissed, it is not clear that the two are equivalent in this context. The religious and moral convictions that motivate objectors to refuse to facilitate same-sex marriage simply cannot be marshaled to justify racial discrimination.[16]

Really? On what basis are we to draw this conclusion? Religiously based descriptive moral judgments about the worth of Blacks were certainly sufficient to justify the ownership of human beings as chattel property for the better part of three hundred years in this country[17] and to undergird a system of segregation that would last at least another hundred years.[18] Frederick Douglass believed that "[r]evivals of religion and revivals in the slave-trade [went] hand in hand together."[19] He was so honestly critical of the role that the established Christian religion played in the formation and perpetuation of the slave economy that, when Douglass published his first book, his publisher prevailed upon him to publish an appendix to the book explaining why Douglass was not personally hostile to Christianity.[20] In opposition to the Civil Rights

law, as methods of power, is seldom present in judicial thinking. *Loving* is one of the few authentic exceptions. *Romer v. Evans*, 517 U.S. 620 (1996), may be another.

[16] Wilson, *supra* note 4, at 101.

[17] Slaveholders and their churches looking for biblical sanction of slavery did not have to go far. Approval of slavery is as obvious in the Bible as is condemnation of same-sexuality. Things get off to a rousing start in Genesis 9:20–27 with the curse on Ham and Canaan. Slaves were just part of the cultural background when one reads passages like Exodus 21:2, 20–21, Leviticus 22:10–11, and Leviticus 25:44. In Deuteronomy 15:12 (jubilee year discussion), provisions were made for the release of Hebrew slaves, but not foreign ones. Abraham had slaves, as did other patriarchs (Genesis 16:1), and Saint Paul, in Philemon, had a perfect opportunity to denounce slavery but did not. Philemon 1:8–21.

This note is indebted to the quick reference assistance of Rev. Susan Parker.

[18] See, e.g., Kinney v. Commonwealth, 71 Va. (30 Gratt.) 858, 869 (1878) ("[T]he destiny to which the Almighty has assigned [the races] on this continent … require[s] that they should be kept distinct and separate, and that connections and alliances so unnatural that God and nature seem to forbid them, should be prohibited by positive law, and be subject to no evasion").

[19] FREDERICK DOUGLASS, NARRATIVE OF THE LIFE OF FREDERICK DOUGLASS, AN AMERICAN SLAVE 118 (1845, 1963).

[20] It is left to the reader to judge how convincing he was:

> [B]etween the Christianity of this land, and the Christianity of Christ, I recognize the widest possible difference – so wide, that to receive the one as good, pure, and holy, is of necessity to reject the other as bad, corrupt, and wicked. To be the friend of one, is of necessity to be the enemy of the other. I love the pure, peaceable, and impartial Christianity of Christ: I therefore hate the corrupt, slaveholding, women-whipping, cradle-plundering, partial and hypocritical Christianity of this land. Indeed, I can see no reason, but the most deceitful one, for calling the religion of this land Christianity.

Act of 1964, Senator Robert Byrd read Genesis 9:18–27 (Noah's curse of the descendants of Ham) into the Congressional Record.[21] In *Loving*, the Virginia trial judge offered an explicitly religious rationale for upholding Virginia's antimiscegenation law.[22] The slaveholders of history and the segregationists of today make no distinctions between their biblically based religious beliefs and the systems of subordination they seek to institutionalize as part and parcel of and in the name of those same religious beliefs.[23] My question to Professor Wilson is this: If they make no such distinction, why should we? Of course, if she had made this analogy, the conversation would be quite different. Readers would instantly rebel at the idea of a county clerk being able to refuse a marriage license to a Black and white couple, as she suggests clerks should be able to do on moral grounds when faced with a Gay couple.[24] But we are not having this conversation because, as Professor Wilson demonstrates, Gays and Lesbians remain the last group against whom it is permissible to discriminate openly and then call that discrimination "religion."

Ignoring the race analogy makes it easy for Wilson and Laycock to hypothesize that Gay rights are something other than those the law already knows how to address. It allows them to suggest that addressing the Gay rights question requires complicated theorizing and historic compromises. The truth is that the law has dealt with religiously motivated discrimination – as rationalization or sincere belief – before. Certainly, this was true with race. Despite staunch opposition to integration on religious grounds, the Civil Rights Act of 1964 contained no broad religious exemptions.[25] It is fair, given

I look upon it as the climax of all misnomers, the boldest of all frauds, and the grossest of all libels.... He who is the religious advocate of marriage robs whole millions of its sacred influence, and leaves them to the ravages of wholesale pollution.

Id. at 117–118.

[21] Byrd also invoked Genesis 1:21–25, Leviticus 19:19, and Matthew 20:1–15. 110 CONG. REC., 13,206–08 (1964); see also TAYLOR BRANCH, PILLAR OF FIRE: AMERICA IN THE KING YEARS, 1963–65, at 334–335 (1998).

[22] "Almighty God created the races white, black, yellow, malay [*sic*] and red, and he placed them on separate continents. And but for the interference with his arrangement there would be no cause for such marriages. The fact that he separated the races shows that he did not intend for the races to mix." Loving v. Virginia, 388 U.S. 1, 3 (1967).

[23] Jerry Falwell, for example, believed that segregation was biblically mandated. "If Chief Justice Warren and his associates had known God's word and had desired to do the Lord's will, I am quite confident that the 1954 decision would never have been made." He later recanted this position. Max Blumenthal, *Agent of Intolerance*, NATION, May 16, 2007, http://www.thenation.com/doc/20070528/blumenthal (quoting Jerry Falwell's statement).

[24] Exactly this sort of outcry arose recently when a Louisiana justice of the peace refused to marry an interracial couple on "conscience" grounds. He eventually resigned under public pressure. See *Louisiana: Justice of the Peace Resigns*, N.Y. TIMES, Nov. 4, 2009.

[25] Civil Rights Act of 1964, Pub. L. No. 88–352, 78 Stat. 241 (1964) (codified at 42 U.S.C. §§ 1981–2000 [2006]).

their treatment of Gay civil rights, to ask the authors whether they believe it should have.

Professor Wilson's preferred analogy of abortion – preferred over race – is an analogy to which gender is undeniably central. But women have fared just as poorly at the hands of religionists. Women have been as much the chattel property of men, first of their fathers and then of their husbands, as Blacks have been the property of whites. The Fourteenth Amendment was argued not to apply to women, with Congressman Thaddeus Stevens pointedly declaring that "[w]hen a distinction is made between two married people or two *femmes sole*, then it is unequal legislation; but where all of the same class are dealt with in the same way then there is no pretense of inequality."[26] In another context, that of suffrage and Section 2 of the Fourteenth Amendment, Senator Howard explained that by "the law of nature ... women and children were not regarded as the equals of men."[27] The prevailing cultural attitude regarding women was neatly summed up by the North Carolina Supreme Court, which held that a woman did not have grounds for divorce when her husband had disciplined her by horse whipping her.[28] The court, citing Genesis 3:16, "Thy desire shall be to thy husband, and he shall rule over thee," declared that being beaten in this way was not cause for divorce as a matter of law.[29] Even as Black men received the right to vote, women were still denied it. The rape of women by their husbands went unrecognized because women were to become "one flesh" with their husbands.[30] Women have been denied employment because of patriarchal attitudes reinforced through religion, and as to abortion particularly, they have been denied reproductive control largely by effective campaigns organized by religious ideologues.[31]

Professor Wilson argues that it is permissible for businesses and even state employees to discriminate against Gays on religious-conscience grounds.[32] I think it is fair to ask her whether there should have been similar religious-conscience exceptions to Title VII for those who do not wish to hire or otherwise accommodate women. Why have we drawn the line at Gays? Whatever the answer to this query, the claim, like Wilson's, that Gays are the target of an

---

[26] CONG. GLOBE, 39th Cong., 1st Sess. 1064 (1866).

[27] Id. at 2767.

[28] Joyner v. Joyner, 59 N.C. (6 Jones Eq.) 322, 325 (1862).

[29] Id.

[30] Genesis 2:24.

[31] See DALLAS A. BLANCHARD & TERRY J. PREWITT, RELIGIOUS VIOLENCE AND ABORTION: THE GIDEON PROJECT 250–255 (1993).

[32] Wilson, *supra* note 4, at 81.

especial religious animus justifying their subjection to especially discriminatory treatment is, as a matter of history, simply untrue.

Ignoring the race analogy also allows the authors to rationalize blatant discrimination. For example, Professor Laycock writes, "I would have no objection to a requirement that merchants that refuse to serve same-sex couples announce that fact on their website or, for businesses with only a local service area, on a sign outside their premises."[33] He reasons that this would avoid "unfair surprise"[34] to Gays and then muses, "Whether the gay-rights side would want such a requirement is a harder question."[35] I doubt that our "side" would care for his proposal, especially considering that most of us have believed for some time now that the segregation question has been answered in the negative.[36] But the reduction of the harm of this kind of economy of abuse to "inconvenience" looks, I suppose, more reasonable when the entire question has been totally divorced from any consideration of equality *qua* equality. It allows Laycock to go on to write offhandedly, almost glibly in the context of the surrounding prose, that "[i]n more traditional communities, same-sex couples planning a wedding might be forced to pick their merchants carefully, like black families driving across the South half a century ago."[37] This casual invocation of Jim Crow offers scarcely a shade of reproof, merely extension by analogy to the sexual apartheid of the twenty-first century.[38]

Certainly, Professor Laycock is quick to point out that he supports Gay rights.[39] He offers this qualification to the reader – perhaps especially to the doubting Gay reader – as an assurance that what he suggests is for the reader's own good. His proffered bona fides in this regard are persuasive. When I wrote a close friend to lament his having signed onto Professor Laycock's letter lobbying for religious exemptions to pending marriage laws, he wrote back quickly to say – to remind me – that "Laycock's letter emphasizes that he supports same-sex 'marriage'."[40] Yes, indeed, it does. But what, exactly, does

---

[33] Laycock, *supra* note 5, at 198.

[34] Id.

[35] Id.

[36] For example, Blow v. North Carolina, 379 U.S. 684, 685–686 (1965) (finding that a restaurant serving "whites only" violated the Civil Rights Act of 1964).

[37] Laycock, *supra* note 5, at 200.

[38] Nor does Professor Laycock mention that changing these deplorable circumstances was the central purpose of the Civil Rights Act of 1964 or that the change was accomplished *without* religious exceptions.

[39] Laycock, *supra* note 5, at 190.

[40] Email from Michael Perry, Professor, Emory Law Sch., to author (May 5, 2009, 17:48 EST) (on file with author).

this support entail? Support of same-sex marriage, but not of a right to marry that is equal to the right straight people enjoy, because it is riddled with exceptions and segregated so as not to offend traditionalist sensibilities, is support that exists in theory only. It is a little like saying, "I'm for absolute protection of free speech but not *for* the cross burning that my absolutist view necessarily protects." It is the sort of posturing that makes for small comfort when you are the one with the burned cross on your lawn.

Professor Laycock casts religious conservatives as marginalized and oppressed.[41] Before denouncing harassment law as an effort "to suppress expression of traditional moral views," Laycock states his agreement with "Robin Wilson's succinct formulation, [that Gays] show every sign of seeking 'to take same-sex marriage from a negative right to be free of state interference to a positive entitlement to assistance by others'."[42] People whose worldview is demonstratively privileged are suddenly transformed into an endangered minority when their ability to subordinate those denominated "inferior" – socially, legally, or both – is even slightly ameliorated. In this, sadly, Professor Laycock and ex–Ku Klux Klan leader David Duke are of one mind. Duke has said that "the time has come for equal rights for ... white people."[43] Laycock similarly suggests that the time has come for equal rights for conservative religionists.[44] In a self-delusion common to the social reactionary and the structural liberal alike, neither pauses to acknowledge that there has never been a time when they did not already have them.

Perhaps the difference in Laycock's and my definition of who needs protection stems from the fact that he is writing from a different perspective than I am reading. How one sees victimization is often wrapped up with one's own group identity. But in this, as in all things, some realism is desirable. Professor

---

[41]   Several of Laycock's phraseologies cast Gays as a menace to an endangered people, especially his admonition that "religious marriage will be much safer if it is cleanly separated [from civil marriage]" now that Gays want in. Laycock, *supra* note 5, at 207. He also characterizes Gays as having "organized the opposition that killed the proposed Religious Liberty Protection Act" and as "organizing the opposition to the proposed Workplace Religious Freedom Act." Id. at 191. The underlying epistemologies that have fictionalized a world in which such "protection" and "freedom" acts are needed to "protect" religious conservatives is nowhere examined. Neither is the fact that religionists are constantly on the offensive to ensure that subordinating, anti-equality messages are ever-present to warp the identities of young Gay people and to make certain that Gay adults are kept in precarious positions economically and physically.

[42]   Id. at 192.

[43]   Peter Applebome, *Ex-Klansman Puts New Racial Politics to Test*, N.Y. Times, June 18, 1990.

[44]   Or if one prefers to adopt the pious individual rights rhetoric that saturates the book: "[A]ll people have a basic human right to preserve their own heritage." DavidDuke.com, http://www.davidduke.com/index.php?p=266 (Mar. 12, 2005, 8:14 EST).

Laycock says that religious conservatives are in need of protection. I say that Gays are in need of equality. The essential question then becomes: How do you know when a group is, in fact, subordinated and consequently in need of these things? Perhaps it is when the group can be assaulted, battered, and murdered at whim, and the law and those charged with executing the law look the other way or labor mightily against admitting it.[45] Perhaps it is when a group is denied a whole range of opportunities, rights, and privileges of citizenship, and few bother to question why, or worse still, if they do, they conclude that it is somehow the group member's own fault.[46] Or perhaps it is when a group is made the object of malicious lies[47] or abusive jokes honed to killing sharpness, or is constantly reduced to something trivial and inconsequential, and very few bother to question why the jokes make them laugh.[48] Or perhaps it is when every hard-won escape from the caste is propagandized into an attack on the liberty of the people who created the caste system and put you in it. All of these things are true for Gay people.[49] Are they true – *really* true – for Christian conservatives in this country?

Of course, Laycock, and David Duke for that matter, are in rarefied company; their brand of doublethink is reflected in judging as well. It reached

[45] Take, for example, the case of South Carolina youth Sean Kennedy. The facts of his violent death are recorded in Shannon Gilreath, A *Climate of Violence Against Gay People*, RALEIGH NEWS & OBSERVER, May 28, 2008, http://www.newsobserver.com/opinion/columns/story/1087382.html. His killer's charges were reduced to manslaughter. Or consider that U.S. Representative Virginia Foxx (R-N.C.), in expressing her opposition to new hate crimes legislation, called Matthew Shepard's brutal murder a "hoax" to further the Gay agenda. Editorial, *Matthew Shepard Act*, N.Y. TIMES, May 6, 2009.

[46] See, e.g., Daniel E. Bontempo & Anthony R. D'Augelli, *Effects of at-School Victimization and Sexual Orientation on Lesbian, Gay, or Bisexual Youths' Health Risk Behavior*, 30 J. ADOLESCENT HEALTH 364, 371 (2002); Rich C. Savin-Williams, *Verbal and Physical Abuse as Stressors in the Lives of Lesbian, Gay Male, and Bisexual Youths: Associations with School Problems, Running Away, Substance Abuse, Prostitution, and Suicide*, 62 J. CONSULTING & CLINICAL PSYCH. 261, 267 (1994); Gay, Lesbian & Straight Educ. Network, GLSEN's 2005 *National School Climate Survey Sheds New Light on Experiences of Lesbian, Gay, Bisexual and Transgender (LGBT) Students*, GLSEN.ORG, Apr. 26, 2009, http://www.glsen.org/cgi-bin/iowa/all/library/record/1927.html (noting that "overall, gay students were twice as likely as the general population of students to report they were not planning to pursue any post secondary education"). For a thorough discussion, see Chapter 4, this volume.

[47] Gays continue to be accused, by supposedly credible sources, of everything from inflated incomes to the routine consumption of blood. For a thorough discussion of anti-Gay propaganda, see Chapter 4, this volume.

[48] For a discussion, see SHANNON GILREATH, SEXUAL POLITICS: THE GAY PERSON IN AMERICA TODAY 39–41 (2006).

[49] They are also true of the group to which Gays are analogized by the authors: women. See Catharine A. MacKinnon, *Excerpts from MacKinnon/Schlafly Debate*, 1 L. & INEQUALITY 341, 343–345 (1983). The formulation of this paragraph is indebted to Professor MacKinnon.

an apogee in the Supreme Court's 1989 decision of *City of Richmond v. Croson.*[50] Justice O'Connor's opinion for the Court brought down the individual rights hammer on state and municipal affirmative action programs aimed at ameliorating generations of antiequality law and social practice. O'Connor writes:

> The rights created by the first section of the fourteenth amendment are, by its terms, guaranteed to the individual. The rights established are personal rights. The Richmond Plan denies certain citizens the opportunity to compete for a fixed percentage of public contracts based solely upon their race. To whatever racial group these citizens belong, their personal rights to be treated with equal dignity and respect are implicated by a rigid rule erecting race as the sole criterion in an aspect of public policy decision making.[51]

The opinion's doublethink disconnects affirmative action programs from a whole backdrop of inequality and from their responsive purposes, namely remedial efforts aimed at a caste system in which Blacks were (and are) oppressed on the basis of their *group* identities. The shift in focus from group-based equality rights to individual rights was necessary for an increasingly reactionary Court to accomplish its transmutation of whites into the embattled and subordinated. Suddenly, through the judicial looking glass, whites were as "suspect" and vulnerable to systemic racism as Blacks. Of course, any serious look at the *group* realities that define the existence of historically marginalized and subordinated peoples, in this case Blacks, makes the Court's decision obviously laughable. At bottom, *Croson* amounted to the translation of white privilege into a constitutionally guaranteed individual right. In a fitting revelation of their transparency, it did not take a lawyer to see the lacunae in this rationale. Philosopher Richard Mohr wrote, "[I]n an inversion of history the oddness of which perhaps only a Foucault or a cynic could fully savor, a purely formalist reading of *Brown* in *City of Richmond* has now become a chief guarantor of white power."[52] The philosopher understands my point, apropos *Same-Sex Marriage and Religious Liberty*, that the institutionalization of power privilege as the individual (and individuating) rights of the already powerful is not clever judicial manipulation only; it is the philosophy by which the world (the United States, anyway) is ruled.[53]

---

[50] 488 U.S. 469 (1989).

[51] Id. at 493 (internal quotations and citations omitted).

[52] RICHARD MOHR, GAY IDEAS, OUTING AND OTHER CONTROVERSIES 76 (1992).

[53] In wondering why the other side opposes same-sex marriage, no one seems to want to believe that opponents might have a very real stake in straight supremacy and in its entrenchment through institutionalization – including the institution of marriage. Clever lawyers attempting to spin a theory to justify inroads into marriage equality even in the few places where it

The authors having rejected the analogy to racial discrimination, their pro-posed analogy – the abortion analogy – is developed by Professor Wilson.[54] This analogy underscores the lack of equality analysis in the authors' combined effort. Professor Wilson wants same-sex marriage analogized to abortion so that mar-riage can be subject to innumerable conscience clause exemptions, allowing those in the general business of facilitating marriage to opt out when they disap-prove of same-sex couples – in the same way that hospitals and physicians can opt out of abortion and even less controversial reproductive control measures on religious grounds.[55] For example, Professor Wilson cites approvingly the "Church Amendment," which gives a private hospital receiving federal funding the right to refuse the use of its facilities for "any sterilization procedure or abortion … prohibited by the entity on the basis of religious beliefs or moral convictions."[56] Congress enacted the Church Amendment in direct response to *Taylor v. St. Vincent's Hospital,* in which a Montana woman sued a local nonprofit hos-pital in Billings, Montana, because it refused to permit her willing physician to perform a tubal ligation for her during the cesarean delivery of her child.[57]

Professor Wilson believes that putting the "moral convictions" of an "entity" ahead of the reproductive choices of a woman – in *Taylor* with the agreement of her physician *and* her husband, and where the hospital in question was the only local hospital available to her – is wise.[58] It is telling that Professor Wilson puts this discussion under the subheading "Protecting Providers from

exists have the convenience of this studied inability to call sexualized dominance what it is. Gays and Lesbians, however, cannot afford to indulge in this myth.

    For her chapter in *Same-Sex Marriage and Religious Liberty,* Professor Chai Feldblum, an out Lesbian and longtime proponent of Lesbian and Gay equality, complains that "[t]hose who advocate for laws prohibiting discrimination on the basis of sexual orientation tend to talk simply about 'equality'." Chai R. Feldblum, *Moral Conflict and Conflicting Liberties,* in Same-Sex Marriage and Religious Liberty, *supra* note 4, at 123, 124. Instead, she adopts the obfuscating rhetoric of her coauthors, writing about "identity liberty" and "belief liberty." Id. She gets caught up in the feelings versus feelings game that is descriptive moral counterbalancing, which allows Professor Laycock to characterize her argument, not unfairly, as one in which "the insult of being refused service and the inconvenience of going elsewhere … almost universally outweighs the harm of forcing the merchant to violate a deeply held moral obligation." Laycock, *supra* note 5, at 197. It makes her argument easy to dismiss, at least from Laycock's perspective. Of course, equality is not about insult or inconvenience. I am certain that Professor Feldblum knows this. Unfortunately, because she does not face up to the evasive rhetoric, she cannot face it down.

54 Wilson, *supra* note 4, at 77.

55 See id. at 79.

56 Id. (citing the Church Amendment to the Health Programs Extension Act, 42 U.S.C. § 300a-7(b)(2)(A) [2006]).

57 369 F. Supp. 948, 950 (D. Mont. 1973).

58 Id. at 949. This is an important fact that Professor Wilson leaves out of her description of the case.

Coercion by Patients."[59] Coercion implies power; Professor Wilson theorizes on the basis of a world where a hospital, with a monopoly on health care, and an individual patient, attempting to exercise reproductive freedom, are fundamentally equal. Alas, this world bears no relation to material reality.

This dissociation with reality that underlies Professor Wilson's argument is laid bare at its origination. Professor Wilson begins by characterizing *Roe v. Wade* as providing a "very strong constitutional right[] to abortion."[60] How so? As we have seen, *Roe v. Wade*,[61] in contrast to *Loving v. Virginia*,[62] was decidedly not an equality case.[63] In *Roe*, the Court placed the right to choose an abortion in privacy on the outer fringes of constitutional thought. By locating abortion rights on this fringe, the Court ensured that women's equality quickly became subsumed by the needs of male-dominated, heterocentric society and made possible the future subordination of women's collective equality needs to the desires of straight male supremacy. The assault on *Roe* and on women's equality in the name of individual rights defined from the male perspective has continued unremitting, namely in the form of the very conscience clause legislation Professor Wilson endorses.[64] What Wilson describes as a "very strong constitutional right to abortion" has been reduced to a "Potemkin Village."[65]

By anchoring her arguments about marriage and religious liberty in *Roe* and its aftermath, Professor Wilson rewrites the question of what is at stake in the culture wars over marriage from the perspective of civil libertarianism and its attendant focus on individual rights. The equality-based claims of Gays and Lesbians are thereby translated, through the rhetoric of individual rights, into the realm of descriptive moral counterbalancing. This means that the asserted rights of the dominant straight ideology almost always win, because it is this ideology that controls how individual rights are defined and satisfied. So despite her concession to the inevitability of same-sex marriage,[66] Professor Wilson does not argue for an expansion of marriage rights. For the most part, she explicates so-called solutions to the controversy that will seriously limit the content of the right to same-sex marriage anywhere it may be recognized.[67] The right to same-sex marriage is eviscerated, riddled with morals-based

---

[59] Wilson, *supra* note 4, at 82.
[60] Id. at 79.
[61] 410 U.S. 113 (1973).
[62] 388 U.S. 1 (1967).
[63] See Chapter 3, this volume.
[64] Wilson, *supra* note 4, at 97–101.
[65] Planned Parenthood v. Casey, 505 U.S. 833, 966 (1992) (Rehnquist, C. J., concurring in part and dissenting in part).
[66] Wilson, *supra* note 4, at 79–80.
[67] Id. at 93–97.

conscience exceptions in exactly the same way that reproductive freedom was and continues to be eviscerated.

While reproductive capacity itself has been used to subordinate women socially – by the politicization of pregnancy as a means to define women, to keep them immobile, and to patronize them in the name of exalted mother-hood – the congressional efforts that Professor Wilson praises have been used to subordinate women legally, by significantly eroding the meager measure of reproductive control the law secured for women through *Roe*. To her credit, Professor Wilson does not pretend here; she states outright that

> [t]he lesson of *Roe* and *Griswold* is that the individual's right to be free from the state's interference with reproductive and contraceptive choices is just that – the right to be free from government interference. It does not translate directly into a right to assistance, a fact that legislatures have chosen to make clear by statute.[68]

Consider, for example, how Professor Wilson characterizes the Alaska Supreme Court's decision in *Valley Hospital Ass'n v. Mat-Su Coalition for Choice*, in which the court held that a private, nonprofit hospital could not burden the ability to procure an abortion under state law.[69] "[I]t was saying to the provider that the right to abortion matters more than an objector's interest in not participating. That decision was tantamount to saying that 'not only does the patient deserve an abortion, but you, the provider, are going to per-form it,' " she writes.[70] The talisman of individual rights has more than once been invoked to keep the government out of places it should otherwise go to secure the equality interests of subordinated people. Professor Wilson faults the court for refusing to maintain the status quo in this way.[71] The court, instead, was saying that a woman's interest in sex equality matters more than a hospital's desire to burden women's equality. This is the fairer way of framing the case. Abortion *is* a sex equality issue. Calling it privacy and subjecting it to balancing with individual rights was perhaps the most we could hope for from the all-male (ostensibly all-*straight*-male) *Roe* Court that could identify with the abortion dilemma only by objectifying it. Is it wrong to hope for more consciousness from a woman scholar with a substantial body of work on bioethics?[72]

---

[68]   Id. at 97.

[69]   948 P.2d 963, 969 (Alaska 1997).

[70]   Wilson, *supra* note 4, at 94.

[71]   See id.

[72]   See, e.g., Robin Fretwell Wilson, *The Limits of Conscience: Moral Clashes over Deeply Divisive Healthcare Procedures*, 34 AM. J. L. & MED. 41, 45 (2008).

Professor Wilson's logic, which is the logic of *Roe*, consummated in *Harris*, and translated by analogy to same-sex marriage, is a means of subordinating the collective equality rights of Gays and Lesbians to the imperatives of individual religious dissenters. The concentration on so-called dignitary rights of Gays and Lesbians rhetoricizes the harm inherent in the proposed system as an individual harm only: sustained only by the Gay couple that is embarrassed, insulted, or inconvenienced in the moment that this individual couple is embarrassed, insulted, or inconvenienced. Such an individualized harm can then easily be balanced against the individual rights of religious objectors. But it is important to recognize that this is a system of inequality. The significant source of power in any system of inequality is the ability to distinguish the "inferior" from the "superior." Defining same-sex marriage as something from which the superior can withdraw, by simple assertions of individual religious expression and without regard to the group-based equality rights of Gays and Lesbians not to be subordinated, subordinates Gays and Lesbians *in fact and in law*. Professor Wilson's focus on individual rights and her utter lack of equality analysis amount to the right of a new breed of supremacists to subordinate all Gays and Lesbians one at a time – or perhaps in the marriage context, two by two.

As I mentioned, Professor Wilson's arguments aspire to something better. She says her approach will sweep away grounds for opposition to same-sex marriage by assuring religious dissenters that they need not, and will not, be required to participate.[73] Essentially, she argues that her position is good for Gays, too, because it will make them more palatable to heterosociety by modulating the sweep of the change that Gay marriage will work in the straight world.[74] The fundamental gap in her logic is that Gay marriage *is a big* change. No amount of public relations or placation can disabuse people with power of the notion that they are losing it – when they actually *are* losing power. As stated before, every system of inequality depends upon the ability to distinguish the "superior" from the "inferior," and heterosexism is no exception. Ceding marriage, the paradigmatic heteronormative institution, means, from the perspective of the Heterarchy, losing an important tool of supremacy. A world in which Gay people can marry on their own terms will be a world in which Gay people *are more equal*. Powerful people know this, and nothing new is communicated to them by the insertion of moral conscience exceptions to equality. Something very real is, however, communicated to the Gay

---

73 Wilson, *supra* note 4, at 100–102.

74 Id. at 81 ("Because weighing competing moral values can be a 'zero-sum' game, perhaps the best we can hope for is a live-and-let-live solution, one that permits refusals for matters of conscience, but limits those refusals to instances where a significant hardship will not occur").

community, the powerless in the equation. That real something is that even in the few states where their equality has been advanced, it must, according to Professor Wilson, once again be subordinated to the discriminatory practices of straight supremacy – which its proselytes insist upon packaging as bona fide religious conviction.

Wilson's approach leaves out the myriad ways in which Gays are subordinated through the social institutionalization of petty prejudices and patronization, the ways in which Gay humanity is simultaneously violated and exploited by underscoring difference (Gay versus straight) socially. These social differences are then constructed into legal differences that matter. Far from contending with the social subordination of Gays – which a substantive equality approach that recognizes dominance would do – Wilson's approach is a product of the same politics, operating in and through the same context of straight over Gay domination. It would effectively enact into law sexuality classifications, namely those in which Gay relationships are inferior to straight relationships, which until very recently were not questioned because they were so civically powerful and all-pervasive.

The alternative approach, the one grounded in a substantive understanding of equality and our constitutional commitment to it, would ask an entirely different question: What if equality meant more than that which is defined by people with power, who tend to see equality as an issue only when people sufficiently like them (as defined by the definitions they write) are treated irrationally? Instead, Professors Laycock and Wilson ask Gays to give up legal equality and depend instead upon the goodwill of straights or, worse, on "market forces."[75] But any system of subordination exists and subsists by rendering the inferior dependent upon the superior. In a tortured paradox, subordinated people are asked to depend upon the people who subordinate them to protect them from subordination. The "gay-rights side" ought surely to resist this. Instead of protection and goodwill or tolerance, we want equal rights. But from the perspective of Wilson and Laycock, recognizing we deserve better and demanding it make us "oppressors."[76] Professor Wilson concludes her argument with more unmitigated praise for the subordination of women accomplished through *Roe* and its aftermath[77] in the guise of women's rights:

[T]he history of litigation after *Roe* provides a convincing prediction about the trajectory that litigation after *Goodridge* and the *Marriage Cases* is

---

[75] *Wilson Letter, supra* note 3; *Laycock Letter, supra* note 3.
[76] *Laycock Letter, supra* note 3; see also Laycock, *supra* note 5, at 192–194.
[77] I do not mean to come off too hard on *Roe* here. *Roe* certainly did promote women's equality to an extent. My major complaint is that it did not do enough.

beginning to take. States can deflect this litigation, as they have with abortion and other deeply divisive questions in healthcare, by deciding now whether issues of conscience matter.[78]

I'd like to suggest a different ending: Perhaps we could, for once, decide that equality *really* matters.

The coup de grâce of *Same-Sex Marriage and Religious Liberty* is Professor Laycock's proposal to unwind the civil status of marriage from its religious status entirely.[79] The idea that Americans should go to the courthouse to be civilly united and to the church to be "married," and that thereby we might end the marriage controversy, is not new[80]; but the recent marriage developments give Laycock's formulation of this nominalism a new urgency. I have no objection to the outcome he proposes, but reading his argument to make marriage "safer" by clearly defining the distinctions between religious and civil commitment, I couldn't help but remember Andrea Dworkin's pithy observation that abortion was finally legalized because men realized that "getting laid was at stake."[81] Could it be that this ultimate concession to split marriage off from its civil status is made because religionists realize that marriage, as they understand it – in other words, patriarchy – is at stake?

The two predominating themes of the Wilson/Laycock argument – reproductivity and marriage – have from the perspective of straight male dominance defined what power is. Denial of reproductive freedom for women, in and out of marriage, and denial of marriage generally to Gays have been powerful weapons in the caste arsenal. A demand for something better is treated as an omnipresent threat to religious liberty because religion has always been a primary tool to subordinate women and Gays. There *is* a politics to this; "concealed is the substantive way in which [the *straight*] man has become the measure of all things."[82] Because these denials happen almost exclusively to women and Gays, they are not considered to raise equality considerations. The religious liberty argument combines conservative social and political values with the rhetoric of individual rights – a rhetoric that many liberals are instinctively drawn to and are seemingly powerless to

---

[78] Wilson, *supra* note 4, at 102.

[79] Laycock, *supra* note 5, at 201–207.

[80] Id. at 206.

[81] ANDREA DWORKIN, RIGHT-WING WOMEN 95 (1978).

[82] One of feminism's great insights was that male power maintains itself through the subterfuge that it is natural and inevitable because it is already always omnipresent. On this point, see CATHARINE A. MACKINNON, FEMINISM UNMODIFIED 34 (1988). But I feel compelled to underscore what feminism has often forgotten to mention, namely that this *male* power is necessarily only *straight* male power. Gay men, as Gay men, have been as alien to the so-called natural order of things as women have been, perhaps more so.

resist.[83] The result is a smoke screen to subvert the group-based equality rights of women and Gays, subordinating them to the individual rights of religious dissenters – the defenders of the religious politics, in America predominantly that of Christianity, that was created by men for men and that remains the chief vehicle for the delivery and static enforcement of patriarchy. Whether the discussion is about sex, marriage, or both, patriarchy is overwhelmingly the imperative, and religion is its metaethics.

From this perspective, heterosexuality itself is an institution of inequality, with women's inferiority centrally enacted through sex.[84] But Gays present the possibility of sex between gender equals, thereby presenting the possibility that sex itself can actually be equal. The legally recognized joining of two people in a "marriage" that was not from the get-go based upon gender differences constructed into legal significances would be no small blow to the system of gender inequality, which is sexuality discrimination – which is patriarchy. This kind of destruction of the central unit of the whole system of patriarchal power is, from the perspective of straight male dominance, nothing short of revolution. Is this the new center of gravity for homophobia? Gays, because we have experienced what we have experienced and lived what we have lived, can't help but wonder.

There is one more point worth making here, and that is that the law is circuitous in many ways. It both embodies prejudices and begets them, often enforcing and suggesting forms of bias simultaneously. American law, in particular, exemplifies this economy of oppression. The Constitution itself once baldly proclaimed the inferiority of African Americans by denominating the Black man as three-fifths of a man (thus by omission underscoring the inhumanity of women of any race or color). The apartheid of Jim Crow, toward which Professor Laycock seems to tilt in his treatment of Gays and Lesbians, enshrined biases of the most vicious variety into law, creating a caste system built upon and perpetuating centuries-old ideas about Black inferiority and white superiority. Through the mythology of caste oppression, powerful whites were made martyrs to Black aggression and the virtue of white women cried out for defense by the Galahads of the Klan. An understanding of the status of women can also be found by examining the law, as it was and is. Restrictions on access to abortion of the kind Professor Wilson lauds continue to ensure that women cannot escape the walking-uterus class to which straight men have assigned them – especially poor and minority women, who

---

[83] See, e.g., José Gabilondo, *When God Hates: How Liberal Guilt Lets the New Right Get Away with Murder*, 44 WAKE FOREST L. REV. 617, 619–620 (2009).

[84] See Chapter 8, this volume.

generally have the least say-so of any women over the when, where, and how of pregnancy.

The assault on the equal humanity of Gays and Lesbians through efforts to give religionists special rights to discriminate against Gays is more of the same in this inventive, if cowardly, tradition of American law. The law enforces and encourages patterns and practices of oppression; these practices perpetuate old prejudices and generate new ones. But more than this – more than simply being a source and reflection of prejudice – the law *can be* violence. When the law does violence, creates it, the law *is* violence. States with anti-Gay marriage amendments have seen increased levels of physical violence against Gays and Lesbians.[85] The slow, inevitable (sometimes not so slow but still inevitable) slide from conceptual liquidation to physical liquidation is evident. Likewise, to exploit marriage equality, in the few places where it does exist, to underscore just how alien Gays and Lesbians are, by explicitly allowing the "good" people to recoil from us under the imprimatur of the state, is to make of Gays Untouchables and to brand us for other forms of maltreatment. Violence against Gays and Lesbians, more often than not born of religious prejudice, is the essence of Gay life in America – really its *quintessence*, for it is always there, inescapable, smothering. In this context – this reality – of violence and abuse that is everyday life for Gays and Lesbians, a proposal like Wilson and Laycock's looks like open season on Gays caught up as a gift.

The most cursory examination of history reveals that many hearts, but also many bones, have been broken in the name of religious piety. Antimarriage amendments and proposals like those of Wilson and Laycock (the next-best things to antimarriage amendments from the perspective of straight supremacy) are part of a culture of religiously fueled violence that breaks not only Gay hearts, but also Gay bones. The imprimatur for violence enshrined in law in the name of religious freedom both obfuscates the Heteroarchy's purpose and ensures its success. Whether Wilson and Laycock are willing to admit it or not, the proposals they are peddling are really proposals for the institutionalization of violence against Gays, with impunity for it, in law. It is imperative that we understand their proposals for what they really are, because they show no signs of stopping.[86]

---

[85] See, e.g., *D.A. Blames Prop 8 for Anti-Gay Violence*, BAY AREA REPORTER, Jan. 28, 2010, http://ebar.comnews/article.php?sec=news&article=3839.

[86] Professor Wilson intervened most recently in the debate over legalizing same-sex marriage in the District of Columbia, testifying before the city council and lobbying for explicit conscience exemptions for religionists. In a letter made public, council member David Catania accused Wilson of several "misrepresentations" that he believed to be calculated and unethical. The full text of the letter is available at http://www.washingtoncitypaper.com/blogs/citydesk/files/2009/11/1112catania.pdf.

APPENDIX

Wilson Letter:

May 1, 2009

The Honorable Governor John Baldacci
Office of the Governor
#1 State House Station
Augusta, ME 04333–0001
governor@maine.gov

Re: Religious liberty implications of S.P. 384

Dear Governor Baldacci:
We write to provide you with an analysis of the effects of S.P. 384 on religious liberty. Those effects would be widespread and profound. If S.P. 384 is passed in its current form – without adequate religious-conscience protections – many religious organizations and individuals will be forced to engage in conduct that violates their deepest religious beliefs, and religious organizations would be limited in crucial aspects of their religious exercise. Instead of passing S.P. 384 in its current form, the Legislature should take the time and care necessary to ensure that the legalization of same-sex marriage does not constrain the fundamental right of religious liberty.

Wide-ranging conflicts recognized by legal scholars

In the only comprehensive scholarly work on same-sex marriage and religious liberty to date, legal scholars on both sides of the same-sex marriage debate agreed that codifying same-sex marriage *without* providing robust religious accommodations will create widespread and unnecessary legal conflict – conflict that will work a "sea change in American law" and will "reverberate across the legal and religious landscape." The conflicts between religious liberty and same-sex marriage generally take one of two forms. First, if same-sex marriage is legalized without appropriate religious accommodations, religious organizations or individuals that object to same-sex marriage will face a wave of new lawsuits under state anti-discrimination and other laws. So will many small businesses, which are owned by individual conscientious objectors. Likely lawsuits include claims that:

- A religious college that offers special housing for married students can be sued under housing discrimination laws for offering that housing to opposite-sex, but not same-sex, married couples.

- A religious school or university that has a code of conduct prohibiting same-sex sexual relationships can be sued under anti-discrimination laws for refusing to admit students (or children of parents) in a same-sex marriage.
- Religious individuals who run a business, such as wedding photographers, florists, banquet halls, or bed and breakfasts, can be sued under public accommodations laws for refusing to offer their services in connection with a same-sex marriage ceremony.
- Religious camps, day cares, retreat centers, counseling centers, or adoption agencies can be sued under public accommodations laws for refusing to offer their services to members of a same-sex marriage. A church or religious non-profit that fires an employee, such as an organist or secretary, for entering a same-sex marriage can be sued under employment discrimination laws that prohibit discrimination on the basis of marital status.

Second, religious organizations and individuals (or the small businesses that they own) that conscientiously object to same-sex marriage will be labeled as unlawful "discriminators" under state law and thus face a range of penalties at the hands of state agencies and local governments, such as the withdrawal of government benefits or exclusion from government facilities. For example:

- A religious university, hospital, or social service organization that refuses to provide its employees with same-sex spousal benefits can be denied access to government contracts or grants on the ground that it is engaged in discrimination that contravenes public policy.
- A religious charity or fraternal organization that opposes same-sex marriage can be denied access to government facilities, such as a lease on government property or participation in a government-sponsored charitable campaign.
- Doctors, psychologists, social workers, counselors and other professionals who conscientiously object to same-sex marriage can have their licenses revoked.
- Religious fraternal organizations or non-profits that object to same-sex marriage can be denied food service licenses, child-care licenses, or liquor licenses on the ground that they are engaged in unlawful discrimination.
- Religious universities or professional schools can have their accreditation revoked for refusing to recognize the validity of same-sex marriages.
- Church-affiliated organizations can have their tax exempt status stripped because of their conscientious objections to same-sex marriage.

All of these conflicts either did not exist before, or will be significantly intensified after, the legalization of same-sex marriage. It is, of course, impossible to predict the outcome of future litigation over these conflicts, and religious liberty advocates will litigate these claims vigorously under any protections available under state and federal law. At a minimum, however, the volume of new litigation will be immense. And religious liberty advocates can also be expected to sue state and local governments for implementing, or even considering implementing, policies that harm conscientious objectors. Thus, two things are certain: S.P. 384, in its current form, will have numerous unintended and detrimental effects on religious organizations and individuals. And it will spawn years of costly litigation, not only for religious organizations and individuals, but for small businesses owned by conscientious objectors across the state.

Examples of conflicts in Maine

To take just one specific example of conflict, many universities in Maine, including religious institutions such as Saint Joseph's College, can choose to provide special married student housing to their students. Enacting S.P. 384 with inadequate religious-conscience protections, however, would force religious universities either to extend married student housing benefits to same-sex couples, thus violating their religious beliefs, or to eliminate the housing benefit altogether. That would benefit neither education nor the state.

Moreover, legal recognition of same-sex marriage would create entirely new classes of litigation activity. For example, Maine's sexual orientation discrimination statutes contain accommodations for certain religious organizations. But with the codification of same-sex marriage, a plaintiff could bring the exact same claim under Maine's gender discrimination or marital status discrimination laws, none of which include religious accommodations. At a minimum, changes to the marital status and gender discrimination statutes should be made as "part of a legislative package" with same-sex marriage.

Precedent for providing religious accommodations

This wave of conflict between same-sex marriage and religious liberty is avoidable. But it is avoidable only if the Legislature takes the time and effort required to craft the "robust religious-conscience exceptions" to same-sex marriage that leading voices on both sides of the public debate over same-sex marriage have called for.

Maine would not be breaking any new ground by providing religious accommodations. Other states have already provided religious accommodations in their same-sex marriage legislation. In Vermont, for example, the same sex marriage bill includes protections for religious organizations that refuse to provide "services, accommodations, advantages, facilities, goods, or privileges" related to the solemnization or celebration of a marriage.[3] And in Connecticut, the same-sex marriage bill includes protection from "state action to penalize or withhold benefits" from religious organizations, and protections for religious organizations that provide "adoption, foster care or social services."

Although Vermont's and Connecticut's protections are important, they leave out a number of the foreseeable collisions between same-sex marriage and religious liberty described above. In Connecticut, for example, a Catholic university that offers married-student housing would have to offer housing to married same-sex couples or risk violating state law. Similarly – and sadly – neither state protects individuals or small businesses. So, for example, wedding advisors, photographers, bakers, and caterers who prefer to step aside from same-sex ceremonies for religious reasons receive no protection. Despite these shortcomings, however, the fact that both Vermont and Connecticut adopted conscience protections in their same-sex marriage bills confirms an important principle: the conflicts between same-sex marriage and religious liberty are real, and they deserve legislative attention.

Maine's existing laws provide additional precedent for religious accommodations. For example, as noted above, Maine's sexual orientation discrimination statutes contain important accommodations for certain religious organizations. Similarly, federal statutes provide protections for religious and conscientious objectors in many different contexts. In short, protecting conscience is very much part of the American, and Maine, tradition. The Legislature should make the effort to continue that tradition.

Inadequacy of existing religious accommodations

Some may argue that Section 5 of S.P. 384 already provides sufficient protection for religious conscience. Section 5 provides:

> This Part does not authorize any court or other state or local governmental body, entity, agency or commission to compel, prevent or interfere in any way with any religious institution's religious doctrine, policy, teaching or solemnization of marriage within that particular religious faith's tradition as guaranteed by the Maine Constitution, Article 1, Section 3 or the First Amendment of the United States Constitution. A person authorized to join persons in marriage and who fails or refuses to join persons in marriage is not subject to any fine or other penalty for such failure or refusal."

This provision is a good start, but it has several serious deficiencies. First it protects only "religious institution[s]." Unlike other Maine laws, it does not protect religious individuals (including small business owners) and it does not clearly protect nonprofit organizations that are controlled or operated by a religious institution. Thus, Section 5 notwithstanding, wedding advisors, photographers, bakers, and caterers can be forced to participate in a same-sex marriage ceremony in violation of their religious beliefs. Similarly, a nonprofit social service organization, such as Mercy Hospital, which is sponsored by the Roman Catholic Church, could be forced to provide its employees with same-sex spousal benefits in violation of its religious beliefs.

Second, Section 5 protects only a religious institution's "doctrine, policy, teaching or solemnization of marriage." Protections for "doctrine," "teaching," and "solemnization" are largely unnecessary because such blatant interference with the internal operations of a church would clearly violate the First Amendment. The protection for "policy" is better, but quite vague. It unclear whether many, if any, of the conflicts mentioned above would fit the definition of a religious "policy."

Finally, Section 5 protects only those rights that are already "guaranteed by the Maine Constitution … or the First Amendment of the United States Constitution." This language renders Section 5 both superfluous and narrow. It is superfluous because, by its own terms, Section 5 provides only those rights that are already "guaranteed" by the United States Constitution. It is narrow because, under the Supreme Court's current interpretation of the Constitution, many of the religiously-motivated actions listed above will not qualify as rights "guaranteed by … the First Amendment," and will therefore be completely unprotected.

Proposed conscience protection

Because Section 5 is too vague and narrow to cover most of the conflicts listed above, stronger, more specific protection is needed. Maine can provide that protection by adopting a simple "marriage conscience protection" modeled on the existing language in Maine's sexual orientation discrimination laws. The "marriage conscience protection" would provide as follows:

> No individual, no religious corporation, association or organization, and no nonprofit organization owned, controlled or operated by a bona fide religious corporation shall be penalized or denied benefits under the laws of this state or any subdivision of this state, including but not limited to laws regarding employment discrimination, housing, public accommodations, licensing, government grants or contracts, or tax-exempt status, for refusing to provide services, accommodations, advantages, facilities, goods, or privileges related to the solemnization of any marriage, for refusing to solemnize

any marriage, or for refusing to treat as valid any marriage, where such providing, solemnizing, or treating as valid would cause that individual, corporation, association or organization to violate their sincerely held religious beliefs, *provided* that

(a) a refusal to provide services, accommodations, advantages, facilities, goods, or privileges related to the solemnization of any marriage shall not be protected under this section where (i) a party to the marriage is unable to obtain any similar services, accommodations, advantages, facilities, goods, or privileges elsewhere and (ii) such inability to obtain similar services, accommodations, advantages, facilities, goods, or privileges elsewhere constitutes a substantial hardship; and

(b) no government official may refuse to solemnize a marriage if another government official is not available and willing to do so.

This language has several important benefits. First, as noted above, it is modeled on existing protections in Maine law for any "religious corporation, association or organization" and for organizations "owned, controlled or operated by a bona fide religious corporation, association or society." This language also provides vital protections for religious individuals who own small businesses.

Second, unlike the vague protection for "policy" in Section 5 of S.P. 384, this language grants specific protections modeled on the Vermont and Connecticut same-sex marriage laws. Those laws protect the conscientious refusal "to provide services, accommodations, advantages, facilities, goods, or privileges ... related to the solemnization of a marriage."

Third, this language lists the primary areas of law where the refusal to treat a marriage as valid is likely to result in a penalty or denial of benefits ("laws regarding employment discrimination, housing, public accommodations, licensing, government grants or contracts, or tax-exempt status").

Fourth, this language provides protection only where providing services related to a marriage, solemnizing a marriage, or being forced to treat a marriage as valid would "violate ... sincerely held religious beliefs." This phrase is drawn from numerous court cases discussing the First Amendment to the U.S. Constitution and ensures that the religious-conscience protection will apply only to a "violation" of "sincere" and "religious" beliefs – not to situations that merely make religious people uncomfortable, not to insincere beliefs asserted as a pretext for discrimination, and not to non-religious moral beliefs.

Finally, this language recognizes that religious accommodations might not be without cost for same-sex couples, such as the need to find a new wedding photographer or caterer if the original choice must step aside for reasons of conscience. In order to address this issue, the proposed language ensures that a same-sex couple can obtain service, even from conscientious objectors, when the inability to find similar service elsewhere would impose an undue hardship on the couple. But because this hardship exception could force organizations or individuals to violate their religious beliefs, it should be available only in cases of substantial hardship, not mere inconvenience or symbolic harm. The language also ensures that no government employee (such as a court clerk) may act as a choke point on the path to marriage. So, for example, no government employee can refuse on grounds of conscience to issue a marriage license unless another government employee is available and willing to do so. These sorts of hardship protections are common in other laws protecting the right of conscientious objection.

In short, this "marriage conscience protection" would alleviate the vast majority of conflict between same-sex marriage and religious liberty, while still allowing for full recognition of same-sex marriages. It has ample precedent in both Maine and federal law. And it represents the best in the American and Maine tradition of protecting freedom of conscience.

Conclusion

Enacting S.P. 384 without robust religious accommodations will lead to damaging, widespread, and unnecessary conflict between same-sex marriage and religious liberty. The Legislature should avoid that conflict by crafting an appropriate religious accommodation provision. On that note, we would welcome any opportunity to provide further information, analysis, or testimony to the Legislature.

Very truly yours,

Thomas C. Berg
St. Ives Professor
University of St. Thomas
School of Law (Minnesota)

Carl H. Esbeck
Professor of Law
University of Missouri

Robin Fretwell Wilson
Professor of Law
Washington and Lee
University
School of Law

Richard W. Garnett
Professor of Law
University of Notre Dame
Law School

Laycock Letter:

Gov. John Baldacci
#1 State House Station
Augusta, ME 04333–0001

Re: Religious liberty implications of SP 0384, LD 1020

Dear Gov. Baldacci:

I urge you to insist that SP 0384, LD 1020, on same-sex marriage, be amended
to provide robust and specific protections for religious liberty. I have studied and
written about the law of religious liberty for many years, and I have written about
how to protect both sexual liberty and religious liberty in my co-edited book,
Same-Sex Marriage and Religious Liberty (2008). I write in my personal capacity,
and of course the University of Michigan takes no position on these issues.

I heartily endorse amendments on the lines proposed in the separate letter
that Professors Thomas C. Berg, Carl H. Esbeck, Richard W. Garnett, and
Robin Fretwell Wilson are sending you. I have not signed their letter, because
I come to these issues from a rather different perspective, but their analysis of
potential legal conflicts is accurate, and their proposed statutory language is
necessary to legislation that is fair and just to all sides.

I support same-sex marriage. I think the pending bill can be a great advance
for human liberty. But careless or overly aggressive drafting could create a
whole new set of problems for the religious liberty of those religious believers
who cannot conscientiously participate in implementing the new regime. The
net effect for human liberty will be no better than a wash if same-sex couples
now oppress religious dissenters in the same way that those dissenters, when
they had the power to do so, used to oppress same-sex couples.

Nor is it in the interest of the gay and lesbian community to create religious martyrs in the enforcement of this bill. To impose legal penalties or civil
liabilities on a wedding planner who refuses to do a same-sex wedding, or on
a religious counseling agency that refuses to provide marriage counseling to
same-sex couples, will simply ensure that conservative religious opinion on
this issue can repeatedly be aroused to fever pitch. Every such case will be in
the news repeatedly, and every such story will further inflame the opponents
of same-sex marriage. Refusing exemptions to such religious dissenters will
politically empower the most demagogic opponents of same-sex marriage. It
will ensure that the issue remains alive, bitter, and deeply divisive.

It is far better to respect the liberty of both sides and let same-sex marriage
be implemented with a minimum of confrontation. Put religious exemptions

in the bill, and at a stroke, you take away one of the opponents' strongest arguments. Let the people of Maine see happy, loving, same-sex marriages in their midst; let them see (this cannot be helped) that some of those marriages fail, just as many opposite-sex marriages fail; let them see that these same-sex marriages, good and bad, have no effect on opposite-sex marriages. Let the market respond to the obvious economic incentives; same-sex couples will pay good money just like opposite-sex couples. Let same-sex marriage become familiar to the people, and do these things without oppressing religious dissenters in the process. Same-sex marriage will be backed by law, backed by the state, and backed by a large and growing number of private institutions. Much of the dissent will gradually fade away, and nearly all the rest will go silent, succumbing to the live-and-let-live traditions of the American people. The number of people who assert their right to conscientious objection will be small in the beginning, and it will gradually decline to insignificance if deprived of the chance to rally around a series of martyrs.

Exemptions for religious conscientious objectors will rarely burden same-sex couples. Few same-sex couples in Maine will have to go far to find merchants, professionals, counseling agencies, or any other desired service providers who will cheerfully meet their needs and wants. And same-sex couples will generally be far happier working with a provider who contentedly desires to serve them than with one who believes them to be engaged in mortal sin, and grudgingly serves them only because of the coercive power of the law. Religious exemptions could also be drafted to exclude the rare cases where these suppositions are not true, such as a same-sex couple in a rural area that has reasonably convenient access to only one provider of some secular service. Such cases are no reason to withhold religious exemptions in the more urban areas where most of the people – and most of the same-sex couples – actually live.

Section 5 of the pending bill attempts to protect religious liberty, but it addresses only part of the problem. The first sentence arguably protects only what is already constitutionally guaranteed, and what is constitutionally guaranteed will inevitably be litigated. Apart from that problem, the first sentence protects religious marriages but it does not unambiguously provide that religious institutions need not recognize same-sex civil marriages. Must a religious counseling service counsel same-sex couples? Must a religious adoption agency place children with same-sex couples? There is no reason for the state to intrude into these religious institutions, or to force them to litigate over ambiguous protections. But the first sentence of Section 5 is unclear. The second sentence of Section 5 is clear, but it protects only those who officiate at marriages and only with respect to the choice whether to officiate.

8

Trans/Sex

Transsexualism: Patriarchal Ontology and Postmodern Praxis

To men a man is but a mind. Who cares what face he carries or what he wears? But woman's body *is* the woman.

Ambrose Bierce, *The Devil's Dictionary*

There is a gap between the way in which transgender is theorized and transsexuality is practiced. The gap is patriarchy.

Myself, *The End of Straight Supremacy*

There can be no doubt that in the culture of male–female discreteness, transsexuality is a disaster for the individual transsexual. Every transsexual, white, black, man, woman, rich, poor, is in a state of primary emergency as a transsexual.

Andrea Dworkin, *Woman Hating*

Men are men, but Man is a woman.

G. K. Chesterton, *The Napoleon of Notting Hill*

In this chapter, I provide a Gay liberation analysis of the phenomenon of transsexuality. To do so is to risk being greatly misunderstood – being labeled transphobic or, perhaps worse, a gay conservative. Nevertheless, transsexuality, in its more modern, politically correct incarnation of transgender,[1] has shifted to the center of "gay rights" organizing in ways I find distressing. This crystallized for me during the 2007–2008 debates over the Employment Non-Discrimination Act. Transsexuals and their supporters rallied to condemn the legislation and its proponents, most notably Congressman Barney Frank.[2]

---

[1] I use the term "transsexuality" in this chapter exclusively, because I believe it is the most accurate descriptor of the phenomenon I am analyzing. There is a gap between the way in which transgender is theorized and transsexuality is practiced. The gap is patriarchy. In most cases, it swallows the theory whole, leaving only patriarchal practices of gender and sexual hierarchy.

[2] For my observations then, see Shannon Gilreath, *In Defense of the Employment Non-Discrimination Act*, GAY CITY NEWS, Oct. 24, 2007.

Such action seemed to me particularly hostile to Gay people, given that trans-sexuals already had/have greater antidiscrimination protections at the federal level than do Gays.[3] In this and other obvious ways, transsexuality has become increasingly central to the "gay rights" movement and it is increasingly cel-ebrated as a path to liberation by movement leaders and by the postmodern canon working to rob Gays of Self-possession even before we have it.

DEFINITIONS

Some definitions are in order. By "transsexual" I mean to refer to a person who believes that he/she is actually of the sex opposite to that of his/her body – a person whose "gender identity" or "psychological sex" does not comport with the actual physical body to which he/she was born. On account of this, he/she wishes to become the other sex, with its attendant gender convention, including dress, mannerisms, as well as bodily presence – thus living the sex and gender that are in his/her head. Transsexuality is the process, generally medicalized, by which this (re)gendering of biological sex is accomplished, often involving, for the male-to-female transsexual, castration, a penisectomy, estrogen therapy, and the creation of a vagina. Breast implants, hair removal, a tracheal shave (to remove the visible Adam's apple), and various facial femini-zation procedures are also often undertaken in order to make the transsexual's appearance more conventionally gendered-feminine.[4] By focusing on this medicalized process, I mean to draw a distinction between the transgender-ism that has always been a part of Radical Gay culture – for example, the gender bending of *femme* Gay men, as seen in the likes of Harry Hay, or butch Lesbians, represented by Jess Goldberg in Leslie Feinberg's autobiographical

---

3   For example, there is a growing trend of protecting transsexuals under a Title VII theory of sex stereotyping. See, e.g., Smith v. City of Salem, 378 F.3d 566 (6th Cir. 2004); Barnes v. Cincinnati, 401 F.3d 729 (6th Cir. 2005); Mitchell v. Axcan Scandipharm, Inc., 2006 WL 456173 (W.D. Pa. 2006); Schroer v. Billington, 424 F. Supp. 2d 203 (D.D.C. 2006); Lopez v. River Oaks Imaging & Diagnostic Group, Inc., 542 F. Supp. 2d 653 (S.D. Tex. 2008); Glenn v. Brumby, 724 F. Supp. 2d 1284 (N.D. Ga. 2010).

4   For female-to-male transsexuals, the process involves testosterone treatments, double mas-tectomy, often closure of the vagina, and the creation of an artificial penis and scrotum filled with plastic implants to simulate testes. Needless to say, in a country like the United States, where insurance does not pay for such procedures, the cost is colossal. The desperation for "sex change" that most acute transsexuals say they experience coupled with the financial hurdles has given rise to an industry of preop transsexual prostitutes, in which transsexuals trick in an attempt to earn the funds necessary for the "sex change." The use of the preop-erative transsexual body in this way underscores my point about the sexualization of the body inherent in transsexuality (see section entitled "Transsexuality and the Pornographic/Patriarchal/Heteroarchal Worldview," this chapter).

novel *Stone Butch Blues*[5] – and transsexualism. With Gay transgender, the object is to be differently gendered – to challenge gender – not to become the other gender by disciplining the body into heteroarchal gender prescriptions. Gender disruption – indeed destruction – has always been a goal of Gay liberation.[6]

Transsexuality, on the other hand, as the conversion of a biologically male body to a female body, or of a biologically female body to a male body, through hormone "therapy" or surgical alteration is acquiescence in, indeed, is ritual celebration of, patriarchal/heteroarchal gender roles and is incongruous with Gay liberation. In direct contravention of Gay liberation, transsexuality presents gender as ontological (biological, even spiritual, in some cases), not epistemological (social).

Much, of course, has been made of the supposed biological link between sex and gender, so that what is actually transsexual (to the extent that that can actually be accomplished) is heralded as transgender. In the context of straight supremacy, the supposition of a biological link between sex and gender is useful to make gender seem like a product of nature instead of politics; thus, challenges to gender are rendered less likely. In the context of the gay rights movement, gender identity is propagandized as biology in order to analogize it to homosexuality, certainly claimed to be biological; thus, making a political kinship between sexuality and gender identity seems reasonable. But perhaps as much as any phenomenon of patriarchy, transsexuality exposes the fact that neither sex nor gender, nor sexuality for that matter, as a category of difference that matters, has much to do with biology. Transsexuality is better understood as the social meaning of biology when biology is social, as in the case of the need to alter biology to conform to patriarchal notions about what gender means. Thus, transsexuality is patriarchy succeeding ontologically, in the sense that reified dominance producing surgical alteration to conform to gender norms does not look epistemological in the context of transsexuality. Instead, it is taken as, theorized as, defended as, and promoted as biology, thus bringing new meaning to Catharine MacKinnon's observation that "dominance reified becomes difference."[7] Quite literally, here, gender epistemology is reified as biology – is made biological (or, at least, physiological) – through the "sex change" operation.[8] A purely biological mode of gender division, in

---

5   See Leslie Feinberg, Stone Butch Blues (1993).
6   As a political statement and strategy, for example, members of the Gay Liberation Front in the early 1970s adopted intentionally androgynous dress and grooming. This was not an identification with heteroarchal gender disciplines, but a pointed rejection of such disciplining.
7   Catharine A. MacKinnon, Toward a Feminist Theory of the State 238 (1989).
8   This is now referred to in the medical community as "sex reassignment surgery" or "gender reassignment surgery."

the sense that one simply either *is* a man or *is* a woman, in the gendered sense, by birth is reinforced. Nothing here challenges the construction of gender or its hierarchy.

It is this epistemic surrender that I think has given some feminists difficulties with transsexualism, conceptually and politically – that transsexualism basically accepts the notion that gender is difference rather than hierarchy in operation.[9] In the transsexual system, gender is distinctly bipolar, with one pole being male/masculine and the other pole being female/feminine; each pole is possessed of some inherent attributes that define what it is to be male and female; each pole is complementary. While a transvestite – a man in a dress – might do something to disrupt gender, obscuring the difference between what is social and what is biological, a transsexual essentially reinforces straight male dominance by reinforcing sex difference by presenting gender binarism as static and natural. Whatever discomfort transsexuals face is thus taken as a natural biological harmony somehow disrupted (by being born in the wrong body?) that can be restored through lopping off the penis, or the breasts, et cetera, by the "science" of "gender reassignment surgery." Quite to the contrary of Gay liberation's aim of destroying patriarchal/heteroarchal gender categories, transsexualism says flatly that gender is all we have.

Thus, the liberalism that celebrates transsexualism is not much different from the conservatism that would condemn it. For each, what is nature, thus natural, is simply a reflection of how the socially dominant see themselves. For liberals, that natural self is ultimately an autonomous self. Hence, the complete autonomy over the body that is a condition of transsexuality is simpatico with a liberal politic. This is fairly easy to see. Less obvious are transsexuality's links to conservatism. Oddly, transsexualism, condemned, of course, by religionists, is actually a mutated clone of natural law theory. Essentially, transsexualism says that Self-alienating gender stereotypes and sexual roles are part of an immutable (divine?) plan – certainly, they are a part of nature. Any transsexual you ask will tell you that this plan is clearly knowable through (and here is the note of evangelical Protestantism) personal revelation. In fact, transsexuals say this personal revelation comes very early; they say they know long before puberty that they are "in the wrong body."[10] Transsexual

---

[9] See., e.g., Janice G. Raymond, Transsexual Empire: The Making of the She-Male (1979); Mary Daly, Gyn/Ecology: The Metaethics of Radical Feminism (1978).

[10] This has led to the troubling practice of medically suspending puberty in identified "transgender" children. The idea behind the practice is that it will prevent the onset of the "wrong puberty" in a "transgender child." Thus, for male-to-female transsexuals, this would mean avoiding thickening of the vocal cords, masculine body hair patterns, increases in size of musculature and skeletal composition, and other "masculinization" of the body attendant on increases of testosterone in males at puberty.

fundamentalism says that there is male and female, as you shall know them. The important question is how you know them. Transsexuality's answer is really that of conservative religion: You know them by gender, which is *holy* for the transsexual and the religionist alike.

Curiously celebrated by the gay rights movement as a path to liberation, transsexualism is actually more akin to religious dogma, standing in the way of authentic personhood, which is Self-creation, not mimicry by ritual or other means. To say that sex exists only coextensively with gender in the head, which must be moved to the body, is not an autonomy claim, much less a creative one. It's handing back any autonomy, by moving to one's *predetermined* place. From the transsexual perspective, gender and sexuality in most cases, and possibilities for reinvention relative to either or both, are severely limited by rigid, predetermined roles. Gay liberation, by contrast, recognizes the ambiguity of the authentic Self, which cannot be encapsulated in abstractions in the form of gender or subverted through concrete distortions in the form of rigid sex roles. In this much needed analysis, Gay liberation understands patterns of relating sexually as subject to social evolution, not as defined by "nature." Gay liberation has always been first and foremost about liberating all human beings from the murderous condition that is Heteroarchy; it cannot, therefore, celebrate surrender to the bedrock principles of Heteroarchy, which are sex roles and gender hierarchy. Gay liberation's act of questioning and protesting what Janice Raymond named the "Transsexual Empire"[11] may thus aid in the breaking down of gender that is necessary for true, Radical change.

TRANSSEX/TRANSGENDER

The prefix "trans" signals that transsexuality and its conceptual umbrella, transgender, are conceived of as marking a movement across the gender spectrum. Indeed, the surgical and/or hormone-induced alteration of the sexed body (male/female) to craft a "new," explicitly gendered body (male-to-constructed-female/female-to-constructed-male) involves movement. The degree of the movement, and concomitantly its political content, is what is of most interest in a Gay liberation analysis. It is in this respect that I think the trend in the modern gay rights movement of accepting the conflation of "transgender"

[11] My citation of Raymond's well-known work on transsexuality (RAYMOND, *supra* note 9) is not intended to be an endorsement of some of her more exotic and dated claims, for example that male-to-female transsexuals are part of a patriarchal plot to spy on women by infiltrating women's spaces. I no more believe that than I believe Gore Vidal's fictionalized account of the male-to-female transsexual whose sole purpose is to torture straight men. See GORE VIDAL, MYRA BRECKINRIDGE (1993).

with "transsexual" is a serious mistake.[12] A disruption of gender to the extent that conventionally understood gender hierarchy is unsettled by gender-bending activity has political moment; comparatively bland migration from one gender pole to the other is not revolutionary – is not a movement toward personal, much less, social liberation. In fact, acceptance of transsexualism in the guise of transgenderism may be more dangerous than it at first appears. In actuality, transsexualism is about more than understanding gender separately from sexuality, as many proponents of transsexualism argue.[13] Transsexualism amounts to a technologized remedicalization of Gays and the endorsement of the possibility of a medical "cure" for homosexuality. In the West, where reality (especially in academic circles never much concerned with reality anyway) is obfuscated by postmodernism and an insistence on derealization as progress, as well as a fetish for "choice" that makes choice apparent where it is not real, these facts are obscured. In other places, however, the view is not so obscured. In Iran, for example, where homosexuality is punishable by particularly grue-some manifestations of the death penalty, transsexual surgery is paid for by the state.[14] In Iran, a Gay man can become a "straight woman" to avoid this kind of punishment. It is the "final solution" for homosexuality. Thus, when Iran's President Ahmadinejad says that there are no homosexuals in Iran, thanks to state-mandated transsexualism, he can mean it.[15] Now, of course, critics will immediately point out that the United States is not Iran, protesting that the kind of harsh legal discipline for sexuality present there no longer exists here, or that what happens in Iran is a direct result of Islamist despotism. But Sandra Bartky, building on Foucault's theory of institutionalized disciplining of "docile bodies," explains that overt legal discipline is not always necessary to accomplish gender (and sexuality) discipline.[16] In fact, once the discipline is no longer overtly legal – once it is invisibilized and made over to a question of social practice and good taste – it may be even more effective, for once obvi-ous coercion disappears so too does much of the impetus for rebellion. The

[12] David Valentine does an excellent job of tracing the development of this trend in *Imagining Transgender: An Ethnography of a Category* (2007).

[13] Dr. Norman Spack, a leading proponent of medicalized transsexuality, has said definitely that "being transgendered is not about sexual orientation." Dr. Spack's use of the term "trans-gendered" here is equivalent to its use in the mainstream gay rights movement to mean medical alteration of the body through hormones or surgery – the definition of "transsexual" as used in this chapter. See Ellen S. Glazer, *Demystifying the Transgendered: Renowned Brookline Physician*, BROOKLINE MAGAZINE, Apr. 2005, at 22–27.

[14] TANAZ ESHAGHIAN, BE LIKE OTHERS (2003) (documentary film).

[15] See Helene Cooper, *Ahmadinejad at Columbia, Parries and Puzzles*, N.Y. TIMES, Sept. 25, 2007.

[16] See SANDRA L. BARTKY, FEMININITY AND DOMINATION: STUDIES IN THE PHENOMENOLOGY OF OPPRESSION (1990) (esp. ch. 5).

specter of choice once materialized is all that is necessary to raise the idea of agency, which in democratic societies is all that seems to be required to turn the oppressive into the romantic.

Nevertheless, liberal theory continues to talk about transsexualism as though it were transgenderism – as though it really has something to do with abolishing gender as we know it. Professor Judith Butler, for example, reiterates transsexual activist Kate Bornstein's premise that a transsexual cannot accurately be described as a "woman" or "man," but must be understood in terms of verbs that articulate a process of continuous transformation – of "in-betweenness."[17] But transsexuals can't have it both ways. They can't claim some paradigm-shifting move and then go about living gender polarity as if it were natural. There is a certain "in-betweenness" inherent in a chromosomally sexed male living with a vagina, but when that constructed-vaginal female then presents him-/herself as gendered female, with makeup, dress, stilettos, and so on, the "in-betweenness" loses any political value (if it had any) from the standpoint of Gay liberation. Transsexuality is, especially outwardly, a normative project, and, as such, it relinquishes part of what is at the core of Gay liberation, namely the destabilization of gender as a category of authority. Under transsexuality, one is a woman or a man only according to the gender framework of the Heterarchy, and to call into question gender norms for the transsexual is to lose one's place in gender – a place no Gay person has ever had. Illuminatingly, when Kate Bornstein attended one of my speeches on pornography, he/she, also a pornographer, spoke from the floor in response to my assertion that Gay pornography reduces Gay people to sex. "Everybody's got to be about something," he/she said. "What's wrong with being all about sex?"[18] As a transsexual, Bornstein is all about conventional/patriarchal gender, whether or not he/she is willing to admit it.[19]

---

[17] Judith Butler, Gender Trouble: Feminism and the Subversion of Identity xii (1999).

[18] This speech was given at the 2008 Southeastern Unity Conference, held at the University of North Carolina, Chapel Hill. If Bornstein's "theory" wasn't such a mass of contradictions, this position would be exceedingly odd given that, in *Gender Outlaw*, Bornstein pointedly recognizes pornography as a form of "force" – of coercion. See Kate Bornstein, Gender Outlaw: On Men, Women and the Rest of Us 233 (1995).

[19] Kate Bornstein's theory of gender, outlined in *Gender Outlaw* and in subsequent work, though fraught with internal contradictions and inconsistencies, is worth reading. Bornstein, himself/herself a postoperative transsexual, gives a compelling account of his/her early life as a man (something he/she says he/she never was) and a rundown of the surgical process as well as its aftermath. He/she also makes some politically salient points about gender and power. But in the end, Bornstein's own theory about the social construction and consequent mutability of gender is belied by his/her own actions of presentation as a gender-female and day-to-day "passing" (see, e.g., id. at 48), which is the transsexual phenomenon of not identifying

Butler, too, celebrates the revolutionary capacity of transsexualism in her best-known book, paradoxically entitled *Gender Trouble*.[20] The title and the entire work are paradoxical because Professor Butler proceeds from the premise that gender is entirely a product of social discourse – a premise with which I am not inclined to disagree. The paradox develops, however, because Butler understands there to be no reality outside of social discourse – no meaningful distinction between apparent reality and truth – thus indicating that gender is an imitation without an original. No Self that has been captured/gendered exists in Butler's postmodern philosophy, and thus for Butler, gender is all that there is. And yet Butler understands gender as capable of being revolutionized and transsexuality as a revolutionary enterprise. She writes:

> Indeed, if we shift the example from drag to transsexuality, then it is no longer possible to derive a judgment about stable anatomy from the clothes that cover and articulate the body. That body may be preoperative, transitional, or post-operative; even "seeing" the body may not answer the question: *for what are the categories through which one sees?* The moment in which one's staid and usual cultural perceptions fail, when one cannot with surety read the body that one sees, is precisely the moment when one is no longer sure whether the body encountered is that of a man or a woman. The vacillation between the categories itself constitutes the experience of the body in question.

> When such categories come into question, the *reality* of gender is also put into crisis: it becomes unclear how to distinguish the real from the unreal. And this is the occasion in which we come to understand that what we take to be "real," what we invoke as the naturalized knowledge of gender is, in fact, a changeable and revisable reality. Call it subversive or call it something else. Although this insight does not in itself constitute a political revolution, no political revolution is possible without a radical shift in one's notion of the possible and the real.... At this point, the sedimented and reified field

---

as transsexual (as Bornstein prescribes) but of identifying solely with the gender to which the transsexual has transitioned (some transsexuals have described this covert transsexuality to me as "going stealth"), and of his/her insistence on the moral relevance of gendered pronouns to describe transsexuals (see id. at 126). Bornstein seems genuinely oblivious to the fact that his/her stated aim of destroying gender (id. at 112) is undermined by his/her insistence on "living ... as a woman" (id. at 149), with his/her "sex change" being the most obvious outward manifestation of both the actual relationship under patriarchy between sex and the gender binary *and* the most convincing evidence that, in living the binary and claiming revolution, Bornstein doesn't get it. Orwell didn't know Bornstein, but Bornstein certainly knows doublethink. Still, in *Gender Outlaw*, there are glimmers of hope. At the book's conclusion, Bornstein claims that "girl" is "an identity I'm working my way out of" (id. at 238). In this endeavor, I wish him/her well.

[20] BUTLER, *supra* note 17.

of gender "reality" is understood as one that might be made differently and, indeed, less violently.[21]

But what Butler is describing here is a change – often explicitly violent, in the case of sex reassignment surgery – in anatomical sex, not in gender. Gender, the social practice, is what drives surgical alteration of an anatomically male body to make it appear female. Because the anatomy does not comport with the gender the transsexual feels compelled to live socially, the body is altered. Sex changes in this scenario (although, of course, not at a chromosomal level); the meaning of gender doesn't. Nothing is made different; compulsory heterosexuality is reinforced; the heterosexual/heteronormative complementarity of bodies is reinforced. The only subversion is the subversive desire of a man to be a woman. But this is less subversive when one pauses to consider that perhaps the only thing worse than being a woman, from the heteroarchal perspective, is being a Gay man. To be Gay in patriarchy/Heteroarchy is to be alien from the gender hierarchy, and thus separated from power, to be inhuman. Transsexuals generally believe they are not intelligibly human unless they conform to naturalized understandings of what sex is to gender and gender is to sex. The body of the transsexual thus becomes a reification of the power transsexuality is theorized to oppose: It is mutilated in a real sense by and for the compulsory heterosexuality it is said to disrupt – and it is affected by and affects gender in ways that are irreducibly traditionally patriarchal/heteroarchal. Mutilation of the body, usually the female body, in the name of an idealized gender complementarity has, after all, been a long-standing patriarchal practice – a long-standing and effective way of gendering power and, indeed, of sexualizing power as exclusively heterosexual along gender lines.

The pathological view of humanity as a stasis of the male positive and the female negative has been inscribed on women's bodies for the whole of patriarchal history. The necessary physical distinguishing between the male and the female – necessary to keep the powerful male ethos dominant – has been physically enacted through countless mutilations. For one thousand years in China, for example, women's feet were bound from early girlhood.[22] When a girl was about seven or eight years old, her feet were washed in a chemical to cause shrinking and then bound as tightly as possible, usually by the girl's own mother, with all toes, except the big toe, bent inward to the sole of the

---

[21] Id. at xxiv (emphasis in original).
[22] For excellent discussions of footbinding in China, see ANDREA DWORKIN, WOMAN HATING (1974) (ch. 6: *Gynocide: Chinese Footbinding*). See also DALY, *supra* note 9 (ch. 4: *Chinese Footbinding: On Footnoting the Three-Inch "Lotus-Hooks"*).

foot. Bones broke. This procedure was repeated frequently for approximately three years – a fresh agony visited on the girl each time the bandages were loosened, so that the foot could be washed and tightened again. The ideal end product would be the three-inch "lotus foot" – the idolized object of Chinese men's sexual pleasure.[23] In reality, of course, the fetishized sexual (and obviously gendered) foot was a rotting, oozing, puss-filled stump. Toenails grew into the sole of the foot, circulation all but stopped, sometimes toes fell off, flesh blackened and rotted. Girls were forced to walk – or more accurately to hobble – on these rotting stumps. Of course, they were also taught always to conceal the true nature of their mutilated feet from men, so that even during sex the female feet were never naked.

This atrocity of footbinding committed against Chinese women's bodies was done in the name of sex roles, male–female complementarity, and gender identity, all to the tune of straight male desire. In other words, footbinding communicated the patriarchal message about *what a woman looked like* in imperial Chinese culture or, even more specifically, what a *desirable* woman looked like – thus revealing gender itself to be a kind of sexual fetish. To have one's feet bound was to be definitively and definitionally female: The outward sign of the lotus foot communicated the feminine identity. To be born biologically female and not to have bound feet was to be robbed of one's status (albeit the lower status in patriarchy) of being a *desirable* woman. Thus, woman, thoroughly sexualized, *is made* through the social process of gender.

Of course, one might say that transsexuality is qualitatively different than footbinding because of the difference in degree of apparent agency in the two practices. Transsexuals, it could be said, themselves choose to alter their bodies surgically. Chinese girls, by contrast, had body alteration forced on them by their mothers or aunts or older female relatives (actually, of course, by the Chinese patriarchs who forced these practices on all women). But I remember seeing a news program many years ago featuring an elderly Chinese women, taking the tiny, hobbling steps that are the result of footbinding. This woman, a young woman when the revolutionary regime outlawed footbinding, continued to bind her own feet out of a gender-motivated desire to be "beautiful," in the gendered sense, and attractive to men – that is, to be a woman. The Hindu practice of *sati* is another example of body destruction in the name of gender in which the compulsion necessary to sustain the practice is rendered

---

[23] Another sexualization of the bound foot involved the myth that the way in which women with bound feet had to walk resulted in a strengthening of the vaginal and rectal muscles of these women, thus making the vagina and anus tighter and more enjoyable for males during penetration.

invisible, rendered merely *cultural*.[24] Indian widows were seen to leap "willingly" into the funeral pyres of their husbands and burn to death. Perhaps in a state of captured consciousness some did go "willingly" to their deaths (although some women had to be physically forced).[25] But social compulsion was/is at work.[26] Perhaps physical destruction seems to some widows a practical response to prevailing social deprivation and ostracism.

Other forms of body destruction and negation continue, usually in the form and practice of patriarchal religions denominated "culture" (whose culture?) by relativists: female genital mutilation or negation of the female body through the Islamist practice of veiling are examples.[27] In the case of the veil, "feminist" cultural relativists defend the practice as one of female agency, invisibilizing the patriarchal religionist compulsion that causes women to smother

---

[24] It also shows the inherently patriarchal/heteroarchal nature of marriage, of which the practice of widow burning is obviously derivative. Marriage and gender are inextricably intertwined. See Chapter 6, this volume. *Sati* is a consummation of both. For an excellent, feminist excavation of *sati* and its meanings, see DALY, *supra* note 9, at 114–127. Daly's critique is not without its problems. For one thing, Daly's criticism of god-centered patriarchal religion does not necessarily translate to Hinduism, which certainly has sustained a harsh patriarchal society but is nevertheless a religion that features many powerful goddesses. Also, I am cognizant of some transnational feminist work rejecting the possibility of antipatriarchal critique that can be applied cross-culturally. See, e.g., CHANDRA MOHANTY, FEMINISM WITHOUT BORDERS: DECOLONIZING THEORY, PRACTICING SOLIDARITY (2003); UMA NARAYAN, DISLOCATING CULTURES: IDENTITIES, TRADITIONS AND THIRD WORLD FEMINISM (1997). In the end, though, I'm left with a fairly basic question: Do women matter or not? I think they do, and they matter equally everywhere, including in places where obviously gendered practices like *sati*, although not widespread, accomplish their destruction.

[25] Daly discusses the force necessary in many instances. DALY, *supra* note 9.

[26] I use the past and present verb form here because, although it was outlawed in India in 1829, *sati* persists in some areas. See, e.g., *Woman Jumps into Husband's Funeral Pyre*, TIMES OF INDIA, Oct. 13, 2008.

[27] Although the mutilation of female bodies has certainly been more prevalent, males have not escaped entirely unscathed from the anatomical fixations of the patriarchal world. There are, for example, the practices of penis elongation, whereby heavy weights are attached to the penises of young men in some areas of Africa. But there is also the practice, so common in the United States as to go nearly unremarked, of male circumcision. This custom, perpetuated as a patriarchal religious practice of Judaism, involves excision of the skin covering the glands of a male child's penis. In the Jewish tradition, this male mutilation is ritualized in the *bris*, a ceremony in which a rabbi (not a doctor) performs the surgery, while onlookers gawk at this sadism and celebrate it as a religious rite. Deritualized male circumcision has been exported to the West, especially to the United States, where it is foisted on male children, per their parents, by doctors who claim it is medical necessity.

In fact, circumcision – penile cutting – may be an original form of transsexualism. It was necessary for Jewish men, who invented the idea of subservience to one, consummately male god, to relinquish some of their manhood, to become, in contrast to their omnipotent male god, feminine. This they accomplished through penile cutting. Through the cut, bleeding penis, they became/become like women in function – as Andrea Dworkin put it, they became/become "menstruating males."

themselves under layers of stifling clothing, even covering their mouths and noses.[28] Still subtler forms of gender inscription on the body exist for the supposedly liberated Western woman, in the form of stiletto heels or layers of face-obscuring makeup (and, of course, much more). Even pregnancy, with its real physical dangers, is often (usually) an imposed state of Self-negation, with women conned into seeing pregnancy as a unique source of fulfillment in the system of gender polarity, induced to embrace the delusion that they are having children because *they want to*. Meanwhile, pregnancy and ensuing child rearing are actually used to fix and make static a woman's inferiority to men. She *is* punished – professionally, economically, intellectually, et cetera – for her unique capacity to bear children.[29]

I offer these examples of traditional gender-based mutilations to ask this question: Can women in patriarchy – women who "choose" to bind their feet or walk into the flames, or veil their faces, or have their third or sixth or eighth child, or hobble around on stiletto heels – really be said to be exercising meaningful agency over their own bodies? My premise is that the gender compulsion affects transsexuals in similar, powerful ways.[30] The historical negation of the female through destruction of the body – a practicality in no uncertain terms in many situations – is carried forward into a new, technologized age where, in spite of the same advances in knowledge that make the process of "sex change" possible, in the name of compulsory heterosexuality's compulsory, pathological vision of gender polarity, the body, this time the body of a Gay man,[31] must still be negated, must be mutilated. No one is dragging the transsexual to the surgeon's knife or the hormonal needle, but the compulsion is real.

---

[28] But when affinity for the veil is counterpoised against escalating danger in aggressively patriarchal Islamist cultures, veiling is revealed to be not so much an act of agency as one of survival. Egyptian activist Nawal El Saadawi has observed that when she was in medical school in the 1950s there were no veiled women in the school, but that in the 1990s close to 80% of women in schools were veiled (the number is probably greater now). Saadawi has said flatly that "[f]undamentalism is why women in the Islamic world are now veiled again." See Mary Daly, Quintessence ... Realizing the Archaic Future: A Radical Elemental Feminist Manifesto 80 (1998).

[29] For a lucid discussion of this point, see Andrea Dworkin, Our Blood: Prophesies and Discourses on Sexual Politics 100–101 (1976).

[30] Interestingly, Kate Bornstein recognized gender as this kind of force. *See* Bornstein, *supra* note 18, at 233.

[31] See the following section of this chapter, "Transsexuality as Gay Erasure," for elaboration. Of course, in transsexuality, the body of a woman is also mutilated in the case of female-to-male transsexuals. Cases of female-to-male conversion seem less frequent, but when they do occur it can be fairly said that double and historically connected negations occur – negation of both the female body and the Lesbian Self.

And what of the related, but certainly less physically violent practice with which Professor Butler begins her discussion of transsexuality cited earlier: what of drag? Professor Butler sees drag as illumining the social construction of gender and, importantly, as disputing its naturalness.[32] But to tell the whole truth about drag, one must distinguish between drag that is "female impersonation" and drag that is "gender-fuck."[33] Drag as gender-fuck may involve a man, identifiable as a man, in a dress. Encountering an identifiable man in a dress is startling. It sends messages about gender roles that, obviously, contradict those roles.[34] It is disruptive. Drag as female impersonation, on the other hand, is simply the ritual reenactment of the patriarchal/heteroarchal feminine eternal – the role attributed to women as the product of nature and accepted as such. Female impersonators pantomime and pander to traditional gender roles, often in exaggerated fashion, reenacting the feminine stereotype with dramatic flourishes: the sensual dance, the provocative gesture, the lip-synched sexual ballad or club groove.[35] These are parodies of woman; they are not liberatory. The Self is not liberated; even in drag, the Self *is still gendered.*

Perhaps the reason that Professor Butler does not respect this difference is that she cannot understand it, largely because she does not believe there is a Self beyond the veneer of social construction. This is an obscurantism that is hard to understand fully, a discussion of gender that takes gender to be an imitation that has no original or referent. Her understanding of the body in these same terms is perhaps what leads her to her conclusion that transsexuality is liberation. As Richard Mohr observes, Butler "presses further [than Foucault]. She claims that the body is even less than a blank slate, and that Foucault is wrong in maintaining a body prior to its cultural inscription."[36] So there is no sexed body, only a gendered body. From Butler's perspective then, perhaps there is only transgender, and what is transsexual is transgender by the default of Butler's position, which has here drifted into Derrida-land, that there is no being outside of social context.[37]

---

[32] BUTLER, *supra* note 17, at 123, 138–139, 148–149.

[33] On this point see RICHARD MOHR, GAY IDEAS: OUTING AND OTHER CONTROVERSIES 144 et seq. (1994).

[34] I'm thinking here of Harry Hay, the original prophet of Gay male Radicalism, who, often appearing bedecked in Native American jewelry and sometimes in a dress, understood the importance of disrupting gender hegemony in the heteroarchal model.

[35] Certainly, drag is also sometimes a sexual fetish. This too is tied to heteroarchal understandings of the communication of (hetero)sexuality through gendered modes of dress.

[36] MOHR, *supra* note 33, at 279 n. 8 (1992) (citing BUTLER, *supra* note 17, at 130).

[37] The groundlessness of Butler's take leaves me, with Mohr, wondering "what in the end she does mean." MOHR, *supra* note 33, at 279 n. 10. This coming to nothingness is perhaps what

Popular rationalization and defense of transsexuality is different from Professor Butler's postmodern musings on the subject. The transsexual politic is quite distinctly one of biology, naming as a product of nature or biology the psychological sex that must be appeased through surgical modification of the body. And yet there are resonances of Butler's theory in transsexual politics, for in a very real way, transsexuality suggests that the corporeal body does not really exist – not authentically at least – until the social inscriptions of compulsory heterosexuality's gender have been imprinted on it. The principal distinction in the concreteness of transgender politics and the spuriousness of postmodern nothingness, however, is that transsexual advocates say that gender is a priori – is always. Butler says that gender, despite the fact that she devotes tomes to it, never *really* was. Herein lies the chief principle of resistance of Gay liberation to Gay erasure through transsexual Self-mutilation and postmodern nihilism: This principle is the existential assertion of Self – the *I am*. I am a Gay man, and no transsexual lobbyist or postmodern theorist is going to disabuse me of that fact.[38] And this should in no sense be read as an

---

packs tenure dossiers these days, but it, like all postmodernism, is of little use for problems in need of solutions. I have to admit that I laughed out loud to discover that Butler's entry in Mohr's index was succeeded by the entry for "buttfucking." Given some of Butler's exotic claims, the nonexistence of the body (above) or the transferability of the phallus (see Butler, Bodies That Matter: On the Discursive Limits of "Sex" (1993)), I half expected to find Butler's name under a heading for "mind-fucking." Thirty-four pages on the "lesbian phallus" are, even by postmodernist standards, hard to swallow. Pun intended.

[38] Postmodernism is dangerous for Gay liberation principally because it paralyzes activism. A brilliant young scholar I know told me recently of his confusion at having his invited paper at a symposium simultaneously praised and maligned by a famous Harvard postmodernist professor. My friend was told his work was brilliant except for the fact that it condescended to offer solutions to real-world problems. Go figure – the "problem" is that your scholarship might actually matter in the real world.

For postmodernists, an identity claimed by a motley assortment of characters whose work has little in common, not the least of which is consistency, there can be no reality of Gay life because a central epistemic notion for postmodernism is that reality does not exist. What takes reality's place as a subject (but, then, there are no subjects in postmodernism either) is generally a blathering on unto nothingness that leaves one wondering about the point. The fact that much of this is coming out of the most prestigious universities and being published in the most prestigious places is not surprising, since one may fairly suppose that this is the eventual product of elitism left alone with itself for long enough: obscurantism in the guise of profundity. Many are fooled, not the least of whom, it seems, are postmodernists themselves. The perfect example of this kind of blind elitist snobbery is the publication of an essay, which was in fact inscrutable blather, in a leading postmodern journal. See Alan D. Sokal, *Transgressing the Boundaries: Toward a Transformative Hermeneutics of Quantum Gravity*, 46/47 Social Text 217 (1996). Sokal said that he engaged in his satirical infiltration of the postmodern noise machine because he "never quite understood how deconstruction was supposed to help the working class." Alan Sokal & Jean Bricmont, Fashionable Nonsense: Postmodern Intellectuals' Abuse of Science 269 (1998).

assertion of male power. I hope I would be equally emphatic about my identity if I were a Gay woman – a Lesbian.

TRANSSEXUALITY AS GAY ERASURE

As alluded to earlier, I have often wondered how much of transsexualism can be explained by an appalling Self-hatred, an overwhelming need not to be Gay – in other words, a Self-liquidating homophobia. From this perspective, transsexualism is a way of avoiding being a *femme* Gay man or a butch Lesbian. Instead a *femme* Gay man can actually be a "straight woman," and a butch Lesbian can actually be a "straight man." Of course, I am aware that there are cases of postoperative male-to-female "Lesbians" and of female-to-male "Gay men." Kate Bornstein, for example, professes to be a transsexual Lesbian. As in any system, there are counterfactuals and outliers. Still, the outliers often aren't really as far out as they appear. The climax of Bornstein's *Gender Outlaw*, for example, is the revelation that his/her "lesbian lover" is "becoming a man."[39]

For my theory of transsexuality to make sense at this point, one must pause to remember the importance of the gendered body and its relationship to compulsory heterosexuality under patriarchy/Heteroarchy as "a direct locus of social control."[40] I know from experience that it is not uncommon for little Gay boys, who often instinctively identify with women because they sense that

Postmodern, elitist detachment from reality and the utter desperation of Gay people living under straight supremacy have merged in the emergence of marriage and transsexuality as central liberation themes in gay rights discourse and politics. What I see as the erasure of Gay identity cannot be understood this way by a postmodern politics because postmodernism denies the existence of any coherent Gay reality or experience to erase. Postulating otherwise – that, for example, Gays share the identity of subordination under straight supremacy – is sneered at as "essentialist." And the acme of aggrandized heteroassimilation in marriage and its twisted cousin, transsexuality, are reconstituted as revolution.

[39] See Bornstein, *supra* note 18, at 225. Bornstein is in many ways an "exceptional" transsexual, in the sense that he/she continues to identity as transsexual and as a transsexual activist. Using him/her as a reference in order to discuss transsexuality highlights the fact that discussion of transsexuality nearly invariably involves discussion of exceptional cases. Generally, we are denied the ability to critique the product of transsexuality because the product is invisibilized in straight supremacy. The practice of "going stealth," as it was named for me by a male-to-female transsexual, which is the process of living as one's "new" gender, with life as the prior gender rendered as undetectable as possible, means that the particulars of transsexuality and its relationship to straight supremacy are harder to analyze because we cannot always readily see and evaluate them. Nevertheless, I believe that the transsexual project naturalizes gender binarism particularly and naturalizes heterosexuality in the ways I have suggested – thus naturalizes the heterosexual imperative.

[40] Susan Bordo, Unbearable Weight: Feminism, Western Culture, and the Body 165 (1993).

they are being instinctively kept at a distance by the men in their lives, to be chastised for being "too feminine." Gender nonconformists have the biggest burdens to bear in the heteroarchal system because they least approximate the heteroarchal gender norms that serve as access points to power – and, if not to power, at least to safety.[41] To anyone who might ask why there are so many closeted Gays, this is the why: To be out is to be vulnerable to straight sadism. Gays learn quickly that gender conformity/assimilation means safety.

Gays also learn that assimilating when we can provides a chance to claim some of the Heteroarchy's dominance, however briefly. This hypothesis can be substantiated by the literature on transsexualism. In one of the earliest case accounts of the psychoanalysis of what we would today call a transsexual, J. Allen Gilbert labeled the condition "homo-sexuality."[42] In 1954 the psychiatrist Emil Gutheil speculated that transsexuals were homosexuals "with an unresolved castration complex."[43] In 1955 Frederic Worden, a UCLA psychoanalyst and his clinical partner, James Marsh, opined that transsexuality is driven by a desire for "escape from … sexual impulses."[44] Indeed, in the first case study of Christine Jorgensen, his/her Danish endocrinologist described him/her as "suffering from homosexual tendencies."[45] Transsexuals, of course, see transsexuality as wholly separate from homosexuality, as they surely would if they were using transsexuality as an escape route to normalcy. Jorgensen, in a recorded interview, said, "I identified myself as female, and consequently my interests in men were normal."[46] Clearly, Jorgensen's choice of adjectives shows the process of rationalization at work, her normal (read: heterosexual, even in her preoperative state) interest in men compared with the abnormal (read: homosexual) interests of Gay men – of what she was before her sex "changed." This process of normalizing, of mindbinding, begins early and is carried into the adult reality of Gay men and women.

The gendered, physical destruction inherent in transsexuality is thus a product of the destruction of the mental and intellectual capacity of Gays under Heteroarchy. This, too, is like the destruction of women's mental and intellectual capacities by the patriarchs. Such circumscription is necessary

---

[41] Gays are *really* transgender in that, by fucking people of the same sex, we dispute compulsory heterosexuality and, thereby, gender.

[42] Joanne Meyerowitz, How Sex Changed: A History of Transsexuality in the United States 104 (2002).

[43] Id. at 106.

[44] Id. at 108.

[45] Jorgensen's male-to-female transformation with the aid of Danish doctors is celebrated as the beginning of the transsexual movement. Throughout his/her life, he/she acted as a spokesperson for the trans movement. Id. at 171.

[46] Id. at 183.

to create the (un)consciousness necessary to sustain patriarchal deceptions. Under Heterarchy, Gays are conditioned from birth to submit willingly to our own Self-annihilation. Might transsexuality not be this conditioned submissiveness to annihilation in its most acute form – the radical annihilation of the Gay Self through gendered conformity of the body to compulsory heterosexuality?

Understanding transsexualism in this way actually provides clarity of insight into the prevailing politics of the "mainstream" gay movement. For example, Bruce Bawer's *A Place at the Table* was received enthusiastically by liberals and neo-cons because it told them what they wanted to hear, largely that straight-assimilated Gays were just normal folks who wanted all the normal heterosexual things out of life.[47] Except for a distaste for heterosexual sex, Gays *are* straights. Gays who rebel against gender roles and sex stereotypes and the conventional institutions enshrining them (like marriage) are to be distrusted, even punished.[48] Bawer's, like the politics of all gay conservatives, is a politics of Gay erasure. Transsexuality, of which Bawer disapproves, is simply the extreme-liberal-Left version of what he preaches – erasing the Gay identity to conform to straight rules. Both ideologies are built around rigid gender conformity and nonconformists' erasure. In the way it sees gender (not to mention politics), Gay liberation is substantially different in perspective. When a male-to-female transsexual seeks affirmation as a woman, he/she seeks affirmation of a woman's body as the biological determinant of a woman's role in society. Gay conservatives, like Bawer, see gender roles as assigned by sex and as basically immutable. Gay liberation, on the other hand, understands what it means to be a man or a woman as process-driven, subject to social evolution – to change. To have a social meaning imposed on the body – which is the process of gender – is therefore Gay liberation's anathema.

TRANSSEXUALITY AND THE PORNOGRAPHIC/PATRIARCHAL/ HETEROARCHAL WORLDVIEW

Transsexuality, like marriage and pornography, is part of the heteroarchal worldview.[49] The relationship between transsexuality and the pornographic

---

[47] Bruce Bawer, A Place at the Table: The Gay Individual in American Society (1993).

[48] Lisa Duggan has aptly named this state the "new homonormativity." See Lisa Duggan, *The New Homonormativity: The Sexual Politics of Neoliberalism*, in Materializing Democracy: Toward a Revitalized Cultural Politics 175–195 (Russ Castronovo & Dana D. Nelson, eds., 2002).

[49] With regard to the transsexual argument from "nature" and natural law jurisprudence arguments about marriage, namely the narrow, obsessive focus on "sexual complementarity or bodily union in coital acts," (see Sherif Girgis, Ryan T. Anderson, & Robert P. George, *Marriage:*

worldview (i.e., the heteroarchal worldview) is plain in the 1968 book *Take My Tool: Revelations of a Sex-Switch*, the blatantly pornographic autobiography of a male-to-female transsexual.[50] As the book's author, writing under the assumed name of Vivian Le Mans, proclaimed, "[I]n bed performing sexually, I can finally fulfill myself and my male partner as much as can any other women – and probably better than most!"[51] Le Mans contrasts stories with his/her less than fulfilling sex life as a Gay man with the transcendent pleasure of sex in the female form, underscoring the transsexual belief that the "sex change" is rooted in heteroarchal understandings of the gendered roles and purposes of male and female bodies.

Joanne Myerowitz, writing about *Take My Tool* in her excellent book, *How Sex Changed: The History of Transsexuality in America*, sees *Take My Tool* and its blatant eroticism of the transsexual as marking a sexualization of transsexuality.[52] But, in fact, sexualization of physical identity is an inherent component of transsexuality inasmuch as it is a practice of heteroarchal understandings of gender, which have always been explicitly sexual and bipolar, and understood in terms of sexual complementarity. This polar binary is dissected in Jane Caputi's analysis of an advertisement for a perfume called "Happy." The ad "shows a white man and woman in 1950s-type garb suggesting total gender role conformity. She wears a pink party dress and holds out a birthday cake. He sports a football uniform, holds a ball under his arm, and has assumed a running stance."[53] "Happy?" Professor Caputi wryly remarks. "I wonder."[54] "This portrait might more aptly be dubbed 'Misery', for the image portrays one originally whole psyche, now split and divided against itself."[55] The key to "step[ping] out of these fetishized roles" is to dispute them and the sexualized hierarchy grounded in them by refusing to acquiesce in the "gender porn"[56] built on the Self-alienated psyche they represent.

No Avoiding the Central Question, http://www.thepublicdiscourse.com/2011/01/2295), the parallels are undeniable. I wonder if George and company would become enthusiastic supporters of "transsexual marriage," if not "Gay marriage," if the mad scientists could figure out a way to give transsexuals a functioning uterus.

[50] *Take My Tool* is the best/worst example. VIVIAN LE MANS, TAKE MY TOOL (1968). Other autobiographies of transsexuals of the period have obviously pornographic perspectives. See, e.g., LYN RASKIN, DIARY OF A TRANSSEXUAL (1971); PATRICIA MORGAN & PAUL HOFFMAN, THE MAN-MAID DOLL (1973).

[51] LE MANS, *supra* note 50, at 8.

[52] MEYEROWITZ, *supra* note 42, at 170.

[53] JANE CAPUTI, GODDESSES AND MONSTERS: WOMEN, MYTH, POWER, AND POPULAR CULTURE 79 (2004).

[54] Id.

[55] Id.

[56] Id.

Pornography[57] is materially a visual enterprise, whether the visual is created in the mind's eye, as in written pornography, or, as is the case predominantly in the video/DVD/Internet age, in the physical eye, through actual images of actual women subordinated through the act of heterosexual fucking and its equivalents. The relationship between sex and gender is fixed and perpetuated through pornography as visual aide – as a guide to interpreting sex difference that has been gendered. The body and its parts are fetishized in pornography, and functionality is communicated through the pornographic visual medium. The male penis is gendered/pornographed into the phallus, permanently erect, ever-ready, engorged, pulsating, and aggressive. In straight pornography, the female body, virtually every part of it, is sexualized according to the gender script. The concentration is usually on the vagina and the breasts. Even the smoothness of a woman's skin is fetishized – even her skin is used as a sexual organ. The physical parts of her define her as a woman, and the visual cues are of utmost importance to the pornographic gaze. In photographic pornography, in which consumers cannot benefit from actually seeing the vagina identified by the penis thrusting into it, as is the case in video pornography, tricks must be employed to keep the pornographic gaze in focus. The vulva may be painted purple, for example, or splayed and propped open by toothpicks to make it appear three-dimensional, so that the pornographic gaze is directed to its appropriate object – there can be no space for imagination. Sexual dominance communicated socially as gender polarity – that is, the physical sex differences between men and women imbued with political meanings and consequences – is dependent on visual cues in pornography and in the everyday.

Rather than disputing the primacy of bipolar gender complementarity, transsexuality parrots patriarchy by calling gender *difference* natural (biological, inevitable) and by embracing its visual propaganda. In an incredible reversal, the postmodern ethic of the transsexual politic intent on derealizing reality actually reifies the patriarchal reality of gender difference made into dominance by intentionally replicating the patriarchal gender hierarchy. Historian Gerda Lerner locates the birth of patriarchy in the "invention of hierarchy."[58] Transsexualism, as a product of the medical/scientific age, might aptly be said to be patriarchy's rebirth through cloning.[59]

---

57 To qualify the noun "pornography" with the adjective "gender," in the way that Professor Caputi did in the preceding excerpt, is actually a redundancy, since all pornography is about gender; gender is irreducibly pornographic – the two exist entirely in codependence with one another.

58 GERDA LERNER, WHY HISTORY MATTERS: LIFE AND THOUGHT 133 (1997).

59 Readers may wonder how a man becoming a woman could actually be replicating patriarchal ideas about dominance and power when a man is relinquishing that power voluntarily by adopting a female body and a feminine persona (I concentrate on the male-to-female

CONCLUSION

What can be made sense of in normal terms cannot be deviant. It is the convention of many Gay men I know – especially younger Gay men – to refer to other Gay men as "she." This is in part, I think, a conscious effort at creating distance from straight men, who are the oppressors. But it is also symbolic of the fact that, in the Heteroarchy's system of gender polarity, to be fuckable is a state of being – a functionality – which is gender-female. As Monique Wittig noted, "The mark of gender, according to grammarians, concerns substantives. They talk about it in terms of function."[60] So the invocation of the feminine pronoun by Gay men in friendly conversation with each other is a kind of mental note – a way of making intelligible their sexual practices in a heteroarchal world. Transsexuality is, I think, a fringe outgrowth of this same kind of coping with same-sex desire under straight supremacy. It is a way of making sense of what seems senseless. Judith Butler describes an "intelligible gender" as one that will "in some sense institute and maintain relations of coherence and continuity among sex, gender, sexual practice, and desire."[61] I can think of no better description of what transsexuality is. In transsexuality, gender *is*, so that a definite and identifiable gender exists and is discernible even when, anatomically, the body does not agree. On the other hand, gender follows from sex, such that it can be experienced fully only if and when the physicality that is anatomical sex is made to conform. This physical sex conformity makes possible the fullness of gender expression/identity, and the gender conformity makes possible, from the transsexual perspective, the

---

transsexual here because a woman wanting to become a man is more understandable from the patriarchal perspective). But many of the male-to-female transsexuals I meet have not undergone castration or penisectomy procedures. These transsexuals may have breast implants and other surgical alterations, but the penis and (often) testicles remain intact (sometimes there is castration, but the penis is maintained). One transsexual I asked about this put it most succinctly when he/she said, "I don't want to get rid of my dick; I respect it." Even the celebrated Christine Jorgensen had some difficulty relinquishing male identification entirely. Interestingly, the apolitical term "bisexual" was popularized by doctors in the early twentieth century as a direct result of the push to redefine sexuality on transsexuals' terms. Beginning in the 1950s, Jorgensen used his/her celebrity and by most accounts incredibly persuasive personality to push doctors to redefine their terms. "Bisexuality" emerged as an important explanatory tool, endorsed by Jorgensen, to explain his/her situation as one in which both masculine and feminine elements were present but the feminine predominated. One might also recall Vivian Le Mans's telling remark that "I can finally fulfill myself and my male partner as much as can any other women – *and probably better than most!*" LE MANS, *supra* note 50 (emphasis added). Implicit here is that Le Mans brings his/her old masculine superiority to his/her new female sexuality.

[60] Monique Wittig, The Mark of Gender (1984).
[61] Butler, *supra* note 17, at 23.

fullness of sexual expression.[62] Transsexuality thus serves a more or less compulsory heterosexuality. Once-Gay/once-men can now have sex as women
with men.[63] Hegemonic heterosexuality is reinforced.

I have no doubt that the desire for a sex change in transsexuals is an urgent,
even desperate drive. Testimonies of this urgency are part of transsexuality's
narrative history,[64] as well as part of more recent case law.[65] But this desperation, which is understandably for the transsexual rationalized as a product "of
nature," is not necessarily a biological phenomenon. All manner of physical
mutilations in the name of gender conformity have been rationalized as natural, and the drive for them has been heady, even for their victims, because of
either captured consciousnesses or the practicalities of survival.[66]

Nothing I have said is meant to suggest, even in the slightest, that transsexuals should be marked for any legal disadvantage on account of their transsexuality. Quite to the contrary, I support legal protections for transsexuals.[67]
I also think that it is the duty of society, so long as Heteroarchy prevails, to
provide the means of "sex change" to transsexuals who are desperate for it.
Transsexuality is a product of straight society and is therefore a *straight emergency*. Having thus created the problem, straights owe transsexuals the right
of survival and of life lived on the terms of their choosing. Support for the
taking of emergency measures in exigent circumstances, however, is not a
determining factor for the ethical perspective of Gay liberation on gender.
To what degree does a belief that no human being should be punished for
conforming to the heterosexualization of anatomy and desire through gender – after all, we all conform to a greater or lesser degree – preclude serious inquiry into what possibilities might exist for improving life if this same

---

[62] See the sexual exuberance of the author of *Take My Tool*, for example. LE MANS, *supra* note 50.

[63] As Gordene MacKenzie explains, the modern, liberal embrace of transsexuality has also
created a dilemma for transsexuals. MacKenzie notes, "The dictionary definition [of trans-
sexuality] also implies that by undergoing prescribed medical treatments, transsexuals can
attain the physical characteristics of the opposite sex. Nothing could be further from the
truth. This medical promise that sex-reassignment surgery will provide physical characteristics of the 'opposite' sex promotes unrealistic expectations about the physical capabilities of
sex-reassignment surgery and ignores the hidden cultural agenda of a bipolar society." See
GORDENE O. MACKENZIE, TRANSGENDER NATION 13 (1994). Indeed, a wealthy, professionally accomplished male-to-female transsexual told me privately that he/she was disappointed
with the results of his/her agonizing and expensive surgeries. Some things like voice, skeletal
size, and height simply cannot be altered. Because he/she feels that the surgery does not
really allow him/her to "pass," he/she often feels like a sort of "freak-show" to be "stared at."

[64] MEYEROWITZ, *supra* note 42.

[65] See, e.g., Kosilek v. Maloney, 221 F. Supp. 2d 156 (D. Mass. 2002).

[66] See the earlier discussion of footbinding, *sati*, etc.

[67] I am inclined to see the situs of such legal protection properly in disability law, not in the
discourse – legal or otherwise – of Gay liberation.

conformity were *really* challenged? What might a day look like when gender itself is delegitimized and removed to reveal a state of authentic sexuality? What if we were to arrive at a day when concepts of gender polarity and rigid role playing were replaced by androgynous fluidity – in this case meant as a referent for a world in which the sexed body is not politicized into a means of tyranny? Transsexuality would disappear as the conditions that produce it disappeared. Human capacity might be realized in that world and on that day. When gender no longer constrains the politics of Gay liberation, we will be closer to that day. A world made new through Gay liberation would mean the ability to live out our lives and our sexualities in ways that are not scripted for us by gender stereotyping.

Gay liberation is at its core a movement for freedom through societal transformation. No Gay people, or any people, will be truly free until the system of gender polarity on which so much tyranny of mind and body is predicated is eradicated from society. The polar identities in this system, phallic identity in men and "masochistic nonidentity" in women,[68] must and will be destroyed. As these gender identities are destroyed, so too will transsexuality be destroyed. Real liberation is found in this revolutionary Gay reality, not in the Self-negation of transsexuality or postmodernism as its partner in derealization.

---

[68] See DWORKIN, OUR BLOOD, *supra* note 29, at 110. In her inimitable way, Dworkin describes the result of the gender binary as a "division of human flesh into two camps – one an armed camp and the other a concentration camp." Id.

(Non)Epilogue

Flaming, but Not Burning

For our God is a consuming fire.

Hebrews 12: 29

I'm whole, then I'm flames. I burn; I die. From this light, later you will see. Mama, I made some light.

Andrea Dworkin, Mercy

The most poignant conversation I had in the roughly three-year period during which I spoke and wrote the words that make up this book was with a young, Gay male college student. This was no Gay man with a straight man in his head. He had recently come out of the closet in ethnic and religious circumstances that made this action one of particular bravery. He had heard me lecture, he had read my books and articles, and he sought me out to tell me that I still had not answered the most important question he had about his own life: that I had not, to his satisfaction, provided him with an answer as to where he fits into the world as a Gay man. He asked a question as bewildering as it was marvelous in its metaphysical complexity: What is Gay identity? For example, when I said that the aim of Gay liberation is a new order in which homosexuality is something other than the absence of heterosexuality and where Gay people are more than a counterfactual to straight supremacy, that its aim is a world in which Gay people are finally accepted as irreducibly human, he wanted to know what this humanity will look like. What will its content be? When I said that in order to be free Gay people must overcome the identity we have been raised to, which has been primarily as the masochistic counterpart to heterosexuality's sadism, he wanted to know what identity would take its place. And he said with deep understanding that perhaps the reason so many Gay youth resort to suicide is that they are disconnected from any sense of community, of history – of identity.

The answers he wants are not easily given, nor are the questions even fully articulable at this time. One cannot know now, at the rough beginnings of a process, what sexuality unconditioned by sex inequality, and male supremacy in particular, might look like. Certainly, the answer is not accessible through mere phenomenological observation. The systematic erasure of Gay experience and point of view has made discovery more difficult and the need for a process of discovery – of becoming – more urgent. Questions, and hopefully answers, become apparent through time, but also, importantly, through resistance and opposition, which is to say through effort.

MORE ON META-MEMORY

> Time comes into it.
> Say it. Say it.
> The universe is made of stories,
> not of atoms.
>> Muriel Rukeyser,
>> "The Speed of Darkness"

It is useful to revisit the concept of Meta-Memory, which I introduced in Chapter 6. Specifically, I said:

> "Meta-Memory" is my way of conceptualizing the idea of a Memory that creates insight from a deeper consciousness that breaks through the heteroarchal false possibilities of everyday that are designed to capture Gay consciousness and thwart authentic Radicalism. In a sense, this kind of Meta-Memory is the act of un-remembering the false memories prescribed for us by our heteroarchal rulers, both civil and religious. Again, noting that the prefix "Meta" means "beyond," I mean to signal here a transcendence of known possibilities through tapping into Gay creativity and imagining new ways of being with the purpose of actualizing a new reality. Part of such a process must be drawn from our past experiences, but much of it will have to come from the courage to imagine possibilities that we may not be able to envision clearly because we have never been allowed under Heteroarchy to control our own destinies.[1]

One key to accessing Meta-Memory is to understand when and through what processes our history and identity are taken from us. In his Memory-sparking work, *Beyond Shame: Reclaiming the Abandoned History of Radical Gay Sexuality*, Patrick Moore posits not only that Gay history exists, but that it reached a zenith in the 1970s. AIDS, however, Moore explains, came along

---

[1]   See Chapter 6, note 53, and accompanying text.

and extinguished much of that history. AIDS became an effective offensive weapon for the Heteroarchy in combating Gay Radicalism. At first, the heteroarchal inclination was to let AIDS play out, killing as many Gays as possible. The Reagan and Bush administrations actively blocked advances in AIDS care for a significant period, resulting in astonishing and unnecessary (in light of available medical and pharmaceutical technology) death. Partially because of pressure from ACT UP and other Gay-initiated efforts to protect Gay lives, policies changed and advances in treatment came. But the stigma of AIDS remained, and was nurtured and nourished by a heteroarchal propaganda campaign aimed at cutting Gays off from ourSelves and each Other. Heteroarchal media, law, and politics converged to make AIDS not only a metaphor but a metonym for Gay existence. Gay politics, in turn, driven by this fear campaign, became rapidly assimilationist. The goal became distance – distance from a past of Radical Gay sexuality, distance from AIDS and its stigma.

The incredible transformation of the Gay consciousness in this period, which continues now, gives a new poignancy to the truth revealed in Sartre's observation that the anti-Semite creates the Jew. Indeed, Gays were made (made over) by the sado-sublimation of our creative energy and political capacity accomplished through sado-sublimation in the guise of AIDS prevention.[2] I'm not here suggesting that "safe sex" is a bad idea. I think it's a good idea for those people who want to have sex in ways that minimize the transmission of HIV and other sexually transmitted infections. But I am suggesting that the hysteria surrounding AIDS – even now, when HIV is basically a manageable chronic illness for those with access to appropriate medication (and who use that medication responsibly) – is used to urge the extinguishment of Gay community and creativity. The stigma attached to HIV is used to encourage the privatization of our energies into the nuclear unit.[3] The breaking of the very ability to foster Gay community follows. Patrick Moore's most Radical claim in *Beyond Shame* is the claim that Gay creativity and, therefore, Gay culture are directly tied to the liberty of Gay sexuality and that a Radical Gay sexuality ought to be reclaimed as a way to take back our creativity and reclaim our culture.[4] I agree with him. I also believe that the penultimate heteroarchal institutions[5] of sado-sublimation and sado-sublimation – pornography,

---

[2] See the introduction and definition of these terms in the preface.

[3] This is admittedly the impetus for the call to marriage by such widely divergent personalities as Larry Kramer and William Eskridge.

[4] Audre Lorde also associates the erotic with creativity and resistance in her classic essay, "The Power of the Erotic."

[5] I say these are penultimate institutions because the ultimate heteroarchal institution is systematized death for Gay people.

marriage, and transsexuality – are actively blocking our creative capacities and our Radical return to our own cultural and creative dimensions through Meta-Memory in the Here and Now. These concrete institutions of sado-sublimation/sublimation work together with liberal politics and theology to erase Gay identity through assimilation and subliminal seduction into heteronormative patterns. And these realities together with allegedly AIDS-driven closure of loci of Gay community, such as bathhouses, have deprived us of opportunities for political organizing and Radical creativity.

The active cultivation of Meta-Memory, through the active engagement with our very real history, would be a first step out of sado-sublimation/sublimation and into real freedom. This, of course, is not easy. It is one of the Big Commitments I named in the introduction to this book. The process to Meta-Memory will require loosing the mind from its heteroarchal mind-bindings and deciding, again, what matters for Gay people and why. The bathhouse, just mentioned, is an instructive example. Despite the reputation – the product of heteroarchal invention – of bathhouses as purely sex-driven, they always functioned – and in some few places continue to function – as much more. They are places for Gays, Gay men especially, to come together for sex, conversation, and organizing.[6] Bathhouses are also democratic in a sense – in the sense that Whitman understood democracy – in that they cut across the economic, social, and cultural divisions that usually keep us separate and engender powerlessness.[7] To see the sex that takes place in bathhouses as always merely meaningless is to suppose a metatheory of sex that is thoroughly heterosexual. In heterosexuality, sex is a private, isolated (and often isolating) experience of invasion. For Gays, on the other hand, sex often takes place in the understood context of community and connectivity – as a

---

[6] The mention of bathhouses here and of their link to Gay men is not to suggest that Lesbians have escaped heteroarchal social and legal control. Discrete loci of Gay community organizing have traditionally been extant only in urban areas. As John D'Emilio explains, capitalism has traditionally discriminated on the basis of gender, offering greater opportunities outside the home and, consequently in urban and otherwise "public" spaces, to men. See J. D'Emilio, *Gay Politics and Community in San Francisco Since World War II*, in Hidden from History: Reclaiming the Gay and Lesbian Past 458 (Martin Duberman, Martha Vicinus, & George Chauncey, Jr., eds., 1989). Consequently, it is no surprise that Gay male life has often been more discernibly "public" than Lesbian life. Traditional patriarchal norms have tacitly thwarted Lesbian organizing in ways every bit as tangible as more obvious closures of bathhouses.

[7] Certainly, not everyone sees the bathhouse in such a light. See Leo Bersani, *Is the Rectum a Grave?* 43 October 197 (1987). Admittedly, hierarchy is present in bathhouses: hierarchy based on looks or muscularity, or youth, or cock size. But I think such reifications of hierarchy are more a testament to the fact that pornography has nearly totally captured the imaginations of Gay men, including those who go to bathhouses, than they are damning for the notion of the democratic *possibilities* of the bathhouse as a location for organizing.

process to multiple consciousness. This understanding of Radical Gay sexuality has been largely supplanted by understandings of Gay sex born from AIDS mythology. Nevertheless, vestiges of it remain, as with, for example, groups of Radical Faeries who meet for communal sex and consciousness-raising. The two, sex and consciousness-raising, are not separate in this context: energy and consciousness are both raised through the sharing of Gay sex. Dare I call this a spiritual understanding of what sex is to Self? Such a definition would surely defy even the liberal theology we are told to rely on for Gay spiritual sustenance. When the Gay-identified character "Jack" in the popular television sit-com *Will and Grace* had a dream in which Cher appeared as god(dess), Jack's query as to whether "you *really are* God" prompted Cher to reply, "Depends on which bathhouse you pray at." Here was a glimmer of deeper insight, even if it was, as I suspect it to have been in this context of opportunistic humor, merely accidental.

As Harry Hay suggested, Meta-Memory also means reconnecting to that "long-ago-cast-out shadow-self," by (re)claiming and celebrating our own and by acknowledging that Gay history has been actively stolen from us. Black Lesbian feminist Barbara Smith wrote of attending the funeral of writer James Baldwin, whom she credits as the greatest influence on her own career as a writer, and of the sadness she felt that not a single eulogizer – no one, not Maya Angelou, not Toni Morrison, not Amiri Baraka, not one of Baldwin's most intimate familiars – spoke of Baldwin as Gay. Although Baldwin was never particularly political about his homosexuality, he certainly never hid it. Smith wondered about the silence, wondered why "[i]n those two hours of remembrance and praise, not a syllable was breathed that this wonderful brother, this writer, this warrior, was also gay, that his being gay was indeed integral to his magnificence."[8] Smith also explains why naming Baldwin's Gayness as "integral to his magnificence" is no mere indulgence in collective ego.

> If I were writing this for a straight publication with a largely heterosexual readership, undoubtedly the question would be looming now: "But what difference does it make if he was gay? Why bring it up especially at his funeral, when the point was to remember the best about him?" Well, Baldwin's being gay and having written about it with such depth and courage at a time when there was no movement nor even a few friends to back him up was definitely "the best" about him.

> If all of who James Baldwin was had been mentioned at this funeral in New York City on December 8, 1987, at the Cathedral of St. John the Divine, it

---

8   BARBARA SMITH: THE TRUTH THAT NEVER HURTS: WRITINGS ON RACE, GENDER AND FREEDOM 79 (1998).

would have gone out on the wire services and been broadcast on the air all over the globe. Not only would this news have geometrically increased the quotient of truth available from the media that day in general, it also would have helped alter, if only by an increment, perceptions in the Black communities all over the world about the meaning of homosexuality, communities where those of us who survive Baldwin as Black lesbians and gay men must continue to dwell.

You see, Baldwin grew up like so many Gay people, in poverty, on mean streets, and in a family and community gripped by the sort of religious hysteria that poverty breeds and that, in turn, breeds an especially desperate homophobia. It was Baldwin's experience of living through these circumstances that sparked his particular genius. The fact that this facet of Baldwin's personality is what may be most valuable to Gay people is precisely why it went unremarked. Certainly, there were likely other concerns at work: a respect for Baldwin's family perhaps most of all counseled against drawing attention to his sexuality. But beyond this, the cultural need not to connect Baldwin to some greater Gayness, because Gayness is unseemly or simply irrelevant, as it is for most liberals, who prefer to see sexuality as only an incidental part of personality – except when their own straight personalities are at issue – was operable in the omission of Baldwin's sexuality from remembrances of him. What Alfred Douglas named "the love that dare not speak its name" continues to be unspeakable and continues itself to be largely voiceless. The Gay sexuality of countless people of historical notoriety continues to go unspoken, and revelation about those on whom research has been done – Eleanor Roosevelt, Bayard Rustin, Virginia Woolf, Vita Sackville-West and Harold Nicholson, Abraham Lincoln, and Leonardo Da Vinci, to name a few – is often met with dismissive scorn. Some intellectuals, including Jonathan Ned Katz, Neil Miller, Barbara Smith, and John D'Emilio, have, of course, done important work in this still underdeveloped area. But if as many Gay intellectuals spent their time uncovering Gay history as those who spend their time distorting or denying it, then all Gay people would be better off. The silence with which Gay people are greeted when we inquire about our history is more than coincidentally related to the silence still present in too many Gay lives. If we stopped, as Barbara Smith put it, "burying our dead twice," it would be a step toward ensuring that more Gay people could stop living double lives.

THE COURAGE TO BE

Plato thought that the problem with heterosexuals – different sexers, baby makers, whatever – was their lack of eternity. My view is that their problem is lack of equality.

Richard Mohr, *Gay Ideas*

ways of sacrificing Gay being for and to straight supremacy. I have also said, in my critique of inequality, that one should look at the effect of a law or practice, not at its intention or goal. I have suggested in discussion of each of these heteroarchal institutions that authentic Gay being is oppositional being, and this supposes that, to some extent, Gay being is defined by its relationship to the Heteroarchy, by what it is in opposition to, which is to say that, to some extent, it is socially defined and contextualized. Thus, an important query arises: If the Heteroarchy is overthrown, if straight supremacy is dissipated, won't this be an end of Gay being? Won't Gay being be sacrificed? The answer is "yes, and no." The answer is "yes" in the sense that the object of Gay desire would no longer be identifiable for its relation to hierarchy, as it often is now, with many Gay men preferring men who fit the pornified image of masculinity. Even functions of Gay being that I have elsewhere praised, or at least have praised as better alternatives to total Gay erasure, for example *femme* and butch roles for Gay people, likely would disappear (in the case of *femme* and butch roles, would disappear as gender disappears entirely as a category of analysis). But at the end of the process of Gay liberation – the process by which Gay creativity is set free – straight supremacy will not emerge stronger, which is the result of the sacrifice of the Gay Self to straight people's "equality," and to gay pornography, marriage, and transsexuality. Vanquishing the Heteroarchy would mean that straight people, too, would no longer exist as they now exist. They, too, would be freed to relate to one another *and* to Gay people without the limits and limitations of sexual hierarchy. Homosexuality and heterosexuality would still exist at a physiological level of attraction. I have never disputed that sexual attraction at some level is *natural*. Instead I have been protesting what is done to that state of nature through political processes, to its co-optation as a means for some people to gain absolute power over other people. The end of Gay liberation is a day when sexuality is not a means to power for straight men at the expense of roughly half of the straight population and of all Gays. On that day, sexuality will continue to be, in a very real sense, Gay, in that sexuality itself will stand in opposition to the reinstitution of hierarchy and tyranny through sex. Gayness, as an ethic of appreciating and protecting the creative capacity of one's Self and of the Other, will be its bulwark.

This new day of freedom will mean an explosion of creativity unparalleled in history because it will mean a world in which the creative capacity of every individual is connected to that of every other individual through a network of friendships – friendship as it does not now exit, or as it exists now only extraordinarily – outside the heterosexual identity. This is precisely why many of the short-term strategic compromises of the gay rights movement are not worth their prices when the results are a distortion of Gay liberation's larger counterculture morality. The principal problem with the modern gay rights movement is that it takes the cultural assumptions and, therefore, the limitations of the Heteroarchy – thus, the heterosexual identity – as largely indisputable. It does little to critique these same assumptions and limitations and, it must be said, precious little truly to reform the social and legal institutions that arise from them. These institutions and the injustice that pervades them do real injury to Gay identity in the sense that they prohibit us from exercising the moral agency necessary to establish the independent Self. I think it was the eventual understanding of the capacity of Gayness for revolution through creativity, inferred originally from homosexual sex acts and the destabilizing capacity of homosexual sex to the heterosexual identity, that led to the regulation of Gay sex. The diabolical manipulation of AIDS by our heterocratic rulers to propel Gays into heterosexually domestic forms of relating meant that it finally became safe to decriminalize homosexuality, stripped as it was in the post-AIDS world of any real revolutionary virility. Perhaps reclamation of our abandoned Radical sexuality will mark the end of assimilation and the beginning of liberation.[12]

OTHERNESS, IDENTITY, AND COMMUNITY

As they become known and accepted by us, our feelings and the honest exploration of them become sanctuaries and spawning grounds for the most radical and daring of ideas. They become a safe-house for that difference so necessary to change and the conceptualization of any meaningful action.

Audre Lorde, *Sister Outsider*

Something of how I understand Gay sexuality as relating to the independent Self and to meaningful community through networking with other Selves is embodied in Professor Tim Dean's assertion of a "positive ethics of cruising."[13]

---

[12]   Changing the sexual as a means of changing the social has been recognized in various Gay theories, including, but not limited to, Michael Warner, The Trouble with Normal (1999); Jeffrey Weeks, Sexuality (1989); Dennis Altman, Global Sex (2006).

[13]   See Tim Dean, Unlimited Intimacy: Reflections on the Subculture of Barebacking (2009). Dean's work is by no means unproblematic. Accordingly, I am interested more in the concepts he introduces than in the content he ultimately assigns to them. The principal deficit in Dean's critique is that it fails to distinguish between Gay sexuality and sexuality that is commodified and propagandized in the straight model through gay pornography and everyday sex practiced as pornography, which is to say as inequality, which Dean apparently endorses. Dean, like leatherman Scott Tucker, on whose work he relies, fails to see that criticism of pornography is not necessarily a criticism of Gay sexuality. To state it as simply and revolutionarily as possible: We need more *experiences* of Radical Gay sexuality, not more *images* of heteroarchal sexuality. Radically Gay sexual experiences are those in which

"Cruising" is a slang term for meeting strangers for sex and has long been an integral concept to Gay, especially Gay male, sexuality, especially in the pre-AIDS years. To paraphrase Dean with some gloss, the importance of Radical Gay sexuality – its revolutionary potential – is found in its ability to protect the "otherness" (*Otherness*) of one's sexual partner. Or as Dean begins his inquiry: *Why should strangers not be lovers?* In other words, Gay sex takes place as an exchange of energy and pleasure without any lasting physical or mental sacrifice on the part of either partner.[14] As Dean understands it, "cruising" is an ethic of openness to the possibility of erotic union with those around you.[15] In this sense, preservation of Otherness is entirely conducive to community. This is distinguishable from single-minded cruising in which the myopic focus is on fucking only, or "narrowing ... the attention to crotch level," as Dean puts it, but also from the accepted paradigm of monogamy and attendant privatization of energy and emotion away from the community and into the nuclear unit.

---

sexuality is not practiced as inequality, in which violence is not perpetrated or hierarchy reified. Although I believe it aspires to be more, Dean's theory is problematic in this regard in that it accepts and defends the normalization of sexual violence in numerous and insidious ways. Dean's defense of the pornographic film *Niggas' Revenge*, with its overt racism – a concrete form of violence in itself – as well as its glorification of physical violence and sadism as sex (discussed in Chapter 5, note 51) is simply one example. However, Dean does seem to understand, at least obliquely, the role that pornography, especially as disseminated through the Internet, has had in privatizing the spatial dimensions of Gay sexuality, in many respects domesticating Gay sexuality by pushing it more and more into the home, where DVD players and computers are located. Online hookup sites, normally saturated with pornography, now do the work of facilitating the kind of sexual encounters that once took place in bathhouses, for example. What's missing now, of course, is the conversation and networking that took place in the bathhouses. The bathhouse as a physical space occupied by many people could deliver, in this respect, what the Internet cannot (see DEAN, id. at 193–194).

[14] Both Dean and I distinguish sex that preserves "otherness" and sex that is designed to avoid encountering "otherness" altogether (see DEAN, id. at 180). For me, at least, the latter category would include purely anonymous sex, exemplified by the "glory hole," in which sex is accomplished by sticking the penis through a hole in the wall and into the receptive mouth or anus waiting on the other side. This type of sex, I think, is actually driven by a need to dissociate from Gay community and cannot be, therefore, a means to community.

[15] DEAN, *supra* note 13, at 210–211. I do not personally believe that an "erotic union" necessarily means a "sexual union" in the strictest sense. Rather "erotic union" refers to the sharing of energy that may be physical, psychic, emotional, or intellectual – energy in all its positive forms. It is true, of course, that such an ethic of openness to erotic union with Others cannot solve all problems. For example, how open one *can* be to such possibilities may depend in large part on the point from which one begins in the hierarchy under which we, all for the worse and separated only by degree, currently exist. Perhaps it is easier for those with relatively more money, and thus more security socially and legally, to be more open. In any event, as an aspiration – as an ethic – such openness may be an important step in eradicating even the boundaries of wealth and class.

Such a sexual ethic stands in stark contradiction to heterosexuality, in which one partner, usually the woman, is subdued, domesticated – independent identity and creative capacity inevitably surrendered. Heterosexuality is, in fact, predicated on subduing the stranger, which we call, euphemistically, seduction. Indeed, some scholarly interpretations of the biblical story of Sodom, from which later prohibitions on homosexuality, called "sodomy" laws, take their name, concentrate on ancient Hebrew customs surrounding "strangers."[16] In that bellicose time, admission of strangers into fortified cities required permission of the city elders – a crude procedure of threshold, minimal domestication. Lot, apparently, in inviting his angelic visitors into his home at Sodom, failed to secure the requisite permission. The attack on Lot's visitors was therefore motivated by their status as undomesticated strangers – by their Otherness. Thus, even if the Sodom story was really more a story about interaction with strangers, the analogy later made to sex, specifically the revelation it entails about the fundamental difference in heterosexuality and homosexuality, is still particularly apt. What I'm saying here is that even had the *men* of Sodom succeeded in raping Lot's *male* visitors, this rape – this domestication of the stranger – would have been thoroughly *heterosexual*. And if God's wrath rained on Sodom because of the Sodomites' lack of hospitality, the story seems more accurately interpreted (parabolically anyway) as a condemnation of heterosexuality than of homosexuality, for in the latter the strangers' Otherness is respected and preserved.

From this perspective, Gay sexuality stands in real opposition to patriarchy and its moral and political imperatives. The *authentic* Gay Self, which may be difficult or illusive conceptually, is, in this light, clearly an oppositional Self – one that resists the heteroarchal limitation of possibilities or, in the case of pornography, marriage, and transsexuality as politics, resists surrender to the Heteroarchy as a possibility. Pornography, marriage, and transsexuality are each propagandized as ways of being or as preconditions of existence. Pornography, as it is propagandized, simply is existence – *is being*. Marriage is taken to be a vehicle to a more fulfilling existence. Transsexuality is taken as a condition of existence for transsexuals. In actuality, each forecloses being – Gay being. Each, as a way of surrendering, of giving up and giving in to the imperatives of the Heteroarchy, is an antithesis of Gay liberation and of the authentic Gay Self. And, from this perspective, formal/liberal equality theory, with its obsessive focus on "sameness"; *Lawrence v. Texas*, with its domestication of the Gay men involved; modern free speech law, in its failure to protect

---

[16] See Shannon Gilreath, Sexual Politics: The Gay Person in America Today 66–69 (2006).

the Other from pervasive anti-identity propaganda; compulsory marriage and its attendant compulsory domesticity; and transsexuality, with its goal of gender and sexuality normativity: all are anathema to Gay Selfhood – to Gay *being*. And Radical Gay sexuality, inasmuch as it respects and preserves *Otherness*, in that sex can begin and end without the faintest hint of an agenda of domestication, also brings us together in ways that do not and, perhaps, cannot exist in other contexts. The Courage to Be not only would change our understandings of and appreciation for the products of our own invention, but would change the goals of the legal arm of our Movement. If we could understand the connection of the Gay individual to the Gay community, then a model of progress based only on individual exceptionality would seem less reasonable, if not entirely fictional. The resources expended for the few, on marriage and military, might be directed toward advocacy for universal health care, comprehensive sex education, and, centrally, effective employment non-discrimination legislation that would allow every Gay person – every person – to explore Gayness without fear of ostracism, homelessness, destitution, and hunger.

CONCLUSION: REALIZING GAY LIBERATION

Derrida says that the problem with democracy is that it is too homosexual. I say that its problem is that it is not homosexual enough.

Richard Mohr, *Gay Ideas*

What I have said in this book is truth in the face of a great deal of obfuscation. In the Western tradition, truth tellers are called heretics. Indeed, in my refusal to be politely grateful for small favors, that is exactly what I am in the mind (and, yes, they are acutely single-minded) of the gay establishment. Like James Baldwin before me, I am sick to death of *their progress*.[17] Please, please, for God's sake – for the sake of that great, heterosexual god who does not exist – do not tell me anymore about liberal progress. I am forever grateful to those six, ostensibly straight, old men and women of our Supreme Court who magnificently and magnanimously decided that fucking in the way that comes naturally to me does not warrant a prison term. But gratitude has its limits. Must I also be grateful that Radicalism has been nearly smothered to death by an obsessively domestic agenda? That Gay people seek straight approval just as battered children seek the tender side of an abusive father? That the

---

[17] See James Baldwin, *The Price of the Ticket*, in THE PRICE OF THE TICKET: COLLECTED NONFICTION, 1948–1985 (1985).

marriage craze means that those not blindly accepting monogamy as gospel are labeled deviant *even in homosexual terms*? That Gays are now duped into believing that even we must participate in the procreative project despite the fact that Gays have the evolutionary benefit of not having to procreate in order to exist (since heterosexual intercourse – at its most fruitful – produces Gay offspring)?

With all possible deference to self-congratulatory liberals and their progress, I cannot fail to notice that there is not a single institution in this generous nation that is not thoroughly heterosexist and homophobic. That is the truth. Every institution that now exists hates us and has as its mission if not our undoing at the very least the defense of a status quo in which we are less than straight people. This is true of the court system and the tax system and the education system (what's left of it, at least). It's also true of the churches, even those who claim to be inclusive, all of them trying to save our souls from something – something never yet satisfactorily explained to me. If they are trying to save me from mySelf, I'd like to have a Self that is totally mine before I'm obliged to lay it on the altar; thank you, very much. And our newest victory – the military: what a joke. Gay people, already bearing a disproportionate brunt of the free world's violence, can now go to the frontlines of a campaign to bring *our* "freedom" to other people? *This* is progress by the straight liberal's definition? How indescribably cruel that is.

James Baldwin said, "The will of the people, or the State, is revealed by the State's institutions." Larry Kramer asks straight people, "Why do you hate Gay people so much?" Need another word be written? Baldwin also said that the purpose of the State is "to keep the nigger in his place." Well, with Baldwin (and Karr), I say, truly, *plus ça change, plus c'est la même chose*. And under present circumstances, I see no particular reason to read our most authentically American pejorative particularly narrowly. Perhaps this gives a whole new dimension to John D'Emilio's assertion that "there are more of us than there used to be."

But it is Baldwin's warning, his lament – that some Black people can become the worst of what is "white" without realizing it – that is perhaps most relevant to the Gay struggle, in law and in life generally. Some Gay people may be becoming what is the worst of straight in terms of the valorization of what "straight" means politically. Will liberal assimilation politics cost us, finally, our identity as Gay people, leaving in its place heteronormativity cum homonormativity? Will the sado-sublimination accomplished through pornography, and marriage, and gender politics in the form of transsexuality, and otherwise render the formulation and expression of a Gay point of view unthinkable or impossible? Will Gayness as integral to a Gay person's magnificence be replaced by an assimilationist politics arguing that sexuality is simply an incidental part of existence confined to what happens behind closed bedroom doors, where formal legal equality is content to leave it? Will straight liberals, who are really no better at separating their politics from their theologies than conservatives are, with the politics of the former being no less than the sado-ritual worship of the straight identity found at the core of the theology of the latter, demand conversion in exchange for salvation? In other words, will Gay people trade the very real possibility of physical destruction for conceptual destruction, which is also existential destruction?

This final query highlights for me, again, that the acute difference between the liberal and me, the way in which we measure progress – the liberal counting noses but failing to stop, as the Radical does, to notice whether the attached body is living or dead – will forever separate us. Never having faced such a raw loss, the straight liberal cannot fathom the momentous truth contained in Emily Brontë's simple prophecy: "I cannot live without my life." Too many Gay people have tried for too long the half-life of the living dead that Heteroarchy mandates for us. But in time we ache with a pain that is neither phantom nor imaginary – an ache for the missing identity excised from us by the Heteroarchy: We ache for our identity like someone aches for a missing limb. They had no authority to take it from us, but they, our hetero-captors, have the power to give it back. If, in the end, we can make them see that they must give back this identity – or at least leave us free to invent one – then, and only then, will I swallow hard and allow them a little self-congratulation.

When no amount of difference manufactured in hierarchy and animated by stigma can justify the low-caste treatment of Gays as an identifiable and Self-identified people, then the question of Gays' inequality to straights that began this book might finally have an answer that is substantively equal. Then and only then will Gay women and men, and the children who might one day grow up to be us, have a fighting chance in the world. That day will dawn and the question will be answered when Gay people start asking it in OUTRAGE instead of in trepidation.

Index